THE
HOOSIER STATE

READINGS IN INDIANA HISTORY

THE HOOSIER STATE

READINGS IN INDIANA HISTORY

INDIAN PREHISTORY TO 1880

Edited by
RALPH D. GRAY

WILLIAM B. EERDMANS PUBLISHING COMPANY
GRAND RAPIDS, MICHIGAN

To Jan,
and to our other joint productions,
Karen, David, and Sarah,
this one is affectionately dedicated.

Copyright © 1980 by Wm. B. Eerdmans Publishing Co.
255 Jefferson Ave. S.E., Grand Rapids, Mich. 49503

Library of Congress Cataloging in Publication Data

Main entry under title:

The Hoosier State.

  Includes bibliographical references.
  CONTENTS: v. 1. Indian prehistory to
1880.—v. 2. The modern era.
  1. Indiana—History—Addresses, essays,
lectures. 2. Indiana—History—Sources.
I. Gray, Ralph D.
F526.5.H66   977.2   80-12496
ISBN 0-8028-1842-0 (v. 1)
ISBN 0-8028-1843-4 (v. 2)

CONTENTS

v

ACKNOWLEDGMENTS

Many people and organizations have contributed, more than they realize, to the compilation of this reader. I have benefited from the counsel and occasional recommendation of items to be considered from several fellow historians at Indiana University, including members of my department in Indianapolis, Professors James H. Madison and Donald F. Carmony in Bloomington, and Professors Patrick J. Furlong and Victor M. Bogle in, respectively, South Bend and Kokomo. My research in the libraries of the Indianapolis area—especially at the Indiana Historical Society, the Indiana State Library, and the Indianapolis Public Library—and in the libraries of Indiana University at Indianapolis and Bloomington has been aided by the talents and good graces of their staffs. I am particularly grateful to Mr. Francis L. Brey of the Indiana University library in Indianapolis, Mr. Jeff Gunderson, reference librarian, and Mr. Tim Peterson, picture librarian, of the Indiana Historical Society Library, and Mr. F. Gerald ("Jerry") Handfield, Jr. and his many colleagues at the Indiana Division of the Indiana State Library.

The administration of Indiana University-Purdue University at Indianapolis supported the early stages of this work through a sabbatical leave, and some of the illustrations used were copied for me by the Instructional Media Systems office of the university. I am also grateful to Mr. Frank Ramsey, chief photographer of the Indianapolis *Star,* and to Mr. James L. Green, director of the Indiana University News Bureau in Bloomington, for supplying a few of the illustrations. I also want to recognize the labors and writing of all of the contributors, living and dead, to these pages, for whose talents and writing abilities I have an increased respect since undertaking this assignment. Most importantly, I want to express my thanks to Mr. Reinder Van Til, editor of the American History Series at Eerdmans, for his confidence in me at the outset, and for his quick but careful and judicious editing of the manuscript, and to Ms. Sandra Nowlin, managing editor of the press, for her interest and helpfulness throughout. The final acknowledgment belongs to my family, to whom these volumes are dedicated, for such works are always cooperative enterprises.

LIST OF ILLUSTRATIONS

PREFACE

There has been a renewed interest in the study of state and local history in recent years, stemming from such diverse stimuli as the growing fascination with the past sparked by the nation's bicentennial observation and the runaway popularity of Alex T. Haley's *Roots*. There is also a reaction building against the anonymity and temporariness of modern life styles. Although historical studies in general are "in crisis," according to a 1975 report to the Organization of American Historians, there is vitality and widespread appeal in community and state historical activities and studies. Such study has become more sophisticated and particularistic without being parochial, more analytical and specialized without being antiquarian.

The problem of readily available and inexpensive books and articles for the beginning student, however, still exists. The market for monographic state studies is not yet sufficiently broad in most cases to justify commercial publishing expenses, which means that the often abundant materials for community and state history have appeared mainly in expensive hardbound books and relatively small circulation journals or state agency publications. This book, intended as a partial corrective to the situation, makes available a sampling of the rich variety of sources that exist for the study of Indiana history. For the most part, I have selected recent secondary accounts and interpretations taken from journal articles or chapters in books; but I have occasionally used contemporaneous accounts and documents. I have even selected a few passages from works of fiction and poetry to help recapture the flavor and drama of Indiana's past.

Indiana is now well into the fourth quarter of its bicentennial period, having been admitted into the Union in December 1816. The first state to be created amid the westward rush following the War of 1812, its roots are the ones common to the other states of the area now known as the Old Northwest. But Indiana quickly developed a distinctive quality and character. By the end of the nineteenth century it was the most rural and homogeneous state of the region, with the highest number of Southern-born—and, conversely, the lowest number of foreign-born—citizens. Although the state is now both heavily industrialized—steel, automotive parts, pharmaceuticals—

and urbanized, with most of its population living in cities between 10,000 and 100,000 in population, Indiana has retained its folksy, rural image.

Both the people, with their rural and southern orientation, and the land, devoid of any natural boundary except along the southern and southwestern edges, have contributed to Indiana's unique flavor. Because of the swampy terrain in parts of northern Indiana, that area encountered by the migrating hordes from New England, New York, and Pennsylvania after the southern third of the state had been settled, fewer remained there as permanent settlers than moved on westward into Illinois, Wisconsin, and Iowa. Consequently, the southern influence, so clearly recognized in the southern hills of Indiana, extended also into the flat, fertile plains of central and north-central Indiana. This contributed to the state's political and cultural orientation in the nineteenth century, its comparatively poor educational system—but, perhaps symbiotically, its rich tradition of oral and then written narratives—and its sympathy for slavery and the slaveholder. Although Indiana was unquestionably Unionist during the long, bloody struggle of the Civil War, "copperhead" influences were present, and Indiana was often a reluctant partner in the Reconstruction policies of the Republican party.

During the late nineteenth century, Indiana emerged as an important industrial state. This development, significantly boosted by the discovery in the latter 1880s of a huge but soon exhausted natural gas field, was first based on the processing of Indiana's large and diversified agricultural crop and livestock production. Subsequently, the location of giant steel-producing plants in northwestern Indiana, as well as the development of an indigenous automobile industry, magnified the state's role as a manufacturing center.

During this same period Indiana entered what has been called a "golden age" in terms of both politics and literature. Once the sixth largest state in the nation in terms of population and thus electoral votes, and with two evenly matched political parties, Indiana was the scene of political contests that were often fierce. And because both parties considered Indiana's "swing" vote essential, an unusually large number of Indiana politicians appeared on the national party tickets. Indeed, between 1868 and 1916 there were only three elections in which Hoosiers were not nominated by one or both of the two major parties. During those years one Hoosier, Benjamin Harrison, was elected president, and four Indiana men—Schuyler Colfax, Thomas A. Hendricks, Charles W. Fairbanks, and Thomas R. Marshall—were elected to the vice-presidency. Hoosier authors were also remarkably active and successful during this period, especially the so-called Big Four of Booth Tarkington, James Whitcomb Riley, Meredith Nicholson, and George Ade. And the literary output of the state has remained strong since that time.

In the twentieth century, Indiana has become known as the home of the world's richest automobile racing event, the Indianapolis 500, and of some of the nation's finest high-school and college basketball and football teams. It has a broadly based and diversified economy, which is contributed to almost equally by industrial business and agribusiness, and its blend of medium-sized urban and small-town communities share the landscape with still rustic rural countrysides. Many of the state's scenic historical and recreational sites have been preserved in an actively expanding state park and state memorial system. These include the sand-swept Indiana Dunes along the shores of Lake Michigan, the homes and studios of such artists and writers as T. C. Steele and Gene Stratton Porter, and the unsurpassed beauty of pristine forest land in such parks as Turkey Run and McCormick's Creek in central Indiana and Spring Mill and Clifty Falls in southern Indiana. Once evenly balanced politically—but always strongly conservative— Indiana has become more Republican in recent decades. It has also become more cosmopolitan, with a number of outstanding colleges and universities, lively civic and cultural groups throughout the state, and countless national and international business and professional organizations with headquarters in the state. Many economic, social, and racial problems remain, but the outlook is bright for "The Crossroads of America," which has been Indiana's motto since 1937 and is increasingly appropriate.

RALPH D. GRAY

INTRODUCTION

There have been countless interpreters of Indiana, using many different modes of expression. The earliest include missionary and military reports for the preterritorial period, travel accounts by intrepid adventurers during the early nineteenth century, as well as letters, essays, and poems by residents or visitors, including John Finley's "The Hoosier's Nest," an 1833 poetic tribute to the pioneers which may have irretrievably attached that epithet to the people of Indiana. There were also attempts at formal histories of the state, beginning with John B. Dillon's typically long-titled work of 1843: *The History of Indiana from its Earliest Exploration by Europeans to the Close of the Territorial Government in 1816 with an Introduction Containing Historical Notes of the Discovery and Settlement of the Territory Northwest of the River Ohio.* Since then the flow of poetry, essays, and histories about Indiana has been enormous, with some of its interpreters transcending local appeal and reaching national and international audiences. George Ade, Booth Tarkington, and James Whitcomb Riley are perhaps the best-known popular writers; Logan Esarey, Jacob Piatt Dunn, Donald F. Carmony, William E. Wilson, and John Bartlow Martin are among the most important historians of the state.

It is the purpose of this brief introductory chapter to provide some general information about Indiana, its location and natural features, its people and their character, and at the same time to present examples of three different types of writing about the state during this century. For fuller but still brief treatments and assessments, see especially John Bartlow Martin, *Indiana: An Interpretation* (1947), Irving Leibowitz, *My Indiana* (1964), and Howard H. Peckham, *Indiana: A Bicentennial History* (1978), the most recent one-volume interpretation of the state.

1

Indiana: The Land and the People

WILLIAM E. WILSON

Professor William E. Wilson provides a good introduction to the Hoosier state, crisscrossed by the nation's main east-west highways and railways. After describing its geographical features, he reviews its geological past, its economic base, and glances at its better-known nonagricultural products—writers and politicians. This selection is from the introductory chapter of *Indiana: A History*, a fine interpretive history written for the state's sesquicentennial in 1966, when the author was a professor of English at Indiana University in Bloomington. He made a substantial contribution to the anniversary observance with this publication, while adding to his long list of books dealing with Indiana history. Professor Wilson's writings include *The Angel and the Serpent: The Story of New Harmony* (1964), *The Wabash* (1940), a volume in the Rivers of America series, and juvenile biographies of George Rogers Clark and Tecumseh, as well as a number of works of fiction.

Indiana: A History is one of the most recent histories of the state to appear. Other useful introductions to this subject are in John D. Barnhart and Donald F. Carmony, *Indiana: From Frontier to Industrial Commonwealth* (2 vols., 1954); Charles Roll, *Indiana: One Hundred and Fifty Years of American Development* (2 vols., 1931); Jacob P. Dunn, *Indiana and Indianans: A History of Aboriginal and Territorial Indiana and the Century of Statehood* (5 vols., 1919); and John Bartlow Martin, *Indiana: An Interpretation* (New York, 1947). Meredith Nicholson, like Wilson, stresses the state's literary tradition in *The Hoosiers* (1900); see also R. E. Banta (ed.), *Hoosier Caravan: A Treasury of Indiana Life and Lore* (new ed., 1975).

The state of Indiana points southward 276 miles from the lower end of Lake Michigan toward the Gulf of Mexico and so stands athwart one third of the path that any east-west traveler must take on an overland journey across the United States. Because the fastest east-west interstate highways and the majority of railway trunk lines pass through the northern and central portions of Indiana and because modern tourists are intent mainly upon arriving anywhere other than where they are, and in the greatest possible hurry, the impression of Indiana left in the minds of such east-west transients is often incomplete and not altogether accurate. A flat land is what most of them remember, a flat land of rectangular fields planted mostly in corn, a flat land ornamented occasionally by small lakes and tree-shaded villages and scarred in one or two places by unprepossessing industrial areas.

Fewer travelers from outside the state cross Indiana in a north-south direction than those who make the east-west journey. One reason is that fewer direct highways run north and south through Indiana; another is that there are fewer places to come from or go to in a hurry on such routes. If there were more of these north-south tourists, the image of Indiana in outsiders' minds would be considerably altered. Corn would remain among the travelers' principal impressions; corn is everywhere in Indiana; but added to the flat land and the lakes and villages and industrial areas would be hills and ravines, caves and deep woodlands, and winding rivers.

Two thirds of the distance from Lake Michigan to the state's southernmost tip—or as far down as Terre Haute on the western border and Lawrenceburg on the eastern side—Indiana is monotonously 145 miles wide, even where it invades the southern loop of Michigan's waters and boldly approaches Chicago's lakefront. The state is thus straight-sided from the waist up because lawmakers and surveyors corseted it along meridian lines when Illinois was separated from Indiana Territory in 1809, with slight alterations in 1816 when Indiana became a state. Below the waistline— from Terre Haute and Lawrenceburg down to the tip of Posey County, where the Wabash River joins the Ohio—the width of the state varies with the temperamental meanders of these two rivers.

Every Hoosier schoolboy learns to say that Indiana is bounded on the north by Michigan, on the south by Kentucky, on the west by Illinois, and on the east by Ohio. In the main this is so, but a close look at a map shows that Kentucky bounds some of the east of Indiana as well as the south. The Wabash River definitely forms the western boundary of the state below Terre Haute, but the Ohio River, commonly called the southern boundary, is more eastern than southern along one third of its edging of Indiana. Most people, including most Hoosiers, forget that the Ohio flows in a sharp southwesterly direction and that when Hoosiers cross it to leave the state in many places above Jeffersonville they are headed east, not south.

The reason for such different views of Indiana as those of the east-west and the north-south travelers across the state is that Indiana is two distinct regions instead of one. Geologists like to think of it as three, but Hoosiers generally see their state divided by the Old National Road, now U.S. Route 40, and are likely to say, if asked where they are from, either "Northern Indiana" or "Southern Indiana." Within Indiana's boundaries, the Old

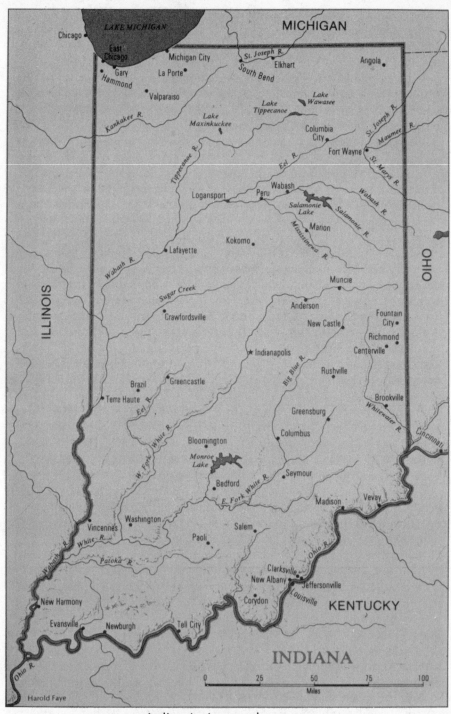

Indiana's rivers and towns
Courtesy of the American Association for State and Local History
(In H. H. Peckham, Indiana: A Bicentennial History, 1978)

National Road, surveyed by a Quaker named Jonathan Knight and cleared of outcropping geodes for its first traffic by 1832, is only a few miles longer than the state's width, entering Indiana from the east just below the 40th Parallel at Richmond, passing through the heart of Indianapolis, and departing for Illinois a short distance west of Terre Haute and the Wabash River.

Above this highway, Indiana is indeed a far-horizoned land, if not altogether flat. Here the great prairie begins its gradual upward tilt toward the Rockies a thousand miles away, and here, hardly distinguishable among lakes and marshes, is the watershed between the systems of the St. Lawrence and the Mississippi. This land is fabulously fertile for the growing of corn, wheat, oats, soy beans, and tomatoes, except in the Calumet area near Chicago, where a Colossus of comparatively recent industrial development stands astride a stretch of singing sand dunes along the shore of Lake Michigan.

The Calumet takes its name from the river Calumet, christened by the early French as the Chalumeau, which means a hollow reed of the sort that pipestems can be made of. It includes Gary, Hammond, East Chicago, and Whiting, each one contiguous to another and with a combined population close to half a million. Outside the Calumet there are two other large cities in the north, South Bend and Fort Wayne, each with metropolitan populations above 200,000; and there are a half-dozen smaller cities of 40,000 or more north of the Old National Road: Anderson Elkhart, Kokomo, Lafayette, Marion, and Muncie.

Below the Old National Road, the scenery of Indiana changes to hills, smaller farms, smaller towns, and fewer cities. Large man-made reservoirs are beginning to dot this area, but it is not naturally lake country. Here in the south, however, are most of Indiana's major rivers, among them the two-forked White and the two-forked Whitewater, the Blue, and the lower Wabash, and many rambling creeks. They flow toward all points of the compass, but eventually each fingers its way southward and in time its waters join those of the Ohio. Some of these rivers and creeks provide rich bottomlands in the Ohio Valley, and on the good land of the south corn, soy beans, and tomatoes prosper, but not in such great abundance as in the north. The southwestern corner of the state, known as "The Pocket," is famous for its melons as well as these other crops.

Here, on the Ohio, is the region's largest city, Evansville, a community of ups and downs in its growth throughout its century and a half of history, but with a metropolitan population in 1960 of 200,000. The only other large urban concentration in the south is the New Albany-Jeffersonville area on the Ohio, across from Louisville, Kentucky, with about 60,000 people in 1960. Vincennes, the state's oldest town continuously inhabited by white men, is in southern Indiana, as is Corydon, the first state capital. The population of Vincennes was less than 20,000 in 1960; Corydon is a village of a few thousand people.

Geology explains, in part, the difference between the two halves of Hoosierland. After the receding of the pre-Cambrian Sea, which once covered the whole area, three glaciers invaded what is now the state of Indiana. The first, called the Illinoian, moved down as far as the Ohio River and beyond it, except for one north-south strip that runs through the central part of the state and is known as the Crawford Upland. The second, called the Early Wisconsin, stopped about two thirds of the way down the stage at a line that is sometimes almost visible in the abrupt change of scenery that one witnesses as one drives along a north-south highway. The last, the Late Wisconsin, came only halfway down the state.

The result of the triple invasion of ice in the north was the leveling of hills and their crumbling into fine glacial subsoil, which in some of the farm land is many feet deep. In the once-glaciated and the unglaciated sections of the south, on the other hand, the hills remain tall and sometimes steep, and the land is not so fertile. Where there was no glaciation at all, there is almost no subsoil, and the bedrock is eroded into deep canyons and sharp ridges.

This unglaciated area, the Crawford Upland, which extends in a band down from Parke and Putnam counties to the Ohio River, is the most scenic of the state. It is the location of Marengo and Wyandotte caves—Wyandotte is the third largest in the United States—and of "Jug Rock" and "The Pinnacle" near Shoals, and its geological history accounts for the beauties of Shades, Turkey Run, McCormick's Creek, and Spring Mill, four of Indiana's score of state parks. In this unglaciated strip, as in the rest of southern Indiana, the hills generally run east and west, and streams and rivers have a difficult time wending their way south. Across the entire southern half of the state, there are seven bands of alternating upland and lowland, three such combinations occurring in southeastern Indiana, three in south-central Indiana, and one in the southwest.

. . . .

Indiana's farmers raise horses, beef and dairy cattle, and some sheep, although from pioneer days to the present mutton and lamb have never been widely popular in the Hoosier diet. But the four-legged creature that dominates the Indiana farm scene is the hog. In pioneer times, hogs were seldom fenced and were allowed to roam the woods and feast on mast. Later, with improved fencing, their diet changed to corn. By 1860 there were two hogs for every person in the state. Today, with roughly 60 per cent of Indiana urban and less than 40 per cent rural, hogs and human beings populate the state in about equal numbers, but Indiana still stands third in the nation in hog raising, outclassed in that endeavor only by Iowa and Illinois. A few years ago, Logan Esarey, an Indiana historian, nominated the hog as monarch of the state. "We may sing the praises of all the heroes of Indiana from LaSalle or George Rogers Clark to the present," wrote Professor Esarey eloquently, "but the prosperity of our state . . . has depended on Mr.

Hog. In fat years and lean years... he has come up with his part, even though he does grunt about it considerably."

There are others, however, who argue that corn, and not the hog, is king in Indiana. After all, corn predates the hog in the state, and now that the supply of mast is depleted, the growing of corn must precede the raising of hogs. Corn was a staple of the Hopewellian mound builders' diet in prehistoric times before hogs were domesticated, and of the later Indians' diet before the white men came, and corn was always the first crop the white men planted after they arrived and settled. Although the land area of Indiana is comparatively small—36,291 square miles, less than two thirds of that of Iowa or of Illinois—Indiana ranks with Iowa and Illinois among the three top producers of corn as well as hogs in the United States.

. . . .

In the last one hundred years, Indiana has been more often Republican than Democratic in its politics, but from an outsider's view it has not always been easy to tell which party was in power, for both of them tend toward conservatism. Because of the remoteness of the state from the coasts, the interest of its people concentrates upon domestic problems more often than international affairs, and as a consequence some of the strongest isolationist sentiment in the nation has emanated from Indiana's politicians. In varying degrees of stridency the voice of "one-hundred-per-cent Americanism" has appealed to Indiana voters for the past fifty years. At the same time, the state has produced Eugene V. Debs, the most noted leader of the Socialist Party in American history, and men with broad international views of American destiny such as Albert J. Beveridge and Wendell L. Willkie. Since 1962, the governor and both senators have been Democrats. Seven presidential candidates have been either natives or, for considerable numbers of years, residents of Indiana, and three of them—Lincoln and the two Harrisons—were elected. Of eight candidates for the vice presidency, Colfax, Hendricks, Fairbanks, and Marshall were elected.

A few crusading Hoosiers from the beginning supported public education, and the once backward state now has one of the highest literacy rates in the nation. As early as 1825 Robert Owen was experimenting with new educational theories in his Utopian colony at New Harmony; soon thereafter, William Maclure established in that town the first trade school in the country; Evansville opened the first public high school in the West for both boys and girls in 1854; and for many of the early years of the present century the public school system of Gary was a subject of observation and study among American and foreign educators. There are four state supported institutions of higher learning in Indiana: Indiana University at Bloomington, Purdue University at West Lafayette, Ball State University at Muncie, and Indiana State University at Terre Haute. These public universities are supplemented by branches, or "centers," throughout the state and by thirty-five privately supported colleges and universities, including such nationally recognized institutions as DePauw, Wabash, Earlham, Butler, Hanover, and Notre Dame, which is the largest Catholic university for men in the United States.

This long tradition of emphasis on education may account, in part at least, for the third major preoccupation of Hoosiers after politics and schools; that is, literature. Since the publication of *The Hoosier School-Master* in 1871, Indianans have maintained a steady flow of books from the nation's publishers, not the least of which is the firm of Bobbs-Merrill at Indianapolis, now a subsidiary of Howard W. Sams and Company. The list of Indiana authors includes such widely varied talents and interests as those of Lew Wallace, James Whitcomb Riley, Booth Tarkington, Meredith Nicholson, Theodore Dreiser, George Ade, George Jean Nathan, Elmer Davis, and Eli Lilly. Riley is probably the only poet who ever became a millionaire by writing verse; Lilly is one of very few millionaires who ever became a writer with a genuine literary style.

Today the literary flood flows unabated in Indiana, although its so-called "Golden Age," when Riley, Tarkington, and Company were in their heyday, has passed. Each year Hoosier writers are honored with awards at an Indiana Authors' Day banquet, and in 1965 the Indiana Author's Day Committee had to consider 158 books published in the previous year by 135 natives and residents of the state. That means that about one out of every 20,000 adult Hoosiers got his name on the title page of a book in 1964; it is safe to guess that most of the other 19,999 will keep on trying.

Some Hoosiers who have made a place for themselves in the nation's history by following other avenues than politics, education, and literature are: James B. Eads, builder of the Eads Bridge across the Mississippi; Richard J. Gatling, inventor of the prototype of the machine gun; Elwood Haynes, a pioneer in the making of automobiles; Wilbur Wright, Virgil Grissom, and Frank Borman, pioneers in air and space; Alva Roebuck, co-founder of Sears, Roebuck; Bernard Gimbel, president of Gimbel Brothers; John T. McCutcheon, *Chicago Tribune* cartoonist; Hoagy Carmichael and Cole Porter, popular composers; Knute Rockne, Wilbur Shaw, Don Lash, and Mordecai (Three-Finger) Brown, of the sports world; Generals Burnside and Hershey, of the Civil War and World War Two; and George W. Whistler, civil engineer, the husband of "Whistler's Mother."

The Hoosier then, what is he? His character is not easy to describe, for his is a compound of many contradictory qualities. He is both sentimental and shrewd, provincial and sophisticated, suspicious and generous, nosey and self-contained, quick-tempered and kind, self-righteous and tolerant, egotistical and unpretentious. In another book about Indiana, I once wrote:

> The Hoosier's friendliness and hospitality are universally recognizable. He is easy to meet and quite ready to talk about himself. His eagerness to share his possessions as well as his private life sometimes

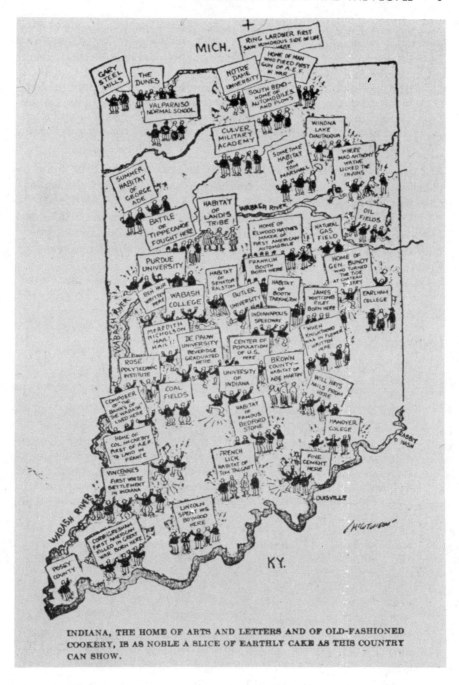

INDIANA, THE HOME OF ARTS AND LETTERS AND OF OLD-FASHIONED
COOKERY, IS AS NOBLE A SLICE OF EARTHLY CAKE AS THIS COUNTRY
CAN SHOW.

John McCutcheon's map of Indiana
Courtesy of the Indiana State Library

appears naïve to the outsider accustomed to the self-protective reticence and suspicion of more thickly populated regions. But the Hoosier is not naïve. He inherits his tradition of cordiality from lonely pioneer days when every stranger was at once a welcome friend and a helpless supplicant; yet from those same early days, he inherits a talent for quick and accurate appraisal of character. You may think that the Hoosier lays himself wide open on short acquaintance; but the chances are that he knows all there is to know about you long before he tells you a single thing about himself.

An adopted Hoosier, Irving Leibowitz, has said the same thing of Hoosiers more recently and more succinctly: "They are country smart and their kids are university educated."

Of late, the Hoosier has broadened his view of the world considerably by travel, by education, and by both adversity and success; but the foregoing quotations still define something basic and immutable in his character.

Indiana in 1916

GEORGE ADE

In the following selection, written in the year of Indiana's centennial, George Ade provides an earlier and briefer statement of the state's essential qualities. Ade, a newspaper columnist, playwright, and essayist, was one of the state's most popular humorists and was known especially for his "Fables in Slang." Fred C. Kelly offers an unhurried look at Ade's life, with generous samples of his prose, in two 1947 publications: *George Ade: Warmhearted Satirist,* and *The Permanent Ade: The Living Writings of George Ade.* For a complete listing of Ade's prodigious literary output, see Dorothy R. Russo, *A Bibliography of George Ade, 1866–1944* (1947). More recent publications include Jean Shepherd (ed.), *The America of George Ade (1866–1944): Fables, Short Stories, Essays* (1960), and Terence Tobin (ed.), *The Letters of George Ade* (1973).

What is a Hoosier? Also, why?
A Hoosier is the happy average. Happy, because he lives in Indiana.
One state in the Union does not borrow its atmosphere from the neighbors.
Indiana has a savor not to be detected in Ohio. It is decidedly un-

From "The Glory of the States: Indiana," *American Magazine,* LXXXI (March 1916), 19.

Michigan-like. Although it tinges off toward Illinois on the west and Kentucky on the south, the community is neither nebulous nor indefinite. It has a soul. It is individual.

Indiana is not Out-West or way Down-East or Up-North or south in Dixie. It is the nucleus, and ever so much of a nucleus.

It is true that west of the Platte River Indiana is supposed to be under the wither and blight of Eastern decay. Conversely, as one leaves Columbus, Ohio, and moves toward the region of perpetual seafood, one encounters people to whom Terre Haute and Cripple Creek are synonymous.

The Hoosier refuses to be classified by those who lack information. He knows that his state is an oasis, surrounded by sections. Our people are clotted around the exact center of population. Boston is not the hub. It is a repaired section of the pneumatic rim.

When a state is one hundred years old (Indiana is just that) it escapes the personal recollections of the pioneer, and is still so young that newspapers do not burn incense before the grandchildren of eminent grandparents.

We have grown some ivy, but we have not yet taken on moss.

Indiana has made history, but it figures that the present and the future are more worthy of attention than a dim and receding past.

Indiana has cemeteries and family trees, but does not subsist on them.

If the Hoosier is proud of his state, it is because the state has lived down and fought down certain misconceptions. Even in Cambridge, Massachusetts, the fact that Indiana produces more gray matter than hoop-poles is slowly beginning to percolate.

For a long time the Hoosier was on the defensive. Now he is on a pedestal.

Forty or fifty years ago the native son who went traveling owned up to an indefinite residence somewhere between Chicago and Louisville. To-day the Hoosier abroad claims Indiana fervently, hoping to be mistaken for an author.

The Indiana man respects his state because it has grown to importance and wealth without acquiring a double chin or wearing a wrist watch.

The sniffy millionaire and the aloof patrician do not cause any trembles in the state of Indiana.

Even our larger cities have no thoroughfares shaded by the gloomy strongholds of caste. Some of the more enterprising comrades are unduly prosperous, but they continue to reside in homes.

The state is short on slums and aristocratic reservations. In other words, we are still building according to specifications.

The number of liveried servants residing within the boundaries is incredibly small and does not include one person born on the banks of the Wabash.

We have a full quota of smart alecks, but not one serf.

"Abe Martin" of Brown County
Courtesy of the Indiana State Library

Because Indiana is not overbalanced by city population and is not cowed by arrogant wealth and has a lingering regard for the cadences of the spellbinder, an old-fashioned admiration for the dignified professions, and a local pride in all styles of literary output, the Hoosier has achieved his peculiar distinction as a mixed type—a puzzling combination of shy provincial, unfettered democrat and Fourth of July orator. He is a student by choice, a poet by sneaking inclination, and a story-teller by reason of his nativity.

Indiana has been helped to state consciousness because a great man has arisen to reveal the Hoosiers to themselves. The quintessence of all that is admirable in the make-up of the native is exemplified in James Whitcomb Riley.

No wonder he is beloved. Why shouldn't we be proud of our own kin?

The state is full of undiscovered Rileys, inglorious but not necessarily mute.

Your passer-by looks out of the car window and sees the Hoosier on the depot platform, necktieless and slightly bunched at the knees. According to all the late cabaret standards, the Hoosier is a simpleton, the same as you observe in the moving pictures.

Alight from the train and get close to our brother before you turn in your verdict.

Forget that he shaves his neck and remember that many a true heart beats under galluses.

Pick out a low, roomy box on the sunny side of the general store and listen with open mind, while he discourses on the crops, and bass fishing, and preparedness for war, and General Lew Wallace, and Christian Science, and the inwardness of the flare-up between Wilson and Bryan, and how to find a bee-tree. Do you want a line on Tom Taggart or Booth Tarkington or John Kern or Uncle Charley Fairbanks? He will give you the most inside information and garnish it with anecdotes.

The Hoosier may wear the wrong kind of hat, but he is alert on men and affairs and living doctrines. For fifty years the state has been a crucible of politics. It was a buffer between crowding factions all during the Civil War.

Just as the Hoosier emerges from the cradle he is handed a set of convictions and learns that he must defend them, verbally and otherwise. So he goes into training. He may turn out to be a congressman or a contributor to the magazines, but even if he escapes notoriety he will always be a belligerent, with a slant toward the intellectual.

What happened away back yonder to make Indiana different? Listen! There were two migrations early in the nineteenth century. From the seaboard there was a movement to the west. From the Carolinas and the mountain regions there was a drift northward across the Ohio River. Indiana was settled by pioneers who had the enterprise to unpack and settle down when they found themselves in the promised land.

Indiana is a composite of steel mills and country clubs, factories and colleges, promoters and professors, stock-breeders and Chautauqua attractions, corn fields and campuses. It grows all the crops and propaganda known to the temperate zone.

If a high wall could be erected to inclose Indiana, the state would continue to operate in all departments, but the outsiders would have to scale the wall in order to get their dialect poetry.

Here's to Indiana, a state as yet unspoiled! Here's to the Hoosier home folks, a good deal more sophisticated than they let on to be!

A Poetic Question

WILLIAM HERSCHELL

This section concludes with a sample of the dialect writing Ade mentions above. The selection below, one of the best-known poems—at least by title—about the state, is from the pen of William Herschell, a journalist who wrote in the vein of, but much less successfully than, James Whitcomb Riley. Herschell (1873–1939) is remembered for his bits of light verse, much of which first appeared in the columns of the Indianapolis *News*, the newspaper for which he worked as a reporter and feature writer for thirty-seven years. A bronze plaque bearing the lines of Herschell's famous paean of praise to his native state rests in the rotunda of the Indiana State Capitol. For brief biographical details on Herschell, see R. E. Banta (ed.), *Indiana Authors and Their Books, 1816–1916* (1949), and Arthur W. Shumaker, *A History of Indiana Literature* (1962).

Ain't God Good to Indiana?

Ain't God good to Indiana?
  Folks, a feller never knows
Just how close he is to Eden
  Till, sometimes, he ups an' goes
Seekin' fairer, greener pastures
  Than he has right here at home,
Where there's sunshine in th' clover
  An' there's honey in th' comb:

From *The Smile-Bringer and Other Bits of Cheer* (1919), pp. 69-70.

Where th' ripples on th' river
  Kind o' chuckle as they flow—
Ain't God good to Indiana?
  Ain't He, fellers? Ain't He though?

Ain't God good to Indiana?
  Seems to me He has a way
Gittin' me all out o' humor
  Just to see how long I'll stay
When I git th' gipsy-feelin'
  That I'd like to find a spot
Where th' clouds ain't quite so restless,
  Or th' sun don't shine as hot.
But, I don't git far, I'll tell you,
  Till I'm whisp'rin' soft an' low:
Ain't God good to Indiana:
  Ain't He, fellers? Ain't He though?

Ain't God good to Indiana?
  Other spots may look as fair,
But they lack th' soothin' somethin'
  In th' Hoosier sky an' air.
They don't have that snug-up feelin'
  Like a mother gives a child;
They don't soothe you, soul an' body,
  With their breezes soft an' mild.
They don't know th' Joys o' Heaven
  Have their birthplace here below;
Ain't God good to Indiana?
  Ain't He, fellers? Ain't He though?

Chapter I
THE FIRST INHABITANTS

Indiana, as its name implies, was the home of many different Indian cultures prior to the arrival of the first French explorers and missionaries in the second half of the seventeenth century; and during the next two centuries Indiana was home to both Indian and white peoples. The Indians of the pre-French period are known as *prehistoric,* while those Indians encountered by the successive waves of Frenchmen, Englishmen, and Americans are termed *historic.* Not only do no contemporary written records exist concerning the prehistoric tribes or nations, but there are no known links between these peoples and the historic Indians, the Delaware, Miami, Potawatomi, Wea, Piankashaw, and others living in the Ohio and Wabash valleys subsequent to 1650. Consequently, our knowledge of the prehistoric Indian peoples and their cultures is limited to that which comes from the archaeological evidence obtained from digs at Indian village sites and ceremonial or burial mounds. This evidence, fortunately, is quite considerable and continues to mount, largely through the efforts of archaeology departments at the state universities and at the University of Notre Dame, assisted by the Indiana Department of Natural Resources and the Indiana Historical Society.

Indians inhabited the region as long ago as 8,000 B.C., and in time, through the four separate cultural traditions that have been defined by archaeologists, made substantial cultural achievements. These included a settled town life, extensive trade and political networks, elaborate mortuary rituals, works of art, and practical items of work and war. The Indians of the Mississippian tradition, the last of the four groupings, either left or were driven out of the Ohio Valley by the seventeenth century, by which time European exploration and colonization in North and South America was well underway.

Spanish explorers and missionaries were the first to follow up on Columbus' discoveries and to build a New World empire. The French and the English moved more slowly, making only tentative moves during the sixteenth century. But both nations established footholds in North America in the early seventeenth century, the British in the Chesapeake Bay and Massachusetts Bay areas, the French in the St. Lawrence Valley.

Samuel de Champlain founded Quebec in 1608, and soon Frenchmen were exploring the sources of the river, then the Great Lakes area and beyond, always searching for trade (particularly in furs), territory, and religious converts. Sometime after the middle of the seventeenth century, the first French explorers reached what is now Indiana. Father Marquette may have passed through the region in 1675 while en route from the Illinois country to the upper reaches of Lake Michigan. But the first documented European visit to Indiana came in 1679. In that year Robert Cavelier de la Salle led a small exploring party across the then rather inhospitable marshlands in the northwestern corner of the state. Much of what is known about his celebrated wintry transit of Indiana is summarized in Ross F. Lockridge's account below.

Subsequently, the French established three bases in what is now Indiana, all located along the historic waterway passage connecting Lake Erie and the Ohio River via the Maumee and Wabash rivers. Although a French settlement at present-day Fort Wayne perhaps antedated the establishment of a post at Fort Quiatanon in 1717, now located a few miles below Lafayette, it was not until five years later that a similar fortified trading post, Fort Miamis, was erected at the former site. The third French post in Indiana, established along the lower Wabash in the early 1730s, was Vincennes. The French developed a substantial fur trade with various Indian tribes at all three locations during the middle years of the century, but they faced growing competition from the English for the furs and the good will of the Indians after 1750. Within little more than a decade, the French were removed from the Wabash Valley and indeed from all of North America.

At the beginning of the eighteenth century, France, according to historian Louise P. Kellogg, "had the most magnificent opportunity that has ever been offered to a colonizing power." The Mississippi Valley stretched out before her, inviting "occupation and exploitation"; but the French were unable to secure their tenuous hold on the valley or even to remain as an imperial power in the New World.[1] Indiana, remote from both centers of French colonial authority—Quebec and, after 1700, New Orleans—played a minor role in the imperial rivalry between France and Great Britain, which culminated in the "Great War for the Empire" of 1754–1763. But the fate of the French in Indiana as well as elsewhere in America was dependent on the outcome of that rivalry.

[1]Louise Phelps Kellogg, "France and the Mississippi Valley: A Résumé," *Mississippi Valley Historical Review*, XVIII (June 1931), 3.

1: Indian Achievements

Centuries before the first Europeans arrived in America, the interior of
North America, including the area that became Indiana, was populated by various "prehistoric" peoples. Archaeological studies, particularly in this century, have revealed much about the misnamed
"Indians" who roamed the forests and plied the waterways of the
mid-continent, and who made significant contributions to the economy and culture of those who followed. Far from being nomadic savages living off the bounty of the land, the evidence clearly indicates a
number of different cultural developments, major agricultural and
commercial achievements, and in time a highly developed town life.
For reasons which have yet to be fully explained, the prehistoric Indians had left the Indiana area and had been replaced by other "historic"
Indian tribes from the north and east by the time the first Frenchmen
reached the area in the mid-seventeenth century.

Indiana's Prehistoric Cultures

JAMES H. KELLAR

Professor James H. Kellar, a leading archaeologist in Indiana, has
summarized the current knowledge of Indiana's prehistoric peoples
and their achievements in an early chapter of *Indiana to 1816: The
Colonial Period* (1971), by John D. Barnhart and Dorothy L. Riker.
Professor Kellar of Indiana University is director of the Glenn A.
Black Laboratory of Archaeology in Bloomington and also serves as
archaeologist for the Indiana Historical Society. His writings include
An Introduction to the Prehistory of Indiana (1973), to which
the reader is referred for a fuller discussion of this theme and for
bibliographic suggestions. See also B. K. Swartz, *Indiana's Prehistoric
Past* (1973), and the older but still useful book by Eli Lilly, *Prehistoric
Antiquities of Indiana* (1937).

All too frequently in an understandable but ethnocentric concern for our own lives and time and their immediate antecedents, it is . . . forgotten that what is presently Indiana had been occupied for many millenniums prior to the appearance of Europeans. The contributions of these earlier occupants, the American Indians, are inescapable to even the most casual observer, although their cultures have long since been obliterated.

The name of the state and its capital city are obvious reminders of Indian occupation, as are the names of four of the immediately adjacent states [and several Indiana counties, rivers, and places]. The native people also made incalculable contributions to the economy of Indiana. The millions of acres of field corn, the leadership in the production of popcorn, the contract tomato crop in the north, and the tobacco harvest in the south all involve plants originally domesticated by the Indian. The same is true of the turkey, the raising of which contributes to the agricultural wealth of the state. Pumpkins, squash, beans, and peppers are other common plant products first utilized by the native inhabitants.

American Indian themes recur in our music and literature and television programming. The last, unfortunately, relies upon the Indian-European conflict for some of its story line, with the result that the contrived events rarely have much real relationship to actual happenings. And the early documentary history, as well as some of the recent, would have been markedly different had there been no human antecedents to contest the European claim to what we have erroneously called a "virgin wilderness."

Unlike the historical record for nearly five centuries of European-derived influence there are no coexistent written sources to document the several thousand years of Indian occupation. Therefore, it is generally impossible to obtain an understanding of individual lives and specific events, or to identify ethnic groups and the languages spoken. It is possible, however, to reconstruct something of the broad picture of cultural change and development through time and comprehend some of the conditions which produced these by reference to the surviving unintentional prehistoric record. This record includes a great variety of manufactured objects (artifacts), remains of plants and animals used by man, human burials, and the man-induced changes in the natural landscape. Careful archaeological excavations in contexts where these occur and the systematic study of the results provide the data whereby an otherwise silent past is permitted to speak.

There are literally thousands of such localities in Indiana and it is a rare river terrace that provides no such evidence. The most common items are the ubiquitous projectile points manufactured from chalcedony or chert. These are often found in association with other materials, such as animal bone, fire-cracked rock, and sometimes bits of pottery, all of which serve to identify the camps and villages of early peoples. Burial mounds are widely distributed, and there are a few hilltop "forts," some geometric earthworks, Indian cemeteries, and "workshops."

Archaeologists working with such materials in the eastern United States have developed a number of generally understood interpretative frameworks; one of these emphasizes what presently appears to be the dominant prehistoric cultural continuities. The continuities are perceived of in terms of four broadly defined cultural *traditions.*

The *Big Game Hunting Tradition* (to about 8000 B.C.) has reference to the earliest well-documented New World populations whose distinctive projectile points have been found in direct association with some of the large Late Pleistocene mammals which are now extinct.

The *Archaic Tradition* (8000 B.C. to 1000 B.C.) makes reference to early groups small in size and seasonally mobile who depended upon hunting, fishing, and plant collecting as the basis for subsistence. There is evi-

Mississippian tradition figurine from Angel Site
Courtesy of the Indiana Historical Society

dence to suggest that this tradition represents a continuation from the preceding with changes resulting from an increasing ability to utilize a variety of natural resources. This ability was undoubtedly given impetus by the slow changes in the environment as the effect of the "ice age" (Pleistocene) was superseded by conditions approximating those of the present.

The *Woodland Tradition* (1000 B.C. to A.D. 900) is generally defined by the presence of pottery, the surface of which has been impressed with cords and/or fabrics, and the development of burial ritualism as exemplified by burial mounds and other earthwork features.

The *Mississippian Tradition* (A.D. 800 to Historic Period) ultimately led to settled "town" life in some areas and greater residential stability in others based upon the intensive utilization of domesticated plants. The presence in the South of flat-topped mounds upon the surfaces of which were erected important structures and a distinctive ceramic complex are definitive characteristics for this tradition. . . .

This interpretive framework applies generally to the whole of eastern North America, of which Indiana is a small and, from the perspective of natural areas, an artificially defined part. Since human populations do move and it takes time for ideas to be transmitted from one group to another, it is to be expected that developments in one area need not occur at the same time as in another or, for that matter, be expressed in precisely the same way once they are present. For example, in Indiana, the "classic" *Mississippian Tradition* sites appear considerably later than in other areas to the west and, even then, only in a very restricted area. Also, cultural expressions in northern Indiana consistently differ from those in the south at every time period. Such situations are undoubtedly accentuated by obvious and subtle differences in the natural conditions encountered by prehistoric man.

. . . .

The beginning of the *Woodland Tradition* is marked by the appearance of fire-hardened pottery containers. This introduction constitutes a technical achievement of no small importance, not only for the vessels produced but also as regards the intellectual endeavor represented. Ceramics are one of the very few native products in which there is a transformation of raw materials into something totally different. Selected clays, tempering, and water are combined and, after drying, sufficient heat is applied to induce a physical reaction with the result being a hard insoluble substance.

Ceramics are also important for the prehistoric archaeologist. Each step of the pottery-making process is susceptible to considerable variation: the choice of clays and the tempering medium, the methods used to form the container, the shape of the vessel itself, types of surface decorations, the presence of handles or other appendages, the temperature of the firing process. All of the foregoing separately and in combination can produce an almost unending variability. However, as with ourselves, what was produced was controlled by group style preferences; these were not universal but differed at particular times and places. Pottery sherds are the most frequently recovered artifact on many sites. This, combined with their systematic variability, permits the establishment of a ceramic chronology to which other associated cultural materials can be related. Wherever pottery has been produced almost invariably archaeologists have used it to establish time scales and, initially at least, to differentiate cultures of the past.

. . . .

The *Early Woodland Tradition* groups, in common with their immediate predecessors, were fundamentally reliant upon hunting, fishing, and collecting for their means of subsistence. The major differences are in the presence of pottery and, in southwestern Indiana, a markedly decreased reliance upon the river mussel as a source of food.

The earliest pottery recognized is a type referred to as *Marion Thick*.

Prehistoric Indian pottery
Courtesy of the Indiana Historical Society

It or related material is present in southern Indiana and northward in the Wabash drainage into the lake region. As the name indicates, it is very heavy, often being over an inch in thickness. The outer surface, sometimes the inner, too, is impressed with heavy cords patterned to suggest that a woven fabric might have been used. . . .

The middle period of the *Woodland Tradition* is typically the time during which ritualism as perceived through burial practices reaches a climax. It, in a sense, constitutes the culmination of trends begun in the Archaic and given additional impetus during the early Woodland period. This is reflected in many ways. Burial mounds are widely dispersed over eastern North America from southern Canada to the Gulf of Mexico and the Appalachians to the Plains. Even more widely spread trade patterns are apparent: obsidian from Wyoming, grizzly bear teeth from the Rocky Mountains, copper from the upper Great Lakes region, pipestone and flint from Ohio, hornstone from Indiana, mica from the southern Appalachians, and marine shells from the Gulf of Mexico region. Also, a few distinctive artifacts and decorative styles occur sporadically in distant sites: copper "pan pipes," bicymbal-shaped copper ear spools, "monitor" type stone pipes, clay human figurines, and some techniques of pottery decoration, i.e., dentate stamping, as well as vessel form. All of these contribute to a picture of considerable social interaction at about the beginning of the Christian Era.

. . . .

The definition of Late Woodland is based largely upon negative qualities; that is, those special features of culture which served to underscore our contemporary view of life during the Middle Woodland period become markedly attenuated or disappear. Earthwork complexes were no longer in use, though a few mounds continued to be constructed. However, these served as general cemeteries in many instances, rather than as repositories for the select few. The trade for exotic raw materials was substantially terminated and such items as mica, obsidian, copper, and marine shells occurred rarely, if at all. Craft specialization suggested by the work produced from these materials, as well as the effigy stone pipes, was no longer apparent. The material culture was often remarkably uniform and lacking in stylistic variation and evidence of experimentation. There was overall a sense of monotony, of sameness, and of local isolation.

A number of explanations have been proposed to account for what amounts to a significant change in the cultural orientation of the Woodland populations. However, most of these are unsatisfactory because they are not susceptible to testing. For example, one proposal is that the limited technological base was ultimately insufficiently productive to support the native institutions responsible for maintaining the inferred ceremonial practices. Another suggestion is that the system itself became so complex and highly developed that further elaboration of the pattern was not feasible. A third hypothesis and one which offers some opportunity for testing is that the Middle Woodland populations were displaced by intruders; the so-called hilltop forts, at least two examples of which are located in Dearborn and Clark counties, are cited as evidence for a struggle for control. This explanation is obviously allied with much earlier statements regarding the demise of the "mound builders," but it rests on the assumption that the intruders were American Indians, as were those intruded upon. A fourth suggestion, and one for which evidence can be marshaled, is ecological in nature. Plant cultivation is present during Middle Woodland, though it does not appear to have been intensively practiced, and it is possible that maize production provided the extra subsistence margin required for the indicated ceremonial development. Being near the northern limits of effective maize cultivation, slight climatic shifts could drastically alter the productivity of the then available seed. And a slight decrease in average temperatures is indicated beginning about A.D. 400, which accords reasonably well with the time when Middle Woodland begins to exhibit "decline." Interestingly, the cultural pattern maintains continuity farther to the south where the natural change would have had much less impact.

. . . .

The *Mississippian Tradition* climaxes in what is the most complex of the several North American cultural developments. Unlike the Woodland apogee which is confined to a limited and somewhat esoteric segment of culture, that during Mississippian is reflected at many levels from the commonplace to the specialized. Also, elements of the development persisted into the period of early European settlement and limited insights were gained by direct observation, specifically in the southeastern states.

The basic tradition was dependent upon the intensive cultivation of maize, beans, and squash, as well as other lesser seed crops and tobacco, which in combination with resident plants and animals, provided an abundant and richly varied food supply. Settlements were permanently established and some evidence of intentional long-range planning is apparent in house distributions, the preservation of open areas within the towns, and the placement of community structures. Some of the larger towns extended over hundreds of acres and must have had populations of several thousand. The raw materials exploited differed little from those available and used for millenniums by the American Indian, but the artifacts produced from bone, stone, and shell and the ceramics were varied and occur in great numbers. The emergent picture is one in which marked social stratification is present and elements of social control are vested in institutions having a religious-political function. Undoubtedly, the town exercised a hegemony over nearby farmsteads.

. . . .

Large mound at Angel Site
Courtesy of the Indiana Historical Society

The outstanding "classic" Mississippian site in Indiana, Angel Mounds, is located a few miles east of Evansville in the flood plain of the Ohio. A summary description of its physical remains serves to convey something of its importance.

The site extended over an area slightly in excess of a hundred acres and was shielded from the mainstream of the Ohio River by a narrow island. The residents undoubtedly were afforded some protection by this natural feature and, additionally, more than a mile of high bastioned stockade made of logs covered with clay daub covered the mainland approaches. A three-terraced flat-topped mound measuring 650 by 300 by 44 feet had been constructed near the approximate center of the settlement; a large structure reserved for a highly esteemed person or group undoubtedly occupied the broad platform. A number of smaller truncated pyramids were erected for yet other community structures. Just west of the large mound was an open plaza. Around this plaza and throughout the village substantial houses were constructed. These were generally square to rectangular in plan and ranged from about sixteen feet to thirty feet on a side. Construction was accomplished by setting upright posts in a trench and then covering the frame with cane mats and these with daub. These houses followed consistent orientations in various segments of the community. While only a portion of the site has been excavated, projections from this suggest that about two hundred dwellings would have been present at any one time. The population estimate based on the number of houses produces a figure of at least one thousand residents. Food reliance was upon cultivated plants, game, fish and mussels, and wild plant products.

The Mississippian occupants of Angel Mounds were skilled craftsmen. They produced a good quality shell-tempered pottery having many vessel forms undoubtedly to serve specific functions. Though most of it is without surface decoration, some painted wares were manufactured. Using stone, bone, and shell, numerous tools necessary for daily life were manufactured in quantity as were other artifacts for personal adornment.

. . . .

Ideally, we should now be in a position, after summarizing ten thousand years of Indiana prehistory, to relate all of this to the Indian occupants of record. Actually, this is for the moment at least, impossible. The explanation for this inability is simple. Various bands of the Miami and Potawatomi occupied the greater portion of the state. Other residents included the Delawares, Shawnee, and a few members of other ethnic groups. These were without exception late migrants into the region. For example, it is not until the late seventeenth century that the Miami apparently moved southeast from Wisconsin and Illinois. The Potawatomi came at about the same time or a bit later. The Delawares did not arrive until the middle of the following century. And at least some of the Shawnee seemed to have wandered over nearly all the eastern United States in the early historic period before returning to what may have been their earlier Ohio Valley homeland. The obvious fact is that the known Indian occupants came into Indiana from the outside and even though they might have lived here earlier, there is no way to relate a fully prehistoric site or culture to a specific ethnic group under these circumstances.

2: The First Europeans

La Salle's Visit to Indiana, 1679

ROSS F. LOCKRIDGE

The journey of Robert Cavelier de la Salle across northwestern Indiana in 1679, over the portage between the St. Joseph and Kankakee rivers, is one of the early benchmarks of Indiana history. La Salle (1643– 1687), whose brilliant career as an explorer and architect of French colonial policy was cut short by his murder while on an expedition to the Gulf coast in 1687, was engaged during the late 1670s in exploring the upper reaches of the Mississippi Valley and planning for the establishment of French settlements there. In the passage below, Ross F. Lockridge describes the La Salle party and the hardships of exploration and quotes from Father Hennepin's account of La Salle's snowy night alone in the woods after he became separated from the others in his group.

Lockridge (1877–1952) was a popular author and lecturer on Indiana topics. In addition to a well-received junior high and high school textbook, *The Story of Indiana* (1951), he wrote juvenile biographies of Abraham Lincoln and George Rogers Clark and a number of pamphlets on New Harmony, where he served as director of the New Harmony Memorial Commission. Lockridge is perhaps best remembered, however, as the founder of the somewhat controversial depression-era "History on Wheels" program, in which he and other speakers and actors presented episodes in Indiana history near the actual sites of the original events, and as the father of Ross F. Lockridge, Jr., author of *Raintree County* (1947), a powerful best-selling novel set in nineteenth-century Indiana.

For additional information on La Salle, see the firsthand account by Father Louis Hennepin, *Description of Louisiana*, translated and edited by John Gilmary Shea (1880), and the biography by Paul Chesnel, *History of Cavelier de la Salle, 1643–1687* (1932); see also George I. Quimby, "The Voyage of the *Griffon*:1679," *Michigan History*, XLIX (June 1965), 97–107.

From *La Salle* (1931), pp. 105–119. Copyright © World Book Company. Reprinted by permission.

La Salle thought it unwise to spend the winter on the frozen shores of Lake Michigan. Most of the Indians, like the birds, had gone farther south, and La Salle decided to go too. Convinced at last that the *Griffon* was lost, he decided to wait no longer. So on December 3, 1679, he and his force of thirty-two men embarked in eight large canoes, or pirogues, and paddled up the St. Joseph River to find the portage which joins the waters of the Mississippi with those of the Lakes. This St. Joseph River, which was best known at that time as the River of the Miamis, is to be distinguished from the St. Joseph which joins the St. Mary at Fort Wayne, Indiana, to form the Maumee.

There were two days of vigorous paddling against the chilly current of the river, which was very swift in places. Sometimes long poles were used. On December 5, 1679, the company landed where they thought the portage was, in what is now the city of South Bend, Indiana. This occasion was dramatic as well as historic, and a detailed record of it was made at the time. . . .

The spot was well suited for making history. The portage was really a key to the continent and had been used for generations, maybe centuries, by the Indians. The portage was less than five miles in length; nearly all of it is included within the present city limits of South Bend.

Portages play a very important part in the history of early exploration and settlement of the Mississippi Valley, and this old St. Joseph-Kankakee Portage was one of the most famous of them. It was the only carrying place of its kind on that long route that La Salle was following from the Atlantic Ocean to the Gulf of Mexico by way of the St. Lawrence River, the Great Lakes, and the Mississippi. Boats and goods had to be carried by land on this trip around the Lachine Rapids and Niagara Falls, and these places were therefore usually called portages; but they were really détours, or run-arounds, rather than portages. Portages, or watersheds, are connecting links of land between great water systems. In this sense of the word, the St. Joseph-Kankakee Portage was the only portage on La Salle's route [and] . . . had peculiar importance for him. Until his arrival at this point we might consider his journey all an upstream progress. He came up the St. Lawrence, up the Niagara, up the Detroit, and up the St. Joseph. Even crossing the Lakes seemed upstream. After portaging over this strip of less than five miles, the rest of the journey was downstream—down the Kanakakee, down the Illinois, down the Mississippi to the Gulf.

This is a fitting point to take note of the personnel of that history-making band that came in true history-making fashion upstream in early winter. In their eight long pirogues they were a picturesque group. True *voyageurs* they were, and well suited to the picturesque setting in which they were placed.

The thirty-two men that La Salle had with him on this occasion may be taken as typical of his associates during his entire career in America. First and foremost, after the great leader himself, was his famous lieutenant, Henry de Tonty. Tonty was a young soldier of a noted Italian family. His father, Lorenzo Tonty, had been an illustrious banker of Naples and governor of Gaeta, and had invented the Tontine system of insurance, which is still in use. Compelled to flee from his native land because of a Neapolitan conspiracy in 1647, he came to France. There he was taken in service by his famous fellow countryman, Cardinal Mazarin, who was then prime minister at the court of the boy king, Louis XIV.

Young Henry de Tonty, who was born in Naples, was brought to the French court as a small baby. He grew up in France, which became his adopted country. At the age of eighteen he entered the French army and fought through several campaigns both on land and sea, suffering many wounds and much imprisonment. His right hand was blown off by the explosion of a hand grenade in the siege of Libissio. Notwithstanding this loss and the six months' imprisonment which followed, he returned to service in the Sicilian campaign. There he served as a volunteer in the galleys until he was mustered out when the troops were discharged because of a general peace. It was soon after this, in 1678, that he joined La Salle at Versailles.

Tonty had been recommended to La Salle by the Prince de Conti. It did not take La Salle long to learn the excellent qualities of his lieutenant. He seems to have trusted Tonty from the first. Shortly after their arrival in Canada, on October 31, 1678, La Salle wrote Conti concerning Tonty as follows:

> His honorable character and his amiable disposition were well known to you; but perhaps you would not have thought him capable of doing things for which a strong constitution, an acquaintance with the country, and the use of both hands seemed absolutely necessary. Nevertheless, his energy and address make him equal to anything.

The lost hand had been replaced by a metal hand, very cunningly fashioned and always covered with a tight-fitting velvet glove, so that there was little or no disfigurement. Tonty goes through history as "Hand of Iron," but he might well have been known as "Heart of Gold." The story of La Salle is literally filled with striking proofs of the golden-hearted loyalty of this devoted lieutenant. Tonty was always faithful to La Salle, even when La Salle's own countrymen abandoned him. He was trusted by La Salle in the forefront of their most desperate enterprises. On many important occasions he stood almost as La Salle's second self. The record shows him to have been a man of noble and intelligent spirit, possessing great physical energy. Being a genuine leader as well as a faithful follower, he inspired the respect and confidence of all his associates. . . .

After Tonty the most outstanding member of that little group was a native American—White Beaver, the Mohican Indian. He was La Salle's hunter and trusted guide. Little is known of White Beaver's first connection with La Salle, and his fate is likewise very obscure; but he looms very important during the most critical years of La Salle's career. He was of gigantic build and possessed in high degree all the speed, the endurance, and the woodcraft skill peculiar to the natives. His unfailing rifle brought down game for the party. His keen eye sought out paths, and his quick ear caught every sound of danger. La Salle could rely upon this naked savage as he relied upon no other except Tonty. Here was an Indian whose unpretentious services, recited in detail in unquestionable journals, show him to have been in truth a noble redman. . . .

In this remarkable party that sailed the waters of the Lakes, there were also the three priests of the Recollect order—Louis Hennepin, Gabriel Ribourde, and Zenobe Membre. All were Flemish friars of the gray robe. It was characteristic of the spirit and policy of La Salle that he should have been accompanied on this hazardous journey of exploration by these holy fathers. He brought them along partly to administer to spiritual wants on the journey but mainly to work in the posts he expected to establish to minister to the Indians and colonists. This Christian knight of France esteemed it quite as much his mission to advance the kingdom of God in the New World as to advance the kingdom of France. He seldom made any expeditions without being accompanied by one or more priests. Where he built a fort, he built a chapel; and where he erected the royal standard of Louis XIV, he raised the Cross of Christ. Shouts of *"Vive le Roi!"* were accompanied by the chanting of *Te Deum*. . . .

The remaining twenty-seven members of the party were a motley crew. Most of them are known by name and to some extent by occupation and service. Some of the men were skilled artisans—such as Moyse Hilleret, the master shipbuilder; Jean Le Mire, a ship carpenter; and Jean Mielleor, the nailmaker, who was known as La Forge. These men were chosen for the building of forts and ships. Some were expert sawyers. Most of the men were soldiers of fortune, wandering *coureurs de bois,* ne'er-do-wells, and adventurers whom La Salle had picked up, some in Paris, some in Quebec, some in Montreal. All were skillful canoemen. Most of them proved entirely untrustworthy. In less than a month from the time of their arrival at the St. Joseph-Kankakee Portage, six of them deserted. And less than two months after that over a dozen more turned mutineers and traitors. It seems probable that some of these men had been placed in this company by La Salle's enemies to stir up mutiny and wreck his enterprise.

One of them, a villain by the name of Nicholas du Plessis, tried to shoot La Salle in the back while crossing this very portage on December 6, 1679. This murderous act was prevented by a faithful member of the party. At various times some of these unfaithful followers of La Salle tried to kill him by putting poison in his food, from which he saved himself by antidotes, which he always carried.

The minor details of La Salle's experiences at this portage have been recorded very elaborately, and they have been given much significance be-

LaSalle at the Portage Landing, St. Joseph River, December 5, 1679

Courtesy of the Indiana Historical Society

cause of the light they throw on the picture of La Salle himself as well as on the obstacles he faced.

As the party neared the portage on the afternoon of December fifth, White Beaver left the boats in order to kill a deer for the evening meal, and without his guidance the *voyageurs* missed the narrow portage path among the bushes. Snow lay thick upon the ground, and the travelers passed the place where they should have landed. They journeyed on around what is known as Pinhook, finally landing about two leagues up the river from the portage, supposedly near where Miami Street meets the river in South Bend.

Here La Salle, realizing that they had missed the portage path, left the party and went out across the swamp alone. He intended to climb the hills south of the river with the hope of being able to see the Kankakee and spy out the way across the prairie. He got lost in the thick overgrown swamps and had a most interesting experience, which Hennepin described as follows:

> We halted to wait for the Sieur de la Salle, who had gone exploring on land; and as he did not return we did not know what course to pursue. I begged two of our most alert men to penetrate into the woods and fire off their guns, so as to give him notice of the spot where we were waiting for him. Two others ascended the river, but to no purpose, for the night obliged them to retrace their steps. The next day I took two of our men in a lightened canoe, to make greater expedition and to seek him by ascending the river, but in vain; and at four o'clock in the afternoon we perceived him at a distance, his hands and face all black with the coals and wood that he had lighted during the night, which was cold. He had two animals [opossums] of the size of muskrats hanging to his belt, which had a very beautiful skin, like a

kind of ermine, which he killed with blows of a stick without these little animals taking flight, and which often let themselves hang by the tail from branches of trees; and as they were very fat our canoemen feasted on them. He told us that the marshes that he met with obliged him to make a wide sweep, and as moreover he was hindered by the snow, which was falling rapidly, he was unable to reach the bank of the river before two o'clock at night. He fired two gunshots to notify us, and no one having answered him, he thought the canoes had gone ahead of him, and kept on his way along and up the river. After marching in this way more than three hours he saw fire on a mound, which he ascended brusquely, and after calling two or three times; but instead of finding us asleep, as he expected, he saw only a little fire among some brush and under an oak tree, the spot where a man had been lying down on some dry herbs, and who had apparently gone off at the noise which he had heard. It was some Indian who had gone there in ambush to surprise and kill some of his enemies along the river. He called to him in two or three languages, and at last, to show him that he did not fear him, he cried that he was going to sleep in his place. He renewed the fire, and, after warming himself well, he took steps to guarantee himself against surprise by cutting down around him a quantity of bushes, which, falling across those that remained standing, blocked the way so that no one could approach him without making considerable noise and waking him. He then extinguished the fire and slept, although it snowed all night.

This is a good picture of the human La Salle, spending the night of December 5, 1679, alone on a bed of leaves in the snow by an Indian campfire. He must have knocked over those opossums "playing 'possum" somewhere east of South Bend near the present site of Mishawaka or Osceola.

When La Salle got back to his party the next day, he was heartily welcomed and warned not to expose himself again in such a manner. Hennepin says, "Father Gabriel and I begged the Sieur de la Salle not to leave his party as he had done, showing him that the whole success of our voyage depended on his presence." In the meantime White Beaver had come up to the party and conducted them back to the portage. Father Ribourde cut some crosses on the trees to blaze the route. At least one of those ancient symbols of Christianity placed by this devoted courier of the Cross is still in existence.

None rejoiced more over the safe return of La Salle than the devoted Tonty, whom Hennepin does not mention at all in this connection. The fact is that Hennepin was jealous of Tonty's prominence in the party, and the reserved Italian had little in common with the boastful friar. Tonty had made a vigorous search for the lost leader and was the first to greet him. He said simply, "The whole party reassembled, which caused us much joy."

. . . .

The party crossed the portage the next day, carrying the big pirogues and the valuable supplies a distance of nearly five miles across the spongy ground then partly covered with snow. There the Kankakee, among quaking marshes, became navigable for the canoes. They went single file by the narrow and deeply worn path through Ox-Head Prairie, where they saw numbers of buffalo horns and bones and partly consumed carcasses. They passed near the abandoned Miami village at the west side of the prairie and saw many canoes that the Indians had left. Crossing the portage was hard work, taxing the endurance of the men and the control of La Salle, who had to look after everything. Everyone took a hand, even the aged Father Ribourde cheerfully bearing his share.

We do not know the weight of La Salle's supplies, but it must have been considerable. The vast amount of tools, trinkets, and guns that he distributed later among the Indians, together with the forge and the bellows, the rigging, and the materials for the contemplated vessels, to say nothing of the arms, ammunition, and regular provisions of the men, must have been a heavy load. It required sixteen men to carry the empty pirogues alone—one at each end of each boat. The remaining seventeen men, including La Salle, had to carry the supplies. They would not weaken the party and endanger the supplies by separating for more than one trip. Having a few men make several trips back and forth would have been a waste of time too. There could be no slackers; all had to work. The portages offered grim, hard work and a stern test of leadership.

In this manner the portage of the St. Joseph and Kankakee was passed by this first memorable band of *voyageurs*. La Salle was to pass this way many times during the next few years of his explorations in the west.

On December 7, 1679, the canoes were launched once more on the winding, marshy courses of the Kankakee, and the hardy *voyageurs* were on their way toward the mighty Father of Waters.

The Failure of French Policy

GEORGE RAWLYK

French presence in the interior of North America was comparatively short. Given the administrative difficulties it was experiencing at home and in the colonies, coupled with the competitive disadvantages under which the French labored while struggling with Great Britain for con-

From "The 'Rising French Empire' in the Ohio Valley and Old Northwest: The 'Dreaded Junction of the French Settlements in Canada with those of Louisiana'" in John B. Elliott (ed.), *Contest for Empire* (1975), pp. 45–50, 51–52, 52–57. Footnotes in the original have been omitted. Copyright © Indiana Historical Society. Reprinted by permission.

trol of the Ohio and Mississippi valleys, France was unable to remain
as a New World power after the mid-eighteenth century. The commercial and military empire of the French fell victim to the more populous
and more powerful English empire. Even the long-standing alliances
between the French and the Indians had been weakened by English
penetration and competition on the frontier. When it came to a military
solution to the problem, the French, by a narrow margin, did not
prevail.

George Rawlyk, a Canadian scholar, here reviews the colonial
policy of France and analyzes its mistakes in strategy that he believes
led to the loss of France's colonial empire. Its quest for military
superiority through dramatic confrontation with the English in the
upper Ohio Valley, rather than by a more prosaic but effective buildup
of trade relations with Indians in the interior, led to an immediate
English response. The resulting French and Indian War brought about
the removal of France from all of North America and left the French-
Canadian people in only a small portion of Canada.

A recent survey with a full bibliography of France's colonizing
efforts in North America is William J. Eccles, *France in America* (New
York, 1972); see also the older work by Louise P. Kellogg, *The French
Regime in Wisconsin and the Northwest* (Madison, 1925). The best
collection of primary documents on New France is still Reuben G.
Thwaites (ed.), *The Jesuit Relations and Allied Documents* (73 vols.,
1896–1901).

Despite the American propaganda barrage concerning the "Rising
French Empire" and despite the widespread fear of "French Encirclement,"
few inhabitants of pre-Conquest New France manifested any real interest in
westward imperial expansion. There was more than enough empty space for
them to fill in the St. Lawrence Valley. It is not surprising, therefore, that
until nearly the middle of the eighteenth century the Ohio Valley was almost
totally ignored by the French authorities. It is true, of course, that after
1701 the French had theoretically adopted a new policy of territorial expansion designed to exclude the Anglo-Americans from the interior of North
America. This policy was implemented by creating Louisiana and by con-
structing fortifications in the Illinois country. The Ohio Valley, however,
was almost completely bypassed. In fact, the upper reaches of the Ohio were
not even explored by the French until Léry's expedition did so in 1729. At
this same time, it should be pointed out, La Vérendrye was already planning
his explorations in search of the "western sea."

In 1721 the British Board of Trade finally responded to news about
French expansion south of the Great Lakes by urging the building of fortifications on the Great Lakes and in the Allegheny passes. But little of consequence was actually done by the British to block the French. In 1726 Fort
Oswego was built on Lake Ontario but nothing was done about the Al-

legheny passes, and the Ohio Valley was as much ignored by the British as it was by the French.

In view of this record of inactivity in the Ohio Valley, it seems both remarkable and ironic that, in the short space of ten years from 1744 to 1754, French interest and behavior in the Ohio country, together with the growing Anglo-American fear of French encirclement, would play such a key role in precipitating hostilities between France and England. The apparent change in French policy seemed to many contemporaries to have been very dramatic. Yet a closer examination of developments in the Ohio country during this period reveals not so much a sudden change in policy as a logical extension of the policy which for decades had guided French activities in North America.

This policy recognized that the fur trade remained the economic pillar of New France. Centered at Montreal, this trade accounted for two thirds of all French-Canadian exports during the first half of the eighteenth century even though agriculture and industry were receiving considerable governmental assistance. The French policy also, it should be pointed out, recognized the relative paucity of settlers in the French North American colonies. Consequently, it was realized that the success of French colonial enterprises in North America was based on a careful cultivation of the various Indian nations. By this means the French had succeeded in obtaining both furs and much-needed allies. It is interesting to note that the French governmental authorities actively participated in implementing this policy. Forts Frontenac, Niagara, and Detroit were maintained as King's posts; goods were sold below cost there in order to entice the Indians away from English posts such as Fort Oswego. Every year a portion of the profits earned from the sale of *congés* and post leases was spent on presents for the Indians to keep them loyal and passive. And before the outbreak of the War of the Austrian Succession in 1744, this policy had, it seems clear, helped guarantee the neutrality or pro-French stance of most of the Indians inhabiting the region south of the Great Lakes.

Nevertheless, such a policy had some obvious weaknesses; one of these was the dangerous French dependence on an uninterrupted flow of trade goods with which to purchase the continued friendship of the Indians. During the War of the Austrian Succession, from 1744 to 1748, this flow was seriously blocked by British naval supremacy in the North Atlantic. As early as 1745, French colonial officials predicted that their Indian allies would automatically turn to Anglo-American traders once the French were not able to satisfy their needs. The commandant of Detroit pointed out in July, 1745, that the English at Fort Oswego were spreading rumors to the Indians traveling to Montreal that the French would soon be short of trade supplies. Within two years the English had made good this threat, and the French post commanders found themselves confronted by a serious dilemma. Their efforts to buy the active assistance of the Indians in the

Illinois country for attacks on the Anglo-Americans, who had penetrated the region in force after 1743, had collapsed because they had nothing with which to make payments to their allies. In disgust and out of need, the Indians began to turn to the very people the French detested and feared— the Anglo-Americans.

Despite these real threats to French policy, some of the French colonial officials, at least in their letters, showed confidence and optimism. Obviously they were eager to impress the minister of Marine that they were still in control of events. However, by the summer of 1747 they could no longer avoid the harsh realities of the new situation. It had become clear to the distraught French post commanders at Detroit and in the Illinois country that a general Indian uprising against the French was being planned. The Anglo-American traders at Sandusky and the area of the Greater Miami River had been extremely active in 1746 and 1747 in drawing many of the Indians away from the French. They had fully exploited the scarcity of French goods and also the Anglo-American victory at Louisbourg in 1745. If the so-called "French Gibraltar of North America" could be captured by a motley collection of Yankees and if the British fleet could virtually drive the French navy from the North Atlantic, the Indians could expect little assistance from their traditional allies. Not only did the Anglo-American traders drive home this point about the shattered French prestige and power, but they also cleverly played on fears of the Ottawa, Potawatomi, Hurons, Chippewa, and Miami, concerning imminent raids by the Iroquois, who were known to be sympathetic to the English. In addition, the Anglo-Americans gave presents to the Indians in an attempt to win them over. These policies were so successful that by the middle of 1747 the Hurons near Detroit were preparing a surprise attack on that settlement. Other tribes, it was hoped, would join in and sweep the upper country and the Illinois country free of the French. Only a fortuitous discovery of the plan by the Baron de Longueuil, the commandant of Detroit, enabled the French to prepare for the uprising and to summon help.

The so-called "Conspiracy of 1747" was nipped in the bud largely because of the arrival of a shipment of trade goods at Detroit, together with an impressive military escort. Once the Indian attack plan was aborted, most of the Indians made loud declarations of loyalty to the French. And soon the correspondence of the colonial administrators regained its earlier sense of optimism.

Nevertheless, this incident had a significant impact on the French and on their policy. As might be expected, the French officials recognized that one of the principal causes of the unrest had been the Anglo-American activities among the Indians. And, furthermore, the refusal of the traditional French-Indian allies to help suppress the uprising persuaded at least the Marquis de La Galissonière, the governor of Canada from 1747 to 1749, that never again should the French allow themselves to be caught in a position where they were forced to rely on the co-operation of Indians: "I think that one of the best ways of forestalling in the future any similar disorder would be to settle a good number of husbandmen at Detroit. Thus that post would be in a condition to subsist almost entirely of itself and to defend all the posts which are nearby." At this point, La Galissonière introduced for the first time the contention that the real threat to the Illinois country came from uncontested Anglo-American access to the Ohio Valley: "I think that is the only way of preventing the English from establishing themselves on the Ohio River, an establishment quite capable of interrupting our communication with the Mississippi which is almost necessary to both colonies."

Here, then, is a statement of the fundamental impact which the "Conspiracy of 1747" had on French policy in North America. Most of the Indians had indicated in no uncertain terms that their support would go to whichever power exhibited the greater military and commercial strength and prestige. Prestige in this sense rested on the ability to maintain a firm grip on trade in the interior, an ability which the French could no longer be certain of exercising in the face of growing British seapower. Unable, therefore, to rely in the future on being able to outbid the English for the co-operation and support of the Indians, the French were compelled to consider the alternative—barring the Anglo-Americans from the interior of the continent altogether. The Comte de Raymond, commanding officer at Fort des Miamis, suggested that this be done through diplomatic channels. More realistically, La Galissonière focused his attention on what could actually be done to plug the Anglo-American conduit to the interior—the Ohio Valley. The geophysical characteristics of the region, it was argued, were such that the existing troops of New France were capable of blocking the Ohio Valley without depending on the Indians for support. . . .

La Galissonière's proposals earned what some would consider to be undeserved praise, both from his contemporaries and from most historians. In a way, of course, his proposals were strategically shrewd. Yet they were neither as realistic nor as original as La Galissonière's admirers would like to believe. The proposals were unrealistic because France had never before succeeded in mounting a sustained immigration and settlement program in North America. They were also unrealistic because the Indians would never have tolerated a major settlement program. One of the few advantages which the French had over the English in North America was that their frontier posts were never transformed into major settlements. Some of them, to be sure, supported small-scale European communities; but these were always designed merely to add to the military strength and security of the post. The Indians had made clear their attitude towards settlement; the English understood this and so did most of the French. Thus, La Galissonière's grandiose proposals were at odds with reality. . . .

Throughout the Ohio Valley and the Illinois country and beyond, the

Indians were very restless and were giving every indication of conspiring once again to try to drive the French from that territory. The new center of the anti-French movement was La Demoiselle's Miami village on the Great Miami River. By 1750 the Anglo-Americans had established a trading post there called Pickawillany, and they had quickly become the predominant influence in the new Indian intrigue. Early in 1750 reports began to circulate among various French post commanders and officials about the possible imminent Miami and Shawnee attacks. . . .

Given the circumstances and his instructions, Governor La Jonquière [La Galissonière's successor] did his best to strengthen the French position in North America. Fort Rouillé (Toronto) was established in 1750 in order to intercept the Indian trade flowing to Fort Oswego. The post at Michilimackinac was strengthened and forts were built at Sault Ste. Marie and at the foot of the Niagara portage. Diplomatic negotiations in 1750 and 1751 secured the neutrality of the Cayuga and Onondaga; these tribes had, following La Galissonière's activities in 1749, feared that the French were eager to force the withdrawal of all Indians from the Ohio Valley. La Jonquière reassured them, promising that "The French, who will go to the Beautiful river, will carry wherewith to supply the wants of those who are there, and will be careful not to disturb them." Only those who proved hostile to the French, declared the governor, would be in danger of expulsion. Finally, in an effort to determine more precisely what was happening in the Ohio country, the governor sent Captain Philippe de Joncaire with a small party to that region.

Despite these efforts, which remained within the limits set by La Jonquière's instructions, the reports sent back by Joncaire and other French officers in the interior indicated that a passive policy would not work. During 1751, at least nine Frenchmen and two slaves were killed in isolated incidents south of Lake Erie. Rumors were circulating of conferences attended by Illinois, Miami, Delawares, Shawnee, Iroquois, and Anglo-American traders. Tension increased when a bad harvest created a scarcity of provisions. Joncaire sadly reported that "the Indians of the Beautiful river are all English."

Faced with this rapidly deteriorating situation, La Jonquière was receptive to any plans offering firm measures against the hostile Indians of the Ohio Valley, especially those at Pickawillany. . . . But once again the plan had to be abandoned. . . .

La Jonquière never had another opportunity to suppress the Indians of the Ohio country. Following an unrelated dispute with Rouillè, he resigned his offices, and before he could return to France, he died, in March, 1752. His replacement, the Marquis Duquesne, was still in France, and so the administration of the colony fell temporarily into the hands of Longueuil, the governor of Montreal.

During his brief term in office, Longueuil attempted to continue La

Jonquière's efforts to suppress the Indian unrest in the interior. He proposed sending a force of four hundred French troops to Detroit that summer, to be followed in the spring of the following year by a slightly larger force. Sometime in 1753, according to the plan, the approximately eight-hundred-man force would then overpower and overawe the hostile Miami and drive out the Anglo-Americans. This plan, in its strategic thrust, was quite similar to La Jonquière's plan of 1751. It differed, of course, in one fundamental way! Longueuil explicitly excluded the Indians from participating. The uncooperative behavior of the Indians domiciled at Detroit in 1751 may have persuaded him not to use any Indians. Or it may have been that Longueuil, expecting the Indians to join the French expedition once they saw its size, deliberately excluded any mention of them because he did not want to alienate his superior.

While Longueuil labored hard to try to put his plan into effect in the summer of 1752, a force of 250 Chippewa Indians from Michilimackinac, under the command of Charles-Michel Mouet de Langlade, had taken the initiative and had attacked and destroyed Pickawillany. La Demoiselle, the Miami chief who had caused so much trouble for the French, was permanently removed from the scene by the simple expedient of boiling and eating him. The terror of a smallpox epidemic contributed further to the collapse of the Indian unrest in the Ohio and Illinois country.

Even before the news of the Langlade expedition had reached him, Rouillé was expressing his displeasure with the extent to which La Jonquière and Longueuil had ignored his orders to avoid entanglements with the Indians. The minister of Marine was determined that the new governor of New France should clearly understand his wishes and conscientiously carry them out. Duquesne was, therefore, warned to ignore the advice of these French Canadians who wanted him to continue the policy of La Jonquière and Longueuil.

Consequently, when Duquesne arrived in New France, he was committed to implementing a military policy independent of Indian allies. He immediately made plans to occupy the upper Ohio Valley in force in order to bar English access to the country and the Indians beyond. An expedition was organized, and in 1753, over two thousand Frenchmen (300 Troupes de la Marine and 1,700 Canadian militia) advanced into the area south of Lake Erie and into the upper reaches of the Ohio Valley. Forts were erected and garrisoned, roads were built, and when the Anglo-Americans tried to protest or resist, they were packed on their way.

This was more than the English colonial governments had bargained for, but most were not keen to finance countermeasures. Nevertheless, a small military force under the command of George Washington, financed by the Virginia House of Burgesses, set out early in 1754 in an effort to force the French to withdraw. The result was rather an ignoble defeat for Washington—but a defeat with major consequences. The mother countries began to participate directly in these affairs, with the result that the Seven Years' War between France and England began, to all intents and purposes, not in 1756 but rather in 1754 in the forested mountain country of the upper Ohio Valley.

What, then, can be said about French policy in the Ohio-Illinois country? La Jonquière, influenced by Canadians such as Longueuil and Bigot, had tried to preserve French authority in the region by forcing the Indians to co-operate. This policy depended on the active assistance of allied Indians. It was a policy rooted in the belief that an exercise of French power and prestige would draw the Indians away from the Anglo-American traders who had already penetrated the territory. But the French ministry of Marine was adamantly opposed to this policy. Maurepas and Rouillé both believed that the expulsion of the Anglo-American traders was the major objective. This could be achieved, they thought, by mounting exclusively French military operations against the traders; no Indian allies would be necessary. As far as they were concerned, the "Conspiracy of 1747" had underscored the fact that the Indians were not to be trusted.

Superficially, the latter policy seemed to be the more effective of the two. Duquesne's expedition, mounted without the help of Indians, had evidently impressed the native inhabitants of the Ohio Valley. Moreover, it had succeeded in sealing the English out of the Ohio country. Thus, it may be argued that the success of the expedition seemed to justify Rouillé's arguments.

Yet Duquesne's accomplishments were not won in isolation nor were they achieved without great cost. The 1752 attack on Pickawillany and the smallpox epidemic had made Duquesne's task that much easier. Yet it must not be forgotten that Duquesne lost four hundred men to disease just in building his road to the Ohio from Lake Erie. This huge cost in human lives confirmed the worst fears of the French Canadians who had opposed the expedition. But most important of all, Duquesne's efforts, by not only claiming but also occupying the upper Ohio Valley, directly threatened the English colonies in North America and helped spark the "Great War for the Empire." La Jonquière's attempts to secure the Illinois country by pacifying the restless Indians through intrigue, diplomacy, and the help of allied Indians probably would not have provoked Great Britain into war. The French Canadians, as has been pointed out earlier, had little interest in the Ohio Valley, except for the few who resented the Anglo-Americans' use of it as a base from which they threatened the Illinois and upper country.

Thus, the metropolitan French perception of the Ohio Valley and the Illinois country had, by 1749, led to the adoption of a policy directed towards the military occupation of the region. Although this was a policy which ran counter to the wishes of many influential French Canadians, it was, nevertheless, only a variant of the policy which had guided French activities in North America for decades. That policy had enabled the French to expand into and exploit the interior of North America without occupying it with settlements. Instead, the French had relied on the respect and co-operation of the Indians. The imperial objectives of France and the commercial objectives of New France were compatibly expressed within the framework of this policy. However, when the commercial disruption caused by the War of the Austrian Succession undermined the co-operation of the Indians, it also undermined the faith of French administrators in the wisdom of that policy. And, consequently, the policy was modified. Reliance on the Indians was discouraged, settlement of the interior was favored, and military operations against the Anglo-Americans were promoted.

Some French Canadians, at least, realized the basic dangers involved in such a policy. It represented, among other things, the abandonment of the traditional French-Canadian approach to North American realities. Metropolitan France was imposing its special brand of ignorance on the affairs of New France. The Conquest owed more to this policy than it did to historical inevitability. As Professor William J. Eccles has observed, "Ineptitude in the French military command and government at home, and the fortunes of war, gave Britain dominion over the vast French territory." It was, it should be pointed out, a close thing. Had Montcalm not adopted such foolish tactics at Quebec on September 13, 1759, the British army might have been destroyed and New France, including the Illinois country, at least, might have remained French territory. But for how long? Historians, of course, must deal with what happened and not with what might have happened. By 1760 the "Dreaded Juncture of the French Settlements in Canada with those of Louisiana" had been dealt a fatal blow. The French-Canadian nation would have to be satisfied with the somewhat restrictive provincial boundaries of Quebec rather than those of a transcontinental Gallic country.

The French Fort At Vincennes

AUGUST DERLETH

Vincennes, the oldest urban settlement in Indiana, was established as a French outpost on the lower Wabash River in the early 1730s. The youthful Sieur de Vincennes had overcome many difficulties in carrying out this mission, but his promising career as a French administrator ended with his death at the stake in 1736 during the Chickasaw wars. The village bearing his name, however, survived, despite general neglect by the British after 1763; and it became the site of stirring conflict

From *Vincennes: Portal to the West* (1968), pp. 4–9, 12–23. Footnotes in the original have been omitted. Copyright © 1968 by August Derleth. Reprinted by permission of Prentice-Hall, Inc.

during the middle years of the American Revolutionary War. Furthermore, with the formation of an Indiana Territory in 1800, Vincennes was designated the territorial capital.

From this place Governor William Henry Harrison oversaw the development of the territory and directed United States relations with various Indian people then living there. In time these relations deteriorated into open hostilities. During the War of 1812 the territorial capital was moved to Corydon, but Vincennes continued as an important commercial and cultural center of southwestern Indiana. At the present time Vincennes has a population of approximately 20,000. And it treasures many visible links with its heritage: the Old Cathedral, erected in 1825 on the site of the original French church; the George Rogers Clark National Memorial; Grouseland, the fine Federal-style mansion of Governor Harrison; the Elihu Stout print shop, the first in the territory; and Vincennes University, the oldest one in the west.

August Derleth, an extremely prolific writer and interpreter of the Old Northwest with over a hundred books, most notably his Sac Prairie and Wisconsin Saga series, is one of the best and most recent historians of Vincennes. In the passages below, Derleth describes both the founding of Vincennes and its final years under French control. For additional material on early Vincennes, see Clarence W. Alvord, *The Illinois Country, 1673–1818* (1920), Louise P. Kellogg (ed.), *The French Regime in Wisconsin and the Northwest* (1925), and Leonard Lux, *The Vincennes Donation Lands* (1949).

On September 30, 1725, the Company of the Indies sent to Périer, the new Governor of Louisiana, a letter proposing that—since Kaskaskia and Cahokia, with Fort de Chartres, held the Mississippi side of the country of the Illinois, and the post among the Ouiatenon the north, an anchor ought to be established in the southeast corner, where the Wabash bent toward the Ohio, thus securing the area—either along the Wabash itself or at the mouth of the Tennessee River.

"M. Périer will reflect well on this subject," the official wrote, "and consider if, by giving eight or ten soldiers to the said Sieur de Vincennes, with the missionary destined for the Ouabache, he will not find himself in condition to assure, by the Indians, the communication between Louisiana and Canada, and to prevent the English from penetrating into our colony, without obliging the Company to construct a fort on the lower Ouabache, of which the expense of the establishment and the support of the garrison make an object of consequence."

To facilitate this venture, Vincennes was confirmed as a halfpay lieutenant attached to Louisiana, though he was not formally detached from Canada. He was then a young man just as old as the century—26. It was hoped that he could persuade a large body of Indians to settle at the place he chose to establish a post wherever he thought best at the bend of the

Wabash, since the King and his ministers seemed to be reluctant to send into the American provinces any substantial number of colonists. The King, however, did instruct the Governor of Canada to release Vincennes for the purpose of establishing the fort on the Wabash.

Delays, notwithstanding orders and instructions, were integral to life in the wilderness. It took a year before Governor Périer got around to sending a load of goods to supply the still non-existent post on the Wabash, but the boat set out from New Orleans so late that it encountered ice and had to turn back. And the next spring Vincennes fell ill, and remained in poor health until midsummer. In the meantime, the Company of the Indies stipulated that the new post was to be manned by ten soldiers and two officers. The Company fixed upon three hundred livres as sufficient for the construction of the fort, and 1,170 livres as pay for the men during the initial year of their occupation of the post. As for presents for the Indians, the Company estimated that 800 livres ought to be enough.

Périer immediately objected to the niggardliness of the allowance. But such parsimony was all too typical of the official approach to the problem of establishing posts and maintaining good relations with the Indians. Périer made clear that the Company was allowing only half enough money to build the fort, and scarcely a fourth of the sum that would be needed if the French were to compete on anything like an equal basis with the British for the favor of the Indians.

When he recovered, Vincennes was in no hurry to select a site for the post on the Wabash. He went back to live for a while with the Miami at Ouiatenon, but there is some reason to believe that he had already made a tentative selection of the Wabash site, though the building of the fort waited upon a more favorable occasion. At some time during 1727 Vincennes and a small group of soldiers made their way down the Wabash and fixed upon a site for the new post—not at the mouth of that river, after all, but approximately a hundred and fifty miles up river from the junction of the Wabash and the Ohio. The post was first called Poste des Pianguichats, after Indians found in the vicinity—one of the numerous branches of the Miami, who had made themselves at home among the remains of the settlement left by the first inhabitants of the area, the Mound Builders, long since vanished.

The site chosen for the post lay along the Wabash in relatively low, flat terrain, with some knolls and low hills bounding it. Vincennes obviously had an eye for settlement, not alone for the building of an isolated fort, for which he might have found a less pregnable position. The chosen site appeared to him to be a fertile one, a site to which French settlers could be drawn; it was a country of many trees—beech, pawpaw, persimmon, sycamore, maple, linden, pecan, red gum, tulip, aspen, ash, cottonwood, elm, wild plum, oak, black locust, and some juniper—one that afforded its wild life, which included elk, raccoons, opossums, wolves, foxes, and porcupines, all manner of natural food—nuts, persimmons, wild strawberries, mulber-

The Wabash (Oubache) River
Courtesy of Ralph D. Gray

ries, wild apples, and other food commonly found in the wilderness of the
continent's heartland. It was a country which, already supporting much
game as well as a great variety of fish in its streams—sturgeon, catfish, pike,
perch, bass, suckers, mullets and pickerel being the most common—would
certainly fit well into the plans of the French governors for the strengthening
of French control by enduring settlement.

Despite the characteristic lack of vigor with which the King and his
ministers pressed colonization of the region, Vincennes, when he returned
from his stay among the Miami, persisted. Limitations notwithstanding, he
had built a fort by early 1732, and on March 7 of that year he wrote to one
of the officials of the Marine in France a letter typical of many that he was to
write:

> I begin by informing you that the Wabash is composed of five
> nations who compose four villages of which the least has sixty men
> carrying arms, and all of them could furnish from six to seven hundred
> men if it were necessary to assemble them for the welfare of the service
> and for their own welfare. On account of the nearness of the English, it
> has been impossible for me to bring together all these nations because
> there has always been a lack of merchandise in this place. The fort
> which I have built is about eighty miles in the Wabash country up the
> river by which the English have been able to descend and open up

commerce with these nations. The place is very suitable in which to build a great settlement which I would have done if I had had troops enough. In regard to the commerce which one can carry on here, a traffic in skins could go on all year to the extent of 30,000 skins.

The Indians, however, wooed by both the French and the English, were troublesome:

I have never had a greater need of troops in these places than at the present time. The savages, the Illinois, as well as the Miami and others are more insolent than they have ever been, especially since the Foxes were defeated. The little experience which I have acquired in the twenty years that I have been among them, causes me to fear some evil trick on the part of these nations and above all, of my own who, seeing a settlement which I had begun, did not seem to wish it to be continued. Since for three years nothing has happened. Except, Monsieur, the migration of all the nations not only of the lakes but also of other places.

Vincennes had no illusions about the "friendship" of the Indians, knowing that that friendship had its price, which the British were far more successful in meeting than were the French, who were forever deprived of merchandise for trade and gifts by the shortsighted insularity of the officials of whom Vincennes and other French commanders addressed repeated representations.

You do me the honor to indicate to me that I send you a statement of the work done and to be done. There is only one fort and two houses within and it will be necessary very soon to build a guard house with barracks in which to lodge the soldiers. Nothing else is possible in this place with so few troops. I need thirty men with an officer. I am more embarrassed than ever, in this place, by the war with the Chickasaws, who have come twice since spring. Only two days ago the last party took away three people and since the French took up tomahawks against them I am obliged every day to put up a defense. I hope, that of your goodness, you will indeed wish to give your attention to this place and to my difficulty for myself as well as for the little garrison which I have. This is the favor which he awaits, from you, who has the honor to be, with profound respect, M., your very humble and very obedient servant, Vincennes.

Vincennes's superiors did little to alleviate his needs. . . . Nevertheless, Vincennes did everything in his power to establish a settlement as well as a fort at the site. In 1733, having built a house apart from the fort, he married the daughter of Philippe Longpré of Kaskaskia, and lost no time in fathering two daughters, Marie Therese and Catherine. Despite the shortage of goods, he kept the local Indians friendly. But, though the land was fertile, and the Indians—when they were impelled to do so, raised maize, beans, squash, and other vegetables, and found the country replete with wild game as the river was with fish—colonists could not readily be lured to a site so deep in the wilderness.

. . . .

By late 1735, Governor de Bienville, exasperated by reports from the outposts of the colony, concluded that the only solution lay in war with the Chickasaw. He needed a pretext for making war and did not have far to look for one. In the course of a recent war with the Natchez Indians, some of the Natchez had escaped from French soldiers and taken refuge with the Chickasaw south of the Ohio; Bienville now demanded that the Chickasaw surrender the fugitives. The Chickasaw, who had been interfering for a long time with the movements of French traders, soldiers and settlers and who, like the Chickasaw north of the Ohio, were trading with the British, refused to give up the Natchez, as the Governor of Louisiana had foreseen. When his ultimatum was rejected, Bienville had the pretext he wanted.

He had his plans made. . . . On the night of March 24, the war party moved into position near the village, French and Indian allies deploying themselves in the most advantageous manner. They waited out the night and attacked at dawn. Unfortunately, it was unlikely that so large a party of French soldiers and Indians could have gone unnoticed in enemy territory. The Chickasaw were well aware of their presence—not only those in the village under attack but also those in the central encampment of Chickasaw. Furthermore, the movement of the soldiers toward the village could scarcely have been unobserved.

The battle had only begun, when several hundred Chickasaw poured in from the woods around the village. Their appearance so dismayed and frightened some of the attacking forces that the Miami fled at once. The French, the Iroquois and the Arkansas Indians were left alone. The battle raged intensely for a while, but the Chickasaw were much superior in numbers, and the French, with their allies, suffered a disastrous defeat.

Artaguiette died in action. Those members of his attacking party who were not slain or could not manage to escape were taken prisoner. One of them, Rickarville, who made his escape months later with the help of British traders among the Chickasaw, said that the prisoners were taken into the Chickasaw village and burned at the stake in an orgy that lasted from three in the afternoon until midnight.

Among the prisoners who were put to the stake was François Bissot, Sieur de Vincennes, who had established the fort and the settlement along the lower Wabash and given the latter his name. . . .

[Follwing Vincennes' death, Goveror Bienville appointed Louis de Bellerive de St. Ange, the son of his venerable commander in the Illinois country, to command the Wabash post. A loyal and dedicated man, St. Ange arrived in Vincennes late in 1736 to take up his new duties, trying to rebuild both the fort and the strained Indian alliances.]

St. Ange went ahead with badly needed repairs to the fort left by Vincennes. It needed to be strengthened, and it needed stone facing. He took steps toward replacing the Indians who had left the area for the north, and at his urging a small band of Indians settled not far away at the site of Russellville, Illinois. But it was clear to St. Ange that what the post at Vincennes needed primarily was not Indians but French settlers, and this problem he could not resolve without help from the government, for the settlers were reluctant to come unless they could own the land they settled.

Bienville, however, still nursed his plan to remove the post to the mouth of the Ohio and was of little help. Yet, in 1742, the Piankeshaw remaining at Vincennes—no doubt with the consent of the Miami nation of which they were part—surrendered the territory trapped by the French to the French. It was a larger territory than that occupied by Vincennes, one embracing more than a million and a half acres lying north and east of Vincennes, though Congress later reduced the amount for Vincennes to five thousand acres, which were given to the Borough of Vincennes and later became known as the "Vincennes Common."

Settlement at Vincennes became more attractive. The government at New Orleans did little to cooperate with St. Ange. Bienville was replaced in 1743 by Governor Vaudreuil, who promised to make the French fur trade once more a flourishing business. He expected to send more traders among the Indians in the colony and intended by this means to increase the influence of the French, thus weakening that of the British. In the face of the niggardliness with which the French government served the colonies' needs, however, this goal was sheer naïveté. . . .

By 1743, however, when Vaudreuil came to the governorship, St. Ange had established himself. Indeed, the post was for a while called "St. Ange" or "St. Anne," though to Bienville it remained the fort of the Piankeshaw and to the traders it was more commonly known as the "little Weas" or "Little Wiaut," both names meaning "Little Ouiatenon" after the Ouiatenon Indians, to which the Piankeshaw were believed to belong. But the name "Vincennes" was even more widely and persistently applied to the post and to the settlement, such as it was.

The settlement was slow to grow. The Piankeshaw village had been called "Chip-pe-co-ke," which meant "scrub brush," but it was now largely deserted. Though the surrender of the Indian lands in 1742 was intended to stimulate settlement by the French, the post at Vincennes was referred to as late as 1746 as "quite inconsiderable," having "about 40 men and 5 negroes," whose occupation was "hunting and the culture of wheat and tobacco." St. Ange was anxious for the settlement to grow, for he wanted to counter Vaudreuil's plan for a fort at the mouth of the Ohio, where, he had been informed, the soil was rich, buffalo were plentiful and the French could deliver goods by water far more inexpensively than the British could carry them over the mountains.

Settlement was expedited by gifts of the commandant at the post, particularly of titles to land. Very probably Vincennes issued no land grants, as the land was in his time still claimed by the Indians. But St. Ange did so, though because of lack of registration no record has been left. The earliest record of a deed is of one issued to François Racine dit Beauchêne, though this deed was lost and was validated by the Federal government long after it was given. The first deed on the legal records of Vincennes was issued in April 1750 to François Filiatreau. None seems to have been for any very great land area; most of the French interested in settling wanted grants of areas about 150 feet square—enough space for a house, perhaps a summer kitchen, an outhouse, a storage building for pork, a place to keep chickens, a stable, perhaps a garden plot and an orchard. And, because the early settlers were engaged in trading, they preferred their land to be located on or near the fort, whereas those French settlers who hoped to engage in farming preferred their land to run back from the shore of the Wabash and liked to own areas of "two by forty arpents," which came to somewhat more than 68 acres. . . .

During much of the decade that followed St. Ange's assumption of command at Vincennes, England and France were at war because of France's part in the War of the Austrian Succession. . . . All this conflict had little effect on Vincennes, save that a few volunteers from that post went to take part in the defense of Fort Duquesne. After the cession of the land by the Indians twelve years before, Vincennes had begun slowly to grow. French-Canadians came to settle there, taking up land on three sides of the fort and back from the Wabash.

With the country around the fort relatively calm and quiet, St. Ange turned his attention to the development of the settlement. The fort itself was improved and repaired. St. Ange undertook to build a chapel next to the fort; he named it "St. Francis Xavier" in honor of the Jesuit priest, Father Francis Xavier de Guinne, who visited the settlement from time to time. He laid out and opened two streets—Busseron Street and Rue de St. Honoré, which led away from the front gates of the fort.

There remained the constant danger of Indian attack, particularly as information reached the fort that the British were patching up all their quarrels with the Indians, including the wavering Iroquois, with whom Benjamin Franklin and other delegates from New England, Pennsylvania, Maryland and New York had conferred at the behest of the British government. They had drawn up a plan of union—a patent indication that the British meant to use their Indian allies against the French. But nothing in the way of unusual depredations by the Indians against the French took place. The settlement was accustomed to learning that an occasional traveler had been set upon and robbed—perhaps killed—by marauding Indians, and

British traders were beginning to appear within range of the fort's command, but no event of an untoward nature took place.

. . . .

On February 10, 1763, the Treaty of Paris ended the French and Indian War. By its terms France ceded to Great Britain all its claims to Canada and the territory east of the Mississippi except for the city of New Orleans. Throughout the years of hostilities—and though the British had seized a French fort as close as that at Ouiatenon above Vincennes—the post commanded by St. Ange took part in no engagement.

Nor were the British in any haste to take over Vincennes. They were principally engaged from May through November of 1763 in dealing with the destructively successful uprising of Indians led by the Ottawa chief, Pontiac, who scourged the region from Niagara west to Detroit, which withstood a seige of five months until Pontiac lifted it in November. Under Pontiac, the Indians had destroyed Fort Sandusky, Fort St. Joseph, Fort Miami, Fort Ouiatenon, Fort Venango, Fort Le Boeuf, Fort Presque—the fort at Vincennes escaped.

Not until the rebellion led by Pontiac had been crushed did the British think again of Vincennes. In May 1764 St. Ange was ordered to take command at Fort de Chartres and to hold it until the British called upon him to turn it over to them. On May 18 he delivered a farewell address to the garrison and people of Vincennes, and, turning the post over to Major Joseph Antoine Drouët, Sieur de Richardville, who was assisted by François de Coindre, he departed for Chartres, leaving behind him close to seventy families, most of them French-Canadians.

Chapter II
THE ERA OF THE AMERICAN REVOLUTION, 1763–1789

Although the British, according to the terms of the Treaty of Paris of 1763, acquired the Illinois country, a vast interior region previously controlled by France, they did not immediately occupy their new territory. Indeed, British policy as expounded in the Proclamation of 1763 was to discourage colonial settlement in the trans-Appalachian area until Indian title to the land was extinguished. This policy, coupled with the limited success of an Indian uprising known as Pontiac's Rebellion, meant that Britain's hold on the Wabash Valley was at best a nominal one for several years. Of the three former French posts in Indiana, the British were driven out of Forts Miamis and Ouiatanon during the Indian war of 1763–1765, and they never had occupied the post at Vincennes. There, after the French commandant Louis de St. Ange departed in 1764, the small French settlement that remained handled its own affairs until renewed British interest in the West during the 1770s. But the British hold was still tenuous until after the Revolutionary War was underway and George Rogers Clark was able to make an initial conquest of the area for Virginia in 1778. He did this merely by dispatching a representative there after he had taken Forts Kaskaskia and Cahokia along the Mississippi River. The loss of Vincennes, however, prompted Lieutenant Governor Henry Hamilton, the officer in charge at Detroit, to personally lead a small British force down the Wabash and retake the fort, thereby setting the stage for Clark's heroic reconquest of Vincennes, the surrender coming on February 25, 1779.

The significance of what Clark did has been debated for many years. Many historians now question the older view that Clark's exploits had direct impact on the negotiations in Paris leading up to the peace settlement of 1783, particularly the generous boundaries the United States obtained in the West. Nevertheless, Clark's dramatic achievement had and continues to have powerful influence on the minds of the people in the nation, especially those in the Old Northwest. Most of the selections in this chapter relate to the classic confrontation between Clark and Hamilton, between a young frontiersman and an aristocratic officer, with contemporaneous and recent examples from the viewpoint of each man.

In 1787, less than a decade after Clark first embarked on his western country mission, the United States adopted a monumental piece of legislation concerning the procedures by which the newly acquired land in the Ohio Valley would be governed and the processes leading to eventual statehood for the area on the basis of complete equality with the original states. This legislation, known as the Northwest Ordinance, also guaranteed to all inhabitants of these lands certain basic rights and freedoms prior to statehood, including a sometimes ignored prohibition of slavery and involuntary servitude.

For further reading on Clark, Hamilton, and the American Revolution in the West, see George M. Waller, *The American Revolution in the West* (1976), Lowell H. Harrison, *George Rogers Clark and the War in the West* (1976), and John D. Barnhart, *Henry Hamilton and George Rogers Clark in the American Revolution* (1951). See also an older account of Clark by an enthusiastic champion of his, James A. James, *The Life of George Rogers Clark* (1928), and the pioneering history by Indianapolis banker and politician William H. English, *Conquest of the Country Northwest of the River Ohio, 1778–1783 and Life of Gen. George Rogers Clark* (2 vols., 1896).

1: The Historians Write

Professor John D. Barnhart was a lifelong student of Indiana and the Old Northwest. A professor of history at Indiana University for many years, Barnhart's major publications were *Valley of Democracy: The Frontier versus the Plantation in the Ohio Valley, 1775–1818* (1953) and, with colleague Donald F. Carmony, *Indiana: From Frontier to Industrial Commonwealth* (2 vols., 1954). Following his discovery of a journal written by Hamilton in 1778 and 1779, which provided the basis for a reexamination of the man's career in North America, he edited the journal, contributed a long introduction, and published it under the title of *Henry Hamilton and George Rogers Clark in the American Revolution: The Journal of Lieutenant Governor Henry Hamilton* (1951).

In that book, and in a related article, part of which appears below, Professor Barnhart presents a view of Henry Hamilton widely at variance to his image as a sadistic, "hairbuying" officer who paid a bounty for scalps turned in by his Indian allies. Barnhart's Henry Hamilton is a sensitive, artistic, and honorable man whose nature left him unsuited for his military responsibilities and whose later life was involved in writing a number of long narratives about his experiences in both the Seven Years' and American Revolutionary wars and defending himself against charges of inhumanity and incompetence.

The Character of Lt. Governor Henry Hamilton

JOHN D. BARNHART

The campaign and victory of George Rogers Clark has generally been treated as a great personal achievement of a most unusual man. As such it is likely the public will continue to consider it, for the people love their heroes and cherish their memories, even the traditions and myths that cling to them. In this instance the dramatic actions of a daring and spectacular

From "A New Evaluation of Henry Hamilton and George Rogers Clark," *Mississippi Valley Historical Review*, XXXVII (March 1951), 643–652. Footnotes in the original have been omitted. Copyright © Organization of American Historians. Reprinted by permission.

leader and his brave frontier soldiers are pictured against a background of cruel Indian warfare in which bloodthirsty savages, directed by a "hair-buyer general," scalped, burned, and ravaged the land. In the hands of a scholar like James A. James, who eliminated the fiction and most of the exaggeration, this interpretation produced a highly interesting and truthful account of the Revolution in the West.

There are certain points, however, at which the picture can be made more complete. No one has made an adequate study of the writings of Henry Hamilton, nor bothered to discover what kind of man he was. Accounts are still colored by the strong prejudices with which the frontier regarded the English and the Indians, and the inadequacies of the British colonial system have not been properly related to the campaign for the Northwest. In other words, the heroism of Clark has been so fascinating that historians have not seen the English side of the conflict and have neglected the larger forces which affected both leaders.

Most of the new information about these men comes from the writings of Hamilton, the extent and significance of which may surprise many. There are probably two hundred letters and small papers that are still in existence, not more than one third of which have been published. In addition there are a group of pictures and four long manuscripts.

Although little value either as historical documents or as works of art can be assigned to some forty pictures, most of which were drawn by Hamilton, they do reveal certain facets of his character which have received very little attention. There are eight small sketches of Indians, two of white men, twenty-eight landscapes, two miniatures, and a portrait of his wife and daughter. They bear witness that he was a family man and a person who appreciated art and nature, and that he considered some of the Indians as persons of character, individuality, and dignity....

More significant than any of these documents is Hamilton's Journal, a manuscript which he began when a messenger arrived at Detroit, August 6, 1778, bringing word that the Americans had taken Kaskaskia, a day by day record of his actions in which he wrote almost daily, and which was discontinued only when he was imprisoned in the jail at Williamsburg, Virginia, and deprived of pen and ink on June 16, 1779. It contains 166 large pages of manuscript in Hamilton's handwriting and is a more detailed and a more significant account of the same events which are found in the "Report" and the Narrative; in fact, both of these were prepared from the Journal. It seems to have been known to few historians, although it contains considerable information about the Indians and their customs, the nature of the country through which Hamilton led his little army from Detroit to Vincennes, the difficulties of traveling by way of the Maumee-Wabash route, the French in the interior of North America, the Wilderness Trace through Kentucky, the characters of Clark and Hamilton, and the conflict between these two leaders.

The Journal in its present form does not seem to be the original, for there are remarks in it which could not have been written on the dates when the entries were first made. Generally, these additions are easily identified; some of them were set off by marks resembling parentheses. The original form was probably shorter than the present, but longer than the "Report." By comparing the Journal with a series of his letters which he could not have changed, it appears that the revision was literary in purpose and honest in character. He did not seek to conceal his mistakes or misrepresent the past in his favor. He must have rewritten it after his release from the Williamsburg jail and before the time he wrote the Autobiography.

By using the various writings of the Lieutenant Governor it is possible to re-evaluate Clark's conquest in the Northwest. This phase of the Revolution appears to be the result of policies and actions which began with the success of the English in the Seven Years' War. Following their acquisition of the French colonies, the British political leaders failed to show much knowledge or appreciation of America. The failure of their policies along the Atlantic coast led to the American Revolution. In the West their unrealistic procedure gave Pontiac his chance, and their declining enthusiasm for colonial possessions led to a temporary abandonment of England's great opportunity. in the interior of North America. The Proclamation of 1763 began to be considered as a fairly permanent division of the continent between the colonists and the Indians, petitions for authority to establish colonies in the interior were rejected, Fort Chartres and Fort Pitt were abandoned, and General Thomas Gage ordered the residents of Vincennes to evacuate the town.

The Quebec Act might have been a wise reversal of policy in the interior had the American Revolution not interfered with its execution. Lieutenant Governor Edward Abbott came to Vincennes for a few months, but his financial budget was so restricted that he considered residence at Vincennes unsafe and therefore resigned. The Lieutenant Governor at Michilimackinac presided over little more than a trader's post. Hamilton's authority at Detroit was never defined, and he worked constantly under this handicap. His relations with the Governor of Canada, Guy Carleton, were very slight and lacking in helpfulness. One of Hamilton's fellow officers wrote a year after the loss of Vincennes: "Mr. Hamilton's disaster proceeded from want of system, uncertain information & want of attention in others as much as from the precipitancy of the measures he took himself, and the want of a regular district correspondence will ever produce such ill effects." One might put it another way by asking whether Clark would have left Kentucky if an officer with even a small garrison and adequate supplies had been located at Vincennes or Kaskaskia. . . .

Hamilton's writings indicate that in addition to British ineffectiveness in the West, the French-Canadian inhabitants played a larger part in Clark's victory than has been realized. The small British army that traveled to

Vincennes was composed chiefly of French Canadians, and not of Englishmen. There were only thirty-three British regulars. The volunteers, the militia, and the officers of the Indian Department were not English. The Lieutenant Governor entrusted his fate to these people who had only a short time before been dissatisfied with British control of the former New France. There was little evidence of dissatisfaction when the expedition started, and all seem to have cooperated very loyally on the way. The inhabitants of Vincennes surrendered readily enough when the British reached their village, but they concealed powder, which they later gave to Clark. Their behavior soon ceased to be satisfactory to the English commander, and they were quickly won over to Clark after he arrived at Vincennes with his army, which contained a number of French from the Illinois villages. Their change of allegiance was serious enough, but Hamilton's entire enterprise was threatened when this attitude began to be shared by members of his own militia. The French of the Illinois Country, of Vincennes, and of Detroit, and, therefore, the soldiers of Clark as well as those in the English force, were fellow countrymen, friends, and even relatives. Views held by one group of these people were likely to be shared by all.

The Indians also had much to do with Clark's victory. Like the French-Canadians, they were dissatisfied with British rule in the interior. In Pontiac's uprising the persistent hope that the French armies would return kept Indian resistance alive much longer than was reasonable. During the year which followed the Lake Indians learned to accept British control. The Shawnee were probably driven to cooperate with the English by the encroachments of the American frontiersmen. But in the Wabash and Mississippi valleys where trade could be carried downstream to the Spanish, the tribesmen were more independent. In proportion as the distance from Detroit increased, the Indians' loyalty to the British decreased. The Lake Indians cooperated wholeheartedly with Hamilton on the expedition and effectually closed the Ohio to prevent American communications by that highway. When, however, they saw the changed attitude of the French, many of them began to take their leave of Hamilton and to return to their homes. Only a few loyal Indians remained at Vincennes when Clark attacked, and no record exists that they rendered any assistance to Hamilton. . . .

Some exaggeration of Clark's victory may now be detected. The number of Hamilton's soldiers and the construction and strength of Fort Sackville have been overstated. It has been said that Clark's men were not one fourth of the combined force of the enemy and his allies. But Clark led 170 men and 46 more were coming by boat, while Hamilton had 79, of whom only 33 were willing to continue fighting and 6 of these were wounded. The inhabitants of Vincennes and the Indians of the lower Wabash were friendly to Clark. The fort had been described as having four blockhouses when there were only two, one of which was unfinished. Professor James A. James wrote, "Clark was surprised to find that this fort . . .

mounting twelve guns and well stored with ammunition, with a garrison of trained soldiers, had been given up so readily." Neither Clark nor Hamilton mention so many guns. The latter described only five: two three-pounders and two small swivels, which were in Fort Sackville when he came to Vincennes, and the six-pounder which he brought with him. As the fighting began, he cautioned the men to be saving of the powder. Clark, however, was more favorable to the British leader, for he wrote, "on Viewing the Inside of the Fort and stores I was at first astonish[ed] at [its] being given up in the Manner it was but on weighing every circumstance I found that it was prudent."

The problems involved in Hamilton's conduct of Indian warfare can now be considered with less bias than in earlier days, but here only in broad outline. He has been charged with recommending to the home government the employment of Indians even though his immediate superior, Governor Guy Carleton, was opposed. Lord George Germain wrote to this effect and Carleton believed him, but no letter of Hamilton's seems to exist which would prove the point. Until the middle of June, 1777, Hamilton tried to keep the Indians around Detroit at peace, although other Indians were being used in the eastern theater of war. He has also been charged with urging the tribesmen to commit brutal and cruel deeds against the people of the Ohio Valley, but his letters and Journal indicate that he urged them to fight only against men in arms and to bring all prisoners to Detroit. Finally, he has been charged with the purchase of scalps of white people in order to encourage the Indians to fight. A lawyer for the defense would have little trouble in discrediting the evidence which has been accepted as supporting this charge. To prove that he did not is hardly possible, but it seems reasonably clear that the charge has not been substantiated. It is obvious that he was engaged in a cruel and barbarous warfare, and that he knew it was inhuman in spite of his efforts to make it less brutal. Possibly his desire to attack Pittsburgh and his eagerness to move against Clark represented a real desire to escape from this unpleasant assignment. The greater the understanding of Indian warfare, the less surprise there is that scalps were brought to Detroit, and the more intimate the acquaintance with Hamilton, the less confidence can be placed in the title "hairbuyer."

The character of Clark and Hamilton can now be defined more clearly. The Lieutenant Governor appears as a man of some education and culture, a descendant of a noble Scots-Irish family, an army man in younger life and afterwards a colonial official in positions of responsibility, an author of an important Journal, and an amateur artist. With an important exception he emerges as a brave, honest, and honorable man. But if his good qualities appear more clearly, the same may be said of his faults. He was too impulsive for his own good, his judgment was sometimes poor, he was intolerant of the vices and customs of the French, and he was not a gifted military leader. His abilities may be summarized as mediocre, for he revealed little evidence of greatness. Even if the charges that he recommended using the Indians in the West and that he bought scalps are rejected until better evidence is produced, and if it is agreed that he tried to teach humanity to the tribesmen, actual events condemn his record. How he rationalized his direction of Indian warfare is not clear, but he persuaded himself that he was changing the Indian method of fighting, and he probably considered his action as in the line of duty.

If service on the frontier involved Hamilton in brutality, it did not leave Clark untouched. Perhaps Hamilton's word will not be accepted as sufficient evidence that Clark participated personally in tomahawking the captured Indians, that he ordered the scalping of a white man, and that he was not very kind to the British after their surrender. There are, however, scattered pieces of supporting evidence in the Clark Papers which, when read with Hamilton's longer Journal, seem to establish his responsibility if not participation. The fundamental traits of his character are further confirmed by the British Lieutenant Governor. His strength of character, his winning personality, his boldness, courage, and perseverance, and his superior military leadership are quite evident. He appears as a man who was straining every nerve and every muscle to win and who suited his methods to the desired goal. The letters which passed among British officers in the Northwest after Hamilton's surrender leave little doubt about the seriousness of the blow which Clark had struck the Indian Department of the British.

The conflict between Clark and Hamilton may now be regarded from the larger aspect of British colonial development. Hamilton's defeat at Vincennes was in reality a part of the larger failure of the British to establish a suitable governmental system in the interior of the continent, to meet the Indians in an understanding and sympathetic manner, and to win the complete confidence of the French habitants. French explorers, missionaries, traders, and officials had left in the minds of their descendants a conception of the greatness of the French king and a memory of the olden days when the fleur-de-lis and the cross ruled the great wilderness—a memory that was not obliterated by two decades of British rule. And the Indian tribesmen scattered along America's inland seas and rivers contrasted the easy camaraderie of the rollicking *coureurs de bois* and *voyageurs* with the brusque hauteur of the British.

Much of the anti-British sentiment of the Middle West that has found its "bête noire" in the "hairbuyer general" should be replaced by an understanding of Indian warfare and of Hamilton as a very human and even likable man. Clark appears as a little more cruel and perhaps a little less great. At least he did not make bricks without straw. The fundamental qualities of his character and the seriousness of the blow he dealt the British in the West are even more firmly established. The English had blundered and a vigorous young red-haired Virginian turned the situation to the advantage of the rebellious colonists, a victory that was soon known in the capitals of Europe.

The Achievements of George Rogers Clark

GEORGE M. WALLER

George Rogers Clark is claimed by several states in addition to Indiana, but it was his Vincennes exploit that provides the basis for his lasting fame. It may also be noted that the Kaskaskia-Cahokia-Vincennes captures by Clark were intended as the preliminary to an assault on Detroit, the keystone of British occupation in the West, but that the Detroit expedition was never mounted. This has led to a considerable controversy over the long-range significance of Clark's actions in the Illinois country, but the scholarly debate cannot detract from the inspired leadership of Clark, the epic heroism of the youthful commander and his men, or the completeness of their victories in 1778 and 1779.

Professor George M. Waller evaluates Clark's activities in the Revolutionary War in their broader context in the following selection. After the war Clark continued in the military defense of the frontier, but his successes were limited and his personal fortune declined. For a short while he lived in Clarksville, part of the 150,000 acres provided to Clark and his soldiers, and the first American settlement in the entire Northwest Territory. But he was held personally liable for debts incurred in the service of his country, and he lost his lands and his reputation. Ten years before his death in 1818, while living in Kentucky with a relative, Clark fell and severely injured a leg, which subsequently had to be amputated.

Professor Waller, a colonial and military historian at Butler University in Indianapolis, where he is chairman of the Department of History, Political Science, and Geography, is the author of *The American Revolution in the West* (1976), as well as other books, including *Puritanism in Early America* (1950) and *Pearl Harbor: FDR and the Coming of the War* (3rd ed., 1976). The article below was based upon an address Professor Waller delivered at a conference on historic preservation in Bloomington, Indiana, in 1975.

[T]he battle between forces under Colonel Andrew Lewis and the Shawnee at Point Pleasant, Ohio, in the fall of 1774 ... was the first out-

From "George Rogers Clark and the American Revolution in the West," *Indiana Magazine of History*, LXXII (March 1976), 1–5, 8–9, 12–13, 17–20. Footnotes in the original have been omitted. Copyright © Trustees of Indiana University. Reprinted by permission.

break of open Indian war in the West since the end of the French and Indian War and Pontiac's Rebellion in the early 1760s. The Battle of Point Pleasant was the only pitched battle of the brief Lord Dunmore's War against the Shawnee. It signaled the reopening of the Indians' struggle against white advance that was to continue during the years of the American Revolution.

George Rogers Clark was a twenty-two year old militia captain in this little "war," holding a commission from the royal governor of Virginia, Lord Dunmore. He marched with a small force that attacked Indian villages on the Muskingum River in southeastern Ohio before joining Dunmore. Clark was not at the Battle of Point Pleasant but joined Dunmore's forces to move against the Shawnee town of Chillicothe on the Scioto River where the Indians in 1774 accepted a preliminary agreement, the "treaty" of Camp Charlotte.

George Rogers Clark in bronze
Courtesy of Ralph D. Gray

Clark was to become one of the leading figures in the American Revolution, fighting against the British with whom he had so recently marched. I think it is appropriate in considering historic preservation to consider the problems of preserving the history of a war and the knowledge of a hero in that war. George Rogers Clark and the Revolution in the West are a kind of historic structure. Like other more material structures they need to be identified and preserved. Like historic buildings they have been altered, added to, and reshaped in the passage of time, in ways irrelevant to their original reality and historic meanings. These changes need to be stripped off—like the porticos added to ancient buildings—the original integrity reestablished, and their meaning for their time and for later times recognized. . . .

A major problem has been that most of us lack a grasp of the order of events, perhaps because the Revolutionary struggle was the longest war we have ever fought, with the exception of the recent affair in Vietnam. It went on for eight tedious, desperate years. Happenings have been confused with other happenings, time sequences have been ignored, misconceptions abound. You are in good company if George Rogers Clark means nothing at all to you. Many people confuse Clark with his youngest brother, William, the Clark in the Lewis and Clark Expedition that explored the Louisiana Purchase area in 1804–1806. Almost everybody who knows something of the Clark story knows mainly of the famous march on Vincennes in early 1779, an epic of endurance and daring. For the rest of the war in the West and Clark's part in it even many historians are confused. To start with, a very brief sketch of the order of events may help.

In late 1776 Indians began to attack across the Ohio River into Kentucky. Clark was instrumental in convincing the Virginia government, which claimed the area, to organize Kentucky as a county, and he became commander of the Kentucky militia with the rank of major. When the British officially unleashed the Indians against Americans on the frontier in 1777, Clark directed the defense of the Kentucky stations from the little fort at Harrodsburg.

Early in 1778 Clark went to Williamsburg, the Viriginia capital, where he received secret instructions from Governor Patrick Henry and the Virginia Council to carry out his plans for an offensive against the British posts beyond the Ohio. His primary objective was Kaskaskia on the Mississippi, though he was also dreaming of an attack on the major British western post, Detroit. Then just twenty-five years old, he was promoted to lieutenant colonel. He secured the surrender of Kaskaskia and other French inhabited villages on the Mississippi, and Vincennes on the Wabash River, by the end of 1778.

Vincennes—primarily inhabited by French settlers—had acceded to the Americans readily when called upon by a visiting delegation of Frenchmen sent by Clark from Kaskaskia. But Henry Hamilton, lieutenant governor of the District of Detroit and the British commander in the West, had marched to retake Vincennes when he heard of Clark's exploits in the Illinois Country. Hamilton succeeded in regaining control of the post late in 1778. In February, 1779, Clark recaptured Vincennes after his legendary march through flooded country between the Mississippi and the Wabash, catching the British commander before Hamilton could mass his forces for a spring attack on Clark. Clark's capture of Hamilton dealt a massive though temporary blow to the British-Indian alliances. It should be noted that Clark remained at Vincennes only a month, returning for another month in July when he tried unsuccessfully to organize a follow up expedition against Detroit. He did not return to Vincennes again until some years after the end of the war, although the town, along with the other French towns in the Illinois Country, remained nominally under American control though much neglected for the rest of the war.

After 1779 American hopes for an early end to the war faded. The war in the West was stalemated. In 1780 Clark supervised the building of a new fort, Fort Jefferson, at the mouth of the Ohio. During the summer he rushed north from Fort Jefferson to assist in the defense of Cahokia, attacked—along with St. Louis—by a motley group of Indians and British traders from Mackinac. Barely back at Fort Jefferson, he again hurried north, overland with two companions, in time to divert a massive attack in June, 1780, led by Captain Henry Bird from Detroit against his post at the Falls of the Ohio but too late to save the defenseless Kentucky stations, Martin's and Ruddle's on the Licking River. In retaliation he led an expedition against the Shawnee in the Miami River valley where he commanded American forces in one of the few pitched battles with the Indians during the war, the Battle of Piqua, killing many Indians, burning their towns and crops.

In early 1781 Clark started to prepare a major expedition against Detroit authorized by Governor Thomas Jefferson of Virginia. In view of the British invasion of eastern Virginia it seems a visionary plan. In fact, Clark himself was temporarily pressed into service with the regular army in the fighting around Richmond where he gave a good account of himself. Traveling back to recruit his forces for the Detroit attack, Clark carried a new commission from Virginia as brigadier general in order to make him senior to the Continental commander, Colonel Daniel Brodhead, at Fort Pitt, a man intensely jealous of Clark. The expedition failed. Brodhead's thinly veiled opposition and a high rate of desertion among Clark's troops culminated in the overwhelming defeat of Colonel Archibald Lochry, a Pennsylvania militia commander who was bringing a detachment down the Ohio River to join Clark. Indians massing to attack Clark fell upon Lochry's small force in southeastern Indiana near the mouth of the Miami River with devastating effect.

Clark remained at the newly completed Fort Nelson at Louisville until the fall of 1782 when he led a last foray against the Shawnee towns across the Ohio but found no Indians to fight. With the war ending, he returned to Richmond, Virginia, and accepted retirement in the spring of 1783.

This short sketch omits any mention of the ongoing defense of the Kentucky stations, of the futile efforts of successive commanders at Fort Pitt to take the offensive against the Indians west and north of the upper Ohio, of allied French and Spanish forces in thrusts against Fort St. Joseph east of the lower end of Lake Michigan and Miamistown at the head of the Maumee, and of many other movements in the war in the West. But moving in for a closer look, one finds many problems.

For instance, what was Clark like? He was tall and well built. He was acknowledged to be a superb leader. Contemporaries are lavish in praising his qualities, but we find no references to his personality and character except what we can infer from his writing or his actions. No contemporary portrait of him exists. One painted from life in his later years shows an embittered old man, his face twisted perhaps in pain. His wartime exertions had a telling effect on his health, his disappointments and lack of rewards on his mind. His excessive drinking right after the war occasioned troubled comment from even his good friends, Thomas Jefferson and James Madison. It had probably set in during the tedious months spent in enforced idleness at Fort Nelson toward the end of the war when severe shortages of supplies, money, and men prevented further campaigning. It doubtless further hurt his health.

Some say Clark was redheaded. No real evidence exists. Do we visualize him with long hair or short? Did he wear a wig? Did he fight in buckskin or in uniform? Did he wear a tricorne or a broadbrimmed hat? Someone even asked recently if he needed dentures, like George Washington. Portraits dating from after Clark's death obviously idealize his image and portray a dignified, retired officer, respected as he actually was after the controversies that swirled around him in the immediate postwar period died down.

A more important question, which I have never found discussed, is how did he find his way in the West? Where did his knowledge of its geography, its people, its Indians, its distances come from? How did he come by the information that enabled him to assess the value of his targets? Some things we know. In the years before the Revolution, Clark worked with a number of other surveyors, ranging widely through Kentucky and well down the Ohio, familiarizing himself with the eastern and southern side of the river from the age of nineteen. In the spring of 1777 before his march on Kaskaskia he had sent Benjamin Linn and Samuel Moore to spy on the place but what led him to do that? In marching overland from near the mouth of the Tennessee River to Kaskaskia he availed himself of a guide, John Saunders, an American hunter who had been there. Further, as a surveyor, Clark knew how to lay out a straight line of march from one point to another.

But to know where the distant point toward which he marched was suggests the use of maps. Here, a figure enters the picture who has not previously been associated with the story of George Rogers Clark. His possible connection would appear to be a matter of interest. He is Thomas Hutchins, born in New Jersey in 1730, twenty-two years Clark's senior. Holding a commission as a British army engineer, Hutchins fought in the French and Indian War and helped suppress Pontiac's Rebellion. He was stationed at Fort Pitt, indeed probably helped to design the fort. He traveled widely in the Great Lakes region and down the Ohio, mapping and sketching the area. He served in the garrisons at Fort Chartres and Kaskaskia until 1772 when he was sent down the Mississippi to help with the building of British defenses in West Florida.

It may be that Hutchins should be called Mapmaker of the American Revolution in the West. His masterpiece, however, was published in 1778 and was thus not available to Clark when the campaign in the Illinois Country took place. Hutchins had gone to London to discuss plans for fortifications in West Florida as well as to arrange for publication of his book and accompanying map providing a "Topographical Description" of the West. He refused to return to fight against the Americans, was imprisoned in England, and after his release returned to America with assistance from Benjamin Franklin in France. He became geographer for the Continental southern army under General Nathanael Greene and then, after the war, geographer of the United States, a title never since conferred on anyone.

. . . .

Notice should be drawn to other problems that arise in attempting to understand this small scale but complex western struggle. Though a dominant figure in this theater of the war, Clark was not the only important American leader, nor were the valiant men who followed him the only ones to fight. In the area between the Great Lakes, the Ohio, and the Mississippi, America was fighting on four frontiers.

On the upper Ohio an impoverished garrison of regulars at Fort Pitt was commanded by a succession of officers appointed by General Washington at the direction of Congress. From this post control was extended to garrisons at Fort Henry (Wheeling), Fort Randolph (at the mouth of the Kanawha River), Fort McIntosh (at the mouth of Beaver Creek), and Fort Laurens (on the Tuscaroras River), as well as small forts north of Pittsburgh on the Allegheny.

A second, inner frontier at the western edge of the Appalachians stretched along the upper Kanawha, the Greenbrier, and the New rivers. The settlements on the Holston, Watauga, Nolichucky, and upper Tennessee rivers made up a third frontier in the southwestern corner of Virginia and western North Carolina, which extended west in 1780 to the Cumberland settlements around what is now Nashville, Tennessee. Clark was prominent in defending the fourth frontier, the Kentucky stations and their western prolongations at Fort Jefferson just below the mouth of the Ohio and in the Illinois Country and Vincennes.

In this area the war was mainly an Indian war. Well before the Revolution the Indians were resisting the aggressive, land hungry frontiersmen. Indians had learned to live with the fur traders, indeed coveted trade, first with the French and then with the British. But the arrival of pioneers who felled the forests, planted trees, and built cabins alarmed them and provoked resistance. During the war the struggle merely took on added seriousness insofar as the Indians were supplied and often led by the British.

On the upper Ohio the Delaware remained peacefully inclined for several years, influenced by Moravian missionaries and the diplomatic skills of George Morgan at Fort Pitt. Attacks across the upper Ohio and against the Kentucky stations even through the Year of the Three Sevens—the Bloody Year of 1777—came mainly from small, roving bands of Mingo (western Seneca), Munsee, and a few renegade Delaware and Shawnee. The Shawnee became the principal scourge of Kentucky only in 1778. By the spring of 1777 the Cherokee had been subdued along the Holston frontier. Except for occasional trouble from the irreconcilable Chickamauga offshoot under Chief Dragging Canoe, this tribe made little more trouble. Clark fought no Indians in his Illinois campaign and encountered Indians willing to fight only in the first of his two raids into Shawnee country in 1780. On the Wabash and Maumee rivers, the Miami, Wea, Piankeshaw, and Kickapoo wavered between the British and the United States throughout the war, did little fighting, and were cowed by Clark most of the time. One Piankeshaw chief, indeed, professed enduring support of the Kentucky Big Knives. Remnants of the Illinois tribe, few, lazy, and debauched, the Kaskaskia and Michigami Indians, did not fight.

Large numbers of the British Indians in Michigan and Canada—Ottawa, Chippewa, Wyandot, Potawatomi, and Huron—joined in attacks on the upper Ohio and in Kentucky only in relatively small bands. A few hundred were the most who took part in any siege or battle out of the thousands presumably controlled by the British. It may be said that offensively the Indians were no real asset to the British, although, paradoxically, it would have been fatal to the British cause in the West if the Indians had not given as much help as they did. Under guerrilla leaders like William Caldwell; Alexander McKee; the Girty brothers, Simon, James, and George; and Captain Henry Bird of the regular British army, along with occasional French Canadian officers, the warriors would attack undefended cabins and weakly held forts. They were too restless to maintain a long siege. The nine days' siege of Boonesborough was the longest. They never attacked a position where Clark was known to be present and rarely risked a pitched battle. The leaders were too few to control them, and renegades like Simon Girty had no inclination to do so. Cruel treatment of their victims, especially the old, the wounded, and women and children was typical.

Yet in negotiations with Clark and his officers, or with Morgan at Fort Pitt, Indian leaders were reasonable, often good humored, and indicated a fair appreciation of America's side of the war. It may be suggested that even fewer would have fought for the British if frontiersmen had not frequently descended to their level and perpetrated equally monstrous atrocities on them. The wanton murders of the friendly Shawnee, Chief Cornstalk, and of White Eyes, who had labored earnestly to keep his Delaware friendly, are only two instances.

The British and their Indian allies were not the only enemies of the American frontiersmen. The men of Virginia were fighting in the West against rival Pennsylvania interests for future possession of the land. Clark's march to the Mississippi and the visionary scheme of a massive Virginia mounted attack on Detroit in 1781 may have originated as much with leading Virginia land speculators as with Clark. Firm evidence is lacking, but Clark's preliminary discussions with Governor Patrick Henry in 1776 may have led the young westerner to conceive his plan. Historians have questioned his choice of targets. They make sense if he was acting to forestall Pennsylvania more than to counter the British, though his proposals would effectively serve both purposes. It is clear, too, that personal interest in western lands as well as official concern for Virginia's claims were combined in the persons of Patrick Henry, George Mason, George Washington, and many other less prominent individuals, and seem to have preoccupied an inordinate amount of their thinking despite their heavy official duties.

The militia of states like Virginia and Pennsylvania were also constantly pitted against the regular army establishment in the western theater of the war. The long time commander at Fort Pitt, Colonel Daniel Brodhead, proved a bitter and frustrated enemy of Clark. Opponents of both the regulars and the dedicated frontier militiamen were an increasing population on the Ohio, in the Kentucky stations, and in older parts of the back country. Such opponents included unpatriotic land seekers, growing numbers of Tories fleeing from eastern hostility, and an influential body of separate state men who denied the claims of any eastern state to the area. Opposition arose, too, between those who favored a defensive war and those, like Clark, who wanted to take the war to the enemy.

Personal rivalry to Clark became evident in the disagreement raised by beleaguered Kentucky defenders facing Indian attack from across the Ohio at a point midway between the last fort on the upper Ohio and Clark's forces concentrated at Louisville. The Warriors' Path crossed near the mouth of the Licking River, a crossing too far from Clark at Fort Nelson to be detected.

Preoccupation with these and many other problems doomed any chance for consistent military effort. The war became a wearying, irresolute seesaw of guerrilla tactics. The Indians were masters of such tactics. Clark was successful when he was able to move swiftly with small forces against unsuspecting targets, when—not by choice but necessity—he had to emulate the Indians and gained their same advantages. Large scale campaigns, whether mounted by the British, the regulars from Fort Pitt, or attempted by Clark, always failed. Major offensives were a logistical impossibility. Equipping, feeding, and transporting large numbers of men, with supplies or artillery, over long distances through difficult terrain proved beyond the means of either side.

Yet in a long war when unity of purpose characterized none of the thirteen states, western Americans at least held their ground, pinned down large numbers of the British and their Indians so that they could not be used against the eastern areas, and gave the United States a claim on the West that American negotiators could fight for at the peace table.

2: The Participants Write

The two brief extracts which follow, one written by George Rogers Clark (1752–1818) and the other by Henry Hamilton (1734–1796), the chief protagonists at Vincennes, describe their travels en route to the lower Wabash and certain aspects of the battle and subsequent surrender of Fort Sackville, the British name for their post at Vincennes. The Clark and Hamilton reports were published jointly in Milo M. Quaife (ed.), *The Capture of Old Vincennes: The Original Narratives of George Rogers Clark and of His Opponent Gov. Henry Hamilton* (1927).

Clark's account was written in 1791 at the urging of James Madison. Some years earlier, in a letter to George Mason, Clark had reported in detail on his campaign in the West, but all copies of the 1779 sketch were lost. The second report, 128 pages long, now rests in the Draper Collection at the Wisconsin Historical Society in Madison. Because various awkward passages render Clark's unedited prose difficult to understand, when Professor Quaife prepared the 1791 report for publication originally in the Lakeside Classic Series in 1920, he modernized its spellings, punctuation, and paragraphing; but the language—"for the most part"—is Clark's own. The Hamilton report, written in 1781, covers his "proceedings" from 1776 through June 1781. It relates the basic facts about his Vincennes expedition and his subsequent imprisonment at Williamsburg, Virginia. This report, written by a well-educated British officer and reprinted a number of times, appears unchanged in the Quaife edition.

Professor Quaife was a distinguished scholar of Michigan, Wisconsin, and the Old Northwest. His major publications include, with Sidney Glazer, *Michigan: From Primitive Wilderness to Industrial Commonwealth* (1948), and a number of edited works. For a recent concise and accurate description of the fall of Fort Sackville, see the National Park Service booklet written by Robert C. Alberts, *George Rogers Clark and the Winning of the Old Northwest (1975)*. See also the more general work by Jack Sosin, *The Revolutionary Frontier, 1763– 1783* (1967), and the older but comprehensive collection edited by James A. James, *George Rogers Clark Papers, 1771–1781* (1912).

Our March Upon Vincennes

GEORGE ROGERS CLARK

We now saw that we were in a very critical situation, cut off as we were from all intercourse with the home government. We perceived that Governor Hamilton, by the junction of his northern and southern Indians, would be at the head of such a force in the spring that nothing in this quarter could withstand him. Kentucky must fall immediately and it would be fortunate if the disaster ended here. Even if we should immediately make good our retreat to Kentucky we were convinced that it would be too late even to raise a force sufficient to save that colony, as all the men in it, united to the troops we had, would not suffice, and to get succor in time from the Virginia and Pennsylvania frontiers was out of the question. We saw but one alternative, which was to attack the enemy in his stronghold. If we were successful we would thereby save the whole American cause. If unsuccessful, the consequence would be nothing worse than if we should not make the attempt. We were encouraged by the thought of the magnitude of the consequences that would attend our success. The season of the year was also favorable to our design, since the enemy could not suppose that we would be so mad as to attempt a march of eighty leagues through a drowned country in the depth of winter. They would, therefore, be off their guard and would not think it worth while, probably, to keep scouts out. If we could make good our advance to Vincennes we might probably surprise and overcome them, while if we should fail, the country would be in no worse situation than if we had not made the attempt. This and many other similar reasons induced us to resolve to attempt the enterprise, which met with the approbation of every man among us.

Orders were immediately issued for making the necessary preparations. The whole country took fire and every order, such as preparing provisions, encouraging volunteers, etc., was executed with cheerfulness by the inhabitants. Since we had an abundance of supplies, every man was equipped with whatever he could desire to withstand the coldest weather. Knowing that the Wabash would probably overflow its banks to a width of five or six miles and that it would be dangerous to build vessels in the neighborhood of the enemy, I concluded, both to obviate this and to convey our artillery and stores, to send around by water a vessel strong enough to force her way, as she could be attacked only by water (unless she should

From Milo M. Quaife (ed.), *The Capture of Old Vincennes: The Original Narratives of George Rogers Clark and of His Opponent Gov. Henry Hamilton* (1927), pp. 118–22, 124–127, 131–132, 134–135, 138–140, 142–146, 149–150. Some footnotes in Quaife's edition have been omitted. Copyright © Bobbs-Merrill Company, Inc. Reprinted by permission.

choose otherwise) since the whole of the lowlands was under water and she might keep away from any heights along the river. A large Mississippi boat was immediately purchased and completely fitted out as a galley, mounting two four-pounders and four large swivels, and manned by forty-six men under the command of John Rogers.[1] He set sail on February 4, with orders to force his way up the Wabash as high as the mouth of White River, and there secrete himself until further orders; if he should find himself discovered he was to do the enemy all the damage he could without running too great risk of losing his vessel. He was not to leave the river until he had abandoned hope of our arrival by land, but he was strictly enjoined to so conduct himself as to give rise to no suspicion of our expected approach. . . .

Everything being ready on the fifth of February, after receiving a lecture and absolution from a priest, we crossed the Kaskaskia River with one hundred and seventy men and at a distance of about three miles encamped until February 8. When we again resumed the advance the weather was wet and a part of the country was covered with several inches of water. Progress under these conditions was difficult and fatiguing although, fortunately, it was not very cold considering the time of year. My object now was to keep the men in good spirits. I permitted them to shoot game on all occasions and to feast on it like Indians at a war dance, every company taking turns in inviting the other to its feast. A feast was held every night, the company that was to give it being always supplied with horses for laying in a sufficient store of meat in the course of the day. I myself and my principal officers conducted ourselves like woodsmen, shouting now and then and running through the mud and water the same as the men themselves.

Thus, insensible of their hardships and without complaining, our men were conducted through difficulties far surpassing anything we had ever experienced before this to the banks of the Little Wabash, which we reached on February 13. There are here two streams three miles apart, and the distance from the bank of one to the opposite bank of the other is five miles. This whole distance we found covered with some three feet of water, being never less than two, and frequently four feet in depth. I went into camp on an elevation at the bank of the river and gave the troops permission to amuse themselves. For some time I viewed with consternation this expanse of water; then accusing myself of irresolution, without holding any consultation over the situation or permitting any one else to do so in my presence, I immediately set to work. I ordered a pirogue to be constructed at once and acted as though crossing the water would be only a bit of diversion. Since but few of the men could find employment at a time, pains were taken to

[1]John Rogers was a cousin of Clark. He saw service in the earlier years of the Revolution, and in 1778 became second lieutenant in Captain Helm's company on Clark's Kaskaskia expedition. As noted here, Clark placed him in command of the war galley sent against Vincennes. After its capture Rogers was sent to convey the British prisoners to Williamsburg.

The George Rogers Clark Memorial at Vincennes
Courtesy of Ralph D. Gray

devise amusement for the rest in order to keep up their spirits. However, the men were well prepared for the undertaking before us as they had frequently waded farther than we must now, although seldom in water more than half-leg deep. . . .

On the seventeenth I dispatched Mr. Kennedy with three men to cross the River Embarrass, which is six miles from Vincennes, charging him to procure, if possible, some boats in the neighborhood of the town, but chiefly to obtain some information if he could do so in safety. He went, and on reaching the river found that the country between it and the Wabash was flooded. We proceeded down below the mouth of the Embarrass, vainly attempting to reach the banks of the Wabash. Finding a dry spot we encamped late at night and in the morning were gratified at hearing for the first time the morning gun of the British garrison. We resumed our march and about two o'clock in the afternoon of the eighteenth gained the banks of the Wabash three leagues below the town and went into camp.

I now sent four men across the river on a raft to find land if possible, proceed to the town, and purloin some canoes. Captain McCarty set out with a few men the next morning with a little canoe he had made for the same purpose. Both parties returned unsuccessful; the first was unable to make land, and the Captain was driven back by the appearance of a camp. I immediately dispatched the canoe down the river to meet the galley, carrying orders for it to proceed day and night. Meanwhile, determined to have as many strings to my bow as possible I directed the men to build canoes in a sheltered place. I had not yet given up hope of our boat arriving; in case she should, these canoes would augment our fleet; should she not come before they were ready, they would answer our purpose without her.

Many of our volunteers began for the first time to despair and some to talk of returning but our situation was now such that I was past all uneasiness. I merely laughed at them; without persuading or ordering them to desist from such an attempt I told them I would be glad if they would go out and kill some deer. They departed puzzled over my conduct. My own men knew that I had no idea of abandoning an enterprise for want of provisions so long as there were plenty of good horses in our possession and I knew that our volunteers could be detained without the use of force for a few days, by which time our fate would be determined. I conducted myself in such a manner as to lead every one to believe I had no doubt of success. This kept up their spirits, and the hunters being out, they had hope of momentarily obtaining a supply of food, besides the expectation of the arrival of the galley. I perceived that if we should not be discovered for two days we would effect the passage of the river.

On the twentieth the water guard decoyed a boat ashore having five Frenchmen and some provisions on board. These men were on their way down-river to join a party of hunters. They informed us that we had been discovered and that the inhabitants were well disposed toward us. They said the fort had been completed and greatly strengthened, and that the number of men in it was about the same as when Mr. Vigo left Vincennes. In short, they gave us all the information we desired, even telling us of two boats that were adrift up the river, one of which Captain Worthington recovered.

Having now two small boats, early on the morning of the twenty-first, abandoning our baggage, we began crossing over the troops and landing them on a small elevation called the Mamel. While engaged in searching for a passage Captain J. Williams gave chase to a canoe but could not take it. The men we had captured said it was impossible for us to make the town that night or at all with our boats. Recalling what we had done, however, we thought otherwise, and pushing into the water marched a league, frequently in water to our armpits, to what is called the upper Mamel. Here we encamped our men, still in good spirits from the hope of soon putting an end to their fatigue and realizing their desire to come into contact with the enemy.

This last march through the water was so far superior to anything our prisoners had conceived of that they were backward about saying anything further. They told us the nearest land was the Sugar Camp, a small league away on the bank of the river. A canoe was sent off to it and returned with the report that we could not pass. I now went myself and sounding the water found it as deep as my neck. I returned with the thought of having the men transported to the Sugar Camp in the canoes, which I knew would consume the entire day and the ensuing night since the boats would pass but

Clark's watery approach to Vincennes
Courtesy of the Indiana Department of Natural Resources

slowly through the bushes. To men half starved the loss of so much time was a serious matter and I would now have given a good deal for a day's provisions or for one of our horses.

. . . .

Now came the real test of our ability. The plain between us and the town was not a perfect level, and the sunken ground was covered with water full of ducks. We observed several men out on horseback shooting ducks about half a mile away and sent off several of our active young men to decoy and capture one of them in such a manner as not to alarm the rest. The information we obtained from this person was similar to that received from those we had taken on the river, with the exception of the news that the British had that evening completed the wall of the fort and that there were a large number of Indians in the town. Our situation was now sufficiently critical. We were within full view of a town which contained upward of six hundred men, counting soldiers, inhabitants and Indians, with no possibility of retreat open to us in case of defeat. The crew of the galley, although numbering less than fifty men, would have constituted a reinforcement of great importance to our little army. But we would not permit ourselves to dwell on this. We were now in the situation I had been laboring to attain. The idea of being taken prisoner was foreign to almost all of our men. In the event of capture they looked forward to being tortured by the savages. Our fate was now to be determined, probably within the next few hours, and we knew that nothing but the boldest conduct would insure success. I knew that some of the inhabitants wished us well, while many more were luke-warm to the interest of the British and Americans alike. I also learned that the Grand Chief, the son of Tobacco, had within a few days openly declared in council with the British that he was a brother and friend of the Big Knives. These circumstances were in our favor. Many hunters were going back and forth and there was little probability of our remaining undiscovered until dark. Accordingly I determined to bring matters to an issue at once, and writing the following address to the inhabitants sent it off by the prisoner we had just taken:

To the Inhabitants of Vincennes—

Gentlemen: Being now within two miles of your village with my army determined to take your fort this night, and not being willing to surprise you, I am taking the measure of requesting such of you as are true citizens and desirous of enjoying the liberty I bring you to remain quietly in your houses. If there are any that are friends of the King of England I desire them instantly to repair to the fort and there join his troops and fight like men; and if any that do not repair to the garrison shall hereafter be discovered they may depend upon being severely punished. Those, on the other hand, who are true friends to Liberty may expect to be well treated. I once more request that they keep out of the streets, for every person found under arms upon my arrival will be treated as an enemy.

. . . .

We advanced slowly in full view of the town, but as it was a matter of some consequence to make ourselves appear as formidable as possible, on leaving our place of concealment we marched and countermarched in a fashion calculated to magnify our numbers. Every person who had under-taken to enroll volunteers in the Illinois had been presented with a stand of colors and these, ten or twelve in number, they had brought along with them. We now displayed these to the best possible advantage, and since the plain through which we were marching was not perfectly level but was dotted with elevations rising seven or eight feet above the common level and running in an oblique direction to our line of march toward the town, we took advantage of one of these to march our men along the low ground so that only the colors (which had been fixed to long poles procured for the purpose) could be seen above the height. While we lay on Warrior's Island our young Frenchmen had decoyed and captured several hunters with their horses; I therefore caused our officers, mounted on these, to ride in and out in order more completely to deceive the enemy. In this manner we ad-vanced, directing our march in such fashion that darkness fell before we had proceeded more than half-way to the town. We then suddenly altered our direction and crossed some ponds where they could not suspect our presence. About eight o'clock we gained the heights in the rear of the town. There still being no enemy in sight, I became impatient to solve the mystery. I ordered Lieutenant Bailey with fourteen men to advance and open fire on the fort while the main body moved in a different direction and took possession of the strongest part of the town. The firing now commenced against the fort, but since drunken Indians often saluted it after nightfall, the garrison did not suppose it to be from an enemy until one of the men, lighting his match, was shot down through a porthole. The drums now sounded and the conflict was fairly joined on both sides. I sent reinforcements to assist in the attack on the garrison, while other dispositions were being made in the town.

. . . .

The garrison was now completely surrounded and the firing continued without intermission (except for about fifteen minutes shortly before dawn) until nine o'clock the following morning. Our entire force, with the exception of fifty men kept as a reserve in case of some emergency, participated in the attack, being joined by a few young men. I had acquainted myself fully with the situation of the fort and town and had detailed information concerning each of them. The cannon were on the upper floors of strong block-houses located at each angle of the fort eleven feet above the ground, and the portholes were so badly cut that our troops lay under their fire within twenty or thirty yards of the walls. The enemy did no damage except to the buildings of the town, some of which were badly shattered, while their musket fire in the dark was employed in vain against woodsmen who were sheltered behind the palings of the houses (the gardens of Vincennes were close to the fort and for about two-thirds of the way around them were fenced with good pickets firmly set in the ground and about six feet high. Where these were lacking breast-works for the troops were soon made by tearing down old houses and garden fences, so that the troops within the fort enjoyed but little advantage over those outside; and not knowing the number of the enemy, they thought themselves in a worse situation than they actually were), river banks, and ditches, and did us no damage except for the wounding of a man or two.

Since we could not afford to lose any of our men, great pains were taken to keep them sufficiently sheltered and to maintain a hot fire against the fort in order to intimidate the enemy as well as to destroy them. The embrasures for their cannon were frequently closed, for our riflemen finding the true direction would pour in such volleys when they were open that the artillerymen could not stand to the guns. Seven or eight of them were shot down in a short time. Our men frequently taunted the enemy in order to provoke them into opening the portholes and firing the cannon so that they might have the pleasure of cutting them down with their rifles. Fifty rifles would be leveled the instant the port flew open, and had the garrison stood to their artillery most of them, I believe, would have been destroyed during the night as the greater part of our men, lying within thirty yards of the walls, and behind some houses, were as well sheltered as those within the fort and were much more expert in this mode of fighting. The enemy fired at the flash of our guns, but our men would change their positions the moment they had fired. On the instant of the least appearance at one of their loopholes a dozen guns would be fired at it. At times an irregular fire as hot as could be maintained was poured in from different directions for several minutes. This would be continually succeeded by a scattering fire at the portholes and a great uproar and laughter would be raised by the reserve parties in different parts of the town to give the impression that they had only fired on the fort for a few minutes for amusement, while those who were keeping up a continuous fire were being regularly relieved. . . .

[The next day the] firing immediately recommenced with redoubled vigor on both sides and I do not believe that more noise could possibly have been made by an equal number of men. Their shouting could not be heard amid the discharge of the muskets, and a continual line of fire around the garrison was maintained until shortly before daylight, when our troops were withdrawn to positions that had been prepared for them sixty to one hundred yards from the fort. Scarcely could a loophole be darkened by the garrison when a rifle ball would pass through it, and for them to have stood to their cannon would have entailed the useless destruction of their men. In this respect the situation of the two parties was much the same. It would have been imprudent in either to have wasted men unless some decisive stroke should require it.

Thus the attack continued until nine o'clock on the morning of the twenty-fourth. . . .

Toward evening a flag of truce appeared with the following proposals.[2] I was greatly at a loss to conceive what reason Governor Hamilton could have for wishing a truce of three days on such terms as he proposed. Many said it was a stratagem to obtain possession of me. I thought differently and had no idea that he entertained such a sentiment, as an act of that nature would infallibly ruin him. I was convinced he had some prospect of succor or of extricating himself from his predicament in some way. Al-

---

[2]Hamilton's proposal, as recorded in Major Bowman's journal, was as follows: "Lieutenant Governor Hamilton proposes to Colonel Clark a truce for three days during which time he promises there shall be no defensive works carried on in the Garrison on condition Colonel Clark shall observe on his part a like cessation of any offensive work, that he wishes to confer with Colonel Clark as soon as can be and further proposes that whatever may pass between them two and any other person mutually agreed upon to be present, shall remain a secret till matters be finally concluded—as he wishes that whatever the result of their conference may be (it may redound) to the honor and credit of each party—If Colonel Clark makes a difficulty of coming into the fort Lieutenant Governor Hamilton will speak to him before the Gate."

though we had every reason to expect a reinforcement in less than three days that would at once put an end to the siege, I did not think it prudent to agree to the proposal. . . .[3]

We met at the church about eighty yards from the fort, Governor Hamilton, Major Hay, Superintendent of Indian Affairs, Captain Helm, who was his prisoner, Major Bowman, and myself, and the conference began. Governor Hamilton produced articles of capitulation containing various provisions, one of which was that the garrison should be surrendered on being permitted to go to Pensacola on parole. After deliberating on every article I rejected the whole proposal. Hamilton then desired me to make some proposition. I told him I had no offer to make other than I had already done, that they surrender themselves as prisoners unconditionally. I observed that his troops had behaved with spirit, and without viewing us as savages they could not suppose they would be treated the worse in consequence. If he chose to comply with my demand, the sooner he should do so the better, as it was in vain for him to make any counter proposition. He must know by this time that the fort would fall and that both of us must regard all blood that might still be spilled as murder on the part of the garrison. My troops were already impatient and begging for permission to storm the fort. If such a step were taken many of course would be cut down, and the consequences of an enraged body of woodsmen breaking into the fort must be obvious to him. It would be beyond the power of an American officer to save a single man.

Various arguments were exchanged for a considerable period of time. Captain Helm attempted to moderate my fixed determination, but I told him he was a British prisoner and it was doubtful whether he could with propriety speak on the subject. Governor Hamilton then said that Captain Helm was liberated from that moment and might act according to his pleasure. I told the Captain I would not receive him on such terms; that he must return to the fort and await his fate. I told the Governor we would not begin hostilities until a minute after the drums should give the alarm. We took leave of each other and parted, but I had gone only a few steps when the Governor stopped me and politely asked if I would be kind enough to give him my reasons for refusing any other terms than those I had offered to the garrison. I told him I had no objection to giving him my real reason, which simply was that I knew the greater part of the principal Indian partisans of Detroit were with him and I desired to be free to put them to death or treat them in any other way I might think proper. I said that the cries of the widows and the fatherless they had occasioned upon the frontiers now

---

[3][Clark's] answer is recorded in Major Bowman's journal as follows: "Colonel Clark's compliments to Mr. Hamilton and begs leave to inform him that Colonel Clark will not agree to any other terms than that of Mr. Hamilton's surrendering himself and Garrison Prisoners at discretion. If Mr. Hamilton is desirous of a conference with Colonel Clark he will meet him at the Church with Captain Helm."

required their blood at my hands and I did not choose to be so timorous as to disobey the absolute command of their authority, which I regarded as next to divine. I said I would rather lose fifty men than to surrender the power properly to execute this piece of business. If he chose to risk the massacre of his garrison for their sakes it was his own affair and I might perhaps take it into my hand to send for some of those widows to see it executed.

. . . .

On the morning of the twenty-fifth arrangements were made for receiving the garrison, and about ten o'clock it was surrendered with due formality and everything was immediately arranged by me to the best possible advantage. On first viewing the interior of the fort and its stores I was astonished at its being surrendered in the manner it had been. However, it was a prudent and lucky circumstance which probably saved the lives of many men on both sides since on the preceding night we had inclined to attempt to undermine it and I found it would have required great diligence on the part of the garrison to have prevented us from succeeding. I found, too, on further examination, that our information concerning the interior arrangements was so good that in all probability the first hot shot after the arrival of our artillery would have blown up the magazine. This would at once have put an end to the siege since the situation of the magazine and the quantity of powder it contained were such that its explosion must have destroyed the greater part of the garrison.

The Surrender of Fort Sackville

HENRY HAMILTON

Major Hay was detach'd with orders to fall down the river, and send to the principal Inhabitants of St. Vincennes, acquainting them that unless they quitted the Rebels and laid down their Arms, there was no mercy for them, some chiefs accompanied him to conciliate the Peankashaa Indians residing at St. Vincennes, and to show the French what they might expect if they pretended to resist. Major Hay secured the Arms, ammunition, and spiritous liquors, as soon as the inhabitants laid down their Arms, and the Officer who commanded in the Fort (Captain Helm) being deserted by the Officers and Men who to the Number of 70 had form'd his Garrison, and

From Milo M. Quaife (ed.), *The Capture of Old Vincennes: The Original Narratives of George Rogers Clark and of His Opponent Gov. Henry Hamilton* (1927), pp. 183–185, 189–192, 194–201, 203. Copyright © Bobbs-Merrill Company, Inc. Reprinted by permission.

were in pay of the Congress surrender'd his wretched fort on the very day of our arrival being the 17th of December 1778. Thus we employ'd 71 days in coming only Six Hundred Miles, which is to be attributed to the extraordinary difficulties of the way owing to an uncommon drought; the severity of the season, and the inevitable delays at the Indian Villages, particularly at Ouiattanon, where the Chiefs who had receiv'd the Rebel colors came in to us from their hunting, acknowledged their error gave up the flags and accused Monsieur de Celoron of having deserted them, besides that he never distributed to them the goods entrusted to him for the Indians.

In the fort we found two iron three pounders, mounted on truck carriages, two swivels not mounted, a very small quantity of amunition, and thirty two stout Horses which had been purchased for Congress, and which I gave to the Indians.

As to the state of the fort we found it a miserable stockade, without a Well, barrack, platform for small arms, or even a lock to the gate. Such was the moderation and good order observed by the Indians, that not a single person had the slenderest cause of complaint, not a shot was fired nor any inhabitant injured in person or property. It is remarkable that tho' on our arrival at this place our number was encreased to 500 Men, there was not one sick, nor had there been a single instance of drunkenness among the Indians or soldiery from the day we left Detroit, tho' rum was deliver'd out on every occasion when the fatigues or bad weather made it necessary. As soon as proper precautions were taken for securing our boats, landing our provisions &c, it became a point of consideration whether we should proceed directly to attack the Rebels at the Illinois, or content ourselves with establishing ourselves in this post where we had these several advantages; the command of the River Ohio by which the Spaniards had supplied the Rebel forts with Powder &c., the cutting off the communication between the Illinois, and the falls of Ohio across the country—The being situated so as to check the River Indians, and encourage the Delawares and Ottawas on white River, further to divide our small force (since we must leave a Garrison in Fort Sackville) appear'd not eligible, and we could not expect the Indians to remain much longer with us. The state of our provisions, the length of the journey (240 miles) and the want of Carriages, added to the nature of the country, subject to innundations all combined to direct our determination to fortify ourselves here, and wait for reinforcements in the Spring.

. . . .

The fort was on the 22nd of February in a tolerable state of defence the Work proposed being finish'd—This day, Mr. François Maisonville return'd from a scout having been in pursuit of Deserters, and brought in two Virginians prisoners, whom he had taken on the Ohio. He took me aside immediately and told me he had discover'd about four leagues below the fort, fourteen fires, but could not tell whether of Virginians or Savages, I instantly sent off Captain La Mothe, Lieutenant Shieffelin and 20 Men to bring me a more perfect account. The Waters being out, the meadows were so greatly overflowed it was necessary to take a circuit. Mr. Maisonville had taken upon him to serve as a guide tho' fatigued. They lost their way night coming on, and were only appriz'd by the firing of Cannon at the fort that it was invested; returning to the Village & finding it impossible to make their way good, they concealed themselves in a barn, sending from time to time one of their Number to explore and make report, but as they emploied Canadians, none of them return'd—The Militia of the Fort had been order'd under arms in the evening. The Major, Le gras, and one of the Captains, Bosseron, with several of the Private Men being reported absent, I suspected treachery, the two Officers however made their appearance at sunset. About 5 minutes after candles had been lighted we were alarmed by hearing a Musquet discharged; presently after some more, I concluded that some party of Indians was return'd or that there was some riotous frolic in the Village, going upon the Parade to enquire I heard the Balls whistle, order'd the Men to the Blockhouses, forbidding them to fire till they perceived the shot to be directed against the Fort. We were shortly out of suspence, one of the serjeants receiving a shot in the breast. The fire was now return'd, but the enemy had a great advantage from their Rifles, and the cover of the Church, Houses, Barns, &c. Mr. McBeath the surgeon having been in the Village when the firing began, push'd to get to the Gate, and narrowly escaped being kill'd, he reported that as soon as the first shots were fired, the Woman of the house where he was told him that Colonel Clarke was arrived with 500 Men from the Illinois. This very house had lately been searched in night on suspicion of a stranger being conceald, but the serjeant and party could not discover any such person—Tho' the night was dark we had a Serjeant Matross and five Men wounded. The weather was still so cold we were obliged to bring the Wounded into our own quarters. The Officers who had continued in tents all the winter were exposed to the fire of the enemy's riflemen as the picketting of the Fort was so poorly set up that one might pass the hand clench'd, between the Stockades. We dislodged the enemy from the Church, and nearest houses by a few cannon shot from the Block-houses, but when day appeared and we saw that the Inhabitants of the Village had joined the Rebels, we despaired of Captain La Mothe's party regaining the fort, but to our great surprize and joy about half-an-hour before sunrise they appear'd and got into the Fort over the Stockades which were upright, and 11 feet out of the ground, with their Arms in their hands. Two Canadians of his Company had deserted the preceding night, and Mr. Maisonville was betrayed and deliver'd to the Rebels by his own Cousin. The firing was but slack after sunrise, and about 8 o'clock a flag of truce from the Rebels appear'd, carried by Nicolas Cardinal a Captain of the

Militia of St. Vincennes, who deliver'd me a Letter from Coll Clarke requiring me to surrender at discretion, adding with an Oath that if I destroy'd any Stores or Papers I should be treated as a murtherer. Having assembled the Officers and read this letter I told them my intention was to undergo any extremity rather than trust to the discretion of such sort of people as we had to deal with. They all approve of this resolution, on which I assembled the Men and informed them of our determination. The English assured me they would defend the King's Colors to the last, adding a homely but hearty phrase, that they would stick to me as the shirt to my back—they then gave three cheers—The French on the contrary hung their heads—I return'd for answer to Col Clarke's Note, that threats would not prevent us from doing our duty as British Subjects, and the Flag having returned, the firing recommenced. La Mothe's Volunteers now began to murmur, saying it was very hard to be obliged to fight against their countrymen and relations, who they now perceived had joined the Americans—As they made half our number, and after such a declaration were not to be trusted—The Englishmen wounded, six in number were a sixth of those we could depend on, and duty would every hour fall heavier on the remaining few; considering we were at the distance of six hundred miles from succour, that if we did not burn the Village we left the enemy most advantageous cover against us, and that if we did, we had nothing to expect after rejecting the first terms, but the extremity of revenge, I took up the determination of accepting honorable terms if they could be procured, else to abide the Worst. . . .

Before anything was concluded the following scene was exhibited, of which I give your Excellency a relation, as it serves to contrast the behavior of His Majesty's Subjects with that of the Rebels, so often celebrated for humanity, generosity, and indeed everything virtuous, elevated, and noble.

About 2 o'clock afternoon a party of Indians with some whites return'd from a Scout, with two Canadians whom they had taken prisoners near the falls of Ohio, probably with information for the Rebels at the Fort. Colonel Clarke sent off a detachment of 70 Men against them. The Indian party was 15 or 16 Men, who seeing the English Flag flying at the Fort, discharged their pieces, an usual compliment with those people, they were immediately fired upon by the Rebels and Canadians, two killed on the spot, one shot in the belly, who however escaped, the rest were surrounded and taken bound to the Village, where being set in the Street opposite the Fort Gate they were put to death, notwithstanding a truce at that moment existed. The manner (as related to me by different people, and among others by the man at whose door this execrable feat was perpetrated) was as follows—

One of them was tomahawk'd immediately. The rest sitting on the ground in a ring bound—seeing by the fate of their comrade what they had to expect, the next on his left sung his death song, and was in turn tomahawk'd, the rest underwent the same fate, one only was saved at the intercession of a Rebel Officer, who pleaded for him telling Coll Clarke that the Savage's father had formerly spared his life.

The Chief of this party after having had the hatchet stuck in his head, took it out himself and deliver'd it to the inhuman monster who struck him first, who repeated his stroke a second and third time, after which the miserable spectacle was dragged by the rope about his neck to the River, thrown in, and suffer'd to spend a few moments of life in fruitless struglings—Two serjeants who had been Volunteers with the Indians escaped death by the intercession of a father and a Sister who were on the spot. Mr. Francis Maisonville whom I formerly mentioned was set in a Chair, and by Coll Clarke's order a Man came with a scalping knife, who hesitating to proceed to this excess of barbarity on a defenceless wretch, Colonel Clarke with imprecations told him to proceed, and when a piece of the scalp had been raised the man stopp'd his hand, he was again order'd to proceed, and as the executor of Coll Clarke's will, was in the act of raising the Skin, a brother of Mr. Maisonville, who had joined the Rebels, step'd up and prevailed on Coll Clarke to desist. The poor man who survived this cruel treatment, and shew'd an unshaken firmness in the minute of impending death, was not afterwards proof to the long confinement he underwent at Williamsburg, the gloominess of his situation affected his spirits first, the apprehension of suffering an ignominious death lower'd them still more, till reason began to be impair'd—The surgeon, a Man of great humanity, tho' attached to the cause of Rebellion, wrote to the Governor and Council of Virginia to solicit a little enlargement for this poor man, as the only means likely to save him, what the answers was I know not, but the unfortunate creature put an end to his miseries and his life, in spight of two persons who watched him and were aware of his situation.

Colonel Clarke yet reeking with the blood of these unhappy Victims came to the Esplanade before the Fort Gate, where I had agreed to meet him and treat of the surrender of the Garrison—He spoke with rapture of his late achievement, while he washed off the blood from his hands stained in this inhuman sacrifice.

He told me it was in vain to think of persisting in the defence of the Fort, that his cannon would be up in a few hours, that he knew to a Man who might be depended on with every other circumstance of my situation, that if from a spirit of obstinacy I persisted when there was no probability of relief and should stand an Assault, not a single Soul should be spared. I replyed that tho' my numbers were small I could depend on them, He said he knew I had but 35 or 36 staunch men, that 'twas but folly to think of a defence with so small numbers so overmatch'd; that if I would surrender at discretion and trust to his generosity, I should have better treatment than if I articled for terms—my answer was, that I would then abide the consequence, and never take so disgraceful a step while I had ammunition and provision.

You will be answerable (said he) for the lives lost by your obstinacy. I said my Men had declared they would die with Arms in their hands rather than surrender at discretion, that still I would accept such terms as might consist with my honor and duty, that knowing what I could pretend to, little time was necessary for drawing up Articles—He said he would think upon it and return in half-an-hour, he returned accordingly accompanied by one of his Captains—I went to meet them with Major Hay, the soldiers in the meantime apprehensive of some ill design, mann'd the East Blockhouse ready to fire at an instant. The conversation was resumed, and Colonel Clarke appeared as determined as before, I then said further discourse was vain, that I would return to the Fort and to prevent mistakes, the firing should not take place for an hour after our parting took my leave & was proceeding to the fort, when Major Hay & Captain Bowman call'd me back, the subject was renewed, and Coll Clarke agreed to my sending terms for his consideration—They were sent that same evening, Colonel Clarke made his alterations and I agreed to them, having first called the Officers together, and exposed to them the necessity of the step. The Men were then assembled, and were convinced that no advantage to His Majesty's service could result from our holding out in the present circumstances. . . .

At ten o'clock in the morning of the 25th, we marched out with fix'd Bayonets and the Soldiers with their knapsacks—the colors had not been hoisted this morning, that we might be spared the mortification of hawling them down. . . .

The terms granted by Colonel Clarke and which I reluctantly signed were as follow—

1st. Lieutenant Governor Hamilton engages to deliver up to Coll Clark, Fort Sackville as it is at present with all the Stores, ammunition & provisions &c &c.

2d. The Garrison are to deliver themselves up prisoners of war, and to march out with their Arms accoutrements and knapsacks.

3d. The Garrison to be deliver'd up to-morrow at 10 o'clock.

4thly. Three days time to be allowed the Garrison to settle their accounts with the traders of this Town.

5thly. The Officers of the Garrison to be allowed their necessary baggage.

Signed at Post Vincennes the 24th day of February 1779.

G. R. CLARKE.

Agreed to for the following reasons—

Hamilton surrendering the Fort
Courtesy of the Indiana Department of Natural Resources

The remoteness from succour, the state and quantity of provisions the unanimity of officers & men on its expediency, the honorable terms allowed and lastly, the confidence in a generous enemy.

HENRY HAMILTON,
Lieut. Govr. & Superintendent.

If it be consider'd that we were to leave our wounded men at the mercy of a Man who had shewn such instances of ferocity as Colonel Clarke had lately done, a compliment bespeaking his generosity and humanity may possibly find excuse with some as I know it has censure from others.

The evening of the day we capitulated, Colonel Clark order'd Neck-irons, fetters and handcuffs to be made which in our hearing he declared were design'd for those Officers who had been employed as partisans with the Indians. I took him aside and reminded him that these persons were prisoners of War included in the capitulation which he had so lately set his hand to, he said his resolution was form'd, that he had made a vow never to spare woman or Child of the Indians or those who were employ'd with them—I observed to him that these persons having obey'd my orders were not to be blamed for the execution of them, that I had never known that they had acted contrary to those orders, by encouraging the cruelty of the savages, on the contrary, and that if he was determined to pass by the

consideration of his faith and that of the public, pledged for the perfor-
mance of the Articles of capitulation, I desired he might throw me into
prison or lay me in irons rather than the others—He smiled contemptuously,
turn'd away and order'd three of these persons to the guard, till the Irons
should be made—The scalps of the slaughter'd Indians were hung up by our
Tents, a Young man of the name of Rainbault was brought into the fort
with a halter about his neck and only for the interposition of the Volunteers
from the Illinois some of whom were his Relations would infallibly have
been hanged without any crime laid to his charge but his having been with a
scouting party; he was half strangled before he was taken from the tree.

. . . .

At length on the 8th day of March, we were put into a heavy Oak
boat, being 27 in Number, with our provision of Flour and pork at common
ration, and 14 Gallons of Spirits for us and our guard which consisted of 23
persons including two officers—We had before us 360 Miles of water carriage and 840 to march to the place of our destination Williamsburgh in
Virginia—

3: An Enlightened Western Policy

The Land Ordinance of 1785 and the Northwest Ordinance of 1787 represent two remarkable achievements of the Confederation Congress. The first document provided for an elaborate and sophisticated system of land survey and sale, the basis of which is still used. It established the congressional township which consisted of thirty-six one-square-mile sections and was laid out in a carefully surveyed and numbered gridiron pattern across the Old Northwest and then much of the rest of the country. Shortly afterwards, in an equally enlightened ordinance that replaced a 1784 plan suggested by Thomas Jefferson, the Confederation Congress established a system of government for the territory "North West of the river Ohio." In broad outline, the Northwest Ordinance provided for a three-step process by which three to five states, equal in all particulars to existing states, would emerge. After an initial phase of an appointed government, the territory was authorized an elected territorial legislature and a delegate to Congress as soon as its population reached 5,000 voters (adult white males). Stage three—statehood—required a minimum population of 60,000 people, not just voters. This legislation, which also contained the famous and precedent-setting prohibition of slavery, as well as a bill of rights, has been acclaimed as a document, in Theodore Pease's words, "secondary only to the Constitution of the United States."

The Northwest Ordinance, 1787

THEODORE C. PEASE

Professor Pease, a student of Midwestern and especially Illinois history during his long tenure as professor of history at the University of Illinois, both clarifies the background and explains the reasons for his admiration of the Ordinance in the article below. It is a revised version of an address he delivered to an American Historical Association meeting in Philadelphia, December 1937. Pease was also the author of *The*

From "The Ordinance of 1787," *Mississippi Valley Historical Review*, XXV (Sept. 1938), 167, 168, 170–80. Copyright © Organization of American Historians. Reprinted by permission.

Story of Illinois (1925) and *The Frontier State, 1818-1848* (1918), and he edited a number of documentary collections.

Meeting in Philadelphia at this season [1937], the American Historical Association appropriately commemorates the 150th anniversary of the Philadelphia convention and of the framing of the Constitution of the United States. While the members of the Mississippi Valley Historical Association join in that commemoration, they naturally remember that another document, secondary only to the Constitution of the United States, is especially intrusted to their historical charge. They remember that on the thirteenth day of July, 1787, the Congress of the Confederation passed an ordinance for the government of the Northwest Territory....

In appraising the place of this document in American history, as it is most fitting to do at this time, it is not essential to seek after novelty or rush frantically in search of unconventional interpretations. All students of western history are familiar with the particulars necessary for a valuation of the ordinance; one of them as well as another may set these forth.

That this is possible is due in great measure to the fact that a generation after the Northwest Ordinance was framed, its authorship became an honor to be contended for. One may pass over the enthusiastic Ohio panegyrist who in 1837 assured his audience that the ancient Romans would have ascribed its composition to the nymph, Egeria! Daniel Webster, in his debate with Robert Y. Hayne, inserted a set eulogy on Nathan Dane as the true author. With other historical partisans ready to press the claims of Thomas Jefferson, of Edward Carrington, of Rufus King, and of Manasseh Cutler himself, large quantities of evidence were collected, preserved, and criticized, so that the main facts connected with the ordinance have long since been set aside to cool.

In appraising its place in American history, the most ardent patriot, the most earnest nationalist need have no misgiving about stating the last iota of the truth concerning it. The importance of that document in American history is past arguing. The devil's advocate may be allowed to say everything that can be said in its disfavor, and when he has done his worst, its sanctity will still prevail beyond all doubt. Historical truth is not singular but diverse; of the infinite number of things which may be said of any historical event or situation, a given number are always sure to be equally true. For instance, there is the saying that under the Ordinance, the United States became one of the most successful colonizing nations of all history; there is Andrew C. McLaughlin's interpretation of the document, along with the Constitution of the United States, as the creation of a system of imperial order toward which the men of the Thirteen Colonies had striven for a quarter of a century, both inside and outside the British Empire. These things are true and many more....

It must also be admitted that the statesmen who labored the passage of the Ordinance do not appear always to have been highminded or disinterested. The great prohibition of slavery, hastily interpreted not to be retroactive, bore, it is true, the original imprint of the humanitarianism of the great Virginians. But for its insertion in the final Ordinance, cavillers have alleged, and with a show of evidence, that smug New England prejudice went hand in hand with the enlightened self-interest of southerners who did not wish slave grown tobacco from northwest of the Ohio to compete with the produce of the Old South.

Further one must admit that if, under the similar Southwest Ordinance, the annals of the Southwest Territory were vacant, in the Northwest Territory personality clashed on personality, governors and governed found no good to speak of each other, and the Ordinance put into practice brought not peace but a sword. One should also recall the corollary that the states formed out of the Northwest Territory did not, in fond memory of the government of their infant years under the Ordinance, inscribe its provisions unaltered in their state constitutions. Quite the reverse. As has already been said, the Ordinance, in the first stage of territorial government, assigned the whole of the legislative, executive, and judicial functions to the governor and judges appointed from above; and hemmed in with property qualifications the offices themselves, and the suffrage grudgingly doled out in the second state of territorial government. In sharp contrast, the first state constitutions of Ohio, Indiana, and Illinois established manhood suffrage and made governors mere figure heads, with scarcely power to do more than draw the meager salaries constitutionally assigned to them; those constitutions rendered courts and judges subject to the election and recall of the legislative representatives of the people. . . .

Having said all these things in dispraise of the Ordinance, one might well ask whence its sanctity, whence its greatness, whence its abiding place of honor in American institutions? The answer is not difficult. Once again one should remember that historical truth is not single and simple but manifold and complex. In the 1820's, the Ordinance was a sacred thing. Representatives of the Northwest Territory in Congress averred that to their constituents it was a pillar of cloud by day and a pillar of fire by night. It could be invoked as a sacred oracle to prohibit the extension of slavery into a state of the Northwest. Friends and partisans of the statesmen who had framed it could contend eagerly over the honor of authorship. "It approaches," said Judge Timothy Walker of Ohio, "as nearly to absolute perfection as anything to be found in the legislation of mankind; for after the experience of fifty years it would perhaps be impossible to alter without marring it." The answer must be that, with all its defects and shortcomings, the Ordinance embodied the policy, the theory of government and the ideal which, in the large, had worked, and worked so brilliantly in the first expansion of the American political system beyond the Alleghenies and to the Mississippi River. A colonizing system so successful that men scarcely recognized it for such, a balance of local autonomy and central authority so exact that it seemed inevitable—those were the things which gave the Ordinance its prestige and its sanctity. Seeing it as the adaptation of an ideal of government to a situation, it can best be appraised in the light of earlier national attitudes toward the West and its settlement.

One might begin with the policy of France in the Old Northwest as it developed from the latter half of the seventeenth century. It would be more true than false to say that with the exception of the settlements in the American Bottom and at Detroit, the French government never wished nor expected an extensive colonization of the West by Frenchmen....

Actually, the French policy in the occupation of the West appears to have been a fine drawn scheme of diplomacy in which the very aptitude of the Indian in that form of politics could be used to involve him in elaborate and far-reaching spider webs of entangling alliances. Once enmeshed, the tribes had perforce to further the ends of French policy, even to lifting the tomahawk against any of their fellow prisoners who struggled to free themselves. French commandants in the West were not so much commanders of frontier garrisons around which settlements might spring up, as military and diplomatic representatives accredited to certain tribes. The commandants at Miamis, Ouiatenon, Vincennes, and St. Joseph were really the French residents near the Miami Confederacy, the Wea, the Piankeshaws, and the Pottawotomie....

When the English, in the negotiations of the Treaty of 1763, bargained for the extension of their frontier to the Mississippi River, they scarcely contemplated any general settlement of the region. Originally, they had entered into the war with the idea of protecting the western frontiers of their colonies against French encroachment. In placing the boundary between the two nations in America at the Mississippi, they intended solely to keep their subjects so far apart that there would be no opportunity for future disputes. When they declared that they would probably never deforest or settle those regions, they were undoubtedly speaking at least as sincerely as diplomats ever do. Actually, Pontiac's insurrection made them acutely aware of French habitants in the West encouraging the Indian resistance. They hastened as soon as they could to occupy the Mississippi line, in the hope of bringing the French frontiersmen to heel; and were disappointed at finding that the French authorities did not take away their inhabitants when they departed. Until 1774 they made no provision for their government, other than autocratic military rule. As Louise P. Kellogg has shown, they seriously considered concentrating all French inhabitants in one village in order to deal with them in easier fashion.

On their own frontiers, however, the English had a somewhat different problem. In the backwoods of their colonies, they had a population recruited from a half dozen nationalities, including half a dozen economic classes, pressing westward with a blind urge which seems subconscious and biological. Anyone who has worked in the sources of the western movement can visualize for himself rough, barbarous families, far more prolific than the red men, now venting on the Indians cruelties as savage as those of the Indians themselves; now pressing in foolhardy fashion to establish their cabins and cornfields close to hostile villages; now fleeing in equally blind panic back to the frontiers. Sometimes they were savages, sometimes cowards, sometimes heroes, but always a force to be reckoned with from their antlike instinct to reproduce their species and to leave their children in a better station of life than they had been. A recurrence of this population in generation after generation, farther and farther west on the advancing frontier has been a commonplace of American history for almost half a century; and the control, the management, the repression of this element, to say nothing of the land speculators who exploited it, was one of the problems respecting the western country that confronted Great Britain.

The un-wisdom with which the British ministry dealt with it is written large across the history of the American Revolution. . . .

The answer to the Quebec Act is the American Revolution, the settlement of Kentucky, the occupation of the Illinois country and the Ohio Valley in the name of Virginia, and the Old Dominion's grandiloquent attempt to extend her frontiers west and northwest to encompass the whole land. Actually, her conquest was but partial. Inspired by land companies possessing speculative titles in the region, Virginia's sister colonies acidly called attention to her neglect of the tasks assigned her in the common cause. In 1781, her great soldier, George Rogers Clark failed in his last attempt on Detroit. With her chance to gain possession of the whole Northwest forever gone, Virginia was perforce compelled to bargain away to the Confederation her title to the fringe of her military occupation along the Ohio and the Mississippi. In doing this, she stipulated a guarantee of her right to Kentucky and that none of the land companies who had banded together and had stirred up the landless states to oppose her wider claims should profit one acre by her cessions.

But the problem of the West remained the most serious one. The Treaty of 1783 had given the United States the title to the Northwest, but only a paper title. Spain or Great Britain or possibly even France might well be expected to wrest the region from the United States, seemingly too feeble to maintain her hold on it by diplomacy or by the sword, or even to begin its economic exploitation. The frontiersmen, treated as step-children by the older states of Kentucky and Tennessee, deprived of all stable government northwest of the Ohio, slipping into anarchy, their trade outlets to the south and to the north controlled by Spain and England, stood on a pivot between older states to which they were tied by blood and by old political habit and the great empires to the north and to the south which seemingly could offer much more in their economic development.

To the rescue of the West two great Virginians stepped forward, each by the method to which his hand naturally turned. While Washington, the man of action, plunged into the wilderness he had known since his boyhood, to search out trade routes by which the two sides of the Alleghenies might profitably carry on commerce with each other, Jefferson, the man of contemplation, thought of political means and of political ideas which might bind the men of the western waters to the men of the Atlantic sea-board. The problem seemed to be two-fold. On the one hand, without strong government, the West might either drift into allegiance to Great Britain or Spain or else by some act of lawlessness involve the infant confederacy in a disastrous war with one power or the other. Central control there must be. On the other hand, if the tidewater was to play the same step-mother's role toward the western settlers that Great Britain had played to the tidewater settlers in the days before the Revolution, the West was as good as gone. If the land speculator buying up his land in vast tracts from a government too lazy to sell it retail, insisted on exacting an exorbitant wholesaler's profit from the men who must till it in the sweat of their brows, an economic revolution must inevitably accompany the political one.

In seeking a solution, Jefferson, even as he had deftly woven the ideas and aspirations of revolutionary America into the Declaration of Independence, brought together things both old and new that might solve the problem. His work during the winter and spring of 1784 as a member of the Congress of the Confederation was as significant as that of any other period of his life. There can be little doubt that the initiative was his in the framing of the Ordinance of 1784. Adapting an earlier suggestion to his end, on the map of the western country, he drew a checkerboard of states from one hundred to one hundred and fifty miles in dimension. The states were plotted in the idea that river systems and large bodies of water were economic unities, rather than boundaries of political division. In each one of these divisions, once the Indian title had been extinguished and the lands put on sale, he imagined a little community of free men meeting together to devise themselves a government. Because little time could be spared to this task from the harsh struggle of wresting a living from the wilderness, because law books would be few and statesmen fewer, he imagined them adopting the constitution and the laws of some one of the thirteen states. Thus he imagined them governing themselves, sending an observer to the government of the Confederation, and finally, once they had attained a population comparable to that of a state, gaining admission to the Confederation on full equality with the older states.

Asking himself what security there could be that the people in this community would remain in due subordination to the central government, or what security they could themselves expect for their admission to the Union in the fullness of time, he recognized immediately that no such system could possibly rest on coercion or force. The most bigoted strong-

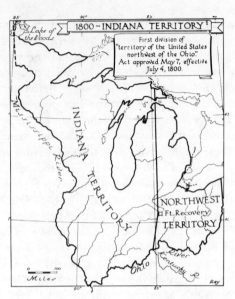

The first territories of the Old Northwest
Courtesy of the Indiana State Library

government man would admit the impossibility of the government's ever using military force to secure obedience in the west country; but the political theory which Jefferson and his fellows had taught in the American Revolution pointed to compact as the true origin of all free government, pointed to free and unforced covenant or agreement as the highest and most sacred sanction for political power known among men. Therefore, to invest the Ordinance of 1784 with the highest sanctity and authority, he inserted in it articles of compact between the people of the older states and the people of the newer West, to bind them forever into political unity, and to serve as the guarantee of the bargains implied on either side. As a great idealist, he inserted also the great prohibition of slavery, north as well as south of the Ohio, only to see it struck out, as he bitterly commented, because of one man's illness in his own Virginia delegation.

Fitting exactly into his larger project, was the Ordinance of 1784 for the sale of lands, later in the Ordinance of 1785 destined to be expanded into the land policy of the United States. Again in his draft land ordinance he borrowed from ideas already current, but he also invented and coordinated. But the underlying concept is a great system of rectangular surveys so simple that a plain man may see for himself where his land lies and its metes and bounds. It is moreover a system in which the government will trouble to sell at retail in tracts so small that a half dozen families may at least club together to buy without paying tribute to a land speculator. Superimpose on this system a series of treaties extinguishing Indian titles, and Jefferson's concept for saving the West by political wisdom stands revealed. . . .

But what of the significance of the Ordinance in the more distant perspective of history? Some months ago one of the most prized members of this association was promoting before a congressional committee an undertaking of vital interest to the Mississippi Valley Historical Association. As he unfolded a plan of action reaching to the year 1949 a congressman asked him if he expected the United States to last so long. The author of this paper admits that he was deeply impressed only by the patient good humor of his fellow member's answer. His own temptation would have been to quote the greengrocer in Shaw's play, "Ah, the world will go on, ma'am: don't you be afraid of that. It ain't as easy to stop it as the earnest kind of people think."

But admitting for the moment that the political civilization of the United States may in the distant future be submerged beneath communism, fascism, race worship, technocracy, or whatever fashions in government that future may bring forth, the fact remains that very often time permits political ideals to outlive the death of the civilization that produces them. The Athenian democracy of Pericles lies buried under more than a score of centuries; it has suffered the drums and tramplings of twenty conquests; it is overlaid by the strata of twenty tyrannies. But there survives that funeral oration of Pericles in which he commemorated men whose lives their country's freedom had made so precious that for that country they freely laid down their lives. That endures and men this night may hearten themselves by it in lands where they must go into their innermost chambers to meditate on it.

And a precious part of the world's heritage in distant ages to come, whatever may have befallen the United States, will be the ideas that men may not permanently by their brothers be held in political subordination and clientage; and that the highest and most sacred guarantee, the most practical and stable cement of states and governments is the free and unforced covenant and agreement of man and man.

Chapter III
HARRISON, TECUMSEH, AND TERRITORIAL POLITICS

Indiana was part of the Northwest Territory from its organization in 1787 until the establishment of a separate Indiana Territory in 1800. The events of paramount importance during this time were the establishment of a government headed by Arthur St. Clair; the eventual defeat of the Indians in Ohio in 1794, after two unsuccessful tries; and the passage of the territory into second stage government in 1798.

Young William Henry Harrison was with General Anthony Wayne as he carefully plotted his moves leading to the decisive Battle of Fallen Timbers. Following that battle came the establishment of Fort Wayne at the strategic three-river site of former settlements of both the French and the Indians; and then came the Treaty of Fort Greenville (1795), which provided for the removal of the Miamis and other Indians westward. Thus Indiana became the area of the next major Indian-white confrontation, culminating in the Battle of Tippecanoe (1811) and the war that followed.

Shortly after the Treaty of Fort Greenville, when the Northwest Territory advanced governmentally into the semirepresentational stage, William Henry Harrison became the first territorial delegate to Congress from the nation's first territory. Appointed to this position in 1798, he served during the 1799–1800 session. Although delegates were not allowed to vote on legislation, they handled all the other duties of congressmen. Interestingly, Harrison is credited with a role in two major pieces of legislation during his brief tenure as delegate: the (Harrison) Land Act of 1800, and the establishment of a separate Indiana Territory. President John Adams then appointed Harrison territorial governor, a post the transplanted Virginian held through three reappointments by Presidents Jefferson and Madison.

During Harrison's tenure as governor of the Indiana Territory from 1800 to 1812, he had the dual responsibility of governing the huge area and of maintaining peaceful relations with the Indians while getting title to as much of the land as necessary. Initially, the Indiana Territory comprised all of the former Northwest Territory except for essentially what was to become the state of Ohio in 1803. But in 1805 the Michigan Territory, and in 1809 the Illinois Territory, which included everything west of the Indiana-Illinois boundary, were given their own governments. Despite the enormity and incongruity of Harrison's tasks, the new governor performed satisfactorily in all areas. By a series of treaties, he obtained title from various Indian tribes to most of the southern third of Indiana, in addition to other portions of land where white men had already settled. When Tecumseh and his brother, known as the Prophet, decided that the Treaty of Fort Wayne (1809) had gone too far, and planned an organized resistance to further encroachments, Harrison took the initiative and the opportunity afforded by Tecumseh's temporary absence from the scene in the fall of 1811 to win an ultimately decisive victory over the Prophet at Tippecanoe.

In the meantime, Harrison had established a government at the settlement at Vincennes, thriving by that time, where he built for himself an imposing brick mansion, Grouseland, which still stands. And he developed into a capable, even astute, frontier politician. There were many issues dividing the small but growing number of pioneers who came to Indiana during its territorial period. However, the political differences tended to be more personally focused as differences between the aristocratic Harrison's followers, who had settled for the most part in southwestern Indiana, and the anti-Harrison people, who were concentrated in the eastern and southeastern sections of the territory. Perhaps surprisingly, slavery in the supposedly slave-free land "North West of the river Ohio" was one of the major issues; others involved matters of local self-government; the location of the territorial capital, especially after the 1809 loss of Illinois from Vincennes jurisdiction; and personality conflicts between Harrison and the eventual leader of the anti-Harrison bloc, long-time territorial delegate Jonathan Jennings.

The War of 1812, despite the early conflict at Tippecanoe, which was continued by the same parties, had little direct impact on the territory. For defenses against Indian raids, a number of blockhouses were erected across the southern tier of Indiana, especially after the bloody massacre at Pigeon Roost late in 1812; but few battles were fought in the region. Governor Harrison resigned his political office early in the war and distinguished himself again as a successful military commander through his invasion of upper Canada. At the Battle of the Thames, his most important victory in the war, Harrison once again confronted Tecumseh, now an ally of the British; but the resourceful Indian leader was killed during the battle.

At war's end, the country resumed its westward march more vigorously than ever before. Soon Indiana had the required minimum population for statehood. In a rapid series of events in 1815 and 1816, including a constitutional convention at the new territorial capital of Corydon in June 1816, Indiana became the nineteenth state of the Union on December 11, 1816.

For information on the territorial period in Indiana, see especially Dorothy B. Goebel, *William Henry Harrison* (1926), and John D. Barnhart and Dorothy L. Riker, *Indiana to 1816: The Colonial Period* (1971). See also Logan Esarey (ed.), *Messages and Letters of William Henry Harrison* (2 vols., 1922), Hubert H. Hawkins (ed.), *Indiana's Road to Statehood* (1964), and Gayle Thornbrough (ed.), *The Correspondence of John Badollet and Albert Gallatin, 1804–1836* (1963).

1: Contrary Patterns in Territorial Life

The Indiana territorial period lasted sixteen years. During most of this time peace prevailed, and Governor William Henry Harrison was primarily involved in administering the area and in obtaining land cessions from the Indians. Although partisan politics was absent, since there were few if any Federalists in the territory, there was much political rivalry based on support for or disapproval of Harrison and his Virginia coterie. In time this opposition was led by Jonathan Jennings, Indiana's territorial delegate from 1809 to 1816, when he became the first governor of the state.

There were, however, a number of issues that divided the growing number of territorial pioneers and enlivened public discussion. They included the court system and the administration of justice, the formation of new counties, advancement into second- and third-stage government, popular participation in political affairs, Indian affairs, and the tormenting issue of slavery. According to the two authors represented below, John D. Barnhart and Jacob P. Dunn, the dominant features of territorial life were, paradoxically, a remarkable growth in democratic practices and the continuation of slavery under another name. At the same time that property qualifications for suffrage were being removed, and election rather than appointment to the upper house of the territorial legislature was being approved, along with popular election of the territorial delegate to Congress, legislative sanction designed to perpetuate slavery under long—even interminable—contracts was also being granted.

In 1805 the Indiana legislature adopted an act permitting slaves to be brought into the territory and, if over the age of fifteen, bound for service "for any term of years."[1] Slaves under fifteen were to be registered and to serve to the age of thirty-five if male, thirty-two if female. Under the terms of this act, which remained in force until 1810, indentures of twenty to forty years in duration were common, and Professor Thornbrough discovered two indentures calling for terms of service of ninety years, and two more of ninety-nine years. After 1810 no new slaves could be brought into the territory and held under indentures; but the existing agreements were not affected. Clearly, the prohibition of slavery set forth in the Northwest Ordinance was not

[1]Emma Lou Thornbrough, *The Negro in Indiana: A Study of a Minority* (1957), p. 9.

absolute. But in the view of historian Jacob P. Dunn, the inclusion of a slavery prohibition clause in the Indiana Constitution of 1816 marked the state's "redemption from slavery."

Professor Barnhart has examined the concurrent growth of democratic practices and their widespread influence in Indiana and surrounding states in his book *Valley of Democracy: The Frontier versus the Plantation, 1775–1818* (1953). A professor of history at Indiana University for many years, he is also the author of a number of articles concerning the sources of migration into the Midwest. Mr. Dunn, in addition to his history of the state to 1816, *Indiana: A Redemption from Slavery* (1888), also wrote *Indiana and Indianans: A History of Aboriginal and Territorial Indiana and the Century of Statehood* (5 vols., 1919).

Democratic Influences in Territorial Indiana

JOHN D. BARNHART

The population of Indiana Territory was approximately twenty-five thousand in 1810, when Indian difficulties were soon to check migration for a short time. The trails as well as the nativities of the early settlers indicate that this population came largely from south of the Ohio River and practically all over trails through Pennsylvania and the Southern states.

The experiences of this frontier population in establishing its social and political institutions form an interesting and significant chapter in the development of frontier democracy. The forces which handicapped the influence of the frontier in the South were absent or so weak as to be unable to control the formation of government and society. Largely lacking were the numerous planters and their slaves. Undemocratic state governments with their policies which favored land speculation, slavery, and aristocracy were not in control. Climate and other geographic forces did not make possible an agricultural regime based upon staple products such as cotton, rice, indigo, or tobacco.

A few aspired to be country gentlemen in imitation of the planter class, farms were often called plantations, a few colored slaves and workers were held as house servants, and land speculation existed on every hand, but more often it was the activity of the small landholder rather than of the rich who dealt in thousands of acres. The little coterie of able men who gathered around Harrison at Vincennes came to be called the Virginia Aristocrats. Negro servants were held by some of them. Aristocratic manners, characteristic of the plantation South or of the old country, had been carried into

From "The Democratization of Indiana Territory," *Indiana Magazine of History,* XLIII (March 1947), 8–11, 13–17, 20–22. Footnotes in the original have been omitted. Reprinted by permission.

this frontier region. General James Dill, a native of Ireland and a Harrison appointee, attended court as a prosecuting attorney in the costume of a gentleman of the Revolutionary period, knee breeches, silver buckles, and cue, "a mild protest against the leveling tendencies of the age" and of the frontier.

But the character of society was not determined by these forces. The larger number of citizens were small landowners and squatters. Until the land was surveyed and placed on sale, nearly all were squatters. When the sales were opened, those who had the money bought small pieces of land. Since the credit system held sway from 1800 to 1820, many a poor man got together enough money to make the first payment and then hoped that industry and good fortune would enable him to meet the succeeding payments before it was too late. The arrears of interest and principal indicate that many had been too optimistic. But the point is that the Indiana frontier was a poor man's home and its development in the formative period was shaped by frontier influences.

The law which created Indiana Territory re-established the same non-representative type of government which existed in the first stage of the Northwest Territory. William Henry Harrison, the governor of the new territory, had gained experience in the former where he served for short periods as secretary and delegate to Congress. He avoided many of the arbitrary acts of St. Clair, but his policies and appointments as governor attracted to him many of the more conservative leaders and antagonized a few vigorous men and a growing number of the newer settlers. Although the secretary, John Gibson, spent his life along the frontier from Pittsburgh to Vincennes, he had little influence upon the government, and the judges were not noted for their sympathy with the ways of the frontiersmen. From the beginning, however, there was much interest taken in the acts of government, and neither the efforts of the people to make the government more democratic nor the governor's critics were suppressed. An almost immediate and continuous movement was begun to make the government not only responsive to the wishes and needs of the people, but also to place it in their hands.

The causes of this movement might be classified as the conditions which produced discontent and the developments which gave the people the opportunity to participate in their own government. Some of them were the lack of unity in a territory which included remote settlements occupied by people of different origins, connections, and interests, as well as the uncertainty of land titles, the activity of land speculators, and the claims of the Indians to large parts of the territory. But the desire of the people for greater self-government, the political ambitions of various individuals, the efforts to legalize slavery, and the difference of opinion as to the best methods of attracting settlers to the country were also involved. Perhaps this latter point has not received enough attention. Persons of aristocratic tendencies placed

William Henry Harrison
Courtesy of the Indiana Historical Society

much emphasis upon the importance of securing men of wealth, family, and education. The closest source of such settlers was the planter class of Kentucky and other Southern states. The planters owned slaves, hence the efforts to legalize slavery. On the other hand, the democratic masses from the South, many of whom had there suffered political, social, and economic discriminations, and settlers from the North were not enthusiastic about the pretensions of the aristocrats to superior talents and they were not willing to pay the price of their coming,—the admission of slavery. It was the old contest of a white man's society with democratic features against the planters' social order with its aristocratic characteristics. Often the contest degenerated into petty quarrels in which every act of the governor was attacked and defended with spirit and acrimony, but if one sees only these disputes, the trees have obscured the forest.

The territorial history of Indiana falls rather naturally into five divisions. There was the unrepresentative stage of territorial government which lasted four years, the early part of the second stage before the separation of Illinois Territory in 1809, the shorter term between the division of the territory and the resumption of Indian warfare, the three years of warfare from the Tippecanoe campaign in 1811 to the end of Harrison's campaign in 1813, and finally the successful struggle for statehood, 1814–1816....

The first period of territorial government came to an end when Harrison reversed his position on the advisability of passing into the second or semi-representative stage of government in 1804. Petitions, he stated, were presented to him asking for representative government. To ascertain the wishes of a majority, he called an election on September 11, at which time the majority of those voting, favored the change. The governor proclaimed the second stage and called an election of representatives for the lower house of the territorial assembly.

Whether the change represented the wishes of the majority or not, a violent newspaper controversy broke out, in which Harrison's critics soon made known their opposition. "A Freeholder of Knox County," who was probably William McIntosh, criticized Harrison's sponsorship of the Vincennes Convention as well as a recent meeting in Vincennes for the purpose of petitioning for the second stage. He asserted that the advance should have come spontaneously and not have been forced by the governor. The meeting to which he referred had adopted an address in which objection was made to the limited legislative powers of the governor and judges, to the power of Congress to countermand their action, to the unsuitability of the laws of other states for Indiana Territory, and to a lack of a voice in any act of the territorial or national government. In extravagant language, the address referred to the first stage of territorial government as the most abominable and tyrannical system ever organized for freemen. The second stage was described as imperfect but as an improvement. It also asserted that the expenses would not be too heavy, that a delegate in Congress was needed, and that able men could be found to serve in the legislative assembly. "Gerald," who was probably Benjamin Parke, asserted that the petitions induced a strong belief that a majority of the freeholders wanted the change in government, while "A Citizen," probably McIntosh, denied this, and a "Plough Boy" defended the governor. Name calling and heat were soon substituted for reasoning, the writers revealed each other's identity, and Parke obviously tried to provoke McIntosh into challenging him to a duel, but the latter asked Parke if calumny was Harrison's last defense.

For a time, however, Harrison and his supporters kept things well in hand. President Thomas Jefferson requested Harrison to choose for him the five members of the upper house of the legislature and Benjamin Parke, Harrison's close friend, was elected delegate to Congress.

The territorial legislature functioned with reasonable wisdom, thus denying the allegation that the territory lacked the necessary men of talents. Two of the measures which seem to demonstrate the good sense of its members were the substitution of a single county court for the earlier complicated system, and the codification of the laws. More important was the gradual assertion and execution of the wishes of the people in a territorial government that was only partially representative. . . .

The territorial legislature soon reflected the sentiment of the people. The second session of the second General Assembly which began on September 26, 1808, indicated a growing appreciation of its powers and of the popular will in contrast to the wishes of the governor and his supporters. The legislative council petitioned Congress that its members should be popularly elected, and the lower house petitioned the division of the territory and the popular election of the delegate to Congress. The representatives may have exceeded their authority to be certain that a federal officer should not have a seat in the legislative council. After a number of petitions opposing slavery were received and after General W. Johnston delivered a very able report against the admission of slavery, the representatives voted unanimously to repeal the territorial act concerning the introduction of Negroes and mulattoes into the territory, but the repeal was rejected by the upper house. The lower house also petitioned that the veto power and other controls over the legislature be restricted. Jesse B. Thomas was chosen to be the delegate to Congress after he pledged himself to work for the division of the territory. It has been pointed out that the election of Thomas was due to a union of the antislavery forces east of the Wabash with the proslavery forces west of the Wabash in opposition to the Harrison party, without recognizing clearly that this union indicated that slavery was not the leading issue. It was Harrison's first serious defeat and from it stemmed the events which gave the popular party control of the legislature after the division of the territory.

Congress responded to these demonstrations of the popular will by providing for the popular election of the councilors and the delegate to Congress, and for the division of the territory by the creation of Illinois Territory. The Harrison group was now face to face with a growing popular party which already included a majority of the people in the new Indiana Territory and which received the opportunity to control the entire legislative branch of the government as well as the delegate to Congress. Harrison remained quite popular, perhaps in part because he was public spirited and above much of the petty politics which accompanied the larger struggle.

The changes in the structure of the territorial government caused a long and acrimonious contest in 1809 which revealed a democratic spirit and procedure in advance of its time. The regular election for members of the legislature was held on April 3, 1809, before official word was received of division. Additional members were made necessary by division and new members and the delegate to Congress were elected on May 22. Throughout the early months of the year, the partisan controversy was waged in the columns of the *Western Sun*, through handbills, and in public meetings. Even after the last election, there were charges and counter charges, explanations for what had happened, and an anti-climactical campaign for and

against the reappointment of Governor Harrison. The election resulted in
the choice of Jonathan Jennings as delegate to Congress in which position he
became the leader of the anti-Harrison forces. The upper house of the
territorial legislature was chosen for the first time by the voters. The legislative results of the election and the protests of the Harrison leaders leave no
doubt of the significance of the results.

. . . .

When the elections for the new legislature were called in 1810, there
was only a slight revival of the contest of the preceding year. Outside of
Knox County the popular party was successful, and in Knox, General W.
Johnston, who was not a Harrisonite, was elected as one of the representatives. This legislature wrote the victory of the popular party into law. New
counties were formed, members of the legislature were apportioned, the
date for the election of the congressional delegate was set, the indenture law
was repealed, and the law requiring servants of color to fulfill the contracts
under which they entered the territory was also repealed. Nothing is more
revealing than Harrison's failure to use his absolute veto upon any of these
acts. No longer was his influence dominant. His friends could not browbeat
a critic into silence, and he was willing to give up the struggle if peace could
be restored.

But some of his followers and many of his opponents were unwilling
to make peace. The people were unwilling to give up the democratic advances and, indeed, wanted to make their government more democratic.
The violent storm in the press, however, ceased and something very much
like a calm ensued. Jennings endeavored to persuade Congress to declare
ineligible for election to the legislature officers appointed by Harrison, to
remove the territorial capital from Vincennes, to grant manhood suffrage,
and to provide for the election of sheriffs in place of appointment by the
governor. He even wrote about filing impeachment charges against the
governor. Two petitions were sent to Congress late in 1811 complaining of
Harrison's interference in elections and asking that officials of the United
States be prohibited from interfering improperly in elections. When Harrison vetoed a bill to move the capital from Vincennes, the people of Jefferson
County petitioned that the veto power be taken from him.

Congress, in response to the wishes of the petitioners, extended the
franchise to free white adult males who paid taxes, and made ineligible to
seats in the territorial legislature the officers appointed by Harrison except
the justices of the peace and the officers of the militia. Jennings was re-
elected in April, 1811, again defeating Thomas Randolph, in fact he served
for the remainder of the territorial period. The territorial legislature transferred the conduct of the elections from the sheriffs to the judges of the court
of common pleas, provided that polls be opened in each township in contrast to one in each county, and changed the method of voting from *viva*

voce to written ballots. It is quite possible that the change in the number of polling places enfranchised more persons than the Congressional act extending the right of suffrage. The seat of government was soon moved from Vincennes to Corydon where the governor's political friends were much less numerous. This measure, however, was not so important as the broadening of the franchise and the election law.

The advance to the second territorial stage of semi-representative government, the division of the territory, the election of delegates to Congress who were representatives of the opposition, the winning of control of the territorial legislature, the repeal of the acts which encouraged the violation of the prohibition of slavery, the extension of the franchise, the democratization of the territorial government, and the subduing of Harrison and his more aggressive supporters constituted a democratic victory of significant proportions. In a very real sense the democratic forces won their victory in the territorial period in contrast to the earlier territories in the Ohio Valley where the popular advance came when state constitutions were adopted. Only the election of the executive, the escape from Congressional supervision of local affairs, and full participation in national affairs, all of which could be secured only when the territory became a state, remained to be won. In Indiana Territory the popular victory was complete except for these. The people had gone as far as they could in creating a democratic government, the final step would complete the victory. That step was statehood.

Slavery in the Indiana Territory

JACOB PIATT DUNN

Naturally the interest of the people was absorbed in the convention. It was the great event of the period. But more than all else they were anxious to know just what would be done in regard to slavery. An estimable lady of Lawrenceburgh, who preserves her faculties unimpaired at the advanced age of eighty-five years, informs me that she remembers clearly the day when the news of the final action reached that place, and that the message which passed from mouth to mouth was, "She has come in free! She has come in free!" Other matters were not of so much importance, and there was a quiet faith that they had been properly cared for. And yet after all this controversy, and all the care of the convention, the slavery question was not yet definitely settled. As to the effect of the Constitution on future importations

From *Indiana: A Redemption from Slavery* (1888), pp. 430–435, 442–444. Footnotes in the original have been omitted.

there was no question, but as to its effect on pre-existent slavery and servitude there remained a wide divergence of opinion. In the eastern counties it was generally considered that slaves and servants were emancipated, and masters acted on that theory, though still feeling themselves charged with the care of keeping their old servitors from want. One master told his negro man and woman that they were free, and might do whatever they liked. If they desired it, he would give them a cabin and bit of land and they might take care of themselves; or, if they preferred, they might continue to live with him, and he would give them a wage allowance and care for them. After a protracted consideration of the subject they concluded to remain. Another master made a similar proposal to his negro woman, but she replied, "No, damn you! I'll go to Cincinnati and soon be as rich as any of you." And sure enough she did locate at Cincinnati, opened a little eating-house, and acquired a competence. This difference of sentiment was due only to the spirit of the negroes, for they were all treated kindly.

In the western counties a few masters removed their slaves from the State, and some of these were afterwards released by the courts of Southern States, as we have seen. The great majority, however, simply continued to hold their slaves in Indiana. The idea which commonly obtained was that the Constitution could have no effect on preëxisting slavery; that the property in slaves was a vested right, secured by the Ordinance, and could not be impaired. Even the courts in that section proceeded on this theory. The first case in which the question was involved came to trial on October 5, 1816, before David Raymond, president judge of the first circuit. It was a replevin suit brought against Thomas Jones by Mason Pecongar *alias* The Owl, an Indian who had adopted civilized life and settled near Vincennes, for the recovery of a colored girl and a cross-cut saw. The jury found for the plaintiff as to the girl, but a new trial was granted and the case was continued. It was settled out of court, for no further mention of it occurs in the records. In 1817, Bob and Anthony, held as slaves by Luke Decker, Jr., brought suit for their freedom in Orange County. They were sons of Dinah, a female slave brought by Luke Decker, Sr., from Virginia, prior to 1787. They gained their freedom, but not until the case had been fought for five years in various courts, and after the question involved had been decided by the Supreme Court in another case, which we will examine presently.

The masters of indented negroes in this section also held to their servants, probably from an enlargement of that quality of the mind which gives one a vague sense of ownership in anything he has once owned. In fact many of them were not sufficiently versed in the intricacies of the law to perceive any distinction between their cases and those of the ancient inhabitants. If this point of vested rights was of any importance, they had their slaves before the adoption of the Constitution as well as the older settlers. Of course there was understood to be a reservation of rights to the ancient inhabitants by the Ordinance, but what did that amount to? The property of a freeborn American less sacred than that of a Frenchman? Perish the thought! This was the line of argument of the statesman from "Egypt" with the *lucus a non lucendo* name, Mr. John Grammar, who said in the Illinois legislature, on a proposition to emancipate indented slaves: "I will show that are proposition is unconstitutional, inlegal, and fornenst the compact. Don't every one know, or leastwise had ought to know, that the Congress that sot at Post Vinsan garnisheed to the old French inhabitants the right to hold their niggers, and haint I got as much rights as any Frenchman in this state? Answer me that, sir."

It must be confessed, too, that no very strict regard was paid to the rights of indented negroes. An illustrative instance is recorded by Sol Smith, the great theatrical pioneer of the Mississippi valley, who was even more famous and popular in his day than his namesake Sol Smith Russell is now. In 1819 he served for a time as an apprentice at Vincennes, and in describing his experience there he thus refers to his master's wife: "This lady had been 'raised' in Kentucky, and having been in the habit of commanding slaves, and the laws of Indiana not permitting her to own any of those convenient appendages to a household, she made use of her husband's apprentices in place of them. She had one negro—his name was Thompson—who had been brought from Kentucky under indentures. He was to be free at the age of twenty-one, and he was now at least thirty-five! Mrs. __ made him believe he was but fourteen, and that he had yet seven years to serve. Thompson used to ask us boys in the office if we didn't think he was fifteen years of age. Of course we could not encourage him in such abolitional ideas. So he served on in blessed ignorance, and whether he has yet arrived at the desired age of twenty-one I am not informed." There may be some slight exaggeration in this, for Sol Smith was not a man to let a story be spoiled for lack of a little color; but in its general tenor it would have applied to many cases in Indiana. The negroes were ignorant, and there were few persons who were willing to incur the enmity of their neighbors by interfering in their behalf. Hence there arose, as G. W. Johnston had reported in 1808, "the most flagitious abuse" of the indenture system.

It should be borne in mind that there was nothing secret or clandestine about slaveholding in the western counties. It was the common opinion that the Constitution had no effect on preëxistent slavery. Indented negroes and other slaves were advertised and sold publicly, and it is hardly necessary to say that this would not have occurred, for lack of purchasers, if there had been any serious question as to the titles to them. The custom continued with so little interruption that in the census of 1820 there were still reported one hundred and ninety slaves in Indiana,—only forty-seven less than there were in 1810. One hundred and eighteen of these were held in Knox County, thirty in Gibson, eleven in Posey, ten in Vanderburgh, and the remainder scattered in Owen, Perry, Pike, Scott, Sullivan, Spencer, and Warrick. In the other twenty-four counties no slaves were reported....

If the writer has done his work properly, the reader now realizes that the slavery of Indiana, small as was its actual extent, was the chief agency in the moulding of our infant growth. It made political parties that otherwise would never have existed. It put men in office who but for it might have lived in obscurity. It excluded men from office who but for it would have been on our lists of public men. It put laws on our statute books, and erased them. It put articles in our first Constitution. It was the tap-root of our political growth,—the great central matter of controversy to which all other questions were subordinate. It drew broad party lines here when national party lines were practically blotted out; and when those lines were drawn, leaders of the dominant party were excused for offenses that would otherwise have ended their political careers, while leaders of the opposition suffered for the merest trifles. In short, it made a quarter of a century of our political history, and, at the end of that time, left the people of Indiana more strongly opposed to the institution of slavery than they ever could have been without it. It had some effect, too, in the councils of the nation, long after it had been disposed of; for when in the debate on the California bill, in June, 1850, the question arose as to slavery in the territory acquired from Mexico, the refusals of Congress to admit slavery to Indiana served as precedents against it.

More than this, if our work is well done, justice has been given to an almost forgotten generation of Indiana men. It has at various times been loosely stated that this man from the North, or that man from the South, saved Indiana from slavery. Not so. The men of Indiana did that. We honor Randolph, and Grayson, and Jefferson for their sentiments, as we do also Coit, and Dane, and King, but these men did not exclude slavery from Indiana, and, if we may believe the testimony that has been cited, they did not intend to do so. That we owe a debt of gratitude to the Congress that made the Ordinance, and to those that persisted in maintaining it as it was framed, is evident; but our gratitude cannot flow to either side of the line between North and South. If we consider the benefits derived from the Ordinance, we see benefactors from Virginia and Massachusetts standing side by side. If we look to the congressional action on petitions, we see that every Congress, regardless of politics, declined to amend the Ordinance. If we look to the composition of the congressional committees that acted on the petitions, we find them divided as evenly as possible between the North and the South, usually with an Indiana man in the balance; and of their six reports, three favoring the admission of slavery and three opposing it, we find two favoring and one opposing by chairmen from the North, and one favoring and two opposing by chairmen from the South; in no instance do we find a minority report. If we look to the sentiment of the nation at the climax of the struggle in Indiana in 1807, we find Congress almost a unit for the abolition of the slave-trade, and yet we find no effort in Congress, from any section, to nullify the indenture law, as the anti-slavery men of Indiana had asked them. If we look to the influence of literature, we find nothing from the North that had more effect in Indiana than Jefferson's "Notes on Virginia." At this day, when it seems fashionable to belittle Mr. Jefferson at all opportunities, we commend to the people of Indiana the consideration of how much of the great anti-slavery report of General W. Johnston, and the revolution of sentiment connected with it, may be justly attributed to the influence of the words of Thomas Jefferson. Nor is this suggestion thrown out for the purpose of bringing him into prominence to the disadvantage of his contemporaries from the North. It is merely to restore, for our own purposes, the historical balance which the reaction of recent years has falsified. Nothing can now detract from the influence he had in determining our early controversies, and nothing should obscure his just credit in our remembrance of it. We do not go beyond the bounds of our State to give praise for the final solution of our local slavery question, for Congress put the solution upon the men of Indiana and they worked it out on Indiana soil. For the privilege of solving it, under the Ordinance, without the interference of Congress, our thanks go abroad, but to no section. As to this we write, as was inscribed on our contribution to the great monument to the greatest of Americans: INDIANA KNOWS NO NORTH, NO SOUTH, NOTHING BUT THE UNION.

2: A Comparative Glimpse, South and North

Only the southern portion of Indiana was settled during the territorial period, and then only in scattered villages in the lower Wabash Valley (around Vincennes), along the Ohio River in the south (Clark's Grant), and in the Whitewater Valley in the southeast (the "Gore"). Not until two years after statehood, in the Treaty of St. Mary's, was the vast central portion of the state acquired from the Delaware Indians and the way cleared for a general movement northward. Vincennes remained the largest settlement in the territory and boasted several cultural developments. These included the chartering of Vincennes University in 1806, the establishment of the Library Company of Vincennes in 1811, and the appearance of the territory's first newspaper, the *Indiana Gazette,* in 1804. This latter accomplishment was the work of Elihu Stout, an 1803 arrival from Kentucky whose pioneer printing shop has been restored and relocated on the campus of Vincennes University. According to local historial Elizabeth M. Denehie in the first selection, Stout's "invasion" of the Old Northwest is of comparable significance to that of George Rogers Clark.

Despite the lack of permanent settlement in northern Indiana during the territorial period, a traveler through this country in 1809 has recorded his impressions of it and its potential, thus providing an interesting contrast between life in territorial Indiana, south and north. The traveler, a man named Johnston, passed through Indiana en route from Fort Wayne to Fort Dearborn, where Chicago now stands. This account was first published in the Peru, Indiana *Saturday Gazette* on August 10, 1839. It was contributed by "J. M. D.," a friend of J. S. Johnston of Piqua, Ohio, whose father had written the "notes." Already in 1839, J. M. D. was moved to comment on the "improvements that have been made upon certain localities," and Johnston's "foresight and penetration, in the selection of the most important points for commercial facilities."

Southern Indiana

ELIZABETH M. DENEHIE

In thousands of Indiana homes today, some member of the family assumes the responsibility of bringing in the newspaper from the front porch or from under the barberry bush where an unruly wind has tossed it. Lucky the individual who gets the first peep at the front page, the sports' section, the comic strips, or whatever individual taste may dictate. Daily distribution of both morning and evening newspapers is enjoyed in almost every city, while in smaller places, or even in the country, at least one daily paper brings news of local happenings as well as that from remote corners of the world to all who can read.

We live in a busy world and are often forgetful of the trail-blazers who made the daily paper. This effort is but an appreciative gesture—a tribute to Elihu Stout, who unassisted and with patient toil, one hundred and thirty one years ago, issued the first number of the *Indiana Gazette,* the first newspaper published in Indiana. This journal, thus founded, with slight interruptions and an early change of name, has continued for a century and more, and therefore has the distinction of being an outstanding pioneering effort.

Elihu Stout, the son of Judiah and Mary Stout, was born on April 16, 1782, in Newark, New Jersey. At an early age, he learned the printer's trade. Judiah Stout fought in the American Revolution, and, ten years after its close, feeling the urge of migrating towards the West, which was then any-where beyond the Alleghenies, he and his family joined the increasing tide, crossed the mountains and settled at Lexington, Kentucky. Here young Elihu obtained employment on the *Kentucky Gazette,* published by the Bradfords, comfortable and wealthy, who became intimate friends of Henry Clay. Ambitious to edit a newspaper of his own, and having faith in the Northwest, he left Kentucky to solicit aid for his undertaking but found little. Undaunted he came to Vincennes in 1803, there to try his fortunes. Governor William Henry Harrison equipped a boat for young Stout in which he journeyed back to Frankfort, Kentucky, by way of the Wabash, Ohio, and Kentucky rivers where he obtained an outfit including a wooden press.

To appreciate the difficulties that confronted Elihu Stout, it is necessary to consider the handicaps of a hundred fifty years ago in Indiana. There were no roads leading from Vincennes to the East at that time. The people were poor. They depended largely upon their own produce from the soil and the forests for the necessaries of life. Money was extremely difficult to obtain and some of it worth less than its face value. Hence the first issue of

From "Indiana's First Newspaper," *Indiana Magazine of History,* XXXI (June 1935), 125–130. Footnotes in the original have been omitted. Reprinted by permission.

the *Indiana Gazette,* on July 31, 1804, in the face of all these obstacles, has a deep significance. It was the urge for expression that motivated the young man of twenty-two years, and the desire to contact the hardy pioneers who were to ask for admission to the Union only twelve years later.

A lengthy but definite statement of the rules governing subscriptions to the *Indiana Gazette* appeared in a number of early issues:

   I. It shall be published weekly on medium paper.
  II. The price to subscribers will be two dollars and fifty cents, payable half yearly in advance. Those who do not come forward at the expiration of the first six months, and make the second advance, will be charged with an additional fifty cents.
 III. No subscriber taken for a term less than one year unless he pays the whole term of his subscription in advance.
  IV. Wherever papers are sent by post, the person subscribing must pay the postage.

The *Gazette* carried as a motto a quotation from Thomas Paine: "Independence is my happiness, and I relate things as they are, without respect to place or persons."

The words of Elihu Stout which were addressed to his readers in the first number of the *Gazette* exemplify his high purpose:

> At length after great trouble and much expense the Public is presented with the first number of the *Indiana Gazette.* Without deviating from the general rule of Newspaper Printers, in the first number the Editor addresses the Public, and lays down the principles which shall govern the publication. His object shall be to collect and publish such information as will give a correct account of the productions and natural advantages of the Territory, to give the latest foreign and domestic intelligence—Original Essays, Political, Moral, Literary, Agricultural, and on Domestic Economics—to collect such fugitive literary productions as will tend to raise "The genius or to mend the heart", etc., etc., shall be the second. The political complection of the paper shall be truly republican but it shall never be prostituted to party . . . . The Editor pledges himself that the columns of the *Gazette* will never be tarnished with matter that can offend the eye of decency, or raise a blush upon the cheek of modesty and virtue. . . .

With the optimism of a young man, Stout probably did not foresee many of the difficulties to be met. For example, a printer had not only to get news and paper but he had to get paid. The first paper mill in the West was completed in 1793 at Georgetown, Kentucky, quite a distance from Vincennes. Early journals of the West were sometimes printed on brown wrapping paper. Tradition has it that a frontier newspaper was once printed with swamp mud for ink and run off on a cider mill. Sometimes only one side of the paper was used. Then after being read by the subscriber, the sheet was supposed to be returned to the printer in order that he might run off the

Territorial capitol (L) and Stout's Print Shop in Vincennes
Courtesy of the Indiana Department of Natural Resources

next issue on the reverse side. Currency was scarce and editors frequently announced that they would take produce in exchange for the paper. Maple sugar, jeans, tow-linen, oats, corn-meal, chickens, deer meat, coon skins, and fire-wood were among the commodities that were prone to reach the printer. Many years after he founded his paper, Editor Stout was compelled to give his subscribers the following in the issue of May 8, 1829: "Want of paper compels me to furnish my readers with but half a sheet. I expect a supply before another publication day."

In April, 1806, a great misfortune overtook the adventurous editor, when his plant was destroyed by fire. The spirit of Stout was not subdued, but he immediately set out for Kentucky determined to prepare for a new venture. While in Kentucky, he obtained another press and a supply of paper which he carried to Vincennes on pack mules over the rude road that followed the old Buffalo Trace. It was more than a year after the fire before it was possible to resume publication.

On July 4, 1807, the first issue of the *Western Sun* is said to have appeared, succeeding the short-lived *Indiana Gazette.* During one hundred three of the years of its existence the *Sun* has been in the hands of three families. The daily edition was started in 1879 by R. E. Purcell. The first copy of the *Western Sun* that is preserved in the Indiana State Library is that of July 11, 1807, which issue is designated as number 2. If the first issue was published one week earlier, it came out on July 4.

Some matter from the columns of the issue of the *Indiana Gazette* and *Western Sun* in the early years may be of interest to readers. An early issue of the *Gazette* carried a poem dedicated

TO A GLASS OF WINE

Thou canst make the heart of man rejoice,
Make blind men fancy they can all things see,
To taciturnity canst give a voice;
And cause e'en infidels to bend the knee;
'Tis pleasant to behold thee, tempting juice,
More pleasant still thy flavour to enjoy;
But much I fear thou smilest to seduce,
And I suspect thou charmest to destroy:
A painted sepulchre thou sometimes art,
Disease and death may lurk beneath that guise,
Or like a Basilisk, thy look may dart
Death to morals,—yet the good and wise
Say thou hast virtue too; then let me try;
Since they have proved thy virtues;
  So will I.

Governor William Henry Harrison's friends in Indiana territory took pride in his importance and achievements. In December, 1811, the members of the Legislative Council and House of Representatives drew up a joint public address to the Governor, which, carrying the signature of the President of the Council (James Beggs) and of the Speaker of the House (Gen'l W. Johnston), was published in the *Western Sun*. The heading of the address ran—"To His Excellency, William Henry Harrison, Governor and Commander in Chief in and over Indiana Territory". The address follows:

When in the course of human events, it becomes necessary for a nation to unsheath the sword in defence of any portion of its citizens—and any individual of society becomes intrusted with the important charge of leading an army of his country into the field to scourge the assailants of its rights—and it is proved by the success of the army that, that individual possesses superior capacity accompanied by integrity and other qualities of the mind, which adorn the human character in a superlative degree. It has a tendency to draw out the affections of the people in a way that must be grateful to the soldier and the man. Such is the light, sir, in which you have the honor to be viewed by your country, and one which the Legislative Council and House of Representatives of the Territory, think you justly entitled to.

And, sir, in duly appreciating your services, we are perfectly sensible of the great benefits and important service rendered by the officers and soldiers of the United States infantry under your command. And it is with pleasure we learn that the officers and militia men of our country acted with a heroism more than could be reasonably calculated upon from men (such as they generally were) undisciplined, and unaccustomed to war.

Resolved, that a joint committee attend to the insertion of the fore-going address in the *Western Sun* for one week.

James Beggs, President of the Legislative Council.

Gen'l W. Johnston, Speaker of the House of Representatives.

On Saturday, May 22, 1819, the *Sun* reprinted from the *National Intelligencer* of Washington, D. C., a "Bird's Eye View of State Politics" in Indiana. Said the *Intelligencer:*

> Politics in Indiana are, in a great measure, personal contests. The latest agitation of her statesmen that we have heard of, is the oppugnation of the lieutenant governor to Governor Jennings' acting as negotiator of Indian treaties under an appointment from the President of the United States. The lieutenant governor, considering the governor as having forfeited the throne, seized upon the reins of authority, as heir apparent, and sequestered the seal of the commonwealth. Gov. Jennings, returning from diplomatic converse with the Indians, walked very deliberately into the secretary of state's office, put the seal into his breeches pocket, hinted that kings and rulers were not accountable to frail mortality, & cooly walked away, and probably whistling lillabullero! The *People*, we presume, will settle the dispute.

The *Western Sun* and its predecessor *(Indiana Gazette)* along with other early Indiana newspapers contain much valuable history of pioneer days. The story of Fulton's Folly, his first steamboat, was published in 1807. Five years later the War of 1812 began, furnishing exciting news. The accounts of battles, campaigns, and the burning of the White House supplied fascinating reading. In 1815, Jackson defeated the British at New Orleans presenting a theme for editors of which much was made. Indiana was admitted to the Union in 1816. Steamboat traffic on the inland rivers expanded rapidly. Mexico won her independence from Spain. After a few years railroad building was started. Indeed the reader of every early Hoosier newspaper finds a great deal of matter that is not only very interesting but well worth perusal. The *Western Sun* chronicled all these important events as history unfolded itself.

Stout and other editors were makers of public opinion in Indiana. Their editorial efforts were fairly good. Dr. Logan Esarey says of their immediate successors: "The old-time editorial of the forties and fifties had a literary style and flavor which one misses in the present day newspaper. Not one of these editors built up a personal following which enabled him to dictate either politically or otherwise".

The modest little *Indiana Gazette* of 1804 blazed the trail for many Hoosier newspapers. By 1854 there were in Indiana twelve daily, two triweekly, one hundred twenty-one weekly, one fortnightly and six monthly newspapers. From any of these it seems a far cry, indeed, to the newspapers of today. Whereas the *Indiana Gazette* reached at most a few hundred subscribers the Indianapolis *Star* passes into the hands of about 150,000 daily. Nevertheless Hoosiers owe a debt of gratitude to the intrepid young editor, Elihu Stout, whose invasion of the Old Northwest with his printing-press is second in importance only to the coming of George Rogers Clark.

Northern Indiana

_____ JOHNSTON

The general course of the road is something north of west. For about three miles the land is thin and timbered with oak, until you reach Spy run, when immediately on crossing this stream a fine bottom commences, which continues for some distance; the timber here is generally sugartree, buckeye and hickory, all of a very large growth. Twelve miles further is Eel river, a tributary of the Wabash.[1] This uncommon little stream is very deep; and at the distance of ten miles on a direct line, and about seventeen by the meanderings of the stream from its source, it is not more than five yards wide and is generally three feet deep, with an uncommonly slow current. The land on this river is remarkably rich and appears to be well adapted to the culture of wheat or hemp. There are but few situations in this region where mills could be placed, owing to the levelness of the land, as all the rivers have their sources in swamps and ponds, and as there are but few springs in the upper country, that is, on the high land which divides the waters of the Lakes from those of the Ohio. Passing on westward you travel through a fine, rich, level country, which bears evident marks of having been under water at some former period. Fifteen miles from Eel river you come to the little Lakes.[2] Here is one of the most enchanting prospects my eyes ever beheld. The traveller after passing through a country somewhat broken for a few miles, is immediately struck with the sight of two most beautiful sheets of water, as pure and limpid as the mountain spring. . . . The soil in the vicinity of these

[1] This Eel River flows into the Wabash at Logansport. It should be remembered that Indiana has another Eel River that flows into the West Fork of White River at Worthington.

[2] In general, the traveler passed northwestward from Fort Wayne to the junction of the Elkhart and St. Joseph rivers. He must have crossed Eel River above Columbia City. The two lakes described were probably in the southwestern part of what is now Noble County, a little way south of Albion.

From "A Trip from Fort Wayne to Fort Dearborn in 1809," *Indiana Magazine of History*, XXXVI (March 1940), 45–49. Reprinted by permission.

lakes is well adapted to the cultivation of wheat or any kind of small grain. The timber is chiefly white and spanish oak, with some chestnut oak. The land is a mixture of sand and clay, and in some places a deep black soil something like river bottom. Eighteen miles further and you come to the Elkhart river, a branch of the St. Joseph of Michigan. For eight miles before you reach this river, you pass through a thicket of young hickory and oaks, about as thick as a man's thumb, and growing so close together that it is impossible to penetrate through it at any other place except where the road runs. This land is as rich as any in Kentucky, and there is not a doubt but that it would prove as fruitful if cultivated. Immediately after crossing the river, which is here about fifty yards wide, a most delightful prospect is presented to view—there is scarcely one tree to the acre of ground for about three miles. Here is an Indian town containing about twenty houses. This village is the place of residence of one of the principal chiefs of the Pottawattamies—his name is Five Medals. This place is beautifully situated on the edge of a fine prairie containing about three thousand acres. About a mile west of this prairie the road comes to the bank of the river, where I found a spring of excellent water, a thing that is very rare in this country. Here the timber is tall and thick on the ground and principally white oak. The soil is white clay. Fourteen miles further is the junction of the Elkhart and St. Joseph. *Here is a place formed by nature for a town.*[3] About half a mile from [above] the forks [junction], these rivers approach within sixty yards of each other. They then separate and form something like an oval piece of ground of nearly one hundred acres, until it comes to low bottom, which appears to be somewhat marshy. This bottom contains about fifty acres, which I suppose is occasionally overflowed. Both these streams are navigable, without any kind of falls, almost to their sources. From the junction down to the Lake, about sixty miles by water, [the St. Joseph] may be navigated with any kind of small craft at any season. It has a deep channel with a gentle current all the way. *There is no situation in this country better calculated for trade, than at the junction of the Elkhart and St. Joseph.* These two streams pass through the richest and dryest part of this country; and I think it would be an object with our government to make a settlement at this place.

Ten miles down this river from the forks, is a portage of three miles west to the Theakiki [Kankakee], a branch of the Illinois river. Fifteen miles below the forks is a French trading house. There are about twenty persons kept here for the purpose of trading with the Indians. These men in the winter season, take each of them a load of goods and ascend some of the branches of the St. Joseph—thence across the portages into the other rivers, and so on to the Indian villages; where they continue until spring—from

---

[3]Elkhart, Indiana, occupies the site described. The junction of the Elkhart and the St. Joseph is just off Main Street near the heart of the city.

whence they then return with their peltry. They all collect together in May and make up their packs, and then proceed down the river into the lake and round to Michillimackinac. It will scarcely be believed that the men perform a voyage of more than a thousand miles in bark canoes, heavy laden with packs, the greater part of the way over a boisterous lake. The soil on the St. Joseph river varies considerably, but there is none but what is equal to our third rate in Kentucky, and has the advantage of being level. There are several fine springs in this part of the country. At the factory [trading post] I was told that there were the remains of a British Fort three miles below, and a fine orchard of apple trees. Twenty miles from the Fort, at the mouth of the river, I was informed a trader had raised several crops of wheat which were as good as could be produced any place.

I crossed the St. Joseph river at the French Factory. Twelve miles west is an Indian village called Terrecoupee. This town stands upon an eminence, and may be seen about seven miles. There is not a tree to intercept the sight for a distance of nine miles. This prairie, I was informed, extends to the Mississippi, a distance of four hundred miles. From this village to Lake Michigan, a distance of about forty miles, the land is about one half timbered and the remainder prairie; but all of a good quality, except about four miles in the vicinity of the lake, where it is very sandy. Here are some of the finest pine trees I ever saw. The road strikes the lake at the most southerly end—at the mouth of the river *Desma*.

I think it is of the utmost importance to the United States, to have this vast region of country settled with Americans as soon as possible. It may be said of that vast tract of country extending from the mouth of the Miami of the Lake[4] to Detroit, and round the peninsula between Lake Huron and Michigan, and round the east end of the latter lake—thence to the mouth of the Chicago river at Fort Dearbourn—thence with the Illinois to the Mississippi, and down that river until it strikes the line of the land purchased from the Indians in the Territories, and up the Wabash to Fort Wayne, and down the Miami to Lake Erie. That about one half of the land is dry, with a rich, level and productive soil. And that about one half of the other half may be divided between marshes and prairies, which would support immense herds of cattle, at very little cost. For it is a fact that salt can be had cheaper at Detroit than it can be at Lexington.

The east or rather the south eastern end of Lake Michigan is bounded by a mountain of sand, about one hundred feet high.[5] This hill has been accumulating since the formation of the lake. The north west wind prevails here the greater part of the year. This wind blowing over an extent of level country, not equalled in the known world, acquires such force when it arrives at Lake Michigan, that on a dry day it will raise such a cloud of sand

[4]The Maumee River was known as the "Miami of the Lake" in the early period.
[5]The famous "Hoosier Slide."

as to completely darken the air; which in time raised up a bank, and every storm has been adding to it, until the present. This mountain is covered with a stunted growth of cedars and juniper trees. I presume there might be as many juniper berries gathered here as would supply the United States with that article. The body of this mountain is always changing. A severe storm will make a break in the top, the regular wind then continues to deepen the breach. The sand is carried back and deposited in the valley behind the hill, which in time becomes the foundation of another mountain. The traveller will see in this country hundreds of these hills [sand dunes] behind the mountain, the whole body of which is carried away in some places for several hundred yards, and deposited behind, and the wind is constantly in motion, taking more and more until the hill will change its place. The lake of course advancing as the bank recedes, so that there is no doubt but that the water has gained considerably on the land. These mountains and hills are not to be found on the west side of the lake. Ten miles along the lake from the point is the mouth of the river Styx, so called on account of a large Indian burying ground. Some of the corpse[s] were in troughs raised up on forks ten feet high; others were folded up in bark and laid on the ground with some sticks over them. There was at the head and foot of every grave, a post upon which was a number of marks thus (XX) which I was informed designated the number of persons they had killed in war. A single line thus (|) was the mark of prisoners they had taken.

The road still keeps along the beach of the lake—and twelve miles further is the mouth of the Grand Calumic [Calumet]. Here the sand mountain ends. Twenty miles farther is the mouth of the Little Calumic [Calumet]. These two rivers are of the greatest consequence to the traders on the lake. They are both about twenty yards wide at their mouths and very deep. One, however, is considerably longer than the other. There is a communication between these two streams, which in case of a storm on the lake, the traders can run up one for several miles, and then cross over into the other, and return down it again into the lake. It is twelve miles from the little Calumic to the mouth of the Chicago river. Here the United States have erected a garrison for the protection of trade in this country. This garrison does great honor to Capt. John Whistler, who planned and built it. It is the neatest and best wooden garrison in the United States.

3: A Classic Confrontation

The most famous and significant confrontation of the térritorial period occurred between Governor Harrison and the great Shawnee leader Tecumseh. After General Anthony Wayne, with whom Harrison had served in the 1790s, defeated the Indians at Fallen Timbers in northwestern Ohio, the next great clash between reds and whites came in Indiana. It was part of Harrison's duties as governor to act as Indian agent and arrange for land cessions. After several previous treaties transferring, at least in the eyes of the United States, land from the Indians to the Union, Harrison entered into new negotiations in 1809 at Fort Wayne. The resulting treaty with Delaware, Potawatomi, Miami, and Eel River tribes conveyed more than 2,800,000 acres of land to the United States, an event which prompted Tecumseh and his brother to begin stiffer resistance to white encroachment. Tecumseh personally explained his views to Harrison in a tense series of conferences in Vincennes during August 1810, after which Harrison increased his military preparations. Talks occurred again in late September 1811, when Tecumseh returned to Vincennes before continuing south in search of new recruits for the Indian confederation he hoped to organize.

At this time Harrison recorded his respect for Tecumseh as "one of those uncommon geniuses, which spring up occasionally to produce revolutions and overturn the established order of things. If it were not for the vicinity of the United States, he would perhaps be the founder of an Empire that would rival in glory, that of Mexico or Peru."[1] Harrison also made plans to act quickly during Tecumseh's absence and attack his base of power at Prophetstown. This led to the battle of Tippecanoe, fought on November 7, 1811.

Professor Marshall Smelser of the University of Notre Dame, a careful student of the early national period of American history, is the author of *The Democratic Republic, 1801–1815* (1968), a volume in the New American Nation series published by Harper & Row. The article from which the passages below were taken was based on an address delivered to the Society of Indiana Pioneers in 1963.

---

[1]Quoted in John D. Barnhart and Donald F. Carmony, *Indiana: From Frontier to Industrial Commonwealth* (2 vols., 1954), I, 129.

Tecumseh, Harrison, and the War of 1812

MARSHALL SMELSER

Indiana Territory had only twenty-five thousand citizens in 1810. When one reflects that the populations of Ohio and Kentucky combined were more than twenty-five times as great, it will be easily understood that the War of 1812 in the Old Northwest was more their war than it was Indiana's. Indiana was only a beachhead in the wilderness. The history of the war as it concerns Indiana is more biographical than geographical, more dramatic than analytic. This paper will treat it that way—as a high tragedy involving two able natural leaders. Like all tragedies, the course of its action gives the feeling that it was inevitable, that nothing could have been done to prevent its fatal termination. The story is the drama of the struggle of two of our most eminent predecessors, William Henry Harrison of Grouseland, Vincennes, and Tecumseh of the Prophet's town, Tippecanoe.

It is not easy to learn about wilderness Indians. The records of the Indians are those kept by white men, who were not inclined to give themselves the worst of it. Lacking authentic documents, historians have neglected the Indians. The story of the Indian *can* be told but it has a higher probability of error than more conventional kinds of history. To tell the tale is like reporting the weather without scientific instruments. The reporter must be systematically, academically skeptical. He must read between the lines, looking for evidence of a copper-colored ghost in a deerskin shirt, flitting through a green and bloody world where tough people died from knives, arrows, war clubs, rifle bullets, and musket balls, and where the coming of spring was not necessarily an omen of easier living, but could make a red or white mother tremble because now the enemy could move concealed in the forest. But the reporter must proceed cautiously, letting the facts shape the story without prejudice.

. . . [O]ur story is a sad and somber one. It shows men at their bravest. It also shows men at their worst. We are dealing with a classic situation in which two great leaders—each a commander of the warriors of his people—move inexorably for a decade toward a confrontation which ends in the destruction of the one and the exaltation of the other. Tecumseh, a natural nobleman in a hopeless cause, and Harrison, a better soldier than he is generally credited with being, make this an Indiana story, although the last two acts of their tragedy were staged in Ohio and in Upper Canada. To understand why this deadly climax was inevitable we must know the Indian policy of the United States at that time; we must know, if we can, what the

From "Tecumseh, Harrison, and The War of 1812," *Indiana Magazine of History*, LXV (March 1969), 25, 28, 30–31, 33, 35, 37–39. Copyright © 1969 by the Trustees of Indiana University. Reprinted by permission.

Indians thought of it; and we must know something about the condition of the Indians.

The federal government's Indian policy was almost wholly dedicated to the economic and military benefit of white people. When Congress created Indiana Territory, the United States was officially committed to educate and civilize the Indians. The program worked fairly well in the South for a time. Indiana Territory's Governor Harrison gave it an honest trial in the North, but the problems were greater than could be solved with the feeble means used. The management of Indian affairs was unintelligently complicated by overlapping authorities, a confused chain of command, and a stingy treasury—stingy, that is, when compared with the treasury of the more lavish British competitors for Indian favor. More to the point, most white Americans thought the Indians should be moved to the unsettled lands in the West. President Jefferson, for awhile, advocated teaching agriculture to the Indians, and he continued the operation of federal trading posts in the Indian country which had been set up to lessen the malevolent influence of private traders. These posts were successful by the standards of cost accounting, but they did nothing to advance the civilization of the Indian. Few white people wished the Indians well, and fewer would curb their appetites for fur and land just to benefit Indians.

The conflict between whites and Indians was not simple. The Indians were neither demons nor sculptured noble savages. They were not the single people Tecumseh claimed but were broken into fragments by language differences. Technologically they were farther behind the Long Knives—as the Indians called the frontiersmen—than the Gauls who died on Caesar's swords were behind the Romans. But they had a way of life that worked in its hard, cruel fashion. In the end, however, the Indian way of life was shattered by force; and the Indians lost their streams, their corn and bean fields, their forests.

Comparatively few white residents of the United States in 1801 had ever seen an Indian. East of the Mississippi River there were perhaps seventy thousand Indians, of whom only ten thousand lived north of the Ohio River. They were bewildered pawns of international politics, governed by the French to 1763, ruled in the name of George III of England to 1783, and never consulted about the change of sovereigns. As Governor Harrison himself said, they disliked the French least, because the French were content with a congenial joint occupation of the wilds while the white Americans and British had a fierce sense of the difference between mine and thine. The governor admitted the Indians had genuine grievances. It was not likely, for example, that a jury would convict a white man charged with murdering an Indian. Indians were shot in the forest north of Vincennes for no reason at all. Indians, Harrison reported, punished Indians for crimes against Long Knives, but the frontiersmen did not reciprocate. But the worst curse visited on the Indians by the whites was alcohol. Despite official gestures at prohibition, alcohol flowed unchecked in the Indian territory. Harrison said six hundred Indian warriors on the Wabash received six thousand gallons of whiskey a year. That would seem to work out to a fifth of whisky per week per family, and it did not come in a steady stream, but in alternating floods and ebbs.

Naturally Indian resentment flared. Indian rage was usually ferocious but temporary. Few took a long view. Among those who did were some great natural leaders, Massasoit's disillusioned son King Philip in the 1670s, Pontiac in the 1760s, and Tecumseh. But such leaders invariably found it hard to unite the Indians for more than a short time; regardless of motive or ability, their cause was hopeless. The Indians were a Stone Age people who depended for good weapons almost entirely on the Long Knives or the Redcoats. The rivalry of Britain and the United States made these dependent people even more dependent. Long Knives supplied whisky, salt, and tools. Redcoats supplied rum, beef, and muskets. The Indians could not defeat Iron Age men because these things became necessities to them, and they could not make them for themselves. But yielding gracefully to the impact of white men's presence and technology was no help to the Indians. The friendly Choctaw of present Mississippi, more numerous than all of the northwestern tribes together, were peaceful and cooperative. Their fate was nevertheless the same as the fate of the followers of King Philip, Pontiac, and Tecumseh.

The Indians had one asset—land. Their land, they thought, belonged to the family group so far as it was owned at all. No Indian had a more sophisticated idea of land title than that. And as for selling land, the whites had first to teach them that they owned it and then to teach them to sell it. Even then, some Indians very early developed the notion that land could only be transferred by the unanimous consent of all tribes concerned rather than through negotiations with a single tribe. Indian councils declared this policy to the Congress of the United States in 1783 and in 1793. If we follow James Truslow Adams' rule of thumb that an Indian family needed as many square miles of wilderness as a white family needed plowed acres, one may calculate that the seventy thousand Indians east of the Mississippi needed an area equal to all of the Old Northwest plus Kentucky, if they were to live the primitive life of their fathers. Therefore, if the Indians were to live as undisturbed primitives, there would be no hunting grounds to spare. And if the rule of unanimous land cessions prevailed, there would be no land sales so long as any tribal leader objected. Some did object, notably two eminent Shawnee: Tecumseh, who believed in collective bargaining, and his brother, the Prophet, who also scorned the Long Knives' tools, his whisky, and his civilization. Harrison dismissed the Prophet's attack on land treaties as the result of British influence, but collective conveyance was an old idea before the Shawnee medicine man took it up. The result of the federal government's policy of single tribe land treaties was to degrade the village chiefs who made the treaties and to exalt the angry warrior chiefs, like Tecumseh, who denounced the village chiefs, corrupted by whisky and other gifts, for selling what was not theirs to sell.

. . . .

By the time he found his life work Tecumseh was an impressive man, about five feet nine inches tall, muscular and well proportioned, with large but fine features in an oval face, light copper skin, excellent white teeth, and hazel eyes. His carriage was imperial, his manner energetic, and his temperament cheerful. His dress was less flashy than that of many of his fellow warriors. Except for a silver mounted tomahawk, quilled moccasins, and, in war, a medal of George III and a plume of ostrich feathers, he dressed simply in fringed buckskin. He knew enough English for ordinary conversation, but to assure accuracy he was careful to speak only Shawnee in diplomacy. Unlike many Indians he could count, at least as far as eighteen (as we know by his setting an appointment with Harrison eighteen days after opening the subject of a meeting). Military men later said he had a good eye for

Tecumseh saving prisoners
Courtesy of the Indiana State Library

military topography and could extemporize crude tactical maps with the point of his knife. He is well remembered for his humanity to prisoners, being one of the few Indians of his day who disapproved of torturing and killing prisoners of war. This point is better documented than many other aspects of his character and career.

The Prophet rather than Tecumseh first captured the popular imagination. As late as 1810 Tecumseh was being referred to in official correspondence merely as the Prophet's brother. The Shawnee Prophet's preaching had touches of moral grandeur: respect for the aged, sharing of material goods with the needy, monogamy, chastity, and abstinence from alcohol. He urged a return to the old Indian ways and preached self-segregation from the white people. But he had an evil way with dissenters, denouncing them as witches and having several of them roasted alive....

One of the skeptics unconverted by the Prophet and unimpressed by the divinity of his mission was Indiana Territory's first governor, William Henry Harrison, a retired regular officer, the son of a signer of the Declaration of Independence, appointed governor at the age of twenty-eight. Prudent, popular with Indians and whites, industrious, and intelligent, he had no easy job. He had to contend with land hunger, Indian resentments, the excesses of Indian traders, and with his constant suspicion of a British web of conspiracy spun from Fort Malden. The growing popularity of the Prophet alarmed Harrison, and early in 1806 he sent a speech by special messenger to the Delaware tribe to try to refute the Prophet's theology by Aristotelian formal logic. Harrison was not alone in his apprehensions. In Ohio the throngs of Indian pilgrims grew larger after the Prophet during the summer of 1806 correctly predicted an eclipse of the sun (forecast, of course, in every almanac) and took credit for it. A year later, when reports indicated the number of the Prophet's followers was increasing, the governor of Ohio alerted the militia and sent commissioners to investigate. They heard Blue Jacket deny any British influence on the Indians. At another meeting later at Chillicothe Tecumseh denounced all land treaties but promised peace. The governor of Ohio was temporarily satisfied, although Harrison still thought the Prophet spoke like a British agent and told the Shawnee what he thought. But in the fall of 1807 there was no witness, however hostile, who could prove that either Tecumseh or the Prophet preached war. On the contrary, every reported sermon and oration apparently promised peace. An ominous portent, however—at least in Harrison's eyes—was the founding of the Prophet's town on the Tippecanoe River, in May, 1808.

The Prophet visited Harrison at Vincennes late in the summer of 1808 to explain his divine mission to the incredulous young governor. Privately, and grudgingly, Harrison admitted the Prophet had reduced drunkenness, but he persisted in his belief that the Shawnee leader was a British agitator. The Prophet went to Vincennes again in 1809 and boasted of having prevented an Indian war. Harrison did not believe him. There is good evidence that in June, 1810, Tecumseh tried unsuccessfully to persuade the Shawnee of the Maumee Basin to move west in order to clear the woods for war. When Harrison learned this he sent a message to the Prophet's town. The "Seventeen Fires," he said, were invincible. The Redcoats could not help the Indians. But if the Indians thought the New Purchase Treaty made at Fort Wayne in 1809 was fraudulent, Harrison would arrange to pay their way to visit the President, who would hear their complaint. Tecumseh privately said he wished peace but could be pushed no farther. These rumblings and tremors of 1810 produced the first meeting of our two tragic protagonists.

Tecumseh paddled to Vincennes with four hundred armed warriors in mid August, 1810. In council he denounced the New Purchase Treaty and the village chiefs who had agreed to it. He said the warrior chiefs would rule Indian affairs thereafter. Harrison flatly denied Tecumseh's theory of collective ownership and guaranteed to defend by the sword what had been acquired by treaty. This meeting of leaders was certainly not a meeting of minds. A deadlock had been reached. A cold war had been started. During the rest of 1810 Harrison received nothing but bad news. The secretary of war suggested a surprise capture of the Shawnee brothers. Indians friendly to the United States predicted war. The governor of Missouri reported to Harrison that the Prophet had invited the tribes west of the Mississippi to join in a war, which was to begin with an attack against Vincennes. The Indians around Fort Dearborn were disaffected and restless. A delegation of Sauk came all the way from Wisconsin to visit Fort Malden. Two surveyors running the New Purchase line were carried off by the Wea.

In the summer of 1811 Tecumseh and about three hundred Indians returned to Vincennes for another inconclusive council in which neither he nor the governor converted the other. Tecumseh condescendingly advised against white settlement in the New Purchase because many Indians were going to settle at the Prophet's town in the fall and would need that area for hunting. Tecumseh said he was going south to enroll new allies. It is important to our story that Tecumseh was absent from Indiana in that autumn of crisis. Aside from this we need note only that on his southern tour he failed to rouse the Choctaw, although he had a powerful effect on the thousands of Creek who heard his eloquence.

At this point it is important to note Governor Harrison's continuing suspicion that Tecumseh and the Prophet were British agents, or at least were being stirred to hostility by the British. British official correspondence shows that Fort Malden was a free cafeteria for hungry Indians, having served them seventy-one thousand meals in the first eleven months of 1810. The correspondence also shows that Tecumseh, in 1810, told the British he planned for war in late 1811, but indicates that the British apparently promised him nothing.

The year 1811 was a hard one for the Indians because the Napoleonic wars had sharply reduced the European market for furs. The Indians were in a state that we would call a depression. And we should remember that while Tecumseh helped the British in the War of 1812 it was not because he loved them. To him the British side was merely the side to take against the Long Knives.

In June and July of 1811 Governors William Hull of Michigan Territory and Harrison of Indiana Territory sent to the secretary of war evaluations of the frontier problems. Hull's was narrowly tactical, pessimistic, and prophetic of the easy conquest of Michigan if the British navy controlled Lake Erie. Harrison's, although in fewer words, was broadly strategic and more constructive: the mere fact of an Indian confederation, friendly to the British and hostile to the Long Knives, was dangerous; the Prophet's town (hereafter called Tippecanoe) was ideally located as a base for a surprise downstream attack on Vincennes, was well placed as a headquarters for more protracted warfare, and was linked by water and short portages with all the northwestern Indians; the little known country north of Tippecanoe, full of swamps and thickets, could easily be defended by natives, but the power of the United States could be brought to bear only with the greatest difficulty. Early in August, 1811, Harrison told the War Department he did not expect hostilities before Tecumseh returned from the South, and that in the meantime he intended to try to break up Tecumseh's confederacy, without bloodshed if possible. On their side, the Indians told the British they expected some deceitful trick leading to their massacre.

The military details of the Battle of Tippecanoe need not be exhausted here. Harrison's forces moved up the Wabash and arrived at Tippecanoe on November 6, 1811. When Harrison was preparing to attack, he was met by emissaries from the Prophet. Both sides agreed to a council on the next day. The troops encamped with correctly organized interior and exterior guards. Here the story diverges into two versions. White writers have said the Indians intended to confer, to pretend falsely to agree to anything, to assassinate Harrison, and to massacre the little army. They allege the Prophet had promised to make the Indians bullet proof. A Kickapoo chief later said to British officers that a white prisoner the Indians had captured told them Harrison intended to fight, not to talk. At any rate, the shooting started at about four in the morning, an unfortunate moment for the Indians because that was the hour of "stand to" or "general quarters" in the white army. Curious Indians in the brush were fired on by sentries. The Indians then killed the sentries. It was then, and only then, the Indians said, that they decided to fight. The battle lasted until mid morning, when the Indians ran out of arrows and bullets and fled. A detachment of Harrison's troops then burned the deserted village and the winter corn reserve of the Shawnee. Two days later the troops withdrew. The depth of the cleavage between Indians and whites is shown by the fact that the Potowatomi Chief Winnemac, Harrison's leading Indian adviser, came up the river with the troops but fought on the side of his bronze brethren. Harrison had 50 Kentucky volunteers, 250 United

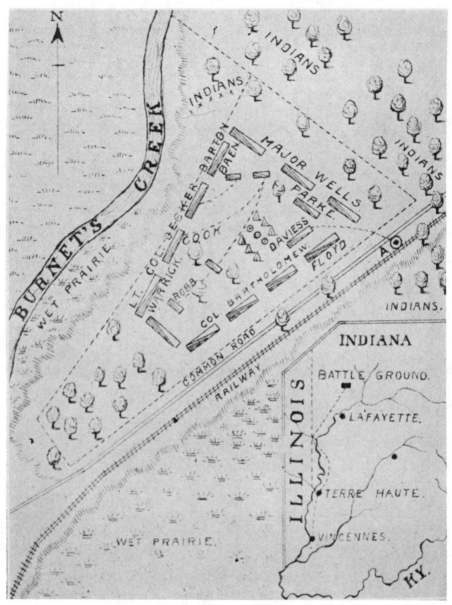

Map of the battleground/Route of march (inset)
Courtesy of George S. Cottman

States infantry, and several hundred Indiana militia, who had been trained personally by him. Reports of losses vary. Indians admitted to losing 25 dead, but soldiers counted 38 dead Indians on the field. This was the first time in northwestern warfare that a force of whites of a size equal to the redmen had suffered only a number of casualties equal to those of their dusky enemies. Heretofore whites in such circumstances had lost more than the redmen had lost. Estimates of Indians in the fighting range from 100 to 1,000. Six hundred would probably be a fair estimate.

As battles go, Tippecanoe cannot be compared with Fallen Timbers in 1794 or Moraviantown in 1813, but it was politically and diplomatically decisive. Its most important effect was to divide the tribes in such a way as to make Tecumseh's dream fade like fog in the sun.

4: The Battle of Tippecanoe

The Battle of Tippecanoe has a significance far beyond that of territorial Indiana. In many ways it represents the beginning of the War of 1812, and its fame lived on to color and influence politics in America during the 1830s and 1840s. The ticket of "Tippecanoe and Tyler Too" was successful in 1840, after Harrison, "Old Tip," had made a strong showing in the 1836 race. President Madison mentioned the "warfare just renewed" in the West when he asked Congress for a war declaration against the British in June 1812.[1]

For all its fame, however, the Battle of Tippecanoe was a costly victory for the United States and the immediate reaction to it carried considerable criticism of Harrison for the heavy losses sustained. Harrison had fewer than 1,000 under arms at Tippecanoe; his casualties totaled 188, including 62 dead. Neither the number of Indian combatants nor the extent of their losses is known, but the estimates range from nearly equal in both cases to considerably fewer in both. The basis for considering Tippecanoe a victory for Harrison at all stems from the fact that he and his troops held the battlefield afterwards and they destroyed Prophetstown the following day before returning home.

One of the more unusual aspects of this clash between soldiers and Indians is that firsthand reminiscences of it exist from both sides. The two selections below contain, first, the recollections of Judge Isaac Naylor, at the time of the battle a twenty-one-year-old volunteer rifleman. Subsequently a lawyer and circuit court judge, Naylor lived in Crawfordsville, Indiana, from 1833 until his death in 1873. The second selection is by Shabonee or Shabonier, a Potawatomi chief (1775–1859) who fought both at Tippecanoe and at the Battle of the Thames (1813), where Tecumseh was killed. A prominent spokesman for the Indians, but known as a peace advocate after 1815, Shabonee became acquainted with Solon Robinson, an agricultural journalist and promoter who founded Crown Point in Lake County in the 1830s. Many years later Robinson published *Me-Won-I-Toc* (1864), a collection of Indian stories which included Shabonee's recollection of the Battle of Tippecanoe.

[1]James D. Richardson (ed.), *Messages and Papers of the Presidents* (20 vols., 1897), II, 488.

For additional information about the battle, see Logan Esarey (ed.), *Messages and Letters of William Henry Harrison* (2 vols., 1922); Dorothy Goebel, *William Henry Harrison* (1926); and John D. Barnhart and Donald F. Carmony, *Indiana: From Frontier to Industrial Commonwealth* (2 vols., 1954); a good, brief account of the battle is by Gayle Thornbrough, "Tippecanoe," *American Heritage,* II (Autumn 1950), 16-19.

An Eyewitness Account of Tippecanoe

JUDGE ISAAC NAYLOR

I became a volunteer of a company of riflemen and, on September 12, 1811, we commenced our march towards Vincennes, and arrived there in about six days, marching one hundred and twenty miles. We remained there about one week and took up the line of march to a point on the Wabash river, where we erected a stockade fort, which we named Fort Harrison. This was two miles above where the city of Terre Haute now stands. Col. Joseph H. Daviess, who commanded the dragoons, named the fort. The glorious defense of this fort nine months after by Capt. Zachary Taylor was the first step in his brilliant career that afterward made him President of the United States. A few days later we took up our line of march for the seat of the Indian warfare, where we arrived on the evening of November 6, 1811.

When the army arrived in view of Prophet's Town, an Indian was seen coming toward General Harrison, with a white flag suspended on a pole. Here the army halted, and a parley was had between General Harrison and an Indian delegation who assured the General that they desired peace and solemnly promised to meet him the next day in council to settle the terms of peace and friendship between them and the United States.

Gen. Marston G. Clark, who was then brigade major, and Waller Taylor, one of the judges of the general court of the Territory of Indiana, and afterward a senator of the United States from Indiana (as one of the General's aides), were ordered to select a place for the encampment, which they did. The army then marched to the ground selected, about sunset. A strong guard was placed around the encampment commanded by Capt. James Bigger and three lieutenants. The troops were ordered to sleep on their arms. The night being cold, large fires were made along the lines of encampment and each soldier retired to rest, sleeping on his arms.

Having seen a number of squaws and children at the town, I thought

From Isaac Naylor, "An Eyewitness Account of the Battle," *The Battle of Tippecanoe: Conflict of Cultures*, ed. Alameda McCollough (1973), pp. 10-13. This account was first published as "The Battle of Tippecanoe, as described by Judge Isaac Naylor, A Participant— A Recently Discovered Account," *Indiana Magazine of History*, II (December 1906), 161-169. Reprinted by permission.

Fort Harrison (1811)
Courtesy of George S. Cottman

the Indians were not disposed to fight. About ten o'clock at night, Joseph Warnock and myself retired to rest, he taking one side of the fire and I the other—the members of our company being all asleep. My friend Warnock had dreamed, the night before, a bad dream which foreboded something fatal to him or to some of his family, as he told me. Having myself no confidence in dreams, I thought but little about the matter, although I observed that he never smiled afterwards.

I awoke about four o'clock the next morning, after a sound and refreshing sleep, having heard in a dream the firing of guns and the whistling of bullets just before I awoke from my slumber. A drizzling rain was falling and all things were still and quiet throughout the camp. I was engaged in making a calculation when I should arrive home.

In a few moments I heard the crack of a rifle in the direction of the point where now stands the Battle Ground House, which is occupied by Captain DuTiel as a tavern. I had just time to think that some sentinel was alarmed and fired his rifle without a real cause, when I heard the crack of another rifle, followed by an awful Indian yell all around the encampment. In less than a minute I saw the Indians charging our line most furiously and shooting a great many rifle balls into our camp fires, throwing the live coals into the air three or four feet high.

At this moment my friend Warnock was shot by a rifle ball through his body. He ran a few yards and fell dead on the ground. Our lines were broken and a few Indians were found on the inside of the encampment. In a few moments they were all killed. Our lines closed up and our men in their proper places. One Indian was killed in the back part of Captain Geiger's tent, while he was attempting to tomahawk the Captain.

The sentinels, closely pursued by the Indians, came to the line of the encampment in haste and confusion. My brother, William Naylor, was on guard. He was pursued so rapidly and furiously that he ran to the nearest point on the left flank, where he remained with a company of regular soldiers until the battle was near its termination. A young man, whose name was Daniel Pettit, was pursued so closely and furiously by an Indian as he was running from the guard line to our lines, that to save his life he cocked his rifle as he ran and turning suddenly around, placed the muzzle of his gun against the body of the Indian and shot an ounce ball through him. The Indian fired his gun at the same instant, but it being longer than Pettit's the muzzle passed by him and set fire to a handkerchief which he had tied around his head. The Indians made four or five most fierce charges on our lines, yelling and screaming as they advanced, shooting balls and arrows into our ranks. At each charge they were driven back in confusion, carrying off their dead and wounded as they retreated.

Colonel Owen, of Shelby County, Kentucky, one of General Harrison's aides, fell early in the action by the side of the General. He was a

The battle rages
Courtesy of Ralph D. Gray

member of the legislature at the time of his death. Colonel Daviess was mortally wounded early in the battle, gallantly charging the Indians on foot with sword and pistols according to his own request. He made this request three times before General Harrison would permit it. This charge was made by himself and eight dragoons on foot near the angle formed by the left flank and front line of the encampment. Colonel Daviess lived about thirty-six hours after he was wounded, manifesting his ruling passion in life— ambition and a patriotism and ardent love of military glory. During the last hours of his life he said to his friends around him that he had but one thing to regret—that he had military talents; that he was about to be cut down in the meridian of life without having an opportunity of displaying them for his own honor, and the good of his country. He was buried alone, with the honors of war, near the right flank of the army, inside the lines of the encampment, between two trees. On one side of the tree the letter 'D' was plainly visible many years. Nothing but the stump of the other tree remains. His grave was made here to conceal it from the Indians. It was filled up to the top with earth and then covered with oak leaves. I presume the Indians never found it. This precautionary act was performed as a mark of special respect for a distinguished hero and patriot of Kentucky.

Captain Spencer's company of mounted riflemen composed the right flank of the army. Captain Spencer and both of his lieutenants were killed. John Tipton was elected and commissioned captain of his company in one hour after the battle, as reward for his cool and deliberate heroism displayed during the action. He died at Logansport in 1839, having been twice elected senator of the United States from Indiana.

The clear, calm voice of General Harrison was heard in words of heroism in every part of the encampment during the action. Colonel Boyd behaved very bravely after repeating these words: 'Huzza! My sons of gold, a few more fires and victory will be ours!'

Just after daylight the Indians retreated across the prairie toward their own town, carrying off their wounded. This retreat was from the right flank of the encampment, commanded by Captains Spencer and Robb, having retreated from the other portions of the encampment a few minutes before. As their retreat became visible, an almost deafening and universal shout was raised by our men. 'Huzza! Huzza! Huzza!' This shout was almost equal to that of the savages at the commencement of the battle; ours was the shout of victory, theirs was the shout of ferocious but disappointed hope.

The morning light disclosed the fact that the killed and wounded of our army, numbering between eight and nine hundred men, amounted to one hundred and eight. Thirty-six Indians were found near our lines. Many of their dead were carried off during the battle. This fact was proved by the discovery of many Indian graves recently made near their town. Ours was a bloody victory, theirs a bloody defeat.

Soon after breakfast an Indian chief was discovered on the prairie, about eighty yards from our front line, wrapped in a piece of white cloth. He was found by a soldier by the name of Miller, a resident of Jeffersonville, Indiana. The Indian was wounded in one leg, the ball having penetrated his knee and passed down his leg, breaking the bone as it passed. Miller put his foot against him and he raised up his head and said: 'Don't kill me, don't kill me.' At the same time five or six regular soldiers tried to shoot him, but their muskets snapped and missed fire. Maj. Davis Floyd came riding toward him with dragoon sword and pistols and said he would show them how to kill Indians, when a messenger came from General Harrison commanding that he should be taken prisoner. He was taken into camp, where the surgeons dressed his wounds. Here he refused to speak a word of English or tell a word of truth. Through the medium of an interpreter he said that he was coming to the camp to tell General Harrison that they were about to attack the camp. He refused to have his leg amputated, though he was told that amputation was the only means of saving his life. One dogma of Indian superstition is that all good and brave Indians, when they die, go to a delightful region, abounding with deer, and other game, and to be a success-ful hunter he should have his limbs, his gun and his dog. He therefore preferred death with all his limbs to life without them. In accordance with his request he was left to die, in company with an old squaw, who was found in the Indian town the next day after he was taken prisoner. They were left in one of our tents. At the time this Indian was taken prisoner, another Indian, who was wounded in the body, rose to his feet in the middle of the prairie and began to walk towards the wood on the opposite side. A number of regular soldiers shot at him but missed him. A man who was a member of the same company with me, Henry Huckleberry, ran a few steps into the prairie and shot an ounce ball through his body and he fell dead near the margin of the woods. Some Kentucky volunteers went across the prairie immediately and scalped him, dividing his scalp into four pieces, each one cutting a hole in each piece, putting the ramrod through the hole, and placing his part of the scalp just behind the first thimble of his gun, near its muzzle. Such was the fate of nearly all of the Indians found dead on the battle-ground, and such was the disposition of their scalps.

The death of Owen, and the fact that Daviess was mortally wounded, with the remembrance also that a large portion of Kentucky's best blood had been shed by the Indians, must be their apology for this barbarous conduct. Such conduct will be excused by all who witnessed the treachery of the Indians and saw the bloody scenes of this battle.

Tecumseh being absent at the time of the battle, a chief called White Loon was the chief commander of the Indians. He was seen in the morning after the battle, riding a large white horse in the woods across the prairie, where he was shot at by a volunteer named Montgomery, who is now living in the southwest part of this state. At the crack of his rifle the horse jumped as if the ball had hit him. The Indian rode off toward the town and we saw him no more. During the battle The Prophet was safely located on a hill, beyond the reach of our balls, praying to the Great Spirit to give victory to the Indians, having previously assured them that the Great Spirit would change our powder into ashes and sand.

We had about forty head of beef cattle when we came to the battle. They all ran off the night of the battle, or they were driven off by the Indians, so that they were all lost. We received rations for two days on the morning after the action. We received no more rations until the next Tuesday evening, being six days afterwards. The Indians having retreated to their town, we performed the solemn duty of consigning to their graves our dead soldiers, without shrouds or coffins. They were placed in graves about two feet deep, from five to ten in each grave.

General Harrison, having learned that Tecumseh was expected to return from the south with a number of Indians whom he had enlisted in his cause, called a council of his officers, who advised him to remain on the battlefield and fortify his camp by a breastwork of logs, about four feet high. This work was completed during the day and all the troops were placed immediately behind each line of the work when they were ordered to pass the watchword from right to left every five minutes, so that no man was permitted to sleep during the night. The watchword on the night before the battle was 'Wide awake, wide awake.' To me it was a long, cold, cheerless night.

On the next day the dragoons went to Prophet's Town, which they found deserted by all the Indians, except an old squaw, whom they brought into camp and left her with the wounded chief before mentioned. The dragoons set fire to the town and it was all consumed, casting up a brilliant light amid the darkness of the ensuing night. I arrived at the town when it was about half on fire. I found large quantities of corn, beans and peas. I filled my knapsack with these articles and carried them to the camp and divided them with the members of our mess, consisting of six men. Having these articles of food, we declined eating horse flesh, which was eaten by a large portion of our men.

Chief Shabonee's Account of Tippecanoe

SHABONEE

It was fully believed among the Indians that we should defeat General Harrison, and that we should hold the line of the Wabash and dictate terms

From J. Wesley Whickar (ed.), "Shabonee's Account of Tippecanoe," *Indiana Magazine of History*, XVII (December 1921), 353–360. Reprinted by permission.

to the whites. The great cause of our failure, was the Miamies, whose principal country was south of the river, and they wanted to treat with the whites so as to retain their land, and they played false to their red brethren and yet lost all. They are now surrounded and will be crushed. The whites will shortly have all their lands and they will be driven away.

In every talk to the Indians, General Harrison said:

> Lay down your arms. Bury the hatchet, already bloody with murdered victims, and promise to submit to your great chief at Washington, and he will be a father to you, and forget all that is past. If we take your land, we will pay for it. But you must not think that you can stop the march of white men westward.

There was truth and justice in all that talk. The Indians with me would not listen to it. It was dictating to them. They wanted to dictate to him. They had counted his soldiers, and looked at them with contempt. Our young men said:

> We are ten to their one. If they stay upon the other side, we will let them alone. If they cross the Wabash, we will take their scalps or drive them into the river. They cannot swim. Their powder will be wet. The fish will eat their bodies. The bones of the white men will lie upon every sand bar. Their flesh will fatten buzzards. These white soldiers are not warriors. Their hands are soft. Their faces are white. One half of them are calico peddlers. The other half can only shoot squirrels. They cannot stand before men. They will all run when we make a noise in the night like wild cats fighting for their young. We will fight for ours, and to keep the pale faces from our wigwams. What will they fight for? They won't fight. They will run. We will attack them in the night.

Such were the opinions and arguments of our warriors. They did not appreciate the great strength of the white men. I knew their great war chief, and some of his young men. He was a good man, very soft in his words to his red children, as he called us; and that made some of our men with hot heads mad. I listened to his soft words, but I looked into his eyes. They were full of fire. I knew that they would be among his men like coals of fire in the dry grass. The first wind would raise a great flame. I feared for the red men that might be sleeping in its way. I, too, counted his men. I was one of the scouts that watched all their march up the river from Vincennes. I knew that we were like these bushes—very many. They were like these trees; here and there one. But I knew too, when a great tree falls, it crushes many little ones. I saw some of the men shoot squirrels, as they rode along, and I said, the Indians have no such guns. These men will kill us as far as they can see. "They cannot see in the night," said our men who were determined to fight. So I held my tongue. I saw that all of our war chiefs were hot for battle with the white men. But they told General Harrison that they only wanted peace.

They wanted him to come up into their country and show their people how strong he was, and then they would all be willing to make a treaty and smoke the great pipe together. This was what he came for. He did not intend to fight the Indians. They had deceived him. Yet he was wary. He was a great war chief. Every night he picked his camping ground and set his sentinels all around, as though he expected we would attack him in the dark. We should have done so before we did, if it had not been for this precaution. Some of our people taunted him for this, and pretended to be angry that he should distrust them, for they still talked of their willingness to treat, as soon as they could get all the people. This is part of our way of making war. So the white army marched further and further into our country, unsuspicious, I think, of our treachery. In one thing we were deceived. We expected that the white warriors would come up on the south bank of the river, and then we could parley with them; but they crossed far down the river and came on this side, right up to the great Indian town that Elskatawwa had gathered at the mouth of the Tippecanoe. In the meantime he had sent three chiefs down on the south side to meet the army and stop it with a talk until he could get the warriors ready. Tecumseh had told the Indians not to fight, but when he was away, they took some scalps, and General Harrison demanded that we should give up our men as murder[er]s, to be punished.

Tecumseh had spent months in traveling all over the country around Lake Michigan, making great talks to all the warriors, to get them to join him in his great designs upon the pale faces. His enmity was the most bitter of any Indian I ever knew. He was not one of our nation, he was a Shawnee. His father was a great warrior. His mother came from the country where there is no snow, near the great water that is salt. His father was treacherously killed by a white man before Tecumseh was born, and his mother taught him, while he sucked, to hate all white men, and when he grew big enough to be ranked as a warrior she used to go with him every year to his father's grave and make him swear that he would never cease to make war upon the Americans. To this end he used all his power of strategy, skill and cunning, both with white men and red. He had very much big talk. He was not at the battle of Tippecanoe. If he had been there it would not have been fought. It was too soon. It frustrated all his plans.

Elskatawwa was Tecumseh's older brother. He was a great medicine. He talked much to the Indians and told them what had happened. He told much truth, but some things that he had told did not come to pass. He was called "The Prophet." Your people knew him only by that name. He was very cunning, but he was not so great a warrior as his brother, and he could not so well control the young warriors who were determined to fight.

Perhaps your people do not know that the battle of Tippecanoe was the work of white men who came from Canada and urged us to make war. Two of them who wore red coats were at the Prophet's Town the day that your army came. It was they who urged Elskatawwa to fight. They dressed

The Prophet (Elskatawwa)
Courtesy of the Indiana Historical Society

themselves like Indians, to show us how to fight. They did not know our mode. We wanted to attack at midnight. They wanted to wait till daylight. The battle commenced before either party was ready, because one of your sentinels discovered one of our warriors, who had undertaken to creep into your camp and kill the great chief where he slept. The Prophet said if that was done we should kill all the rest or they would run away. He promised us a horseload of scalps, and a gun for every warrior, and many horses. The men that were to crawl upon their bellies into camp were seen in the grass by a white man who had eyes like an owl, and he fired and hit his mark. The Indian was not brave. He cried out. He should have lain still and died. Then the other men fired. The other Indians were fools. They jumped up out of the grass and yelled. They believed what had been told them, that a white man would run at a noise made in the night. Then many Indians who had crept very close so as to be ready to take scalps when the white men ran, all yelled like wolves, wild cats and screech owls; but it did not make the white men run.

They jumped right up from their sleep with guns in their hands and sent a shower of bullets at every spot where they heard a noise. They could not see us. We could see them, for they had fires. Whether we were ready or not we had to fight now for the battle was begun. We were still sure that we should win. The Prophet had told us that we could not be defeated. We did not rush in among your men because of the fires. Directly the men ran away from some of the fires, and a few foolish Indians went into the light and were killed. One Delaware could not make his gun go off. He ran up to a fire to fix the lock. I saw a white man whom I knew very well—he was a great hunter who could shoot a tin cup from another man's head—put up his gun to shoot the Delaware. I tried to shoot the white man but another who carried the flag just then unrolled it so that I could not see my aim. Then I heard the gun and saw the Delaware fall. I thought he was dead. The white man thought so, too, and ran to him with his knife. He wanted a Delaware scalp. Just as he got to him the Delaware jumped up and ran away. He had only lost an ear. A dozen bullets were fired at the white man while he was at the fire, but he shook them off like an old buffalo bull.

Our people were more surprised than yours. The fight had been begun too soon. They were not all ready. The plan was to creep up through the wet land where horses could not run, upon one side of the camp, and on the other through a creek and steep bank covered with bushes, so as to be ready to use the tomahawk upon the sleeping men as soon as their chief was killed. The Indians thought white men who had marched all day would sleep. They found them awake.

The Prophet had sent word to General Harrison that day that the Indians were all peaceable, that they did not want to fight, that he might lie down and sleep, and they would treat with their white brothers in the morning and bury the hatchet. But the white men did not believe.

In one minute from the time the first gun was fired I saw a great war chief mount his horse and begin to talk loud. The fires were put out and we could not tell where to shoot, except on one side of the camp, and from there the white soldiers ran, but we did not succeed as the Prophet told us that we would, in scaring the whole army so that all the men would run and hide in the grass like young quails.

I never saw men fight with more courage than these did after it began to grow light. The battle was lost to us by an accident, or rather by two.

A hundred warriors had been picked out during the night for this desperate service, and in the great council-house the Prophet had instructed them how to crawl like snakes through the grass and strike the sentinels; and if they failed in that, then they were to rush forward boldly and kill the great war chief of the whites, and if they did not do this the Great Spirit, he said, had told him that the battle would be hopelessly lost. This the Indians all believed.

If the one that was first discovered and shot had died like a brave, without a groan, the sentinel would have thought that he was mistaken, and it would have been more favorable than before for the Indians. The alarm having been made, the others followed Elskatawwa's orders, which were, in case of discovery, so as to prevent the secret movement, they should make a great yell as a signal for the general attack. All of the warriors had been instructed to creep up to the camp through the tall grass during the night, so close that when the great signal was given, the yell would be so loud and frightful that the whole of the whites would run for the thick woods up the creek, and that side was left open for this purpose.

"You will, then," said the Prophet, "have possession of their camp and all its equipage, and you can shoot the men with their own guns from every tree. But above all else you must kill the great chief."

It was expected that this could be easily done by those who were allotted to rush into camp in the confusion of the first attack. It was a great mistake of the Prophet's redcoated advisers, to defer this attack until morning. It would have succeeded when the fires were brighter in the night. Then they could not have been put out.

I was one of the spies that had dogged the steps of the army to give the Prophet information every day. I saw all the arrangement of the camp. It was not made where the Indians wanted it. The place was very bad for the attack. But it was not that which caused the failure. It was because General Harrison changed horses. He had ridden a grey one every day on the march, and he could have been shot twenty times by scouts that were hiding along the route. That was not what was wanted, until the army got to a place where it could be all wiped out. That time had now come, and the hundred braves were to rush in and shoot the "Big chief on a white horse," and then fall back to a safer place.

This order was fully obeyed, but we soon found to our terrible dismay that the "Big chief on a white horse" that was killed was not General Harrison. He had mounted a dark horse. I know this, for I was so near that I saw him, and I knew him as well as I knew my own brother.

I think that I could then have shot him, but I could not lift my gun. The Great Spirit held it down. I knew then that the great white chief was not to be killed, and I knew that the red men were doomed.

As soon as daylight came our warriors saw that the Prophet's grand plan had failed—that the great white chief was alive riding fearlessly among his troops in spite of bullets, and their hearts melted.

After that the Indians fought to save themselves, not to crush the whites. It was a terrible defeat. Our men all scattered and tried to get away. The white horsemen chased them and cut them down with long knives. We carried off a few wounded prisoners in the first attack, but nearly all the dead lay unscalped, and some of them lay thus till the next year when another army came to bury them.

Our women and children were in the town only a mile from the battle-field waiting for victory and its spoils. They wanted white prisoners.

The Prophet had promised that every squaw of any note should have one of the white warriors to use as her slave, or to treat as she pleased.

Oh how these women were disappointed! Instead of slaves and spoils of the white men coming into town with the rising sun, their town was in flames and women and children were hunted like wolves and killed by hundreds or driven into the river and swamps to hide.

With the smoke of that town and the loss of that battle I lost all hope of the red men being able to stop the whites.

I fought that day by the side of an old Ottawa chief and his son, the brother of my wife. We were in the advance party, and several of those nearest to me fell by the bullets or blows of two horsemen who appeared to be proof against our guns. At length one of these two men killed the young man and wounded the chief, and at the same time I brought him and his horse to the ground. The horse ran, before he fell, down the bluff into the creek, quite out of the way of the whites. The man's leg was broken and he had another bad wound. I could have taken his scalp easily, but Sabaqua, the old chief, begged me not to kill him. He wanted to take him to his wife alive, in place of her son whom the white brave had killed.

I was willing enough to do this for I always respected a brave man, and this one was, beside, the handsomest white man I had ever seen. I knew him as soon as I saw him closely. I had seen him before. I went to Vincennes only one moon before the battle as a spy. I told the governor that I came for peace. This young man was there and I talked with him. He was not one of the warriors but had come because he was a great brave. He had told me, laughingly, that he would come to see me at my wigwam. I thought now that he should do it. I caught a horse—there were plenty of them that had lost their riders—and mounted the white brave with Sabaqua behind him to hold him on and started them off north. I was then sure that we should all have to run that way as soon as it was light. The Indians were defeated. The great barrier was broken. It was my last fight. I put my body in the way. It was strong then, but it was not strong enough to stop the white men. They pushed it aside as I do this stick. I have never seen the place since where we fought that night. My heart was very big then. Tecumseh had filled it with gall. It has been empty ever since.

5: The Nineteenth State

Following the War of 1812, a wave of settlement swept across the New West like pent-up flood waters bursting through a dam. Indiana's population jumped from 35,000 or 40,000 prior to the war to more than 147,000 in 1820, 685,000 in 1840, and over 1,350,000 in 1860. Other western states were growing rapidly too. Beginning with Indiana, a total of six new states entered the Union in the six years between 1816 and 1821.

The statehood movement had been present in Indiana since at least 1811, when the first petition for statehood was submitted to Congress. But, as Professor Carmony explains in the following selection, this sentiment was not a unanimous one, primarily for monetary reasons. Nevertheless, when a second request was approved by the territorial legislature in December 1815, Congress responded with an enabling act on April 19, 1816, which authorized a constitutional convention. Convened in June at Corydon, which had been the territorial capital since 1813, the delegates quickly agreed to proceed with drawing up a constitution. The Indiana constitution was advanced for its time, particularly the education article, which called on the state to provide "as soon as circumstances will permit . . . for a general system of education, ascending in a regular gradation, from township schools to a state university, wherein tuition shall be gratis, and equally open to all."[1] The constitution reflected the prevailing Jeffersonian philosophy concerning republican institutions and limited executive authority, and it required annual elections and meetings of the General Assembly. Given the prevailing concern for the economy in 1816, as described below, it is not surprising that circumstances never permitted the establishment of the comprehensive educational system envisioned, and this article was substantially modified in the new constitution of 1851.

Donald F. Carmony, professor of history at Indiana University and editor of the *Indiana Magazine of History* from 1955 to 1975, is an outstanding student of Indiana history. He is the author of numerous books and articles on the state, including the comprehensive survey he and John D. Barnhart compiled: *Indiana: From Frontier to*

[1] Quoted in Hubert H. Hawkins (ed.), *Indiana's Road to Statehood* (1964), p. 87.

Industrial Commonwealth (2 vols., 1954). The article below is based on research Professor Carmony did for his doctoral dissertation at Indiana University.

Statehood Achieved

DONALD F. CARMONY

Indiana remained at the representative stage from late in 1804 until statehood was achieved in 1816, during which period the total territorial expenditures averaged approximately ten thousand dollars yearly. About two-thirds of this sum was paid from federal appropriations leaving one-third payable from territorial revenues. While at the nonrepresentative level, territorial costs had totaled about $5,700 annually with all but two hundred dollars being provided from the federal treasury.

The meagerness of these totals, especially when the extent of the federal subsidy is considered, is indicative of the fiscal atmosphere in which Indiana became a state. It was generally understood that this federal support would be lost if territorial days were ended, while it was also recognized that statehood would result in added costs. The ensuing discussion has several references to these points of view. With this picture before us, the fiscal aspect of the statehood contest can be observed more nearly from the contemporary perspective and the movement cannot be properly understood in any other manner. Such objectivity is particularly hard to achieve in these days when fiscal expenditures have towered skyward until millions and even billions are spent with less caution and care than the founding fathers of Indiana spent thousands or even hundreds of dollars.

By 1816, Indiana with a population of between seventy-five thousand and one hundred thousand was ripe for statehood. Indian resistance had been crushed during the War of 1812 and English influence around the Great Lakes had waned. Indiana was the first of six states to enter the Union in the half-dozen years beginning in 1816, and the spirit of nationalism reached a new peak causing membership in the Union to be viewed with patriotic pride.

The Mississippi Valley was debtor to the Atlantic Seaboard and Europe, and its financial resources were limited even more than many contemporaries realized, but that frontier spirit of optimism and expansion which led to excessive land speculation and reckless ventures in banking and internal improvements often produced rosy forecasts of future fiscal affairs. The failure of the First State Bank of Indiana in the 1820's and the internal

From "Fiscal Objections to Statehood in Indiana," *Indiana Magazine of History,* XLII (December 1946), 313–314, 316–321. Footnotes in the original have been omitted. Reprinted by permission.

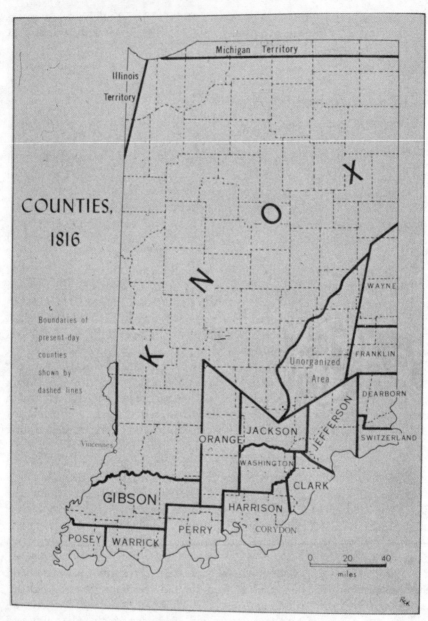

Indiana counties in 1816

Courtesy of Robert C. Kingsbury, An Atlas of Indiana, 1970

improvements debacle of the late thirties and early forties are appropriate Indiana illustrations of this frontier tendency. Some Indiana taxpayers, however, preferred a prolongation of the territorial status to being "weaned" from the federal treasury but such raised their voices in vain.

. . . .

The War of 1812 apparently checked and delayed agitation for statehood. During the years 1812 and 1813, the thoughts and efforts of the people of Indiana were beamed on defense from the Indians and their British allies, although by the end of 1814 the war clouds were dispersing and the immediate future promised a considerable impetus to population and fiscal resources. The Assembly provided for an 1815 territorial census to discover whether the number of inhabitants totaled a minimum of sixty thousand as required for statehood by the Ordinance of 1787. In the summer of 1814, Waller Taylor, in announcing himself a rival for Jenning's position in Congress, rather gingerly advocated statehood: "as soon as the people shall think themselves able to support it, however, I shall expect instructions, and those instructions, whatever they may be, coming from a majority of the people, or from the Legislature, I shall punctually obey."

The 1815 census, taken by the tax listers or assessors, disclosed a population of nearly sixty-four thousand. Newspapers within and without the territory viewed this count as opening the way to immediate statehood. The *Western Eagle,* recipient of the public printing patronage, proudly announced:

> another manly link is about to be added to the bright chain of our glorious republic in the Territory of Indiana . . . . there is a charm, a political magic in the right of self government . . . that attracts our citizens to an independent state government in preference to a territorial establishment even partially at the expense of the Federal government.

The *Eagle* cited the rapid development of Ohio in the preceding decade as ample illustration of the magic of statehood; here the flow of population had been greater than that of the Greeks over the Mediterranean World.

On December 11, 1815, exactly one year before the formal admission of Indiana, the territorial house again approved a memorial for statehood and soon concurred in changes which the Council made therein. Jonathan Jennings, still territorial delegate and leader of the statehood movement, presented this memorial to the lower house of Congress where it was referred to a committee of which he was chairman. After some delay, perhaps arising partly from its association with a similar act for Mississippi, an Indiana Enabling Act was approved by President James Madison on April 19, 1816.

While this measure was pending at Washington, Governor Thomas

Posey, who had succeeded Harrison in 1813, wrote a personal letter to Secretary of State Monroe against statehood:

> Some of our Citizens are very restless to go into a State government. I wish the people were well prepared for the measure, but I may say with propriety that at least two thirds, or three fourths, are not able to contribute but very little, if any thing to the Support of a State; and there is also a very great scarcety of talents, or men of such information as are necessary to fill the respective Stations, & offices of government. No doubt you have seen the memorial of the two Houses of our Legislature to Congress for the purpose of going into a State Government. If Congress should be so benevolent as to grant all ask'd for, there would be no other difficulty except the want of men of good information.

The governor stated that three years would be soon enough to make the proposed transition and solicited the endorsement of Secretary Monroe for another three-year term as governor! Posey, no doubt, realized that his tenure was contingent on a prolongation of the territorial period and this perhaps fortified his position in regard to statehood, while such leaders as Jennings, who would probably gain political advancement, were inclined to soft-pedal the increased fiscal burdens which would result from statehood. . . .

On the eve of the constitutional convention, at Corydon, *The Cornucopia of the West* wisely counseled that to assume the dignified position of a free and independent state would "require the exercise of a degree of fortitude, wisdom and economy. . . ." It was urged that taxes be reduced and shackles be removed from industry. Contemporaries generally consider taxes "too high," but present day Hoosiers may well wonder what shackles then burdened industry. Apparently, the then odious excise taxes which the federal government had reluctantly revived during the war of 1812 were the target of this criticism.

The most complete and best organized of the available statements against statehood came from the pen of "Republican" who addressed his thoughtful remarks "To The Citizens of Indiana." His identity is unknown but he was strongly opposed to Jennings. "Republican's" appeal appeared in the *Western Sun* about one week prior to the convening of the constitutional convention and may have been timed to influence the delegates to decide against framing a constitution as the next step on the road to statehood. "Republican" viewed the crisis as one which seldom occurred and confined his argument largely to the fiscal issue, making no other objection to statehood.

Although taxes in support of the territorial government were heavy, statehood would cause these burdens to be doubled, while by remaining a territory money could be saved to citizens where it was much needed in settling a new country. Indianans were urged to attend for a while to "the opening, clearing, and cultivation of their farms, have a surplus produce for market, invite emigrants, & then we shall be able to pay our state revenue without the sheriff's taking our childrens bread." After such delay the people of Indiana could enter the Union as wise men, but its immediate assumption would result in the tax exemption of all lands sold by the federal government within Indiana for five years from the date of sale; make the salaries of the governor, judges and secretary payable from state rather than federal revenues; and result in additional expense because of more offices. If the territorial government were retained, the expense and the ability to pay taxes would gradually become proportionate to that required to support a state establishment and pay revenue to the United States. There is much to be said for the validity of "Republican's" thesis, but fiscal policy of a government is not always in accordance with valid theories and practices.

On June 10, 1816, the constitutional convention convened at Corydon and next day voted 34 to 8 to frame a constitution and the preponderance of this majority indicates much popular support for the statehood movement. Jonathan Jennings was made chairman of the convention. Less than two weeks later the *Western Sun* quoted from a letter received from Corydon:

> The Convention have determined by a majority of 33 to 8, to launch our political vessel of state, and I am afraid without having a sufficient number of skillful navigators on board, at least to manage the vessel in case of a storm.—But with such an overwhelming majority in favor of a state government, the people must take it as a mad [man] takes his wife, "for better or worse," &c. with but this exception, a divorce cannot be obtained.

Within about three weeks the constitution was framed and during the next few months a state government was organized, but formal admission was delayed until December 11 when President Madison approved a joint-resolution of Congress declaring Indiana a member of the Union. The Hoosier state has never been without a sufficient number of would-be navigators, but not all have been of equal skill as pilots of the ship of state!

The average annual cost of state government during the first decade of statehood was approximately twenty-five thousand dollars, yet this initial decade was a difficult period with much deficit financing involving relatively large issues of state treasury notes. By the mid 1820's, however, the depression had lifted, population and resources were larger, the state debt was almost liquidated, and Indiana was entering a decade in which the fiscal skies would generally be clear, and the state would continue to grow in population and resources at an amazing rate. The fiscal objection to statehood seems to have been largely forgotten as Indiana became proud of her place in the Union.

Chapter IV
LIFE ON THE INDIANA FRONTIER

During the pioneer period in Indiana, approximately the years between the two constitutions of 1816 and 1851, very significant changes were occurring in practically all walks of life. Most apparent were the demographic changes. Both the central and northern portions of the state were settled, partly by the northward movement of Hoosiers into the fertile flatlands that characterize all but the southern third of Indiana, and partly by the northern and western migration of people from the upper South, Ohio, and the middle Atlantic states. But prior to 1850, particularly, the number of foreign immigrants was small.

In 1825 the General Assembly held its first meeting in the new state capital of Indianapolis, the new "city of Indiana" located and laid out for that purpose only four years earlier near the geographical center of the state. Even the regions surrounding the swampy and marshy wetlands in the north were settled during the 1830s and after; and most of Indiana's present number of counties were established by 1840, and by 1860 all ninety-two had been organized.

The primary economic activity of Indiana's first generation was, of course, agriculture. Most pioneer farmers eked out a living from the soil, provided most of life's essentials through their own and their family's sweat and skills, bemoaned the lack of adequate transportation to town and market, and worried about the Indians. Work-related tasks such as barn raisings, corn huskings, and road building were turned into social affairs for entertainment; politics and religion also provided diversions from the usual routine of work from dawn to dusk.

Pioneer Indiana was also the scene of one of the best-known Utopian communities in America, Robert Owen's New Harmony. The village itself, located on the lower Wabash several miles south of Vincennes, had been established by Father George Rapp in 1814. He and his followers prospered in the area during the decade they remained; but the Rappites returned to Pennsylvania in 1824–1825, after Robert Owen, a Scottish industrialist and reformer, had agreed to the purchase of New Harmony. The communal society Owen founded was much less successful than George Rapp's had been, but many of the intellectuals attracted to the town by

Owen's advanced ideas concerning society, education, equality, and the rights of labor remained in Indiana after the New Harmony experiment collapsed in 1827, thereby enriching the quality of life in the state. The same may be said of Robert Owen's five children, who played important roles in the scientific, educational, political, and military history of the state during the next half-century.

A major concern of Hoosiers in the early nineteenth century was transportation. The growing populace needed improvements in and additions to the natural routes of travel provided by rivers and streams, buffalo traces, and Indian trails. In the 1820s a major north-south connection known as the Michigan Road was laid out from Madison on the Ohio River through Indianapolis and South Bend and on to Michigan City at Lake Michigan. The leading east-west thoroughfare in the 1830s, the National Road, traversed the state from Richmond in the east to Terre Haute in the west, via Knightstown, Indianapolis, and Brazil. The state's transportation network was further enriched by canal construction during this decade, and by the appearance of the railroad in the state in the 1840s. Unfortunately, the state became involved in a disastrous Mammoth Internal Improvement program in 1836, in which it decided to use state funds and credit to underwrite an ambitious, eight-project plan designed to crisscross the state with improved roads, canals, and railroads at a cost of some $10,000,000. The Panic of 1837 intervened, followed by a severe depression from 1839–1843. Some of the state's money was embezzled, and none of those projects of the 1830s was completed by the state, which was now saddled with an enormous debt and still in need of improved transportation. In time the projects themselves were taken up and completed by private concerns, and the state slowly extricated itself from debt. But the episode profoundly affected the people at the time and has had a continuing impact.

Indian relations, and the eventual removal of most of the Indians living in Indiana, is another aspect of pioneer Indiana. In the Treaty of St. Mary's, or the New Purchase Treaty, concluded in 1818, the Delaware Indians agreed to leave central Indiana within three years. Their departure actually occurred one year earlier, in 1820, when they moved into the trans-Mississippi West. The transplanted Indians included the first wife and children of William Conner, a prominent Indian trader and settler in central Indiana. In the 1830s a major Potawatomi removal occurred, the forced-march route from Indiana into Missouri being designated another "trail of tears." In the 1840s a third and final large-scale removal involving the Miamis in the Fort Wayne area took place. Although some Indians remained on land granted to them in previous treaties, the Indians as a threatening presence had disappeared. That fear, as well as a contemptuous attitude of some whites toward all Indians, had precipitated the now famous massacre at Fall Creek, in north central Indiana, in 1824.

The readings that follow, written by both pioneer contemporaries and by writers and historians afterwards, describe various aspects of pioneer life in Indiana. The state is indeed fortunate in the number and quality of its reporters on pioneer life. In addition to the works represented in the selections below, particular notice should be given to the Pulitzer-Prize-winning book by Professor R. Carlyle Buley, *The Old Northwest: Pioneer Period, 1815–1840* (2 vols., 1950); and to such primary sources as Emma S. Vonnegut (trans. and ed.), *The Schramm Letters: Written by Jacob Schramm and members of his Family from Indiana to Germany in the year 1836* (1935); Hugh McCulloch, *Men and Measures of Half a Century: Sketches and Comments* (1888); and Sandford C. Cox, *Recollections of the Early Settlement of the Wabash Valley* (1860).

1: Pioneers

The Settlers

L. C. RUDOLPH

A good summary statement about the heavily southern origins and often indolent nature of the first Hoosiers has been written by the Reverend L. C. Rudolph. In the first section of his book on the early history of Presbyterianism in Indiana, he has written eloquently and understandingly about "the settlers" and the hardships of their life on the frontier; but he also discusses their optimism, their willingness to share meager resources, and their good humored acceptance of the limitations imposed on them by circumstances. There is also a brief passage concerning the problems of travel in an area with almost no roads worthy of the name.

Reverend Rudolph, a former member of the Louisville Presbyterian Theological Seminary faculty, is now acquisitions librarian at the Lilly Library on the campus of Indiana University at Bloomington. In addition to *Hoosier Zion,* he has written about the origins of Methodism in the United States in his biography *Francis Asbury* (1966). For more information on pioneer life in Indiana, see R. Carlyle Buley, *The Old Northwest: Pioneer Period, 1815–1840* (2 vols., 1950); see also the reminiscences of Oliver Johnson, as recorded by his son, Howard Johnson, in *A Home in the Woods* (1951, reprinted 1978).

Most of Indiana's earliest settlers were from the southern backwoods. It has been customary to think that southern Indiana was settled from the south while northern Indiana was settled from the north and east, the National Road being a rough division. After a painstaking check of census data, Elfrieda Lang concludes that early Indiana was even more southern than most scholars had supposed. Miss Lang's calculations show that in

From *Hoosier Zion: The Presbyterians in Early Indiana* (1963), pp. 4–11. Some footnotes in the original have been omitted. Copyright © 1963 by Yale University Press. Reprinted by permission.

Indiana the southern population moved right on into the north. Indiana was insulated from the northern and eastern population streams by swampy land that blocked the way to the more desirable Wabash country. The lake port at Michigan City was backed by sand dunes, and the persistent "Kankakee Pond" extended from the Illinois line to South Bend. The Yankees bypassed Indiana because they could not, or thought they could not, get in. As Power concludes, "Paradoxically, although the state lay directly in the path of the westward-moving thousands, thousands moved westward and never saw it."[1]

On the other hand Indiana was open to the south. From the Cumberland Gap the watercourses ran northwest. The famous Wilderness Road led to Kentucky and to the Ohio River at points below Cincinnati. Limestone formations and the best soils ran in nearly perpendicular belts northward from the Ohio. These corridors connected Indiana with the Appalachian back country, the great reservoir of land-hungry pioneers.

From these Appalachian valleys came Indiana's early settlers. To be sure, a few members of the seaboard plantation stock migrated to the Old Northwest: Charles Willing Byrd, William Henry Harrison, Edward Coles, and the father of Edward Eggleston are examples. There were also population islands, like the French at Vincennes, the Swiss-French wine producers at Vevay, English settlements near Evansville, and the Owen settlement at New Harmony. The towns at the commerce centers quickly attracted and developed a merchant class. But for every handful of these gentry there was a woodsfull of marginal settlers. They may have been Scotch, Scotch-Irish, German, English, or even French in their origin, but they had been pioneering for one or more generations before reaching the Ohio. Their pioneering had been done in the back country of Virginia and especially in North Carolina. The view that the main current into Indiana came from North Carolina is supported by careful students of the population movements.

As a rule the southern settlers were poor. The better lands of Kentucky soon commanded a higher price than new settlers could pay, so they pressed on into Indiana. Though there were few navigable streams reaching back more than forty miles from the Ohio, the settlers pressed across the great river, settled along the available streams, and then assaulted the forest directly. The hills of southern Indiana were not yet exploited or eroded, and the natural drainage provided healthful living sites. Moving to the woods of Indiana meant an outlay of several hundred dollars if one held a Yankee farmer's standard of comfort and equipment. There had to be money for horses, a wagon, boat transport, land, cabin, barn, and subsistence, both for the trip and until the first crop could be harvested. The great body of southern pioneers had no such standard. They strapped the articles which

[1]Richard L. Power, "Wet Lands and the Hoosier Stereotype," *Mississippi Valley Historical Review*, XXII (1935), 41, 46.

they felt must be moved upon the backs of their family and animals and set off "jinglety bang." Many had absolutely nothing to lose and were going "no where in perticklar." If they had any money and avoided getting cheated by land sharks, they bought land. If they had no money, they "squatted," hoping to buy later when their situation improved. If their situation did not improve, they became part of that useful group of shifting pioneers who sold their improvements for what they could get and moved on to "squat" and tame more wilderness.

In the woods of Indiana these southern settlers became specialists in subsistence living. Most of them had been "patch farmers" in the back country, and that was what the occasion seemed to demand. There was the perpetual matter of wresting food, clothing, and shelter from the forest and taking care of the family. That was all time permitted. They soon learned that keeping such demands on their time to the minimum allowed more rest for tired and often sick bodies. Their first shelter was likely to be a half-faced camp, a sort of pole pen with an open side before which a fire burned, followed by a rough log cabin. Either may merit description by a traveler as a "pen," a "miserable hole," or a "dirty hovel." William Faux found little to please him on his American tour in 1819, and Indiana frontier cabins were no exception:

> Saving two comfortable plantations, with neat loghouses and flourishing orchards, just planted ... I saw nothing between Vincennes and Princeton, a ride of forty miles, but miserable log holes, and a mean ville of eight or ten huts or cabins, sad neglected farms, and indolent, dirty, sickly, wild-looking inhabitants. Soap is nowhere seen or found in any of the taverns east or west. Hence dirty hands, heads, and faces every where. Here is nothing clean but wild beasts and birds, nothing industrious generally, except pigs, which are so of necessity ... Nothing happy but squirrels; their life seems all play, and that of the hogs all work.

But even such a warm friend of the West as Richard L. Mason recorded in his travel account that same year, as he passed from Louisville through newly settled country to Vincennes, that accommodations were poor and charges high, the people impolite, and their private shelter woefully inadequate to protect them from the severe weather. In time, if the settler stayed and prospered, he might improve the first round-log shelter as a kitchen and attach it by a sort of breezeway to a new and larger hewn-log house.

When the demands of subsistence living allowed it, the southern settler did not think leisure a sin. It was a constant scandal to the Yankee population that the Hoosier made little hay, planted few fruit trees, built few barns, and seemed content with the most scrubby breed of livestock. Neither the zeal of the Yankee nor the thrift of the peasant German marked him. Crawford County farmers climbed the beech and the oak trees in spring to observe the amount of bloom. If they thought the bloom forecast enough beechnuts and acorns to fatten their shoats, they planted little corn.

A host of early writers undertook to characterize the settlers. Some, plainly resentful, called them ignorant, coarse, lazy, lawless. Those accustomed to deference because of prestige or money found the frontiersmen unimpressed by either. Hoosiers did not call a traveler "sir," they called him "stranger." Samuel J. Mills and Daniel Smith, reporting on their travels through the "Territories," declare, "the character of the settlers is such as to render it peculiarly important that missionaries should early be sent among them. Indeed, they can hardly be said to have a character." On the other hand, some have become romantic about the frontier and its settlers. John E. Iglehart is moved by strong passages from Frederick Jackson Turner's essays, especially: "Western democracy was no theorist's dream. It came stark and strong from the American forest." . . . State patriots and historians for local anniversary occasions are also prone to idealize the pioneers.

The way of the frontier farmer was most often hard. He was sick or his horse was lame or the squirrels were eating the corn. But things were about to be different. Every farmer seemed prepared to draw from his pocket a lithographic city and grant the merest acquaintance the favor of taking a few building lots. In spite of present difficulties boundless optimism seemed the mood, and it went with a fierce frontier loyalty that was not anxious for outside counsel. Akin to this was the brashness, buoyancy, and confidence of public figures or candidates—a willingness to support all claims with a fight. The frontiersmen called it a "pushing" spirit and R. Carlyle Buley has attributed to it the ability of young Hoosier doctors to undertake difficult cases without a qualm, and of untried lawyers to plead their cases with unwarranted, flowery eloquence.

The early Indiana settler was willing to share what he had. If there was to be preaching, he would make his house a sanctuary and send out the word—"give out preachin." If travelers needed shelter, they were welcome to the cabin with the rest. In fact, some have charged the Hoosier settler with hospitality beyond his facilities. "Traveled over a fertile country four miles to Steenz, making a distance of thirty-four miles. At this dirty hovel, with one room and a loft, formed by placing boards about three inches apart, ten travelers slept. There were thirteen in the family, besides two calves, making in all, with my friend and self twenty-three whites, one negro and two calves." Problems of dressing or undressing for bed in such large and mixed companies seem to have troubled eastern travelers much more than Hoosiers. For understandable reasons, the settler was willing to share what he had—short of his money. This was too scarce. In the new settlements almost all trade was carried on by barter of goods and service. If the store account could be paid in tow linen, "sang" (ginseng), hides, or "chopping," no cash was forthcoming. When a whole acre of bottom land, trees and all, might be had for less than two dollars, parting with silver was parting with one's best hopes for a farm. This has a real bearing on church subscriptions. Cash was not for trade or pledge; it was for land.

Only if he lived beside a heavily traveled road might the woodsman make some charge for accommodations. When he did so, he would most likely add one room to his cabin, hang out a sign to "keep public," and dignify the whole by the name of tavern. The tavern-keeping settler is by no means the typical citizen of Indiana's frontier, however—there were few

The State Seal
Courtesy of the Indiana Department of Natural Resources

roads of any importance. "Zane's trace across Ohio had no real parallel in Indiana, and the settlers stuck to the navigable streams with unfailing persistence." The earliest major road in Indiana was the Vincennes Trace or the "Buffalo Trace," from Louisville to Vincennes. It amounted to a westward extension of the Wilderness Road and became the chief land route for southerners bound for Illinois.

In frontier usage the word "route" should usually be substituted for "road." As late as 1823 the route from Vincennes to Indianapolis was laid out by dragging a log with an ox team through the woods, prairies, and marshes. Specifications for roadbuilding were very loose, and there was no effective system of maintenance beyond corduroying crucial stretches with fallen logs. A road was a general indication of direction to which one returned between mud holes. There might be bridges or ferries over major streams, and there might be lodging of a sort along the way. Indiana's roads, or lack of them, called forth some purple passages from early travelers. Baynard Hall, a Presbyterian clergyman and the first principal of the new Indiana Seminary at Bloomington in 1823, commented on the roads only thirty miles north of the Ohio:

> The autumn is decidedly preferable for travelling on the virgin soil of native forests. One may go then mostly by land and find the roads fewer and shorter; but in the early spring, branches—(small creeks)—are brim full, and they hold a great deal; concealed fountains bubble up in a thousand places where none were supposed to lurk; creeks turn to rivers, and rivers to lakes, and lakes to bigger ones; and as if this was too little water, out come the mole rivers that have burrowed all this time under the earth, and which, when so unexpectedly found are styled out there—"lost rivers!" And every district of a dozen miles square has a lost river. Travelling by land becomes of course travelling by water, or by both: viz., mud and water. Nor is it possible if one would avoid drowning or suffocation to keep the law and follow the blazed road; but he tacks first to the right and then to the left, often making both losing tacks; and all this, not to find a road but a place where there is no road,—untouched mud thick enough to bear, or that has at least some bottom.

A critic with fewer clerical inhibitions inscribed in the register book of a tavern at Franklin:

> The Roads are impassable—
> Hardly jackassable;
> I think those that travel 'em
> Should turn out and gravel 'em.[2]

---

[2]From the reminiscences of J. H. B. Knowland of Indianapolis, cited by George S. Cottman, "Internal Improvement in Indiana," *Indiana Magazine of History*, 3 (1907), 20.

A Gazetteer's Description

JOHN SCOTT

The first contemporaneous selection comes from the pen and press of an early Indiana printer, John Scott, who compiled *The Indiana Gazetteer or Topographical Dictionary* in 1826. Scott, a native of Pennsylvania, had come to Indiana to ply his trade in the year of statehood. He settled first in Brookville, moved a number of times during the 1820s, and eventually established newspapers in Centerville and later in Logansport. He issued a number of books and maps from his presses in their various locations. *The Indiana Gazetteer,* a product of Scott's Centerville years, represents a genre of writing common to the period. It served as a useful guide and traveling companion for newcomers to the state, because despite the handicaps under which Scott compiled his information, the book was remarkably accurate. Richard E. Banta, in his comprehensive *Indiana Authors and Their Books, 1816–1916* (1949), called Scott's work "the earliest scholarly description of the state, its people, its products, and its resources." And Gayle Thornbrough, in her introduction to the 1954 reprint edition, called early printers like Scott the ones who "in conjunction with the clergy and the schoolmasters saved the frontier from cultural sterility."

One of the earliest books of any published in Indiana, *The Indiana Gazetteer* begins with a general description of the state and its principal towns and transportation facilities, followed by a series of alphabetical entries listing towns and counties. In 1954 the Indiana Historical Society reprinted it, and portions of the book's first pages have been reprinted below.

NAME. The name of the State of Indiana is derived from the Territory out of which it was formed; and, probably, from the Aborigines of the country.

BOUNDARIES. The state of Indiana is bounded on the North by Michigan and Northwestern Territories; East by the state of Ohio; South by the Ohio river, and on the West by the state of Illinois.

SITUATION & EXTENT. It is situated between 38 degrees and 20 minutes, and 42 degrees of North latitude; and between 7 degrees 47 minutes, and 10 degrees 42 minutes of longitude West from Washington City; or between 84 degrees 47 minutes, and 87 degrees 42 minutes of longitude West from London. It is 150 miles in extent from East to West, 282 from North to South on the Western, and but 196 on the Eastern boundary; the Ohio river cuts off so much of its South-eastern quarter, that the state

From *The Indiana Gazetteer or Topographical Dictionary* (1826, reprinted 1954 by the Indiana Historical Society), pp. 27, 32–36, 39–41.

contains an area of but about 190 miles square, which is equal to 36,000 square miles, or 21,040,000 acres. . . .

PRINCIPAL TOWNS. Among the chief towns are Indianapolis, Vincennes, New-Albany, Salem, Madison, Lawrenceburgh, and Richmond. Besides these there are numerous others which are rapidly increasing; among which are Charlestown, Jeffersonville, Bloomington, Brookville, Connersville, Centreville and Fort Wayne, for a more particular description of each, see the proper heads.

POPULATION. In 1820 Indiana contained 149,000 inhabitants, of which 1230 were blacks, but all free. By a census taken in 1825, under the state authority, as a data for apportioning the state representation, it appears that the total number of qualified voters was 37,000; and allowing these to compose one fifth of the whole, the actual population of the state, in 1825, was 185,000; however, it was computed, by competent judges, at the commencement of the present year, at about 250,000; making the increase in five years 100,000.

RELIGION. In religious opinions, the people are much divided; but the Presbyterian, Methodist and Baptist are the prevailing denominations. In the south-western part of the state there are some Shakers; and in Randolph, Wayne, Union, Washington, Henry, Orange and Hendricks counties there are large and respectable societies of Friends, or Quakers. There are a few of almost every denomination, and some of none at all.

CHARACTER & MANNERS. The general character and manners of the people, are as various as their religious sentiments; which is owing, principally, to the circumstance of their having recently emigrated from different sections of the Union. It may not be improper, however, to remark, that the inhabitants are affable, generous, and hospitable. The distinctions in rank, &c. which are observed in the Atlantic and Southern States, are not known here; the people are on an equality; for which they are much indebted to the wise policy of the general government, in the sale of the public lands. These lands are divided into small tracts, and offered at moderate prices, which enables the poor to possess them. Hence, the rich, who are disposed to tyrannize over the poor, are prevented from monopolizing the wealth of the country; and the evils, which necessarily grow out of such monopolies, are not to be found.

LITERATURE. This, like other new settled states has not made great advances in literature. Charters, however, for several Seminaries have been granted by the legislature; some of which are in a flourishing condition. These Seminaries are located in the following counties: Clark, Union, Knox, Monroe, Gibson, and Orange; and the Cambridge Academy in Dearborn county. Common schools are also encouraged, in a greater or less degree, throughout the state.

TRADE AND MANUFACTURES. Considerable quantities of Cotton Yarn and Cloth, and some Woollen Goods are beginning to be made at the several

Factories; and manufactures, of a domestic kind, are made, in great abundance, throughout the state. Of trade, horses, cattle, swine, whiskey, flour, sugar, &c. compose the principal domestic articles of exchange for foreign commodities. These articles are taken, in great abundance, every year, to the Southern and Eastern markets. As yet, but little is taken to the North, but in a few years, when the communication is opened between the Wabash river and lake Erie, we may calculate that large quantities will pass in that way, at least, Farmers and others will have an opportunity of passing with ease, either to the North, the South, the East, or the West, as the different markets may invite.

FORM OF GOVERNMENT. The legislative authority is vested in a Senate and House of Representatives; both of which, collectively, are styled the General Assembly of Indiana. The members of both branches are elected by counties, or districts composed of counties, according to population; which may be seen by a reference to the table of apportionment in pages 9, 10 and 11. The representatives are chosen for one year: and for eligibility a man must be, at least, 21 years of age, have resided in the state one year, and paid a tax. The whole number of representatives must never exceed 100, nor be less than 36; the present number is 78. The Senate is composed of members elected for 3 years, who must not exceed one half, nor fall short of one third of the number in the house of representatives. A senator must be, at least 25 years of age, and have resided two years in the state, one of which within the county, or district, in which he may be elected, if the county or district may have been so long erected; but if not, within the territory from which it may have been taken. The General Assembly has the sole power of enacting all the state laws, but no act can take effect unless approved by the Governor.

The Judiciary system comprises four several grades of courts, to wit: the Supreme, the Circuit, the Probate, and the Justices' courts. The Justices of the Peace are chosen for five years, by the people, in each township respectively. They are conservators of the peace throughout the county; and hold six courts a year, at the seat of justice, for the purpose of transacting county business.

The state is divided into five circuits, in each of which there is a Presiding Judge. The President Judges are elected for seven years, by a joint ballot of both branches of the General Assembly. In each county in the circuit, there are also two Associate Judges, who are chosen by the people for 7 years. These courts are held twice a year, in each county.

The Supreme court consists of three Judges who hold a court twice a year, at the seat of government. They are likewise chosen by the legislature, for seven years.

The supreme executive authority of this state is vested in a governor, who is chosen triennially by the people. For eligibility he must be 30 years of age, a citizen of the United States ten years, and of the state five years. He may be eligible to office 6 years out of 9; is commander in chief of the militia, commissions all officers in the state, civil and military, has power to remit fines and forfeitures, and to grant reprieves and pardons, except in cases of impeachments.

A lieutenant governor is chosen by the people at every election for governor, who holds his office for three years, is president of the senate, and fills the place of governor when vacancies occur.

The secretary, treasurer and auditor of state are elected for 3 years by the legislature.

The Clerks of the circuit courts are chosen by the people, of the respective counties in the circuit, and serve 7 years. Recorders are elected in like manner, and hold their offices the same length of time. Sheriffs and Coroners are chosen by the people biennially.

The governor's salary is $1000 per annum; Supreme and Circuit Judge's $700 each; Associate Judge's $2 per day; and the secretary's, treasurer's and auditor's of state $400....

FACE OF THE COUNTRY, SOIL & PRODUCTIONS. The interior, and the Northern parts of the state, generally, are level, and in some places marshy. A considerable portion of the Southern section, bordering on the Ohio river, is very hilly and broken. The hills, however, differ much from those of the Eastern and Southern states; they are fertile, and not so large as properly to be termed mountains, the greater part of which may be cultivated with ease. The lands between the Wabash and White rivers, and in the New Purchase generally, are not surpassed by any in the western country. Extensive Prairies are found on most of the rivers, particularly on the Wabash and Tippecanoe. The Grand Prairie, perhaps, the largest in the western country, commences a short distance north of the Wabash, near the source of Eel river, and extends, in a south-western direction, into the state of Illinois. It is supposed to be about 300 miles in length, and 100 in breadth. There are many others to be found on Sugar creek, White, Blue, Mississinnewa and Salamania rivers, though far inferior, in point of size, to the Grand Prairie. On these prairies no timber grows, excepting a few scattering trees; sometimes, however, they are found in groves. Many of these prairies are high and dry, and others low and marshy; they are fertile and yield an abundance of grass, from two to three feet in height. Some of this grass is of a good quality, and is cut by the inhabitants for hay.

Among the forest trees are oak of various kinds, hickory, maple of different species, poplar, beech, birch, sycamore, hackberry, cottonwood, ash of several kinds, cherry, spice, pawpaw, buckeye, and various other kinds, whose beautiful foliage and flowers, present a delightful prospect. No soil produces a greater abundance than that of Indiana; from 80 to 100 bushels of corn have been raised, in a year, on a single acre of ground. The animals of the forest are similar to those of Ohio and the other western states. Of mines which have been discovered, Indiana, may boast with any of the states: copper, iron, coal, &c. are found on the Wabash and Tippecanoe. A large body of Zinc has been discovered near the mouth of sugar creek, in Johnson county. Saltpetre has been found near Corydon, in Harrison county: when this cave was first discovered, several hogsheads of this mineral were taken in its pure state, without the labor of purifying it; that which is now taken, however, requires some labor. Salt springs have been also found in different parts of the state, and have been wrought, though not extensively, on Salt creek, in Franklin county, and at several other places.

CLIMATE. The summers are generally warm, and pretty regular: the winters mild, and all the seasons healthy. In some parts fever and ague frequently prevail, but this is owing more to the manner of living, than to the climate. The climate, in general, may be ranked among the healthiest in the world.

A Pioneer's Recollections

WILLIAM M. COCKRUM

William M. Cockrum was a child of the Indiana frontier, having been born in a southern county of the state in 1837. He grew up on the family farm without the benefits of a formal education. Cockrum and his brother James operated a general store and produce business as young men, frequently shipping pork, tobacco, and other goods to New Orleans. During an enforced leisure later in life, Cockrum had both firsthand experience and the reminiscences of older settlers on which to base his history of early Indiana. The same is true for his second book about the underground railroad. The young farmer and merchant had participated in various antislavery activities during the 1850s, and when the Civil War came he volunteered for service in an infantry division, the 47th Indiana. Wounded at Chickamauga, captured and imprisoned for eight months, Cockrum never completely regained his health.

As a farmer and orchardman following the war, Colonel Cockrum, who by his own account had been collecting data on the pioneer period in Indiana for fifty years, published his book in 1907. General Lew Wallace, a comrade in arms who had become famous for his historical romances, particularly *Ben Hur*, encouraged and supported Cockrum in this endeavor. Its strong points are the detailed accounts about day-to-day life—the clothing worn, the food eaten, the tools used, and the customs followed. In the passages below, Cockrum describes the food, housing, clothing, some hardships, and some of the

From *Pioneer History of Indiana, Including Stories, Incidents and Customs of the Early Settlers* (1907), pp. 157–162, 184–196.

more pleasant aspects of frontier life. Cockrum published a second book, *History of the Underground Railroad,* in 1915. He died in 1924 at the age of 87.

The pioneers who first came to Indiana could not have remained for any length of time had it not been for the game which was so abundant on every hand. They often, for weeks at a time, had no other food than the bear, deer and turkey meat. They used every sort of substitute for bread, often roasting the white-oak acorns and eating them in the place of bread with their meat. They would gather the seeds of the wild rice and wild barley and mix it with the roasted acorn, pounding it all up together, making ash cakes of the meal thus obtained. On such food as this with a bountiful supply of meat, the old pioneers and their families subsisted, but as soon as they could raise a patch of corn all this was done away with and the meal made from the corn with beetles, seasoned with the rich bear grease and made into bread was used, and these hardy people prospered and grew fat on it. They were perfectly healthy and the children raised in this way made the strongest men and women. Dyspepsia and kindred stomach troubles were not known. There was but little opportunity of obtaining an education yet they were students of nature and every day learned useful lessons that stood them in need for self-protection and the protection of their families.

In a few years after the first settlers came there were, in most cases, those about the forts or blockhouses who could teach the young people the first principles of education and in after years these people improved the information thus gained by reading the few books that were in the country and many of them became learned in all things needed at that time. The young people were married at a much earlier period in life than the young people of this day. A boy at that time, sixteen or seventeen years old was counted on to do a man's work and to do his part in hunting or in scouting for Indians. The six or eight years now taken to secure an education by our young people to prepare them to be competent to do their part in the great battle of life was spent by their grand and great-grand-fathers and mothers preparing this country so that such great attainments could be secured by the present generation. The difficulties in commencing housekeeping then were not so great as now. They did not have to wait until they had saved money enough to build a fine house and furnish it with the luxuries of life before they got married, thus spending eight or ten years of the best portion of their lives and often failing in their expectations. They were contented to commence life as their mothers and fathers had before them with nothing but what they could manufacture and devise from the cabin down to all their furniture and dress. Instead of spending their time lamenting their sad fortune, they were happy in their love for each other and for the great blessing of perfect health which they enjoyed.

The possessions of these people worried them not at all for neither of them had anything but a small wardrobe of common, warm clothes. They had the great book of nature before them and were happy studying its changing scenes. Neither did they worry about dressmakers for they all made their own clothing from shoe pacs and moccasins to the hats or bonnets which they wore. There was no change of fashion to keep up with and they did not worry about what this or that one had for they all dressed alike and employed their time about more useful things than learning the different styles of making dresses and clothing. They enjoyed life as they found it and loved the simple amusements that all engaged in at that date. Many could go on the puncheon floor and dance for hours without fatigue. They had free use of their bodies, not being encumbered with tight belts that hindered them from breathing and did not know what a corset was, that garment which at this date holds the body of its victims as if in the grip of a vise. Thus they could use every part of their body as freely as nature intended it to be used. In raising their children these hardy women furnished all the food they needed in infancy from their own breasts, thus laying the foundations for strong men and women to take their places.

The clothing of the men and boys was in keeping with their daily life and made for the most part of deer skins. When this was well dressed it made comfortable and serviceable shirts, leggings and coats. Sometimes the women made their petticoats of this very useful and serviceable material. The deer, elk and buffalo skins furnished the material from which all foot-wear was made.

In an early day there were many scattered herds of buffalo in all sections of Indiana but no such innumerable droves as the later hunters were used to see on the great western prairies. The buffalo skin was covered with a shaggy coat of kinky wool. Sometimes this was sheared and when mixed with a small portion of the wild nettle fibre, to give it strenth, it was carded and spun the same as sheep's wool was. Later on, from this coarse thread they wove a cloth using the nettle thread for chain that made strong and comfortable clothing. The buffalo hair was mixed with the fur and hair of other animals, usually the long hair of the bear, then was carded and spun. They knit this into warm, serviceable stockings but without the fiber of the nettle as it was too short to have the needed strength to hold together.

In most cases the first settlers were young men just married, who, with their young wives, their axes and their rifles and such other property as they possessed, came boldly into this then dense wilderness. If they were so fortunate as to find any before them, they would stop a few days and select a place to make their home. They then cut the logs for their cabin and with the help of their new found friends would carry the logs and put them up, covering the cabin with boards made with their axes for frows and putting weight poles on to hold the boards in place. Cracks between the logs were

A pioneer's cabin: the Lincoln home
Courtesy of the Lincoln Boyhood National Memorial, National Park Service

stopped by wedging in pieces of timber and then filling it all full of mud. A hole of the proper size was cut in the side for a door and often the only door shutter was a bear skin. For a fire place and chimney they cut out three or four logs the width wanted, at the end of the cabin and built a three-sided crib on the outside, joining it to the building. Layer upon layer of mud were then put on the inside of the crib making the jambs and backwall as high as needed to be out of danger of the fire, letting the smoke take care of itself.

The floor and carpet were of mother earth. For a bedstead they would drive a fork into the ground far enough from the side and end of the cabin, then put a pole in the fork and into a crack between the logs and another pole the other way from the fork and to a crack in the logs, thus making the end and side rails of the bedstead. After this they put other poles lengthways as close as they wanted and piled fine brush over this, covering the brush with skins of animals. At this time the proverbial blue figured coverlid made by their good mothers in their old North or South Carolina, Tennessee or Kentucky homes would come into use with such other bed clothing as they were fortunate enough to have brought with them. The deficiency, if any, was supplied by bear and deer skins.

They made a table in the corner in the same way as the bed was made only it had for a top thick boards made level with an axe. For seats the back log was used until it was wanted for its place to form the back of the fire, when its mate was put in and used for a seat until it was wanted. If they were fortunate enough to own an auger, three-legged stools were made.

Many of the first settlers for a few years lived in what was called in that day, a half-faced camp, made by putting two large forks in the ground the proper distance from a large fallen tree to make a twelve or fourteen foot pen then putting a pole from fork to fork and other poles from that one to the log as closely as they were wanted and then piling brush on this. They then rolled logs up to the two sides as high as they wanted them leaving the outer end open usually facing the south. Large fires were made at this open end during cold weather, the occupants lying with their feet to it and their heads toward the large log. Usually these camps were made in the dry season and by the time the rainy season came on they would have plenty of skins to cover them and line the sides, thus keeping the rain and cold out and drying the skins at the same time.

These brave people did the best they could to have the comforts of life but they had very little to do with. There was not a nail in a hundred miles of them. The settler's young wife, his cabin, rifle, axe and possibly a horse were all his earthly possessions, but he was rich in good health, determination and pluck. With his axe he cleared a few acres for corn and vegetables, with his rifle he could have plenty of the choicest meats and skins of bear, deer, beaver, otter and raccoon to exchange for salt, ammunition and a few necessities of life, when he could get his furs to market probably seventy-five miles away.

About what was going on in the outside world he knew nothing and cared less for he had a world of his own around him, fresh and crude as nature could make it. Probably he had not more than two neighbors and they three to five miles away, the only means of communication between them being made on foot over a path running around fallen tree tops and over logs, a blaze made on a tree or sapling now and then keeping them in the right direction. He had severed all connection with his old home and the outside world bidding adieu to mother and friends and to the early associations that are so dear to all. With all this sacrifice he was happy and contented and determined to face the great battle of life and to win. Nature's volumes were ever open before him and he studied well, learning the things needful for his protection. He was threatened with danger from the lurking savages who ever watched for an opportunity to destroy him and his home and in many cases did kill and capture the whole family, but still others came to fill their places.

When two or three had settled in the same place they built forts and in dangerous times moved their families into them remaining there much of the time during the summer and fall months. While the women were there their husbands and fathers were in the wilderness watching the slipping enemy, sometimes killing one and again several of them. It got so that the Indians dreaded them and came less frequently. The pioneers determined to drive them away so that the danger to their families would cease. Finally they hunted the Indians in bands and in many battles defeated them. They met them on their own grounds, defeating and driving them out of this region and on the ruins of their savage wigwams this beautiful country has been made.

. . . .

The early settlers, as a rule married when they were young; there was no inequality in the way for all were on the same level. If the young man was a good hunter and a good soldier if need be, that was all the requirements needed. The young girl had no bad habits and was industrious and healthy. She had learned from her mother the simple forms of housekeeping. Probably they did not have a cent of money between them. In many cases it was hard for the father of the sons, who were first married in the wilds of this country to get the needed means for the legal part of the ceremony.

When it first became known that there was to be a wedding, everybody old and young, were in great glee in anticipation of the coming feast and the continued frolic which would follow and which generally lasted until two days after the infare, the wedding reception at the groom's father, and until their house was built and properly warmed by an all night's dancing. Then it was turned over to the young people who assumed their position in society as one more family added to the sparsely settled region. Everybody in the whole neighborhood knew that he would be invited; in fact the custom on such an occasion was that no invitation was needed and the latch string was out to all comers and especially to the neighbors. The custom of the celebration at the home of the bride has been in vogue as long as the United States has been settled by the white people.

It is not to be wondered at that everybody was on the qui vive when a wedding was on hand, for there was no other gathering where all could go. On the day of the wedding the candidate and his best fellows, probably as many as ten, who had been his friends in the chase and on the scout, gathered at his father's home. The first thing to do was to select two of the best mounted who were to run for the bottle which took place when they arrived within one-half mile of the bride-elect. They timed their march so as to arrive about noon, the wedding usually taking place just before the noon meal. When they got to the point near the home, the word was given and the two young men started at break-neck speed trying their best to win. A bottle of corn whiskey was given to the young man who first passed a given point. He then turned his horse and, riding at the top of his speed, carried the bottle to the approaching party and treated them all to its contents. I well remember a tree shown to me some years ago on the Jackson Martin farm near Littles in Pike county, where a Mr. Martin was killed while running for the bottle: the horse became scared at something and ran against the tree fracturing the young man's skull.

After the return of the racing party the company continued to the house where they found all the people of the neighborhood assembled. Nearly every section had some one with ministerial license who would solemnize the wedding; there was no legal light nearer than the county seat, which was often fifty miles away.

After the ceremony was over the feast began, which was a feast indeed of the best things to be obtained in the country; all sorts of meats and bread made from meal, pounded in a mortar and baked on a hoe or Johnny-cake board. Wild honey was there in abundance as a bee tree could be found on any forty acres, often as many as a dozen of them. Possibly the dinner was served on a table or platform, covered with three foot boards seventy-five or one hundred feet long, and over this was laid a piece of linen cloth that had been lying in the garden for weeks to bleach. This cloth was made entirely by the bride. All the dishes in the neighborhood had been borrowed as the supply was very scant, only a few pewter plates, a few pewter spoons, but horn and wooden ones filled the need and the party [was] jovial and happy; everyone enjoying themselves.

After the dinner was over the old folks started for their homes, the younger people making preparations for a dance that was to last until broad daylight. They did not understand the fancy dancing of this day but the figures were four handed reels and what they called square sets. Some of the people from Virginia understood dancing a reel that was called in old Virginia—"hoedown." The musician was usually a middle aged man who was an expert with the violin before leaving the older settled sections.

The infare was the same as the wedding; two young men raced for the bottle and the gathering was the same people as on the day before. The feast of good things was enjoyed by all. After the dinner was over and the old folks had gone to their homes the young folks started the dance in which everyone took part. Their dress was all of home manufacture, bride's and all, they were of the most comfortable sort.

The honeymoon of the young people was not extensive in travel. They did not have the worry of packing large traveling trunks nor were there any old shoes thrown after them for there were none to throw.

The first thing to do after the infare was to build a house to live in, but before they could have charge of their new home there must be the regulation house warming. . . .

After a favorable site had been selected all the neighbors helped in cutting and hauling the logs. The first thing to do was to cut three large logs the length the building was wanted and scutch one side and lay them so they were level, on a range with each other. On this the first two end logs were placed, then the puncheons laid, meeting on the middle log for the foundation. The puncheons were first faced with an ax to cause them to lie level. Then the foot adz came into play, making the floor level and smooth. The side and end logs were laid on and notched down so as to make the cracks as small as they could and the walls strong. Usually the corner men scored the logs, each way half the length, until they met the other corner men. The scores were scutched off, making the walls look much better than round logs with bark on. At the square of the house usually about eight feet above the floor, two end logs projected about fifteen inches beyond the wall and usually other logs were laid across the building projecting the same as the end log and the proper distance apart to receive four foot boards for the loft. The butting logs, as they were called, were laid up notched to fit and pinned to the cross logs. Against the butting logs the first course of boards for the roof rested. The slope for the roof was made by cutting the end logs above the square two and one-half feet shorter. The next side log was laid some two feet from the wall, projecting over at each end two feet. This was called a ridge pole or log for the boards to lie on. The same was continued until the top log was in place where the boards of both sides of the roof met, forming the comb. Small logs were split open the length of the ridge pole for the purpose of weighting the roof so the boards would be level and stay in place. The weight poles were tied at each end with hickory withs to the end of the ridge poles. The door was made by cutting out the logs on one side the width wanted and pinning heavy pieces of upright timbers to the end of the logs by boring a hole through the timber and into the end of the logs, which made it very solid. A similar opening was made at the end, only wider, for a chim-

A home in the woods, 1820: future site of Indianapolis
Courtesy of George S. Cottman

ney. A three sided crib of logs joined to the end logs of the house was made high enough above where the back wall came to form the foundation for the chimney. Timber was driven down to form a place so that clay could be pounded in to make the hearth and raise the fire place even with the floor. After this mud mixed with grass was made and large cats or lumps were pounded in between the boards placed to shape the fire place and the logs, until it was as high as needed and then the chimney was started by drawing it in like a partridge trap until it was of the proper size to draw well, then built with sticks and clay until above the roof. The cracks between the logs of the house were filled with chinking of timber and plastered with mud. The door shutter was made by riving thick boards the length wanted, then putting heavy pieces across called battens then pinning them fast. Heavy wooden hinges were put on by pinning two pieces across the door and auger holes bored through them where they extended over the door's edge, then two butts for the hinges were pinned on the logs inside to a piece called facing with round tenon made on them. The door was then hung by fitting the auger holes over the round tenons. A heavy latch was made that when fastened on the inside could not be opened, without the proverbial latch string of buck skin through a hole in the door and hanging on the outside was used in lifting the latch. When completed the door could not be opened without great power being used. On each side and on the ends of the room a peep hole was left so that what went on on the outside could be seen and if need be could be used for a port hole to shoot from. A heavy piece of timber fitted into these peep holes; windows they could not have as long as there was any danger from Indians.

The gun rack over the door was usually made by fastening the prongs of deer horns in an auger hole. A good lamp was made by forming a cup out of clay and burning it hard. When this was filled with bear's oil, and fitted with a cotton wick, it made a very good light.

Hunting for game through the long days was the most laborious work that could be done. Often when the snow was melting and the creeks and branches overflowing, the hunter waded through the wet all day, at night returning to his humble home all worn out, many times, however, with three to six turkeys tied to his back and again with two to four pairs of venison hams and the hides of the deer. While all were fond of the chase and of necessity had to follow it, yet no labor ever performed by man was more trying on the constitution.

When the spring season came on the deer were poor and they were let alone until the crop was put in. Before planting the crop more acres of ground had to be cleared and the brush and logs burned, the rails made and the fence put around it. This required great labor. Besides his own work the farmer had to assist his few neighbors in rolling their logs so that they would help him in return. Often new comers had to have houses raised. With all his labor he put in his crop in good season and the virgin soil, with little stirring,

Clearing the land
Courtesy of the Indiana Historical Society

produced bountifully supplies of corn and vegetables for his stock and table. If the family had boys they aided their father in the crops from the time they were eight years old. If the mother's side of the house had the most help then the strong healthy girls helped their father in putting in his corn and in tending it. Industry was a virtue that was always in force for there were no idlers. . . .

[The] mother worked from early morning until late at night preparing the needed clothing for the family and doing her household work. The daughters stood nobly by their mother, helping her in every way they could. As the mother grew older they relieved her of the care and weariness of the household duties and went forward in all the needed preparation for the home. The boys, were ever in the fields with their father at work, and when the corn was cribbed they followed him in the chase, killing bear, deer and turkeys for the needs of the family. When winter had come they would go three or four miles away to some neighbor's house where subscription school was being taught for a month or so, thus gathering the first principles of an education.

When these healthy boys and girls came home from school and the daily duties were gone through with, the girls preparing the evening meal, milking the cows and caring for all the household work, the boys attending to their stock and cutting wood for the fire, preparing large back logs to be placed against the back wall of the chimney. After supper was over and the dishes cleared away one of the girls would bring her cards and wool to make the rolls for another who had the large spinning wheel making the rolls into thread. The old people and the rest of the family sat around the fire talking of the events of the day. They had no books but the bible and possibly an old English reader—newspapers they had never seen. After awhile one marries and leaves the old home and then another, until they all have homes of their own clustering around the old homestead which usually fell to the youngest.

This is the way this country has been peopled. True, many have moved to other parts of the country, but in every part of Indiana, second and third generations from the old pioneers yet occupy and control the country outside the towns.

The dress of these people was suitable for the life they had to lead. The hunting shirt was worn by all the men and was made of various sorts of material. It was a loose frock coat coming down below the middle of the thighs. The sleeves were very large. The front part of the garment was made very full, so much so that it would lap over more than a foot on each side, when it was belted. The cape was very large and full, much like the comfortable long capes worn by our cavalry soldiers during the war of the Rebellion. They were ornamented with a heavy fringe around the bottom and down the shoulder seams and a row on the cape about half way from the bottom to the collar. The bosom of these hunting shirts when the belt was fastened was always used by the hunter to carry the things needed for his convenience and comfort. On one side the tomahawk and on the other the hunting knife were each fastened to a loop made in the belt. These two weapons were indispensable and every hunter carried them. The hunting shirt was mostly made out of linsey cloth, some were made out of linen, the cloth made thick by filling made from tow which was gathered from the last hackling of the flax. There were many made out of dressed deer skins for summer and fall wear but they were very cold in the winter time. The skin coats were fantastically ornamented in the fashion of the Indians. The hunting shirts were of any color to suit the fancy of the owner. Some of them were very gay but those intended for the chase or scout were usually a dull color so as not to be easily distinguished. The undershirts, or vests as we now call them, were made of any material they could get. The breeches were made close fitting and over them a pair of buckskin leggins were worn fringed down the outside seams like the Indians. A pair of moccasins for their foot covering and protection were much better for the purpose of hunting and scouting than shoes, which they could not get, as no noise was made in walking. They were made of buckskin in one piece, with a gathered seam along the top of the foot and from the bottom of the heel to the ankle joint. Flaps were left on each side so as to reach some distance up the leg to be covered over with the lower part of the leggins, and all held in place by strong thongs of buckskin tied around just above the ankle joint, to keep the snow and dirt out of the moccasins.

It required only a little time to make a pair of moccasins. For this purpose and for mending the holes worn in them an awl made out of any kind of iron was an indispensable tool, and with a ball of thongs or strings cut from a dressed deer skin, was in the shot pouch or hunting shirt pocket of every hunter. In the winter the moccasins were very cold and dry deer hair was stuffed into them to keep the feet warm. If the wearer owned any red pepper pods a liberal supply of it was put in with the hair. I have heard my father say that in cold wet weather the moccasin was only a little better than going barefooted.

The head dress of the men was as varied as there were kinds of animals. Bear, beaver, fox, raccoon and even the sullen opossum furnished material for headwear. In the summer time they had hats made from the wild oat straw and from the flag that grew in ponds. Even the inside bark of the mulberry roots was cleaned and worked into very light durable hats for summer wear. Gloves were made out of the skins of small animals with the fur on the inside.

The women did not have as elaborate costumes as the men, but they dressed at all times to suit their work and the weather if they had the material to make their clothing from. The linsey skirt or petticoat as it was termed then, worn over some sort of dress of linen or cotton, made much like ladies wear now for night gowns, was the usual costume. If worn in cold weather a waist or jacket was added to the skirt. Their clothing was warm and comfortable. In warm weather they invariably went barefooted, but during the cold weather they had moccasins or shoe pacs, a sort of half moccasin. They made shawls of flannel the same as they made blankets of any color that suited their fancy with bright colored stripes at each end and a heavy fringe sewed on all around it. Later when they got to raising cotton in sufficient quantities, they made a very pretty and serviceable cotton dress with stripes of many colors. For head dress they always wore caps night and day with a frill on the front edge often out of the same goods, very old ladies often wore dark colored caps made of some fine goods brought from their early childhood home. They wore the regulation sun bonnet of that period which differed but little from that worn by many at this time. The head piece or crown was made with casing for splits of wood to keep it in shape with a gathered curtain sewed around the lower edge. These hooded bonnets were good shades from the sun and when taken in connection with the other dress of that day were very becoming to the wearer. For handkerchiefs they had small home-made squares of white cotton cloth of their own spinning and weaving. For gloves leather made out of squirrel hides dressed, was used and they were as soft as the best kid and lasted for all time.

Often it was very difficult to secure the raw material to make this clothing. The flax crop at times failed as the land was too loose for it to do well in. The flax roots are very short and the new soil of that date was a very loose loam and in dry weather the flax would die out and the crop fail. At such time, when the flax failed, some one would go to the rich creek bottoms where nettles grew in abundance and secure loads of the stalks. After it was dried and rotted they broke and worked it the same as they did the flax. A strong thread could be spun from the fiber covering the stems and this thread was woven into cloth and made into clothing. When they had wool and linen thread they wove linsey cloth, the best that could be had for comfort and durability. Every woman was her own weaver. The girls who were fourteen years old could spin and weave and make their own clothing. Their clothing was such as they could make by hand. These early pioneers tanned their own leather. A large trough for a tanning vat back of the smoke house or in it as was often the case, was an indispensable piece of property. The bark of the black oak, carefully secured in the spring when the sap was up, was dried to be used later for tanning their leather. The skins of deer, wolves and later on of bears and cows that had died or had been killed by the panthers were saved and dried until such times as they were wanted to be put into the vat. They were first put in a trough with strong ashes and kept there until the hair became loose and could be scraped off. Then they were put into the vat and the oak bark was pounded up as finely as needed and put in layer after layer as the skins were placed in the trough. When the oak liquor or ooze had been used until it commenced to lose its strength it was drawn off and a new supply of bark put into the vat. After being in the vat for several months the hides were taken out. A board or slab was driven into the ground and the top end was shaved to an edge. Then the hides were scraped back and forth over the edge of the slab until they became pliable; then bear's oil was put on and worked in until every part of the skin was soft. Our people learned from the Indians that the brains of the deer was the best of all material to make the tanned leather soft and pliable and to keep it so. It took nearly three large dressed buckskins to make a leather suit, including a hunting shirt, leggings and two pairs of moccasins.

Senator Smith's Reminiscences

OLIVER H. SMITH

The record of Indiana's historic past has been enriched by a number of contemporaneous writings. One of the most valuable is *Early Indiana Trials and Sketches* by Oliver H. Smith, an attorney, politician (a Democrat, then a Whig), and railroad promoter of central Indiana during the antebellum period. A native of Pennsylvania, Smith came to Indiana in 1817 at the age of twenty-three, and he began his legal career in 1820. Elected to the Indiana General Assembly in 1822, and to Congress in 1826, Smith served a single term in the United States Senate from 1837 to 1843, after which he moved to Indianapolis and devoted himself to railroading. His book began as a series of newspaper articles in 1857 that recalled various incidents associated with Indiana's earliest years of statehood, particularly its robust and personalized system of justice. Because of the popularity of Smith's first installments in the Indianapolis newspaper, he expanded the series to include a number of "sketches" and other material. These were collected and published in book form in 1858, the year before Smith's death.

The selections below are representative of Smith's prose—straightforward, vibrant, and laced with humor and frankness. From his sketches come information on the art of frontier politics, an early Indiana legislature and its members, the important role played by circuit-riding ministers on the frontier, the difficulties of travel in the days before railroads and automobiles, the hardiness and ingenuity of individual settlers, and much more.

Early Condition of Indiana.

WHILE my mind is on Indiana, the reader will excuse me for deferring my sketches of the House of Representatives, the Senate, the Supreme Court

From *Early Indiana Trials and Sketches* (1858), pp. 116-117, 76-77, 80-81, 97, 28-29.

and other matters at Washington, to a more convenient season. And, as these sketches seem to be looked upon as a part of the history of early Indiana, while I make no such pretensions, and refer the public to the authentic history of the State by my valued friend John B. Dillon, Esq., State historian, I may be excused for stating some matters that will be only interesting to the citizens of our State who would like to compare Indiana as she was, with Indiana as she is. I shall not even attempt the comparison, but leave the reader to make it for himself.

At the time I came to the State in March, 1817, there was not a railroad in the United States, nor a canal west of the Alleghany mountains. The telegraph had not been discovered, fire was struck by the flint and steel, the falling spark was caught in "punk" taken from the knots of the hickory tree.—There was not a foot of turnpike road in the State, and plank roads had never been heard of; the girdled standing trees covering the cultivated fields, the shovel-plow the only cultivator, no roads west of Whitewater, not a bridge in the State; the traveling all done on horseback, the husband mounted before on the saddle, with from one to three of the youngest children in his arms—the wife, with a spread cover reaching to the tail of the horse, seated behind, with the balance of the children unable to walk in her lap. We young gentlemen retained the luxury of a single horse; not a carriage nor buggy in all the country. After some years Mr. Lovejoy brought a buggy without a top, to Connersville, from New England. I borrowed it to ride to Wayne county, but I gave up the buggy and took my horse, for fear the people would think me proud, and it would injure my election to Congress.

The finest farms around Connersville in one of the most beautiful countries in the world, cleared, with orchards and common buildings, were $5 to $10 per acre. I bought the fine farm of one hundred and sixty acres, adjoining Connersville, the same now the residence of my friend Hon. Samuel W. Parker, of John Adair, of Brookville, for $9 per acre, in three annual installments without interest. The brick two-story dwelling in which I lived when I was elected to Congress, in the heart of Connersville, twenty-six feet front, well finished, with back kitchen, lot 26 by 180, good stable, I bought of Sydnor Dale for $325,—which was considered a high price at the time. The excellent farm over the river one mile below town, in 1828, I bought of William Denman for $5 per acre, in payments. There was very little money in the country, and produce was equally low in proportion. I bought the finest qualities of stall-fed beef, and corn-fed hogs, for family use, at a cent and a half per pound; corn ten cents, wheat twenty-five cents per bushel, wood delivered and cut short at the door at a dollar per cord; boarding at common houses, with lodging, from a dollar to two dollars a week, and at the very best hotels two dollars and a half. The first year I traveled the circuit, my fees fell short of two hundred dollars; and the second, when they increased to three hundred, I felt as safe as a Stephen Girard. All my wants were supplied, I owed nothing, and had money in my pocket.—No white man had settled more than five miles west of Connersville at that time. . . .

An Early Legislature in Indiana.

In August 1822, I was elected to the Legislature from Fayette, and late in November mounted my pony and started for Corydon, the temporary seat of government. My way led by Madison, then a small village. Late in the evening of the third day from home, I rode up to a little frame house, about the center of the town, to which I was directed as the only hotel. My horse was taken at the steps by a slim, flaxen-haired youth of a hostler. I had a first-rate supper, a sweet, clean bed, a good breakfast, and left on my journey in the morning, the landlord, as I supposed, being from home. The next Monday the House of Representatives met in the old court-house at Corydon. John F. Ross, the clerk, called the roll; "County of Jefferson," when to my surprise, my flaxen-headed hostler stepped forward, in the person of Gen. Milton Stapp, in after years Lieutenant Governor, and one of the most distinguished men of the State. The roll calling progressed, as I stood by the side of the General he bowed and smiled. The "County of Vanderburgh and Warrick:" I saw advancing a slender, freckled-faced boy, in appearance eighteen or twenty years of age. I marked his step as he came up to my side, and have often noticed his air since. It was Gen. Joseph Lane, of Mexican and Oregon fame in after years. The house was composed mostly of new members, and was said to be the greenest ever convened in the State, myself included. We had, however, a few who would pass even at the present day. Gen. Stapp, Isaac Howk, Horace Bassett, John Dumont, Isaac Julian, Pinkney James, Gen. Burnett, William A. Bullock, Lucius H. Scott, Dennis Pennington, Benjamin V. Beckes, Dr. Sylvanius Everts, Nathaniel Hunt, and others. The session lasted six weeks, and perhaps no Legislature ever met and adjourned in the State, doing less harm.—There were a few measures, however, in which I took an active part, that may bear mentioning. The poll-tax system was first established, the exemption in favor of widows, of personal estate to the value of one hundred dollars, from the debts of deceased husbands; and the act giving a representation to "the new purchase," to strengthen the middle and northern parts of the State, in passing the law for the removal of the seat of government from Corydon to Indianapolis. This latter act was warmly contested, debated weeks and finally passed by a very close vote. The first constitution provided that "Corydon in Harrison county, shall be the seat of government of the State of Indiana, until the year eighteen hundred and twenty-five, and until removed by law." It further provided, "the General Assembly may, within two years after their first meeting, and shall in the year eighteen hundred and twenty-five, and every other subsequent term of five years, cause an enumeration to be made, of all the white male inhabitants above the age of twenty-one years; the number of Representatives shall at the several periods of making such enumeration be fixed by the General Assembly, and apportioned among the several counties." The question was whether it was competent for the Legislature to take the census and make the apportionment at any intermediate time, or whether it could only be done at the expiration of every five years. We carried the bill in favor of the first construction, and the seat of government was removed years sooner than it would otherwise have been. We had little important business before us; Gov. Hendricks was inaugurated, and Judge Parke elected to revise the laws.

An Electioneering Operation.

An incident occurred in the election of Treasurer of State that may be instructive to candidates. Daniel C. Lane was the incumbent.—There was no tangible objection against him as an officer, but it was rumored that he could see a short rich man over the head of a tall poor man. His competitor was Samuel Merrill, then of Vevay, afterward for years Treasurer of State, and President of the State Bank. The day for the election was not fixed. I was among the warm friends of Mr. Merrill. Our prospects for his election were very poor—chances as ten to one against us. Mr. Lane, as was the custom, began his course of entertainments, and, as his house was small, he only invited to his first dinner the Senators and the Speaker of the House of Representatives, Gen. Washington Johnston,—intending, no doubt, to feast the members of the House on some other evening before the election.

Next morning the House met, and a few of us understanding each other passed around among the uninitiated, and soon had them in a perfect state of excitement against Lane. The time had now come, and I introduced a resolution inviting the Senate to go into the election instanter. The resolution was reciprocated, and down came the Senate. The joint convention was immediately held, and Mr. Merrill was elected by a large majority, the Senators voting for Mr. Lane and the members of the House for Mr. Merrill, who made the State a first-rate officer. The Legislature adjourned, and I returned home through the woods. This ended my legislative career in the State, as I was never afterward a candidate.

Electioneering.

I HAVE sketched the most important trials that were had during my two years as circuit prosecuting attorney, which ended with the spring term of 1826, when I became a candidate for Congress and resigned. Amos Lane was appointed my successor. The most of the sketches that will be given are of after occurrences.

My competitor for Congress in 1826, the Hon. John Test, was one of the first men in the State, had been on the court bench, was a fine lawyer, a good speaker, and had represented the district three full terms. The contest on my part looked at first almost hopeless. Stump speaking was just coming in fashion. The people met our appointments by thousands. The judge had his high character to aid him, and I brought to my aid a strong voice, reaching to the very extremes of the largest crowds. The judge went for the graduation of the public lands, and I went for home gifts to actual settlers. My position was the most acceptable to the masses. We met in Allenville, Switzerland county, on one occasion. The whole country was there. The judge was speaking, and for the first time introduced the new subject of railroads. He avowed himself in favor of them, and said he had voted for the Buffalo and New Orleans road, and then rising to the top of his voice, "I tell you, fellow-citizens, that in England they run the cars thirty miles an hour, and they will yet be run at a higher speed in America." This was enough. The crowd set up a loud laugh at the expense of the judge. An old fellow, standing by me, bawled out, "You are crazy, or do you think we are all fools; a man could not live a moment at that speed." The day was mine. The judge had ruined his prospects by telling such an improbable story at that day. On another occasion the judge was speaking in favor of the tariff in the highest terms. The people knew but little about it, but what they had heard was decidedly against it; few knew the meaning of the word, and fewer what it was like. One old fellow said he had never seen one, but he believed "it was hard on sheep."

Perils of a Congressional Campaign.

THERE was fun in those days. We had no parties then, and there was some life in a contest—very different from after times, when the candidates had to be engrafted into the party stock, and drew all their life and strength from the party to which they belonged.

On one occasion in after years I was speaking at a battalion muster in Ripley county, and had spoken over two hours. I noticed an old man leaning against a tree in front of me. As I closed he roared out, "Mr. Smith you have made one of the best speeches I ever heard, I agree with all you have said. Will you answer me one question before you leave the stand." "Most certainly." "Will you vote for General Jackson?" "No, sir, I shall vote for Henry Clay." "Then you can't get my vote." The question was between Jackson and Clay, and not between myself and [my] competitor as to who should go to Congress, with the old man then. The contest grew warm, and more and more doubtful. My stock was rising, and with it my spirits. My district covered one-third of the state.

I had not, as yet, visited the county of Allen, some hundred miles north of Randolph. There were no roads, nothing but Indian paths, to travel at that day through the wilderness. In the early part of May I turned the head of my pony north for Fort Wayne. The streams were high and the path for miles under water in places. I rode in that campaign a small brown Indian pony, a good swimmer, a fine pacer, and a fine traveler. The first day after I left the settlements at the Mississinewa, I reached the Indian station at Francis Godfroy's. The chief was [away] from home, but one of his wives came out at an opening in the picketing, and pointed toward Fort Wayne; the chief was there. She could not speak a word of English. I pointed to the stable, then to my horse, then to my mouth, then laid my head on my hands, shut my eyes, and commenced snoring. She seized the reins of the bridle; I dismounted and passed through the pickets into the house. My faithful pony was fed. Night came on at length; supper was announced, by motions; corn bread, venison, and sassafras tea, a bear skin on the floor for a bed, and sound sleeping followed. Breakfast of the same over, and I was about starting alone, when there came up an Indian that could speak a little broken English. I agreed with him for a guide for two dollars for a day to get me over the Salamonia and Wabash rivers. We were soon on our horses, and off went my guide at full speed on his pony, and was soon out of sight. I overtook him, however, at the Salamonia. In we went, he leading. The ponies swam beautifully; and away we started for the Wabash.

Itinerant Preachers.

I SHOULD be false to the history of Early Indiana were I to pass by in silence the itinerant Methodist preachers who contributed so much to the establishment of good order, quiet, intelligence, morality and religion among the first settlers, and without intending to give offense to others, I venture the remark, that early Indiana, nay, more, Indiana to-day, owes more to the itinerant Methodist preachers than to all other religious denominations combined.

Their system carried their churches into every settlement, and where two or three were gathered together, there was a Methodist preacher or exhorter in the midst. They were at the bed-side of the dying man on their knees, and at the grave their voices were heard in songs of praise. Other denominations waited for the people to come up from the wilderness to worship, while the itinerant Methodist preacher mounted his horse, and sought out their cabins in the woods, held his meetings there, carrying the Gospel, and leaving the Bible and Hymn Book as he went.

. . . .

A Sheriff Outwitted.

IN early times, before the first land-sales of the beautiful Whitewater valley, where Connersville, Liberty, Cambridge City, Centerville and Richmond now stand, there lived upon the east bank of Whitewater, a mile above Connersville, a most remarkable woman by the name of Betty

A circuit rider
Courtesy of the Indiana Historical Society

Frazier. She was a small, tough-looking, rather swarthy woman; her husband, George Frazier, was a poor cripple, and with their children was entirely supported by Betty. They had settled upon a small fraction of government land, intending to purchase at the sales. The land-office was at Cincinnati, and General James Findlay was the Receiver. The spring of the year, after a severe winter, had come; the sales were to take place the next winter, and Betty had the season before her to raise the money to pay for her land. She commenced with a young stock of hogs, caring for them daily, driving them to the best mast, and preparing a good patch of corn for the fattening process. She had one horse only to tend her crop, and to ride to Cincinnati when she drove her hogs down to sell, and buy her land.

One day about mid-summer she saw a horseman ride up to her cabin in full uniform. She met him at the bars: "Well, General Hanna, how do you do?" "Very well, Mrs. Frazier." "What on earth has brought you all the way from Brookville to my poor cabin?" "I am very sorry to tell you, Mrs. Frazier, that I am the sheriff, and have an execution against your property." "Well, General, I always submit to the law; come with me to the stable and I will give you my only horse as the best I can do." There were no "exemption laws" then. Betty and the General proceeded to the stable. It was a strong log building with a single door, no window, overlaid with a solid platform of logs, and filled above with hay for the horse. The door fastened outside with a large wooden pin in a log. "There, General, is the horse—

take him." The General stepped in and commenced untying the horse. Betty immediately fastened the door outside, driving the pin into the hole to its full length, and left the General to his reflections while she attended to her household affairs. Time passed away; night came on; but no relief to the captured General. Morning came, and with it came Betty. "Well, General, how did you sleep last night." "Not very well. I am ready to compromise this matter; if you will let me out and show me the ford over Whitewater (the river was muddy and high), I will leave you and the horse and return the execution 'no property found.'" "Upon honor?" "Yes, upon honor." Betty opened the door. The General mounted his horse and silently followed Betty down to the river side. "There, General, you will go in just above the big sycamore, and come out at that haw-bush you see." The General started; at the second step both horse and rider were under water out of sight, and the chapeau of the General was seen floating down the river. Still, he being one of the pioneers, and his horse a trained swimmer, gallantly stemmed the current, and exactly struck the haw-bush, his horse swimming to the very shore, while Betty stood on the bank screaming—"I guess the Brookville officers will let me alone now till I have sold my pigs and bought my land." The General rode on dripping wet to his brigade that mustered that day. But the end was not yet. Time rolled on; the pigs grew to be well fatted hogs. Betty mounted her pony; the little boys started the hogs for Cincinnati; they had ten days to get there before the land-sales; the distance was about seventy miles. Nothing unusual occurred on the road until they arrived at New Trenton, at Squire Rockafellow's. The night was stormy; the snow fell deep; next morning found Betty at the usual hour on the pony, well wrapped, with *an infant a few hours old in her bosom.* She arrived with her hogs at Cincinnati the day before the sale, sold them for cash, and the late General Findlay told me that she stood by his side on the box and bid off her land, with her infant in her arms. Surely "Truth is stranger than fiction."

The Shooting Match

ROBERT CARLTON, ESQ. [BAYNARD RUSH HALL]

Baynard Rush Hall (1798–1863), a graduate of Union College and Princeton Theological Seminary, came to Indiana during its first decade of statehood to take up duties as principal of Indiana Seminary. Later when the seminary became Indiana College (in 1838 it became

From *The New Purchase or, Seven and a Half Years in the Far West* (1843, reprinted 1916), pp. 105–112.

Indiana University), Hall served as professor of ancient languages for three years before returning to the east in 1831. Twelve years later he published a book about his experiences in the central one-third of Indiana, the part acquired from the Indians by treaty in 1818. Although often supercilious in tone and full of ridicule for his unwashed and ill-prepared "scholars," Professor Hall provides a rich and detailed account of people, conditions, and frontier culture. Hall's style is florid, but he has superb descriptive powers as well as a wide variety of experiences to relate.

Professor James A. Woodburn, in his introduction to the Indiana Centennial Edition of Hall's *The New Purchase,* has called it "an immortal book . . . because it contains the most valuable history of this Hoosier land in its early beginnings; because it relates in graphic and racy style personal adventures, western scenes and characters, college jealousies and dissensions, the state of popular culture or lack of culture, and the social conditions in a large part of this new country in its early days. Here are found vivid descriptions of the varied aspects of frontier life that Hall witnessed and of which he was a part,—the modes of travel, the roads, the cabin homes and inns, the settler's hospitality, his food, his clothing, the games, the weddings, the barbecues, the rifle-matches, the stump speeches, the college exhibitions, the court trials, the 'shiv-ar-ree', the pigeon-shooting. Here is history,—not of wars and dynasties and states, but of the life of a people" (pp. ix–x).

The 1916 edition of *The New Purchase* restores the original 1843 volume in full (an 1855 edition had omitted over 100 pages concerning college president Andrew Wylie, with whom Hall had had a prolonged disagreement); it also contains a key that identifies as fully as possible the people and places to which Hall gives fictitious names in the book (e. g., Bloomington is called Woodsville, Indianapolis is Timberopolis). In the selection that follows, Hall describes a frontier "line shooting match" in which he had participated. For more information on Hall, see the sketch by James A. Woodburn in the *Dictionary of American Biography,* VIII, 118–119; see also Richard E. Banta (ed.), *Indiana Authors and Their Books, 1816–1916* (1949), and Arthur W. Shumaker, *A History of Indiana Literature* (1962).

READER, were you ever fired with the love of rifle shooting? If so, the confidence now reposed in your honour will not be abused, when told my love for that noble art is unabated: nay, let me whisper in your ear—

"What yet?"

Yes—in the corner of my bed chamber a genuine New Purchase rifle! And all the forest equipments,—otter skin bullet pouch with a tail gracefully pendent—a scalping knife in a sheath adorned with porcupine quills—a savage little hatchet—a powder horn, and its loader of deer-horn, tied on with a deer sinew and holding enough to prime a shot gun—a mould running three hundred and twenty-five to the pound—wipers—an iron hook to tote squirrels—and some hundred and fifty patches all strung and fastened to the leather strap of the pouch—ay! and a pair of moccasins and pair of green leggins, and—

"Do you ever yet go a gunning?"

Gunning!—alas! is that degrading appellation to be applied to hunting!—but how should they know? Yes, I do steal off sometimes and try to fancy myself in the woods. But what are these *scrawney* little trees fenced in to prevent cattle from eating them down? Where is a squirrel, or a raccoon, or a fox, or a turkey to hide? And where can one lose himself and camp out? No grand and centurial trees here reaching up to heaven and sending roots to the centre of the earth! No hollow caverns in enormous trunks, where wolves and bears may lurk! No vast sheltering expanse of tops where panthers and wild cats may find security. How vain to think of crawling through a thicket of undergrowth to the leeside of a deer, stopping with moccasined foot—stirring no leaves—cracking no twig—shaking no bushes—till one can get within the magical distance, a hundred yards. Nothing, nothing here, to excite dread, call forth skill, reward toil, and show the independence of the hunter.

True, I make-believe, like little girls, playing baby house; I say to myself, "Now Carlton, 'spose that old log away off there was a bear?—or that tame turkey a wild one?—or that cream-coloured calf a deer—or that sharp eared dog a wolf?" And instinctively I catch myself with my side that way, drawing a bead with one eye into the hind sight and fixing the other on the may-be game, and then, clicks goes the trigger. Fortunate, the rifle is not cocked. Indeed, these rehearsals are always without a load; if not, farewell to the integrity of the little knot in the old log—and to the gambols of calf and dog—good night to the eyes of farm turkies and dunghill roosters!

In vain do flocks of black-birds and robbins, and tom-tits rise!—they might perch on my shoulders: for who but a wretched dandy and shot-gun driveller, with a double-barrelled gun, a whole pound of powder! and four pounds of shot! will fire at a flock, killing two and wounding twenty? To be sure a curious stranger will sometimes meet us and politely request to see "a rifle *discharged!*" and with an incredulous smile wonder if a man can really hit a solitary single bird with so "*minute*" a ball! And then we cannot but show off, and so we begin with amazing condescension:

"Sir! do you see that little blue bird?"

"Oh! yes! that tiny creature on the next tree."

" 'Tut, No!—that to your right, on the post."

"What! that away there? too far, Sir, too far."

"Too far!—forty-five yards in a straight line!!"

Reader, we hit at any height or in any direction; but a horizontal or a little below is our preference. The rifle is better balanced, and the light, especially in opposition to the sun, is thus less dazzling and makes the cleanest bead. Hence I select, if possible, on occasions like the present a bird so placed as to render the affair more like our target firing.

"Now, Sir."—we continue—"I shall hit that bird."

"If you do, I will eat it."

"Then you will have your supper in a second or two."

And with that I set triggers—toss down my hat—feel for a level with my feet—cock rifle—turn left side to the mark—raise the piece with my thumb on the cock—incline shoulders back with knees bending outward—till the mass of man and gun rest on the base—let fall the rifle a little below object—and then, ceasing to breathe and stopping my pulse, and bringing into the hind sight a silver bead like a pin's head, I rapidly raise that bead till darkened by the feathers under the throat—and the next you see is a gentle flutter of spread wings as if the poor little creature was flying down for a worm or a crumb.

"Ah! Sir, you've only inflicted a severe wound; but really this is wonderful! I could hardly believe in this skill unless I saw it."

"Well, sir, please pick it up; the poor tit is dead enough, and never knew what hurt him." And of course, reader, it must be so, for the bird's head is off.

Such skill was of course not the work of a day. Ounces of powder and pounds of lead were spent in vain first, and many a squirrel, at the crack of the rifle, would remain chattering or eating a nut, imagining somebody was shooting somewhere; until conjecturing by the third or fourth ball pealing bark some two or three feet from him, that the firing was rather in his direction, away he would scud for fear a chance bullet should maybe hit him! But my heart was in the matter in those days. Hence it is no great marvel if in due time my rifle dealt out certain death second to none in the Purchase. What avail then concealment in the topmost branches; there was the dark spot of a body or a head amid the green leaves. What! a retreat behind crotches or into holes; there was yet the tip of an ear or point of a nose, or twinkle of an eye. Or did a squirrel expand on a small limb till his body above was a mere line of fur on the bark like feathery hair on a caterpillar? in vain, "the meat" was mine.

A squirrel once so stretched himself as to create a doubt whether a squirrel was above the branch or not; but firing *secundum artem* down he came, and, as was necessary, dead.

Yet wound external had he none; he had been killed, as is often the case, although it occurred but once with me, by concussion; the ball having struck the limb of the tree exactly under his heart.

Let none think we western people follow rifle shooting, however, for mere sport; that would be nearly as ignoble as shot gun idleness. The rifle procures, at certain seasons, the only meat we ever taste; it defends our homes from wild animals and saves our corn fields from squirrels and our hen-roosts from foxes, owls, opossums and other "varments." With it we kill our beeves and our hogs, and cut off our fowls' heads: do all things in fact, of the sort with it, where others use an axe, or a knife, or that far east savagism, the thumb and finger. The rifle is a woodman's lasso. He carries it everywhere as (a very degrading comparison for the gun, but none other occurs), a dandy a cane. All, then, who came to our tannery or store came thus armed; and rarely did a customer go, till his rifle had been tried at a mark, living or dead, and we had listened to achievements it had done and could do again. No wonder, in these circumstances, if I should practice; especially when it needed but the flash of a rifle pan to set off our in-bred magazine of love and tendencies towards bullet moulds and horn loaders! No wonder, that, after many failures, even in hitting a tree, Mr. Carlton could be seen in his glory at last, standing within lines of beholders right and left, and at forty-five yards off-hand planting bullet after bullet into the same auger hole! Reader! may you live a thousand years; but if you *must* die, unless somebody will save your life by splitting an apple on your head—(William Tell size)—at fifty yards off-hand with a rifle ball, send for me—shut your eyes for fear of flinching—and at the crack—go, your life is your own.

Old Dick is one hobby often mounted literally and maybe now too often, metaphorically, the rifle is my other: But with *this* by no means must we *bore* you; and, therefore, after narrating my famous shots in behalf of the Temperance Society, we shall for the present put the gun on the rack over the fireplace.

Glenville and myself were once, on some mercantile affairs, travelling in an adjoining county, when we came suddenly on a party preparing to shoot at a mark; and from the energy of words and gestures it was plain enough a prize of unusual importance was proposed. We halted a moment, and found the stake to be a half-barrel of whiskey. If ever, then and there was to be sharp-shooting; and without question, then and there was present every chap in the settlements that could split a bullet on his knife blade or take the rag off the bush.

"Glenville," said I, seized with a sudden whim, "lend me fifty cents; I mean to shoot."

"Nonsense! Carlton; you *can't* win here; and if you could, what does the president of a temperance society want with a barrel of whiskey?"

"John, if I can find a gun here anything like my own, I *can* win. And although I have never before won or lost a penny, I shall risk half a dollar now for the fun of the thing, and to have the satisfaction of knocking yonder barrel in the head and letting out the stuff into the branch here."

After some further discussion Glenville acquiesced, and we drew near the party; where dismounting, I made the following speech and proposal:

"Well, gentlemen, I think I can outshoot any man on the ground, if you will let us come in and any neighbour here will allow me to shoot his gun, in case I can find one to my notion; and here's my fifty cents for the chance. But, gentlemen and fellow citizens, I intend to be right out and out like a backwoodsman; and so you must all know we are cold water men, and don't believe in whiskey; and so, in case we win, the barrel is, you know, ours, and then I shall knock the article in the head. But then we are willing to pay either in money or temperance tracts the amount of treat every gentlemen will get if anybody else wins."

To this a fine, hardy looking farmer apparently some sixty years old and evidently the patriarch of the settlement, replied:

"Well, stranger, come on; you're a powerful honest man any how; and here's my hand to it; if you win, which will a sort a tough you though, you may knock the stingo in the head. And stranger, you kin have this here gun of mine, or Long Jake's thare; or any one you have a notion on. How do you shoot?"

"Off-hand, neighbour; any allowance?"

"Yes; one hundred yards with a rest; eighty-five yards off-hand."

"Agreed."

"Agreed."

Arrangements and conditions, usual in grand contests like that before us, were these:

1st. A place level as possible was selected and cleared of all intervening bushes, twigs, &c. 2d. A large tree was chosen. Against this the target shingles were to be set, and from its roots or rather trunk, were measured off towards the upper end of the cleared level, the two distances, eighty-five and one hundred yards. A pair of very fine natural dividers were used on this occasion; viz. a tall young chap's legs, who stepped with an elastic jerk, counting every step a yard; a profitable measure if one was *buying* broadcloth; but here the little surpluses on the yards were equally to the advantage of all. 3d. Cross lines at each distance, eighty-five and one hundred yards, were drawn on the measured line; and on the first the marksman stood who fired off-hand, while on the second the rests were placed or constructed. Rests depended on taste and fancy; some made their own—some used their own—some used their comrades'—and some rested the rifle against the side of a tree on the line: and of all the rests this is the best, if one is careful to place the barrel near its muzzle against the tree and not to press hard upon the barrel. Some drive in two forked stakes and place on them a horizontal piece; and some take a chair, and then seated on the ground, they have the front of the chair towards them and its legs between their feet, resting the whole gun thus upon the seat of the chair. Again, many set a small log or stone before them, and then lying down flat on their bellies, they place the muzzle on the rest and the butt of the gun on the ground near their face; and then the rifle seems as moveless as if screwed in a vice. In this way Indians and woodsmen often lie in ambuscade for deer at the licks, or enemies in war.

4th. Every man prepared a separate target. This was a poplar shingle, having near its middle a spot blackened with powder or charcoal as a ground; and on this ground was nailed at its four corners a piece of white paper about an inch square and its centre formed by a diamond hole; two corners being perpendicularly up and down. From the interior angles of the diamond were scratched with a knife point two diagonals, and at their intersection was the true centre. With a radius of four inches from this centre was then circumscribed a circle: if beyond this circumference any *one* of the allotted shots struck ay! but a hair's breadth, all other shots, even if in the very centre, were nugatory—the unlucky marksman lost.

5. Each man had three shots. And provided the three were within the circle, each was to be measured by a line from the centre of the diamond to the near edge of the bullet hole—except a ball grazed the centre, and then the line went to the centre of the hole—and then, the three separate lengths added were estimated as one string or line, the shortest securing the prize. This is called line shooting.

6th. Each one fixed, or had fixed, his target against the tree as he pleased; and then, each man was to fire his three shots in succession, without being hurried or retarded. We occupied on an average to-day every man about fifteen minutes.

More than thirty persons were assembled, out of whom had been selected seven as the best marksmen; but these, induced by the novelty, having good-naturedly admitted me, we were now eight. Of the eight, five preferred to shoot with a rest; but the old Achates, the sapling woodman that had stepped off the distances, and myself, were to fire off hand. All the rifles were spontaneously offered for the stranger's use. I chose, however, Tall Jake's; for although about a pound too heavy, it sighted like my own, and went as easy on the triggers, and carried one hundred and eighty to the pound —only five more than mine which carried one hundred and seventy-five.

Auditors and spectators now formed the double lines, standing, stooping, and lying in very picturesque attitudes, some fifteen feet each side the range of the firing, and that away down towards the target tree even, behind which several chaps as usual, planted themselves to announce at each crack the result of the shot. All this seems perilous; and yet accidents rarely happen. In all my sojourn in the Purchase we had but two. The first happened to a fine young fellow, who impatient at some delay, peeped out it is supposed, to ascertain the cause, when at the instant the rifle was fired, and its ball glancing entered his head and he fell dead in his tracks. The next happened to an elderly man, who was stationed behind a large tree awaiting the report, and who at the flash of the gun, fell from behind with one piercing cry of agony, bleeding and dying:—the trunk was hollow and in and opposite the place where our neighbour stood in apparent safety, was a mere shell, through which the ball had gone and entered his heart!

Well, the firing at length began. I have no distinct recollection of every shot. Now and then, a central ball was announced, and that followed by two others a full inch or may be an inch and an eighth even from the centre; and once, where two successive balls were within the diamond, the third, by some mischance of the rest depended on, struck on the very edge of the grand circle. Balls, too, were sometimes planted in three different corners of the paper—very good separate shots—yet proving want of steady and artistical sighting, or even a little experimenting with the edges of the hind sight; which was owing doubtless to drawing the bead to the edge and not the bottom.

A smart young fellow having made two very fair shots, boasted so grandly about his new rifle, that a grave, middle-aged hunter offered to bet a pound of lead, that if the young chap would allow him after the gun was rested for the shot, to rub his hand from the lock to the muzzle, he would so bewitch the rifle that she should miss the big tree. This was all agreed to: and then, such as knew how to bewitch rifles rapidly retreated to our rear, and such as did not, were beckoned and called till they came. All ready, the young man on the ground, and his rifle on its rest, our conjuror ran his hand slowly along the barrel, pausing an instant at the muzzle, and uttering an incantation, and then going behind the marksman, he bade him fire when he lied. This he did; and marvellous enough it was—the ball not only missed the shingle, but struck no where in the tree! Great was the astonishment and mortification of the youth; but as we magnanimously allowed him a shot extra and without witchcraft, his countenance brightened and especially when his ball now spoiled the inner edge of his diamond.

Perhaps you are curious, and wish to learn how to bewitch a rifle? I will tell on one condition:—all the spectators when a rifle is bewitched must be made to come to the rear of the firing party. Here is the recipe: let the rifle-doctor conceal in his hand a bullet small enough for the purpose, and on rubbing as far as the muzzle, let him as adroitly as possible deposit said bullet just within the said muzzle—safely betting any number of pounds of lead, that whatever else the marksman may hit, he cannot hit his shingle N.B. See that the rifle to be bewitched has no triggers set, and is not on cock, otherwise two tartars of a very unpleasant character may be caught by the rifle-doctor instead of one.

One man only took to his belly (the technical term was to fire on his belly), but as his log-rest turned a little at the third shot, the unerring bullet, following the guidance of the barrel, stuck itself plump outside the circumference named, and thus nullifying one true central ball, and one in the lower interior point or angle of his diamond. Another man was still more unfortunate. After two most excellent shots, his gun hanging fire at the third, he bawled out, "No shot!" which being a notification before the shot could be examined and reported, entitled him to another trial; but alas! the ball thus tabooed had grazed the centre! Again his gun hung fire; but now he did not *veto;* and his bullet was found sticking in the tree an honest foot above the top even of his shingle!

And now we, who fired off-hand, and thereby professed to be "crack" shots—(yet most marksmen make a *noise* there)—we began to make ready. We higgled a little as to who should lead off; not to show politeness as well bred folks in entering rooms and carriages, but because all were, the least bit however, cowed, and each wished to see what his neighbour could do first. When that kind of spirit comes crawling over a body in rifle-shooting, it must be banished in an instant. The effect in oratory may be a very good speech—(unless you stump)—but in our art, it is always a very bad shot. Our noble art demands calmness and the most imperturbable self-possession; and that, at the beginning, the middle, the ending of the exercises. And so I said:—

"Well, gentlemen, if you want to see where to plant your balls, I'm the one, I think, to show you"—

"Why no, stranger"—replied the old Achates—"I allow that aint fair nither, to let you lead off. We're all neighbour-like here, and 'tis only right you should see what we kin do fust. I sort a suppose maybe it will save you the trouble of shootin anyhow. So come, Long Jake, crack away and I'll foller—and arter, you, stranger, may shoot or not jist as you like best."

"Agreed, grandaddie," responded Long Jake, "so here goes." And then Jake, after returning from the old beech, where he had put up his target, took his rifle, left a moment leaning against a tree, and with firmness and grace stepped on the line. Two things and only two gave me hopes, viz., he shut his left eye and held on the diamond without rising or falling perpendicularly to it: but then he held that rifle as if it were the true horizon—and then—click—snap—but no report. Lucky snap for me I knew it must have been a central ball: but still better for me—Jake was embarrassed a little. Shaking out the damp powder he primed afresh, and again began his aim. Now, however, a very slight vibration seemed to glimmer on his barrel, and when he did fire, I was not disappointed nor greatly displeased at the cry from the fellows that leaped from behind the target tree—"rite hand corner, grazin the dimind!" Again Jake loaded, raised his piece, and fired at first sight, and the cry now came—"centre!" This increased my neighbour's confidence, and happily lessened his carefulness; for sighting, as he himself afterwards confessed, "a lettle bit coarseish like," the cry now was—"line shot, scant quarter *'bove* centre!"

"Come, grandaddie," said Jake to the old gentleman as he walked up to the line from adjusting his shingle, "you must do a little better nor that, or maybe we'll lose our stingo, for I know by the way this stranger here handles my rifle, he's naturally a hard chap to beat."

This speech was occasioned by my handling the gun, taking aim, setting triggers, &c., in order to get better acquainted with the piece; and which experiments resulted in a secret and hearty wish for my own gun.

"Well, Jake, I allow yours kin be beat a bit," replied our veteran taking his position on the line. At a glance towards his "toot en sembell," Mr. Carlton too, allowed he had met his match—and, perhaps even with his own gun. How grand the calmness—as if in no battle! How alive muscle and feature—as if in the midst of enemies! There he is dropping his bead—ay, his eyes both wide awake, and he raises the piece till that bead dims on the lower point of his diamond—a flash—and from the tree—"centre!" He was soon again ready, and at his second flash, came the cry—"upper edge, fust hole!"—and that cry was answered along the gradually narrowing and crowded lines, by the whole company—"hurraw for grandaddie—hurraw-aw!" His third shot, brought from the tree—"lee-e-tle tor'ds rite corner of dimind—jeest grazed centre!"—and was answered by—"grandaddie forever, hurraw-aw-aw!"

"Carlton," maliciously whispered Glenville, "the stingo is safe—anti-temperance beats!"

I felt honour demanded, however, a trial; and so requesting Glenville to fix as I should direct my target, I stood on the line of firing, sighting several times with open pan and no priming; until the mark exactly suited, when I cried out "stand clear!" And now, supposing Jake's rifle sighted like my own, and threw its ball a little above its head (as indeed is best), I drew up as usual, with rapidity, and fly just as the bead caught the lower tip of my diamond, the report instantly returned being—"inside lower pint of dimind, scant quarter, b'low centre!"

"Blame close, stranger," said the old hero, "but I allow you'll have to mend it to beat me."

"Praise from *you*, my old friend, is *worth* something—I'll try my best to satisfy you."

Jake's rifle was now understood: she sent balls exactly where she aimed, and not as mine, and most good rifles, an eighth of an inch above. Making, therefore, my front sight a hair thicker and fuller in the hind sight, and coming full on the lower angle of my diamond—"Centre!"—was echoed from the tree and along the lines—"hurraw-aw! for the stranger!"

"You're most powerful good at it," said the old gentleman, "but my line's a lettle the shortest yet."

"Well, my good old friend, here goes to make yours a little the longest"—and away, along between the unflinching lines of excited spectators, whistled my third and last ball, bringing back the cry—"lee-e-tle b'low the centre—broke in first hole!" But, while all rushed to the examination and measurements, confined to our two shingles, no exultation burst forth, it being doubtful, or, as the hunters said, "a sort of dubus whether the stingo was grandaddie's, or the stranger's." In a few moments, however, and by the most honourable and exact measurements, it was decided that the old Achates had "the shortest string by near about half the brenth of his bullit!" And then such uproar rose of mingled hurraws,—screams,—shrieks,—yells,—and outcries! an uproar none but true honest-hearted far westers, unadulterated by foreign or domestic scum, ever did or can make.

The hurricane over, the victor mounting a log made the following speech:—

"Well, naburs, it's my sentimental opinyin this stranger's acted up, clean up, to the notch, and is most powerful clever. And I think if he'd a fired his *own* gun as how he mought a come out even, and made up the lettle matter of diff'runce atween us—and that would be near about shootin a little bit the closest of any other chap, young or old, in these 'are diggins—and so, says I, let's have three cheers for the stranger, and three more for his friend."

Oh! dear reader! *could* you have heard the old, dark woods ring then!—I struggled hard, you may be sure; but what was the use, the tears would come!

We both made replies to the compliment; and in concluding, for I mounted the log last, I touched on the wish we really had to do good, and that nothing was better for hardy, brave, and noble woodsmen than temperance.

"Well, strangers, both on you," replied that very grand old man, "you shan't be disapinted. You depended on our honour—and so, says I, if these 'are naburs here aint no objection, let them that want to, first take a suck of stingo for a treat, and then, says I, lets all load up and crack away at the cask, and I'll have fust shot."

"Agreed! agreed! hurraw for grandaddie Tomsin—hurraw for strangers! —hurraw for the temperance society!—load up, boys, load up!—nobody wants a suck—crack away, grandaddie—crack away, we're all ready!" And crack went old Brave's rifle—crack, long Jake's—crack the brave Gyas, and the brave Cloanthus—and crack every rifle in the company: and there rolled the wounded half-barrel, pouring its own death-dealing contents through its perforated heads and sides, till soon the stingo was all absorbed in the moist earth of the forest.

Glenville and I now "gathered hossis and put out," highly pleased with the events: and a few weeks after we were still more pleased, at hearing that all the company at the prize shooting that day had become members of the temperance society. If, therefore, any old fashioned temperance society (such as it was before fanaticism rules it,) wishes champions to shoot, provided "grandaddie Tomsin" will be one, I know where can be found another.

2: Cultural Centers of the 1820s

Among the newcomers to Indiana in the 1820s were the followers of Robert Owen, the industrialist-reformer who established his shortlived experiment in communal living in 1825. Although the Owenite community failed in 1827, a number of the remarkable and talented people who had come to New Harmony remained and exerted a continuing influence on the educational, scientific, and humanitarian developments in Indiana for decades. Among a number of important "firsts" at New Harmony are the first public library in Indiana, the first workingmen's institute, the first kindergarten, and sponsorship of the first geological survey of the state, a service performed by David Dale Owen.

At the time of the New Harmony experiment in southern Indiana, the William Conner farm, an important cultural center of a different sort, was developing in central Indiana. Conner, originally a fur trader and Indian agent with his brother John (who later founded Connersville in southeastern Indiana), had established himself on the White River (above what became Indianapolis) to continue working with the Indians. Following the Treaty of St. Mary's, Conner's Indian wife and her children departed for the West with the migrating Delaware in 1820. The home Conner built for his new wife in 1823, and where the Conners lived until 1837, has become the Conner Prairie Settlement and Museum, a "living history" restoration of pioneer life now operated by Earlham College. It is located a few miles south of Noblesville. Conner, his achievements, and the current use of his home and its surroundings are described below. The best sources on the history of New Harmony, including both the Rappite and Owenite phases, are William E. Wilson, *The Angel and the Serpent: The Story of New Harmony* (1964); George B. Lockwood, *The New Harmony Movement* (1905), and Karl J. R. Arndt, *George Rapp's Harmony Society, 1785–1847* (1965). Arndt has also collected, translated, and edited thousands of Rappite documents for his *Indiana Decade of the Harmony Society, 1814–1824* (2 vols., 1976–1978). See also Richard W. Leopold, *Robert Dale Owen: A Biography* (1940), and Arthur E. Bestor, Jr., *Backwoods Utopias: The Sectarian and Owenite Phases of Communitarian Socialism in America, 1663–1829* (1950). For additional information on William Conner, see Charles N. Thompson, *Sons of the Wilderness: John and William Conner* (1937).

New Harmony: A Youngster's View[1]

MINER K. KELLOGG

In 1886, approximately sixty years after he had first come to New Harmony as a lad of ten or eleven, Miner K. Kellogg described his experiences as a member of one of the first families to join Robert Owen's experimental society. The Kelloggs remained there only eighteen months, after which they participated with a few friends in an even shorter-lived communal society at Jeffersonville. Although born in New York, young Kellogg spent most of his youth in Cincinnati, Ohio, where his father was a successful tailor both before and after his brief sojourns in southern Indiana. The memoirist, a talented musician and artist, eventually became a portrait painter. The manuscript copy of "Brief Notes for an Autobiography of Miner K. Kellogg, 1886" is in the Indiana Historical Society Library. The section dealing with New Harmony, edited by Mrs. Sylvester, associate editor of the *Indiana Magazine of History,* was published by the magazine in 1968, portions of which are reproduced below. Mrs. Sylvester also prepared the selection on Conner Prairie, intended originally as an introduction to a photographic portfolio published in the *Indiana Magazine of History* in 1969.

Up to this time [1825] my father had supported himself by his trade that of a tailor and was one of the most excellent and fashionable of the City [Cincinnati]. Had he been content to follow up his business he might have laid by a competence—but he had no love of money, his heart was in some way inclined another way which lead his mind to the contemplation of those abstract subject[s] which could be of little service in the accumulation of means of immediate and direct benefit to himself. He scarcely ever discussed commercial matters though he did political economy because it was of general concern, or of benefit to the community at large. This wavering between the choice of a line of personal benefit or a line of general good to humanity—kept his mind in just that unsettled condition as prepared it for the reception of any plausible doctrines that promised a revolution in the

[1] In editing this portion of Kellogg's autobiography every effort has been made to retain the author's spelling, grammar, punctuation, and style. Kellogg frequently omitted periods after abbreviations and sometimes failed to place them at the end of sentences. His spelling was not always perfect, and occasionally he did not begin his sentences with capital letters. These lapses and idiosyncracies have been retained and have not been indicated by a [sic] as long as the meaning remained clear. In many instances it was impossible to distinguish between Kellogg's capital and lower case letters and between his periods, commas, and dashes. His intentions regarding paragraphing were also difficult to ascertain. Decisions in these cases were necessarily arbitrary, but whenever possible modern usage prevailed.

From "Miner K. Kellogg: Recollections of New Harmony," Lorna Lutes Sylvester (ed.), *Indiana Magazine of History,* LXIV (March 1968), 45-48, 50-53, 56, 58-61. Some of Mrs. Sylvester's footnotes have been retained. Copyright © 1968 by the Trustees of Indiana University. Reprinted by permission.

accepted order of things and which would create an entirely new System in the organization of society for the good of the human race!

This was just that condition of thought which was ready to receive the ideas of a *new Social system* propounded by that great humanitarian Robt Owen who had just made his appearance on an American Rostrum to propagate such a *social reform,* promising to result in a much happier era in human affairs. To this enchanting doctrine my Father was ready to give ear, when Mr. Owen arrived in Cincinnati and gave lectures in advocacy of his peculiar views, and to gain proselytes to join him in establishing a community in which these views should be carried into execution in a formal and practical manner apart from the old communities which now prevented, through custom and prejudice a favorable result to this new order of social life.[2] The calm logic and good temper of Mr. Owen captivated Father and he became one of the very first proselytes to follow him in an experimental effort to benefit the *"human race"* at the thoughtless risk of the fatal result which might overwhelm the members of his own family in case his new venture should prove a failure! Thus it is with all enthusiastic humaritarians! But I need not dwell on this fruitful subject; it must have been already exhausted by able peers throughout the realm of social Philosophers. Men's minds in all ages give readier acquiescence to the dictates of emotion than to the coolness of reason; and nothing but the actual results of sad experience will correct their fatal delusions.

Father was the victim of emotion; gave up his business, raised all the means he could and embarked in the new Enterprize zealously in the spring of 1824. He became indeed one of the most active Lieutenants of Mr. Owen.[3] Many families of Cincin[n]at[i] were as enchanted with the prospect of a happy change in their social condition as was Father, and joined him in a journey to the "promised Land." They went by Steamboat down the Ohio until reaching Mt. Vernon in Indiana. This was a little village upon the high bank of the river—composed of a few straggling frame buildings and probably two hundred inhabitants. One hotel only.[4] Landing the few trunks and household goods belonging to the party at the water's edge they were left in charge of some one of them whilst the others ascended the bank to the village Inn, where temporary accommodations were found for the women and children. The weather was delightful, & sunny.

[2]Robert Owen arrived in Cincinnati on December 9, 1824, and apparently remained only a few hours before proceeding to Louisville. Kellogg's father must have learned previously of Owen's successful social reform in New Lanark, Scotland, and of his plans to inaugurate a "New Moral World." Contemporary Cincinnati newspapers were not checked, but no other record has been found of Owen's speaking in Cincinnati at this time. *The Diaries of Donald Macdonald, 1824–1826 (Indiana Historical Society Publications,* Vol. XIV, No. 2; Indianapolis, 1942), 236–37.

[3]Other sources do not indicate that the elder Kellogg assumed so important a place in Owen's project, either in Cincinnati or later in New Harmony, as this document suggests. The Macdonald diaries note the Kelloggs' arrival in the Indiana community and state that Miner's father was placed on a committee which apparently served as a kind of preliminary governing body. *Diaries of Donald Macdonald,* 292.

[P]reparations were now made for an onward move to the interior—the objective point of the pilgrimage some fifteen miles distant on the banks of the Wabash River. In the mean time it was determined to send a messenger ahead to make proper arrangements for the reception of the party in "New Harmony," which was to be their future "happy home".

The prospect ahead was enchanting to all. The old folks were children again and moved as actively and as gaily as in the days when picnicks were calling them to the woods for a good old frolic.

Mr. Parsons a young graduate of West Point was of the party and he was chosen to go on to New Harmony to make known our coming to Mr. Owen who was awaiting our arrival. I was to accompany him. He mounted a spirited iron gray colt and I was placed behind him and we made the journey through the uninhabited forest in great glee, everything was fresh and joyous the birds plentiful gay in colors and musical. This in the month of April 1825 The end of our journey took us by surprize from a hill over-looking the beautiful village lying silent, clean and inviting in the plain below, with the silvery stream of the Wabash encircling it in the distance with the bright green canebrakes and prairies of Illinois in the far distance. It was indeed the picture of Paradise to me and I was loth to descend the hill for a nearer view. But we had to move on to our destiny. The village was laid out symetrically in squares bounded by wide streets, clean and white, but not a soul or animal to be seen. It was sunday—every body within their domiciles. We rode slowly through the street fronting us not knowing where to find Mr. Owen. But noticing a goodsized house painted red differing from all others we concluded it to be for public uses and rode towards it—no one yet in sight from whom to get information—when we noticed a man emerge from the house and await us before the door in expectancy. We saluted him and Parsons told him who we were *"from Cincinnati."* It was Robert Owen. He was bareheaded and bald—with a most genial and ben-evolent aspect—bade us welcome in quiet and Fatherly tones, and reaching up for me took me in his arms to descend—greeting me with a kiss, placed me upon the ground with the remark that I was the *first disciple* of *his* that *had yet arrived* to make a home with him in New Harmony. Escorting us into the Hotel—for such it proved to be, a servant took our horse and we were domiciled for the time with the much loved man who was to direct our destinity in the future. He was entirely alone not a member of his family had yet arrived, and Mr. Parsons soon became the recipient of the projects to be carried out in the immediate future for establishing of the Colony.

In a day or so our families arrived from Mt. Vernon and were properly housed and cared for in different parts of the almost deserted Village.

. . . .

[4]An early history of Posey County, Indiana, notes that Mount Vernon became the county seat in 1825, the year of Kellogg's arrival. According to the publishers, "The town took a new lease on life and grew quite rapidly, and was the rival, and even ahead in numbers and commercial importance, of Evansville." *History of Posey County, Indiana* . . . (Chicago, 1886), 361.

As soon as enough children had arrived to form into classes, schools were established for their reception and care. There was one large boarding school which was conducted on the Military Mess system with two long tables parallel in one room. Into this the scholars were marched with military precision to their allotted places, and thus marched out together to the playgrounds where they were dismissed. Indeed the whole exercises were carried out in a prescribed and regular military manner.

Into this school I was placed. The food was of the simplest and cheapest kind—no meats, no eggs, no pies—Nothing in fact but corn mush and milk. This was good and healthy to those that liked it—but I did not—it so disagreed with me that I could not touch the mush. The milk only was sipped up, hence I was nearly starved. Whenever I could do so after dismissal I would slip into the kitchen door and beg for something to eat—and I was often gratifies [sic] by the kind old cook giving me a good sized piece of the hardbaked mush which adhered to the large iron pot. There seemed to be a determined effort to starve me out of my fastidiousness and to keep up the principle of equality among the scholars—all must be treated alike. In the playground—quite a field behind the school, were erected swings bars, poles and other things pertaining to a Gymnasium, and gave great delight and healthy exercise to us all: and here also we were regularly drilled in squads and companies in all military movements by experienced men. Our recitations were conducted in so agreeable a manner that all were interested and studied faithfully—there was no need of severity in any case. In fact the established order of government was one of kindness—persuasion and love: an order more acceptable to the scholars, than agreeable to the teachers— for the latter were compelled to keep a check on their impatience, and to govern their own tempers when sorely tried. I recall one laughable instance of this. One of our best instructors was an Irishman of fine abilities named *Gilmore*. He was marching us down a broad street for exercise and drill formed into one long line across the street. We could keep a line well dressed but for one gawky lazy overgrown boy named Ran Boss, who would persistently fall a step behind. Gilmore would frequently touch him up from behind with a long fishing pole of cane—still he lagged behind—at last Gilmore lost all patience and temper after exhausting kind words—then he brought his long pole suddenly to his aid by a swishing sweep across the back of *Ran* who found his proper place very quickly. But the whole line broke as if by one impulse—the boys scattering in all directions with the cry of "Old School"—Old School"—with Gilmore in great passion following those he could reach with his pole—uttering his malediction as he ran. "*I'll* give you old school, *I'll* give you old school," but he never got us together again that day—and we were never called upon to make any apologies for such rudeness to our teacher—it was so well understood that he had himself violated the Golden Rule of the school. This was the only violation of New Harmony discipline that my memory now recalls.

. . . .

The boys were made useful in various ways—Sometimes we were employed in the fields, hoeing and gathering potatoes or other vegetables—hetchelling flax[5]—shucking corn and other light work. Indeed there seems to have been no end to the employments in which we were engaged and instructed, and by which *a revenue to the Community might be gained at the same time.* We were to be utilitarians in every sense of the word. As the society increased in numbers various trades were established by competent tradesmen and the boys were placed under their tuition and guidance. In the mean time men of learning arrived and took positions as professors of higher branches of study such as botany and natural history—even of languages and Philosophy and they did not lack for students before the final collapse of the great *experiment.* It is a fact of especial interest to know that many of the brightest intellects in the United States found their way to this new social organization in the hope of making it, by the exercise of their exceptional attainments a Model, and an eminent success. Among these accomplished scholars a few may be named as examples, because they have been widely known and acknowledged as such. *Say,* the Naturalist, William Maclure the "father of geology." etc etc Other men of more than ordinary intelligence came into this charmed circle. There was Phiqepal D'Arusmont, afterwards the husband of Fanny Wright who often visited and encouraged the movement by her eloquence and engaging language and noble manners. She had been a very noted and acceptable lecturer on free thought and expounder of the doctrines of Mr Owen throughout the principle cities—and—being the *first* female who had yet appeared upon the American Rostrum drew very large and intelligent audiences whenever she lectured. I think she must have been one of the most original and attractive women who has ever graced the lecture room in the United States. She undoubtedly led the way and gave courage to those of her sex who afterwards enforced their views and sentiments however peculiar or unpopular upon the attention of the public ear.[6]

. . . .

In the Public Square was a large church and a town Hall, leaving about half the square for play ground—in its centre stood a large pump and

---

[5] The word *hetchel* is a variation of *hatchel* or *hackle,* meaning to comb or board with long metal teeth. It is used in connection with dressing flax, hemp, or jute.

[6] In January, 1826, the keelboat *Philanthropist* arrived in New Harmony. Better known as the "Boatload of Knowledge," its passengers were a group of brilliant, eccentric intellectuals whom Robert Owen had recruited in the eastern states. Included among the passengers were William Maclure, geologist, educator, and philanthropist, who was Owen's principal associate and financial partner in the New Harmony venture; Thomas Say, zoologist, conchologist, entomologist, curator of the American Philosophical Society, and professor of natural history at the University of Pennsylvania; and Guillaume Sylvan Casimir Phiquepal d'Arusmont, a Pestalozzian teacher sponsored by Maclure. William S. Phiquepal, as he was known for a while in the United States later married Frances Wright, a social reformer and leader in the free thought movement. Miss Wright first came to New Harmony in March, 1825, and apparently resided

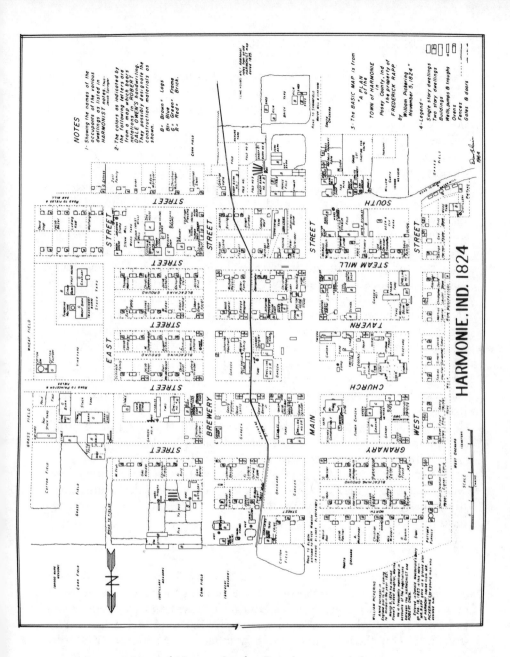

Map of Harmonie, the Rappite community

Courtesy of the Indiana Historical Society

in the Indiana community off and on until 1828. Wilson, *The Angel and the Serpent*, 136–43. See also *Diaries of Donald Macdonald*, 333–37; Victor Colin Duclos, *Diary and Recollections of Victor Colin Duclos*, in Lindley, *Indiana as Seen by Early Travelers*, 537–38.

its trough before it. [T]his trough furnished a basin which served the boys for ablutions, and was a constant resort.

The Church was used on Sundays for religious services by believers of every doctrine—and even by Atheists when they wished to confute the believers in Holy Writ. The Town Hall was used for public meetings. Mr Owen often lectured. At one of these lectures I took a seat in the gallery directly opposite to him, and with a paper on my hat-crown made a first attempt at drawing a likeness. It seemed a pretty fair attempt as the boys recognized it immediately, and made quite a talk after the lecture—Hearing of it Mr Owen sought me out as I was washing my hands at the pump, and asked to see it. I was so mortified at his having found me out that I declined his request—but his words were so kind and encoraging that I took off my strawhat and pulled out the drawing for his examination. He smiled at it, and said he thought it might be very good, and added, patting me on the shoulder, "proceed—proceed, my son and you will make an Artist one of these days" These words from so great a man impressed me for a very long time and were the first to give me corage to "proceed" in making attempts of a similar character. Mr. Parsons assisted me in my labors. He had learned drawing at West Point. Here was a new source of delight and I drew upon it often in trying to copy the outlines of birds butterflies and other beautiful subjects. I cannot imagine a region richer in birds of splendid plumage or insects of greater rarity and variety. The paroquets were so plentiful that flocks of them passed through the thick woods with lightning speed shrieking like a steam whistle—in their rapid flight—their brilliant greenish & goldish tints fitfully flashing across amid the sombre shadows of the forest.[7]

Very little time was occupied in this study of art—so many other duties were forced upon me in the varied trades and exercises demanding attention. But it served the purpose of turning my attention and taste to the beautiful arts.

. . . .

No money was circulated in New Harmony. The principle was barter on the cooperative plan. One store alone sufficed for all the traffic—each purchaser paid in the value of his labor. There was an excitement among us boys one day when some coin was received at the store. It had been a strange object in the town and we were gratified by the opportunity afforded

[7]"Parroquets" were apparently quite common in southern Indiana at this time. Another visitor to the state describes them as follows: "though they have become so familiar; and though they excell all the birds of this country in beauty of plumage,—their scream is so discordant, and their fierceness of disposition so apparent, as to preclude every sensation of attachment.

"These birds build their nests in hollow trees. The strength of their necks is remarkable; and we are assured that when both wings and feet are tied they can climb trees by striking their bills into the bark." David Thomas, *Travels through the Western Country in the Summer of 1816,* in Lindley, *Indiana as Seen by Early Travelers,* 80.

by the storekeeper to handle some few cents of the currency of the outer world! Towards the end of the experiment the exports fell short of the imports needed for our sustenance—and want and trouble stared us in the face—crowds sometimes surrounding the store clamoring for the actual necessities of life. This fact I well remember for I witnessed it in great astonishment and fear. Only think of such a dire result to such magnificent promises. A *collapse must soon ensue* of course.

We were often treated to a ball in the town hall. The only thing different from such an amusement in other towns was the dress of the girls. Here was inaugurated what has since been called the "Bloomer"—short skirts and pantalettes. It was graceful and pretty enough—but above all convenient—and it lasted as a fashion long after the disbanding of the community—possibly does yet among the old residents.[8]

There was one fact deserving notice in that society of comparative strangers to each other—met here from every quarter—there was no thieving nor crime—consequently no police or courts. There were no drinking saloons. I don't think there was an instance of inebriaty known—nor do I believe there was an intoxicating liquor in the place.[9] It was peaceful—every man respecting his neighbor. Religious observances were confined to those whose faith exacted them, but they were not enforced on others—even by general opinion. Free thought on such matters was equally respected, hence no unpleasant collisions of sentiment. Mr. Owen himself did not believe in the inspiration of the Scriptures, nor did his sons, and I suppose many others held that view, but there were no contentions. Every one quietly enjoyed his own belief. *Sunday* was by common consent kept as a holiday— and was enjoyed as each person liked—in repose, in work or in study—in music or in games of recreation.

The church building in the public square was held sacred on Sunday for the uses of religious people—so that when they occupied it on that day the square in front of it was not used for any species of amusement which might disturb worshipers within. There was no law but public sentiment to control such things. There being no Church or other bells, the Sunday was as silent in New Harmony as it is in any Mohammedan town. It impressed

[8]Another resident of New Harmony, Mrs. Sarah Pears, described the female dress as "a pair of undertrowsers tied round the ankles over which is an exceedingly full slip reaching to the knees, though some have been so extravagant as to make them rather longer, and also to have the sleeves long." Mrs. Pears also discussed the men's apparel, "The pantaloons are extremely full, also tied around the waist with a very broad belt, which gives it the appearance of being all in one. . . . They are tied around the neck like the girls' slips, and as many wear them with no collar visible, it is rather difficult to distinguish the gentlemen from the ladies." Thomas Clinton Pears, Jr. (ed.), *New Harmony, an Adventure in Happiness: Papers of Thomas and Sarah Pears (Indiana Historical Society Publications,* Vol. XI, No. 1; Indianapolis, 1933), 82.
[9]According to the Duke of Saxe-Weimar, Owen reported that the Rappites' old distillery was to be torn down because he had forbidden the serving of spirituous liquors in New Harmony. At the time of the Duke's visit, however, wine was still being made; and apparently the towns-people did not maintain complete abstinence. Bernhard, *Travels through North America,* 425.

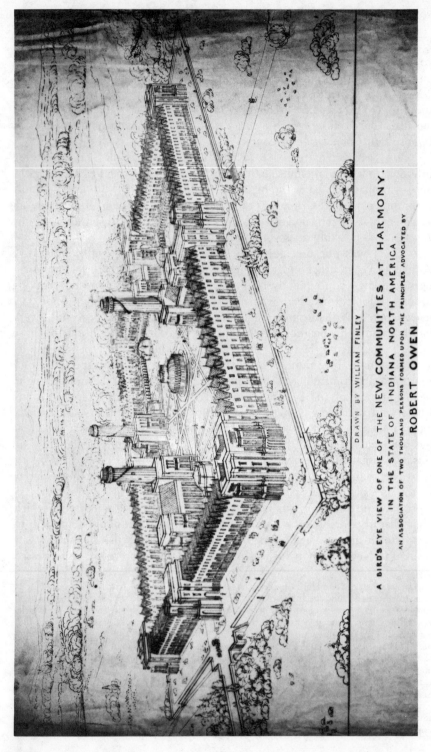

A BIRD'S EYE VIEW OF ONE OF THE NEW COMMUNITIES AT HARMONY.
IN THE STATE OF INDIANA NORTH AMERICA.

AN ASSOCIATION OF TWO THOUSAND PERSONS FORMED UPON THE PRINCIPLES ADVOCATED BY

ROBERT OWEN

DRAWN BY WILLIAM FINLEY

Robert Owen's plan for New Harmony *Courtesy of the Indiana Historical Society* me very greatly the beautiful Sabbath day on which I entered it. It did not appear to be inhabited, and was as silent as Pompeii itself.

The town was laid out in squares enclosing four brick dwellings one at each corner—the inner space was given up to gardens for the families residing in the houses—one family to each. Factories and workshops were placed in the suburbs. Wood only was then used and therefore no black smoke was seen and the atmosphere always clear and healthy—every thing as clean and inviting as a parlor floor.

In bad weather of course the streets were exceptions, as in all such unpaved towns without water works or hydrants. Pumps supplied drinking water, good and plentifully. There were no accidents by fire during the two years of my stay—even had there been—the houses were so isolated that even without an engine no serious conflagration could have occurred.

A few small steamers had ventured to run up the Wabash as far as Terrehaut—but very seldom seen—so small was the Commerce.

In time the evidences of the ultimate failure of this humane but ill-advised project of bettering the social condition of men had so multiplied that even the zealots had given up hopes of success. They maintained however that had there been a proper organization at the first, it must have ultimately succeeded. Of these believers my father was one, and longed for an opportunity to establish another society in some other quarter on a new basis—eliminating all the evils which experience had shown to be pernicious and destructive in the present attempt to ameliorate the ancient condition of the civilized world. After a quiet conference with a few of his old Cincinnati friends in the community and with Mr. Owen it was arranged to take a "New departure". Father was fortunate enough to obtain enough money to help him in this enterprize—he got *twenty dollars* and it was all that Mr Owen could spare—showing the desperate condition of his own finances! But he had confidence enough in the result of such an enterprize as to bless it and lend a hand.

William Conner's Farm

LORNA LUTES SYLVESTER

Indiana Territory was just over two years old in August, 1802. Carved from the Northwest Territory in May, 1800, the new area included all but a sliver of the present state of Indiana, all of Illinois and Wisconsin, about

From "Conner Prairie Pioneer Settlement and Museum," *Indiana Magazine of History,* LXV (March 1969), 1-2, 4-7. Some of Mrs. Sylvester's footnotes have been retained. Copyright © 1969 by the Trustees of Indiana University. Reprinted by permission.

half of Michigan, and a tiny section of Minnesota. The territory's white population of approximately 6,500 lived mainly in Kaskaskia, Cahokia, Mackinac, Detroit, Clark's Grant, Vincennes, and a few other "scattered and isolated islands" of settlement "entirely surrounded by a wide sea of green forest."

By 1802 settlements in the area eventually to become the state of Indiana formed a narrow crescent beginning in the lower Whitewater Valley in the east, south along the Ohio River, and up the Wabash to Vincennes in the west. Except for the sizable Vincennes Tract, surrounding the town of Vincennes; the 150,000 acre Clark's Grant, opposite the falls of the Ohio; the wedge shaped Gore in the east, which would be added to Indiana Territory in 1803; and isolated patches of land granted to the whites by the Treaty of Greenville in 1795, the future Hoosier State in 1802 was entirely Indian country. Here and there roamed the Piankashaw, Miami, Shawnee, Wea, Kickapoo, Potawatomi; and in the territory's midsection, between the two forks of White River, were the peaceful Delaware. The estimated Indian population ranged from 5,000 to 25,000; whites numbered about 2,500. The country which is now central and northern Indiana was, in 1802, "a continuous primeval wilderness. . . . There were no roads other than Indian trails and buffalo traces, no boats except the softly gliding Indian canoes, no towns other than straggling Indian villages, no inns between the white settlement. . . . It was veritably the haunt of wild beasts and savage men."[1] Two missionaries to the Delaware on White River further attested to the isolation of the area in 1802, "the Delaware towns, of which there are nine in all, lie from four to five miles apart, and are scattered along the river. After these towns come other settlements of Indian nations as for instance, the Nanticoke, Schawanos and others. After that there is nothing but meadowland as far as the eye can reach, until the banks of the Wabash."[2]

In this wilderness in the Delaware Indian country, about four miles south of the present site of Noblesville, Indiana, "on a beautiful moonlight night, August 12, 1802 . . . with only the aid of a French Canadian," William Conner completed the construction of a double log cabin which was to serve as a home for his Indian wife and children and also as a trading post.[3] Located on the eastern side of the west fork of White River at a point where the stream made a horseshoe bend, the cabin soon became a landmark in the area. For several years Conner's trading post was the central

[1]Charles N. Thompson, *Sons of the Wilderness: John and William Conner* (*Indiana Historical Society Publications*, Vol. XII; Indianapolis, 1937), 41.
[2]John Peter Kluge and Abraham Luckenbach to Jacob Van Vleck, September 24, 1802, in Lawrence Henry Gipson (ed.), *The Moravian Indian Mission on White River: Diaries and Letters, May 5, 1799, to November 12, 1806* (*Indiana Historical Collections*, Vol. XXIII; Indianapolis, 1938), 476.
[3]Quoted in Thompson, *Sons of the Wilderness*, 46.

market place for Indians in the vicinity, and hundreds of furs left there for Cincinnati via Conner's Trail to John Conner's store a few miles below Brookville, Indiana.

John and William Conner were brothers who had come to the Delaware country from Detroit during the late eighteenth century. Both had married Delaware women—William's wife being Chief Anderson's daughter, Mekinges—both had been licensed traders to the Indians even before building their respective posts, and both were to be extremely influential in the development of Indiana Territory and the Hoosier State. They served as guides on military and diplomatic missions, were interpreters and advisers for many of the treaties removing Indian title to the land in eastern Indiana Territory, fought in the War of 1812, served in the state legislature, helped select the site of Indianapolis, founded towns, and operated numerous businesses in addition to the fur trade.

The Conner brothers had spent most of their lives in an Indian environment. Their parents, Richard and Margaret Conner, were adopted members of the Shawnee tribe, Margaret having lived with the Shawnee from childhood. John, William, their brothers, and their sister were raised among the Christian Delaware in the Moravian mission towns in Ohio and Michigan. At the end of the Revolutionary War the Conner family was living near Detroit where Richard Conner had acquired vast acres of farm land. Before the turn of the century, however, John and William left their father's farms for the Indian country in what was to become the state of Indiana. While John eventually chose to locate in the Whitewater Valley near the border between Indian and white territory, William and his wife, Mekinges, settled in their double log cabin on the west fork of White River near the Delaware towns. Here scores of Indians came to trade their beaver, fox, raccoon, mink, otter, muskrat, and other pelts for the Hudson Bay blankets, trade axes, knives, beads, and similar paraphernalia which Conner stocked. Here Mekinges cared for their six children. From here William left to serve with General William Henry Harrison as guide, interpreter, and soldier during the War of 1812. And to this primitive log cabin in 1820 came Governor Jonathan Jennings and ten commissioners appointed to select a site for the permanent seat of government in the four year old state of Indiana.

The location selected was at the confluence of Fall Creek and White River approximately fifteen miles south southeast of the Conner cabin. By the Treaty of St. Mary's (New Purchase Treaty) at St. Mary's, Ohio, in 1818, the United States had removed Indian title to the land in central Indiana in which the Conner cabin and the capital site were located. Both the Conner brothers had been extremely influential as interpreters and advisers in securing Indian agreement to this treaty. Indeed, according to two of the United States commissioners, Jonathan Jennings and Lewis Cass, the

Conners "had it in their power to have prevented any purchase of Indian title to land on the waters of the White river. . . ."[4] The Treaty of St. Mary's was particularly significant for William, for by it the Delaware agreed to leave Indiana for lands provided by the federal government west of the Mississippi River. According to tribal law an Indian wife must remain with her people, thus Mekinges and the six children would leave with them. Conner himself could have accompanied his wife—some white men married to Indian women did so—but William chose to remain in Indiana.[5]

The Delaware had been given until 1821 to leave the state, but during the late summer of 1820 most of the tribe gathered at the Conner cabin preparatory to departure. They left for the West in August or September, accompanied by Mekinges and her children.[6] Approximately three months later, on November 30, 1820, Conner married Elizabeth Chapman, stepdaughter of John Finch who had moved to the west fork of White River in the summer of 1819. Conner had first met Elizabeth on a trip to Connersville earlier in 1819. According to one writer, whose wife was a great granddaughter of John Conner, William was attracted to her even at this time, and the attraction became mutual after Elizabeth moved to the White River country with her stepfather. The fur trader and his new wife moved into the double log cabin which he had built for his Indian family eighteen years before.

Three years later, however, Conner built a new home for Elizabeth—a two story, brick structure, one of the first such buildings in the New Purchase area. Located approximately one mile south of the cabin site and back from the river, the brick house sat on a small hill overlooking rich river bottoms and the semicircular sweep of White River itself. According to one historian the house was considered "elegant" and "remarkably handsome" at the time of its construction, and he describes it as follows:

> A center hall divides the house, disclosing at one end the broad sweep of the prairie farm and providing at the other the usual mode of entrance from the land which leads to the main road. On entering the yard the old well first meets the eye. . . . Spacious rooms with a fireplace in each, open from the hall, and from it a graceful stairway leads

---

[4]Jonathan Jennings to Senator James Noble, January 27, 1827; Lewis Cass to Senator James Noble, January 20, 1823, in U.S., *Senate Documents*, 20 Cong., 2 Sess., Report 25, pp. 5–6.

[5]For text of the Treaty of St. Mary's see *United States Statutes at Large*, VII, 188–89. Possibly Conner could have arranged for his wife and children to remain in Indiana had he and/or she wished to do so. Indeed, there is some evidence that he attempted to persuade Mekinges to stay, but she apparently decided to go with her tribe. William Marshall, Conner's partner, accompanied his Delaware wife to the lands west of the Mississippi. Thompson, *Sons of the Wilderness*, 109–14, 121.

[6]Vincennes *Indiana Centinel & Public Advertiser*, November 4, 1820, cited in Barnhart and Carmony, *Indiana*, I, 210n. At the time of departure Mekinges took with her sixty ponies, and Conner had agreed to purchase her and the children's interest in the 640 acres of land on White River. Thompson, *Sons of the Wilderness*, 123–25.

William Conner's home, 1823
Courtesy of the Indiana Department of Natural Resources

to the second floor, where there is a similar arrangement of rooms with a fireplace in each. . . . Adjoining the dining room on the south side of the hall is an old-fashioned kitchen containing a spacious fireplace with an oven on one side. A staircase . . . leads to a loft-like room above the kitchen.[7]

William and Elizabeth Conner lived in this home until 1837 when they moved to a 150 acre farm adjoining Noblesville, Indiana. The circuit court of Hamilton County—formed in 1823—also held its early sessions in the brick house, as did the Board of County Commissioners.

Conner's interests in the new state of Indiana were by this time myriad. In 1823 in conjunction with Josiah F. Polk he platted and founded the town of Noblesville which soon became the county seat of Hamilton County. After John Conner's death in 1826 William maintained the operation of his brother's store in Indianapolis, his mills in Hamilton and Fayette counties (including wool carding, gristmill, sawmill, and distillery), his two farms and two town lots. William also served as a member of the Association for the Improvement of Common Schools in Indiana, as commissioner to lay out a road from Indianapolis to Fort Wayne, and as a charter member of the Indiana Historical Society. He still saw occasional service as an

[7]Thompson, *Sons of the Wilderness*, 133–134.

interpreter in treaty negotiations with the Indians. He also served in the state House of Representatives for three terms (1829–1830, 1831–1832, 1836–1837) and accompanied the Indiana militia as a guide during Black Hawk's War in 1832.

When Conner and his wife Elizabeth moved from their brick home on White River to Noblesville in 1837, he liquidated many of his businesses. Until approximately the time of his death in 1855, however, he maintained his interest in internal improvements in Indiana—roads, canals, and railroads —operated a saw- and gristmill about four miles north of Noblesville, conducted a general store on the west side of the public square in that town, and managed nearly three thousand acres of land which he owned in Hamilton, Cass, Wabash, and Marion counties. When Conner died at the age of seventy-eight, he was survived by his wife, nine of their ten children, and a burgeoning state which owed more to his resourcefulness, enterprise, and energy than most of its citizens would ever realize.

Not until May, 1855, about three months prior to his death, did Conner become sole owner in fee simple of the land on White River on which he had built his first cabin and brick home. He had settled there while the area was still Indian country, but when the land passed to the federal government by the Treaty of St. Mary's, the Conner homestead should have been reserved to him, as similar acreage was to other individuals in like situations. Conner, however, when assured that the government would make adjustments later, agreed to postpone his claim. "Later" proved to be thirty-seven years and many legal maneuverings in the future.

After Conner's death the land on White River had a number of owners, and during the twentieth century the house was allowed to deteriorate. This neglect and the passage of time almost erased the original dignity and simplicity of the Conner homestead. In 1933, 110 years after its construction, Eli Lilly, then president of the Indiana Historical Society, purchased the brick house and surrounding acres. After careful and painstaking restoration of the original structure the house was opened to the public on a limited basis. Guests there could see the Jacob Cox portraits of William and Elizabeth Conner as well as furnishings and memorabilia of the Conners and of the period in which they lived. In 1964, after further restoration, Mr. Lilly presented the Conner Prairie Settlement to Earlham College to be operated as a permanent historical museum.

Visitors to Conner Prairie today enter the settlement through a pioneer museum which houses a 150 year old dugout canoe, exhibits depicting frontier farming and the life of William Conner, and a collection of early farm implements, a gift of the Purdue Agricultural Alumni Association. From the museum, guides—dressed in apparel typical of the early 1800s— conduct tours through a log barn, containing a covered wagon and other farm equipment of the period, and a log cabin and log trading post representing the double cabin and trading post which Conner had during the early nineteenth century. As the tour is routed, next come a log distillery and springhouse and a board and batten loom house, which contains all the equipment needed by the pioneer housewife to card, spin, and weave her cloth. (The log buildings in Conner Prairie Settlement were moved there from Brown County, Indiana; the loom house came from the south edge of Carmel, Indiana.) In these buildings Conner Prairie guides demonstrate the uses of the items on display. Visitors can see how an early flintlock rifle was loaded and how candles were dipped, how flax or wool was carded, spun on the old spinning wheels, then woven into cloth on the large looms. In the kitchen of the brick house meat will probably be roasting on the fireplace spit, and possibly bread will be baking in the unique beehive oven. Only in the old distillery—which was plugged by the State Alcoholic Beverages Commission—will there be no demonstrations.

And as the present day guests step out of the old brick house onto the front veranda—added at the time of the restoration in the 1930s—they may well agree with an earlier visitor to the Conner home who wrote, "I never beheld a more delightful scene than when I looked down . . . on a field of three hundred acres of waving corn, some two feet high, with fifteen or twenty merry plowmen scattered over it at work." This writer entered the house "out of nature's forest, only broken by the occasional cabins and small patches of cleared land of the early settlers."[8] Today's visitor enters from the hurried and harried activity of the twentieth century, but the peace, dignity, simplicity, and beauty of William Conner's homestead has endured for almost 150 years and is still there to touch him.

[8]Nathaniel Bolton, A Lecture Delivered before the Indiana Historical Society on the Early History of Indianapolis and Central Indiana . . . (Indiana Historical Society Publications, Vol. 1, No. 5; Indianapolis, 1897), 173.

3: Indian Relations

The story of the Indians in Indiana during the early nineteenth century is the usual melancholy one of commercial and territorial exploitation, occasional hostility and violence, and ultimate removal. During the first two decades of the century a series of treaties transferred ownership of the lower two thirds of Indiana to the white man; a major confrontation at Tippecanoe occurred, followed by continued hostility between Indians and whites during the War of 1812; and the Treaty of St. Mary's (1818), an "American land grab,"[1] transferred the vast central portion of Indiana to the United States and required the Indians to leave the land within three years. This occasioned the departure of the Delawares from central Indiana in 1820, followed by the removal of the Potawatomis in the 1830s and the Miamis in the 1840s. This is partially explained by the influx of white people into all parts of the state, causing Indiana's population to double and then redouble between 1820 and 1840, creating a demand for improved transportation routes all over the state. Most of the Indian treaties after 1820 were formed ostensibly for the purpose of acquiring land needed for transportation arteries such as the Michigan Road or the Wabash and Erie Canal; and the treaties ordinarily provided for a few individual reservations of land to certain prominent Indian leaders and their families.

As the Indian population in central Indiana was declining, an incident in 1824 created a brief furor and led to an unprecedented act: the conviction and execution of white men for the murder of Indians. In the late winter of 1824, five whites—four men and a boy—approached a small Indian camp along Fall Creek allegedly looking for strayed horses. As they were helping in the search, two Indian men were shot in the back; after that the three women and five children remaining in the camp were also murdered. As news of the massacre spread, the people of Madison County called for the arrest of the murderers and protection against any possible retaliation by the Miamis or Senecas. Although the instigator of the event, a fur trapper from Ohio, escaped, the other men and the boy (a son of one of the men involved), were arrested and eventually tried on murder charges. The sentences of death by hanging were carried out except in the case

[1]Bert Anson, *The Miami Indians* (1970), p. 179.

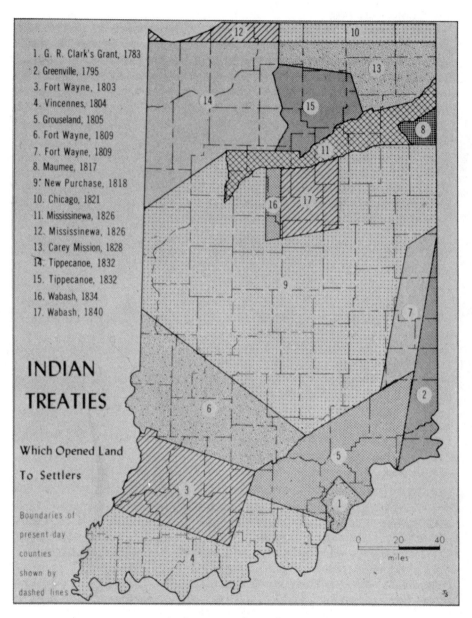

1. G. R. Clark's Grant, 1783
2. Greenville, 1795
3. Fort Wayne, 1803
4. Vincennes, 1804
5. Grouseland, 1805
6. Fort Wayne, 1809
7. Fort Wayne, 1809
8. Maumee, 1817
9. New Purchase, 1818
10. Chicago, 1821
11. Mississinewa, 1826
12. Mississinewa, 1826
13. Carey Mission, 1828
14. Tippecanoe, 1832
15. Tippecanoe, 1832
16. Wabash, 1834
17. Wabash, 1840

INDIAN
TREATIES

Which Opened Land
To Settlers

Boundaries of
present day
counties
shown by
dashed lines

Indian treaty boundaries
Courtesy of Robert C. Kingsbury, An Atlas of Indiana, 1970

of the youth, who was on the gallows when a dramatic last-minute pardon came from Governor James Brown Ray. The pardon saved his life but not his reason.

In 1974, Jessamyn West, an Indiana-born author and novelist, published a best-selling novel, *The Massacre at Fall Creek,* based on this unusual example of frontier justice. One of her basic sources for the facts in the case was Senator O. H. Smith, a prosecutor in the case who described it in some detail in his book *Early Indiana Trials and Sketches* (1858). In the selection below, Chapter Fourteen of West's novel, young Ben Cape, a friend of Johnny Wood and an eyewitness to the massacre, gives his testimony to the court under examination of the prosecutor, O. A. Dilk. The fictional names of the four men on trial are George Bemis, George Benson, John Wood, Sr., and John Wood, Jr. The chapter—as indeed the book as a whole—reveals the mixture of motives and emotions present on both sides in the volatile situation, which becomes in West's hands a microcosm of the fears, passions, and complexities of frontier life in America.

Some twenty years after the Fall Creek Massacre, a brutality of a different sort was enforced on the Miami Indians in northeastern Indiana. After staunchly resisting all efforts at their removal for years, several Miami Indian chiefs agreed among themselves, for unknown reasons, that emigration was now acceptable to them. Accordingly, a new treaty was signed at the Forks of the Wabash in November 1840, which, although it required only half of the Miamis to leave the state within five years, transferred almost all the tribal lands to the United States and thus was acceptable to the people of Indiana. In return, some Miami chiefs received fee-simple title to several sections of land in the area; in addition, a comparatively high cash settlement of $550,000 was agreed to. The city of Kokomo, named after a Miami Indian, was platted in 1844 on land reserved to Francis Lafontaine, the son-in-law of the old revered Chief Richardville. For the Indians required by the treaty to leave Indiana, the treaty provided for a 500,000 acre reservation west of Missouri. In the second selection below, Professor Bert Anson describes the complicated removal process, which was delayed past the five-year period agreed on and ultimately required the threat of force. He also evaluates the leadership abilities of new Chief Lafontaine, whose death in 1847 ended a long period of powerful Miami Indian influence in Indiana and the Old Northwest.

For readers desiring more information on the Fall Creek massacre, the best brief introduction to the complex series of events is George Chalou, "Massacre at Fall Creek," *Prologue: The Journal of the National Archives,* IV (Summer 1972), 109–114; see also, in addition to the book by Senator O. H. Smith, the work by Jacob P. Dunn, *True Indian Stories* (1908), pp. 187–200, and Helen Thurman, "The Fall Creek Tragedy," *Indiana Magazine of History,* XXVII (September 1931), 230–235. There are, however, few sources that bear directly on the Indian removals from Indiana. The Potawatomi removal of 1838 has been described in Irving McKee (ed.), *Trail of Death: The Letters of*

Benjamin Marie Pettit (1941); and Nellie Armstrong Robertson and Dorothy L. Riker (eds.), *The John Tipton Papers* (3 vols., 1942), contain some firsthand information. For more general sources, see also William T. Hagan, *American Indians* (1961) and Bernard W. Sheehan, *Seeds of Extinction: Jeffersonian Philanthropy and the American Indian* (1973).

The Massacre at Fall Creek

JESSAMYN WEST

Court resumed on Monday morning. Judge and side judges were in place. Benson was in the prisoners' pen. Ordinarily a florid, heavy-set man, he was noticeably thinner and paler. Sitting over there in the straw in the jail, cussing and sweating and fuming, had worn him down. He was still cussing and sweating and fuming, but there was noticeably less of Benson for the job.

The Indians, if they found the proceedings tedious, gave no sign of it. Unaccustomed to sitting on benches and chairs, unable to see what went on if they sat cross-legged on the floor, after their custom, they stood. The row of them, straight, motionless, seemingly untiring, attracted about as much attention as the proceedings up front. No one forgot them. Or forgot why they were there. No one was able to attend continuously to the oratory of the lawyers or the testimony of witnesses without turning to see how the Indians were taking it. Had one crumpled, leaned against the wall, sat down? No, there they stood, a handful of red men, surrounded by their enemies, impassive, unafraid, waiting to see the justice they had been promised done.

The courtroom was even more crowded than it had been on Wednesday. Bemis's confession had whetted the appetites of all. Was there more to come? The shooting of two bucks in the open was not as compelling as the slaughter of women and children at the sugar camp. Who had done that? The two Wood men and Benson had boasted earlier in open meeting that they were responsible for the killing. This was before there was any hint of trial or jail. What they had expected was praise. Varmints wiped out. Thieves of the settlement's fish and game taught a lesson. The settlement owed them thanks.

There were some in the courtroom who still felt that way. Those who had lost relatives at the hands of Indians were shedding no tears over the deaths at the sugar camp. It would give them pleasure to hear exactly what had happened, and what had happened they hoped included suffering as well as death.

Even those to whom Indians had done no harm had a sneaking feeling, of which they weren't proud, of wanting to hear the worst. Their throats were dry. They couldn't look their children in the eye.

O. A. Dilk, as assistant to Armitage, wasted no time in asking Ben Cape, the preacher's son, to come to the witness stand. This caused a gasp in the courtroom. Caleb Cape had had a hand in getting Bemis to confess. Was the preacher going to get his comeuppance now? Hear a confession squeezed out of his own son by the prosecutor?

Dilk handled young Cape as tenderly as a china dish. He all but lifted and carried the big lunk of a boy to the witness stand. Moved his own lips in the swearing in as if to show the boy anybody could do it.

Once he got under way the boy didn't need any more help than a sledder going downhill on glazed ice. Dilk kept slowing him down so that there wouldn't be any cracks in his testimony into which the defense could later poke their prying noses.

"How did you happen to go to the sugar camp on the afternoon in question, Benjamin?" Dilk asked.

Did the fact that Dilk didn't like his own name give him a delicacy in his use of the names of others? So no "Ben," but the full dignity of the Biblical name?

"Johnny Wood came by our house with a gun. I thought he was going squirrel-hunting. He's my best friend. My sister—"

"We're not interested in your sister, Benjamin. Now go on. What happened next?"

"I asked Johnny if I could go with him and he said I could. But Pa wouldn't let me take a gun."

"Why not?"

"Saturday afternoon is getting close to Sunday, and Pa thinks that on Saturday afternoon you shouldn't go frolicking."

"Does he think squirrel-hunting 'frolicking'?"

"It's lots of fun," Ben said, as if agreeing with his father.

"But he let you go with Johnny Wood."

"Just to watch and pick up squirrels for him. Not to do any shooting."

"Did you pick up any squirrels?"

"No. Johnny didn't shoot any."

"Why?"

"He was in a hurry to meet his father and uncle."

"George Benson and Wood Sr.?"

"Yes, sir."

"Where?"

"At the Indian sugar camp."

"Were these men glad to have you with them?"

"No. Old Mr. Wood wanted to send me home. But Johnny's Uncle George said, 'Let him stay. It will do him good.'"

"Did he say what it was that would do you good?"

"No, sir."

"Who was at the sugar camp?"

"Besides the Woods and George Benson?"

"Yes."

"The Indians. Three women and four children. One was my friend Folded Leaf. I was learning Indian gospel with him from Black Antler, the preacher."

"How did your father feel about your memorizing Indian gospel, Benjamin?"

"He said that what Black Antler preached was about what he preached. Except the names was different."

"Can you remember any of the words you memorized?"

Ben said, "I know by heart lots that Black Antler preached."

"Just a few lines will do," Dilk told him.

"Black Antler said, 'Our land will decay if we do not think on the Great Spirit. We must renew our minds and think on the Great Being who made us all. Then when we put our seeds in the Earth, they will grow and increase like the leaves on our trees. If any man, whatever he may be, will look on the Great Being above us all and do his will on Earth, when his days are out and the spirits about find he is a good man they will grant him more days to live in the World, and if he lives a good man, doing no evil in those days, when those days are out, the Great Being will take him to himself. The like of this...'"

Charlie Fort, on his feet at once, his resonant tenor bugling his protest, addressed Judge McGowan. "Your honor, I protest. What is this, a court of law or a camp meeting to convert whites to the religion of the Senecas? My understanding was that we were here to try the case of George Benson, indicted by the grand jury for murder. Now if the Great Spirit had a hand in this, I will listen to *his* testimony. Is the prosecution prepared to produce the Great Spirit?"

There were hoots of laughter, the soft thumping of moccasined feet, the high-jinx shouts of play parties and cornhuskings.

Before Judge McGowan could say a word, or even gavel for silence, there was a carrying sound from the back of the room: the ominous hoot-owl call of one Indian signaling to another. This silenced the courtroom faster than any crack of wooden gavel on wooden table. Then, in a muffled drum roll of a voice that had never had to give a command twice, the words, "Let the boy speak."

All turned toward the speaker. Dilk, who had not expected support from this quarter, and wasn't sure he wanted it, said, "What was that?"

All, now looking to the back of the room, saw the largest, most richly dressed, likely the oldest of the Indians take one step forward. He repeated what he had said. Not more loudly, though perhaps more slowly, "Let the boy speak."

Fort, undaunted, ignored the Indian and said, "Your honor, the boy's testimony does not require any further recitation of the doctrine of Handsome Lake as preached by Black Antler. These doctrines have absolutely no bearing on the case we are considering. Further talk about them simply wastes the court's time. We have already been forced to listen . . ."

Judge McGowan did not permit Charlie Fort to finish his sentence. "Objection overruled," he said.

True, it was not customary to permit listeners, red or white, to dictate courtroom proceedings. But this case was not customary in any way. Better, McGowan believed, to permit jurymen and onlookers alike to believe that the chief's request was not unusual. Let the judge lead the jury, by some rebuke to the chief, to believe that the red men were out of order and those twelve jurymen, all with side knives, would be at the back of the room with such speed and fury as might make the sugar-camp massacre a Sunday-school picnic.

"Let the boy continue," McGowan said, as if the order had originated with him.

"Continue, Benjamin," Dilk said, as calmly as if the idea had been, from the beginning, *his*.

Ben, rattled by the interruptions, made a couple of false starts, reconsidered, and finally got under way again.

"Black Antler taught us, 'Never forget to be thankful to the Great Spirit above us all. We will be good friends here and when we meet with the Great Being above we will have brighter and happier days.'"

Ben looked apologetically at his Indian listeners. "I know more, but right now I can't seem to remember. The way we always did it, Folded Leaf would say it with me. He knew it better'n me and I could follow him when I forgot something."

At the back of the room the chief who had spoken made the Indian sign "We are satisfied."

"Continue with the boy's testimony," McGowan ordered.

"Benjamin," Dilk said, "why did you think Benson and the Woods went to the Indian camp?"

"To visit them."

"This is something you have done before?"

"Yes."

"What happened to the squirrel hunt?"

"I thought we would hunt after we ate."

"They fed you?"

"Indians always do."

"Did everybody eat?"

"Yes."

"What happened next?"

"We just talked around for a while."

"How long?"

"I don't know ... 'til we heard the shots."

"What shots? Where?"

"I don't know. I can't remember." Ben dropped his face into the cradle of his arms.

At the back of the room one of the younger Indians spoke. "You tell, boy."

Dilk turned his anvil face toward the Indians. "He is going to tell. You won't help him by yelling at him."

The Indian who had first spoken, the tall, richly beaded and feathered chief, made a sign of rebuke to the younger Indian. "The boy tells well. Let him take his own gait."

"Benjamin," Dilk said, "was the first shot from toward the river or away from it?"

Ben looked up, puzzlement on his face. "The first shot was toward the river."

"Then ... ?"

"Then a single shot from the other direction."

"After that, Benjamin?"

"The killing began. It was then they started doing it."

"Doing what?"

"I told you. Killing. They all started killing the Indians. They started shooting. As soon as the other shooting stopped, they started shooting the women and children."

"Who did the killing?"

"They all did it."

"Did you see anybody in particular?"

"I saw two. First of all I saw what Johnny Wood did."

Charlie Fort was on his feet. "Judge McGowan, I protest. We are now considering the case of George Benson. If the boy has any testimony relevant to the actions of George Benson on the afternoon in question, let him continue. If not, let him step down."

"Your honor," Dilk spoke harshly, "this court will have to make up its mind whether it wants to hear the gentleman from Ohio spiel or whether it wants to hear from an eyewitness an account of what actually happened. I ask the court to remember that the witness is a young lad, and that the horrifying events of the afternoon ..."

Charlie Fort was once again on his feet, his tenor voice high and carrying after Dilk's bass. "Your honor, I object. The prosecutor is prejudicing the minds of the jury by using words to characterize the acts of the men I defend; and no testimony has yet been produced to justify such language."

"Objection sustained," said Judge McGowan.

"I withdraw the word, your honor. But I do ask you to remember that the witness is young. He is unaccustomed to being questioned about a ..." Dilk paused dramatically. "A disturbing event." He paused again, giving

Fort his opportunity to argue that what had happened at the sugar camp was not "disturbing." Fort remained silent. Dilk continued. "As I said, the boy is young and the events he witnessed did not happen in any order or sequence which Mr. Fort may feel most suited to the defense's case. They happened, and Benjamin remembers them as they happened. We will, I assure you, Mr. Fort, get to Mr. Benson. And when John Wood, Jr., is tried for the act for which he has already been indicted by the grand jury, my witness will then repeat for the jury what he saw, in case the jury feels the need to hear that act described once more. But I beg of you, Judge McGowan, out of consideration for the feelings of the boy and out of a judicial concern for the most complete account possible of the events of that day that you permit the witness to tell the court of the happenings in the order that they happened."

"Permission granted, Mr. Dilk. Continue with your witness."

"Benjamin," Dilk said, "you have told us that after you heard the shots fired away from the camp, shooting then began at the camp. You also said that you can only say positively who was responsible for two deaths? Is that true?"

"Yes, sir."

"Which was the first of these deaths you witnessed and who was the killer?"

"When the shooting started, two squaws fell down right away. Everybody thought they were dead. But one of the squaws wasn't dead, because they brought her to church at our house the next day. She died then."

"You said there were three Indian women."

"Yes, sir."

"Did you know the other one's name?"

"Yes, sir. Her name was Wide Eyes."

"Wasn't she hit?"

"Not at first. George Benson told Johnny he was leaving her for him because she was younger than the other women."

"Hadn't Johnny done any shooting?"

"No. He hadn't lifted his gun. When Mr. Benson said, 'What are you waiting for, Johnny?,' Wide Eyes said, 'I am a Christian. The Lord Jesus Christ is my savior. Don't shoot me. I love the Lord Jesus Christ.' Then Mr. Benson said, 'She's a redskin, Johnny. Let her have it.' Then Wide Eyes tore open the front of her dress so that all of her skin down to her waist showed. And she was as white as we are. And she said, 'Brothers, my skin is white as yours.' And it was. But Mr. Benson said, 'She's a breed, Johnny. Her father forced a white woman. Whose side are you on, anyway?' Then Johnny raised his gun and fired. It hit one side of her chest—right in the center. But she just stood there, and not even any blood came out. So Mr. Benson said, 'She's got one more, Johnny. You got one bull's-eye. One more will do it.' So Johnny shot her again—in the same place—on the other side. She went down to her knees like she was going to say her prayers and she said, 'I love the Lord Jesus Christ.' Then she fell on her face and then she died. When she died, Johnny raised up his gun and ran over to Mr. Benson."

"To shoot him?"

"No. The gun wasn't loaded then. To hit him."

"What did Mr. Benson do?"

"He took hold of the gun, and Johnny held on, and Mr. Benson threw Johnny to the ground."

"Did he hurt him?"

"I don't know. Stuff came out of Johnny's mouth, but it was puke, not blood."

Ben leaned over, his face in his hands again.

Dilk said quietly, "So all the Indians were then dead?"

There was no response from Ben.

Dilk repeated somewhat more loudly, "So all the Indians were then dead?"

Ben shook his head. "Not all."

"We can't hear you, Benjamin."

Judge McGowan said, "Mr. Dilk, your witness will have to speak up. This is not a private conversation between you and the boy. It is public testimony given to a jury trying men for their lives."

Ben sat up with a jerk. His eyes were red-rimmed and his round cheeks glazed with tears.

"Hang me," he said.

"Did you kill anyone, Benjamin?" asked Dilk.

"It would've been better if I had."

"You did not kill anyone. Who did?"

Ben stood up and pointed at Benson. "He did."

"Sit down, Benjamin," Dilk said. "You have already told us that both Benson and Wood Sr. fired at the women and children and that with the exception of Wide Eyes, who was killed by Wood Jr., and of Talking Crow, who died next day at your house, everyone was dead when the firing ceased. Have I misunderstood you?"

"Everyone looked dead."

"But everyone wasn't?"

"No, sir."

"Who was alive?"

"Folded Leaf. He was alive."

Having said these words, Ben stood, repeated them again in a strangled voice. "He was alive. He was alive." Then he bolted from the witness stand and appeared to be headed for the door, the street, and the woods beyond. As he passed the bench where the Cape family sat, Caleb Cape shot out an arm and pulled his son down onto the seat Caleb had vacated.

The crowd murmured, but the disturbance was not loud enough to require Judge McGowan's gavel.

If Ben had been seated next to Hannah, he might have buried his face on her shoulder and cried. He was next to his father, and crying on his father's shoulder was an act he wasn't encouraged to perform in private, let alone public. So he leaned forward, head to his knees, and rocked soundlessly, tearlessly, backward and forward.

He heard Dilk say, "The court will understand and excuse the witness's very natural emotional upset. Give him a few minutes to recover and we will continue."

Ben felt his father's arm across his shoulders, supporting him, so that his rocking was easier.

"Ben," his father whispered, "this is a big test for you. The biggest and the hardest you've had yet. You got through this. Now you do what you ought to do here—tell the truth—and things will likely smooth out for you from here on. It don't matter what people think—or what you think they'll think—you just set your jaw and tell the truth. This ain't between you and them—the people out there. It's between you and Folded Leaf and God. And me. You're my son. I set some store in you—and what you got the backbone to do. Telling the truth, no matter how much you wish it could be different, will clean the slate. It'll make everybody who loves you proud."

Caleb had murmured these words in a voice so low Ben hardly knew whether it was his father or his own mind speaking to him. Maybe it was Folded Leaf, forgiving him and whispering to him to tell what had happened. He didn't have to rock any more. The pain in his chest had let loose of him so that he could sit up straight and take notice of where he was.

Dilk said, "Is the witness ready to resume his testimony?"

Ben felt the weight of his father's arm lifted from his shoulders. He stood. He said, "I am ready." His voice had a strange cracked sound in his ears, so he repeated the words to make sure they carried. "I am ready." It still wasn't the voice he was accustomed to, but it carried.

Dilk said, "Please take your seat, and we'll resume where we left off."

Ben reseated himself.

"The witness has already been sworn," Dilk said. "The question, Benjamin, was that though everyone *looked* dead, everyone wasn't dead. Do you remember that?"

"Yes," said Ben. "I remember that."

"The next question was 'Who was alive?'"

"Folded Leaf. He was alive. He'd been shot in the leg and was stunned. But when Wide Eyes was shot, he sat up and tried to crawl to her. He couldn't because his leg was shot and the bone was sticking out. Bone is white like chalk, Mr. Dilk."

"That is a fact, Benjamin. Then what happened?"

"Mr. Benson yelled, 'The damned little bastard is alive!'"

"There are ladies present, Benjamin."

"Do you want me to tell what happened?"

"Everything that has bearing on the trial. Bad language has no . . ."

"I'm keeping back most of the bad language. There was lots more than I've told."

"Thank you, Benjamin. When Mr. Benson saw that Folded Leaf was still alive, what did he do?"

"After the cussing?"

"After the cussing."

"He shot at Folded Leaf but his gun misfired. Then he started toward Folded Leaf, and Folded Leaf called to me, 'Help me, Ben. Help me, Ben.' When he called I ran ahead of Mr. Benson toward Folded Leaf. But Mr. Benson caught me by the arm and said, 'Preacher's boy, if you don't want the same medicine I'm going to give that redskin'—he cussed some more— 'stay out of here.' "

"Did he hurt you?"

"He didn't hurt me bad. I could've stood it. He slung me down. But what he did was scare me. His eyes were popping out and spit ran out of his mouth.

"Then Folded Leaf called again. 'Help me, Ben.' But I didn't run to him."

"Why?" Dilk asked.

"I was afraid of Mr. Benson. When I got halfway up, he turned back toward me and lifted his foot like he was going to kick my teeth out or kick me somewhere."

George Benson, eyes once more bulging, spit at the corners of his mouth, got to his feet. He had been brought into the courtroom ironed, and the chains rattled as he stamped his feet. "That's a lie, that's a lie," he bellowed. "I was trying to save the boy. The redskin was crawling toward him. Ben, you know that's a lie. It was your safety I was thinking of. I pushed you to save you."

Judge McGowan saved Ben the need to reply. "Mr. Benson," he said, "sit down and be quiet or I will instruct the sheriff to remove you."

Benson sat down, but he kept talking. "The boy is lying, Judge. He never did like me. I run him off our place once."

"Sheriff," Mc Gowan said, "will you remove the prisoner?"

Benson stopped speaking. "Mr. Benson," McGowan said, "you will be given all the time necessary to tell your story. But the court cannot give proper attention to two witnesses at once. Now, Mr. Dilk, if you will have your witness continue. I trust we'll have no more interruptions."

Dilk said, "Benjamin, will you tell us what happened next?"

"I didn't go to help Folded Leaf. I was afraid to."

"What did Mr. Benson do?"

Ben put his head in his hands again.

Dilk took hold of Ben's shoulder. "Mr. Benson was right, wasn't he? Folded Leaf tried to kill you."

Ben jerked upright. "He didn't, he didn't. I told you, he couldn't move. His leg was shot in two. When Mr. Benson saw he had me buffaloed, he walked over to Folded Leaf. And Folded Leaf said once more, 'Help me, Ben.' But I didn't move. Then Mr. Benson picked Folded Leaf up by the heels and swung him around in a circle so that he fetched his head up at the end of the swing against the trunk of a big beech. Then he swung him the other direction and did the same thing."

"Did this kill the boy?"

"He didn't have any head left. Mr. Benson smashed his head like an egg. There was a body left, and running down the body was blood and stuff like pus and more little white bones. You couldn't tell if the body was a boy or a girl. Or if it was an animal, except for the clothes."

"What did Mr. Benson do then?"

"He threw what was left of Folded Leaf away. Like hog guts. Then he pulled up some grass and wiped his hands on it. Then he said, 'I reckon that finishes the job.'"

"What did you do then?"

"When he said that, I got up and run."

"Where did you run to?"

"I was heading home. But I was sick a lot of times and I couldn't go fast."

"Did you hear any more shots back at the sugar camp?"

"I couldn't hear anything for a long time but Folded Leaf's head breaking open against the beech tree. And I could hear him ask me to help him. I still can. And I remembered how quiet he was when Mr. Benson picked him up. He didn't beg Mr. Benson. Or ask me any more to help. He knew what was going to happen to him, but he didn't make a sound. But his head made a sound. His head made a sound like . . ."

Judge McGowan said, "We have heard that before. You don't have to repeat it."

"No, you haven't heard it, Judge McGowan. *You* didn't hear it. You don't know what it sounds like. Not the head of somebody who asked you for help. Not the head of . . ."

"Ask your witness to step down, Counselor."

Dilk put his arm around Ben, said something only the boy could hear, then led him back to where his family sat.

The courtroom was silent. No one moved. Judge McGowan stared out at the crowd. They had come to see the monkey show. Well, they had seen it. He thought he could hear heartbeats; he certainly heard hard breathing. He certainly heard Ben Cape crying and George Benson muttering away low enough not to be told to stop, but loud enough to prove no judge could shut him up. Would the crowd sit there silent all day? Did they want to hear more of the same? He gaveled to wake them up.

"The court will adjourn for two hours for dinner."

There was one door. The prisoner, his wife and six children trooping behind him, was taken out first. The Cape boy's account had taken some of the feistiness out of him, but he was far from broken. A white man in chains and Indian bucks parading like peacocks. Benson was rolling a mouthful of spit around like a cow with a cud of poison. There was no target within reach. He carried it as far as the door and loosed it like a hot cannonball on the new spring grass.

Judge McGowan watched him go. Benson would pass through that door someday hearing dreadful words he had spoken. God in heaven, God of mercy, why did he ever become a judge?

The jury followed. *They* would find guilty or not guilty: Sanders, Johns, Roberts, Gunn, Stephenson, Smith, Bentley, Wilson, Kilburn, Morley, Marsh, Fielding. They had listened to something they could not forget. What wrong had that Indian boy done beside being born red? Guilt or innocence was their responsibility. Life or death was his. He wanted to put his face as low in his hands as that boy had, hearing again a head break open with the sound of a pumpkin busted for cattle food, and cry. He wanted to, but he was a man, not a boy, and a judge, to boot; which is hardly a human being, he sometimes thought.

He sat upright, features as impassive, he hoped, as the Indians he faced.

The lawyers, talking, but quiet for lawyers, left together—except for Dilk, who went out with the Cape family. Mrs. Wood, enjoying herself, wife and mother of stars in the play, went out in a prance.

The onlookers left. The trial was many things to them. Most important, human beings instead of trees. Orators battling. A contest between lawyers, with words flying like bullets. The listeners all had real bullets, could make them or buy them. But none of them had a lawyer's store of words to fight with. Blood had been shed and more might flow. The onlookers filed out like fever patients from a hospital, their faces heated and their eyes bright. Judge McGowan had seen this happen time and time again. Considering the vein of cruelty that pulsed in all men, the love of violence, the fascination with death, it was a wonder so few heads were broken, so few breasts mangled with bullets.

He did not believe the Indians were any different in nature from the white men—in spite of Handsome Lake's prophecies and Black Antler's teaching. They, too, were brutal, but their training was different. Their faces were not open books. The Indian boy had not cried out. His kinsmen had not uttered a sound as they listened to the manner of the boy's death. They left the courtroom, their faces as sealed as old tree butts around the living sap that fed them.

Judge McGowan envied them.

When the side judges and Fenton, the clerk, had left the room and he was alone, he did what he had wanted to do before: he put his arms on the table in front of him and his head in his arms. He was not a young man, not old either—thirty-eight. There were strands of white in his brass-colored hair, like a dandelion getting ready to go to seed. He was not ambitious, like Fort and Dilk. He was judicious by nature. Judicious in practice, he had learned, was another kettle of fish. Judicious in practice required that one man, sitting on a bench, Amos McGowan, in his case, declare that in the name of justice one man should die, another serve ten years at hard labor, a third go free. There were hairlines here too fine for the human eye (which was all Judge Amos McGowan had) to see.

A hand on his shoulder roused him.

"Amos, I hope I didn't wake you up."

It was Johnston, the Indian agent. "I wasn't asleep."

"Will you come eat dinner with me?"

"Thank you, Colonel. I don't feel like eating. My stomach turns at the very thought."

"That wasn't a very pretty story."

"I've heard worse."

"I reckon you have."

"There are times I think I should never have been a judge."

"You've built up a fine reputation all over the state."

"Reputation don't chew like food. Happiness neither."

"This sort of thing makes us all bilious."

"There's nothing wrong with my liver. I've got a troubled mind. No one man can hand out justice the way a judge is asked to."

"No one man is asked to, Amos. Behind you is a grand jury that indicts. A petit jury finds guilty or innocent. All a judge is asked to do is to sentence."

"It shapes up that easy to you?"

"Besides the juries, you've got a framework of law and of court practice almost a hundred years old to support you."

"Court practice for the past hundred years won't help me in this case. You know as well as I do no court has ever handed down a judgment against a white for killing an Indian."

"Don't you think it's about time? We've got enough treaties with the Senecas to roll up and make a corduroy road of paper from here to Washington, D. C. We're not at war with them. Don't you think it's about time the law recognized them as human beings, under the law?"

"Oh, it's time, all right, Colonel. God knows it's time. *We* know it's time. But did the men who did the killing know it was time? For two hundred years it was time to kill Indians. How was Benson and the Woods to know the time had come to stop?"

"Something told Bemis. It's a lesson the other can learn in this courtroom.

"All right, string 'em up. What use to a man with a broken neck will that lesson be?"

"Their sons will learn the lesson. The Indians will learn."

"What lesson will the Indians learn?"

"They'll learn there's justice for them, too. They'll learn they don't have to raid and scalp and burn to get it."

"You admit they've done those things?"

"For God's sake, Amos, where do you think I've been for the past fifty years?"

"There's those who wonder."

"There's no need to wonder. I been right here. Born here. Living in Ohio state. Watching the Indians get the dirty end of the stick for fifty years. It's time they got justice."

"Colonel, there's no such thing as justice. There's chance. It won't be justice that hangs these men. If they hang. It'll be chance. The chance that put an Indian agent like you in the Northwest Territory at the time of the killings. It won't be justice that saves them. It'll be the chance of a judge who wonders how settlers can know that time has had a turnabout; that justice, who has had her blinders off and her eyes wide open to see who was red and who was white, has put them back on again; that's what may set them free."

"Chance and justice could go together sometimes, couldn't they?"

"I pray they can, sometimes. In God's name, I pray it, Colonel."

"Leaving justice out of it, Amos, you know what this trial can mean in the matter of saving lives?"

"Oh, I know that, and don't you remind me of it. This court, while I preside, won't be run on the principle of providing victims to appease attackers. We're not savages. I'd rather we'd all be wiped out together than have any man who wasn't found guilty by the jury sentenced by the judge to appease the Indians and save our own necks."

Judge Amos McGowan slumped against the headrest of the tall fan-backed chair brought in from somebody's parlor for the trial. He looked up at the chunky Colonel. The *Colonel's* decision had been made from the minute he heard of the killings. Get the killers hanged. With this promise made to the tribes (time and chance and justice all bundled together for him), he had staved off an Indian uprising and had brought the chiefs to Pendleton to see with their own eyes that his promise was being kept. Behind the Colonel, backing him up, stood the Secretary of War, Calhoun. And behind Calhoun stood Monroe, the President. And both were providing money to transport Indians, fee lawyers, pay the expenses of witnesses.

What did *he* have? McGowan asked himself. The law and his conscience. And the terrible knowledge that all courts up to this time had ignored the law. And that Benson, the Woods, and Bemis had killed out of knowledge of this fact.

"Come on out and have some dinner with me," Johnston urged again. "It'll do you good."

McGowan shook his head. "I think I'll go out to the backhouse and have a good puke," he said. "That's the slant my stomach is taking right now."

The Miami Emigration from Indiana, 1841–1847

BERT ANSON

Jean Baptiste Richardville died August 13, 1841, at his home on the St. Mary's River a few miles southeast of Fort Wayne on the tract he had secured in 1818. At a tribal council held later in 1841 at Black Loon's village on the present site of Andrews, Indiana, Francis Lafontaine, or Topeah, was elected principal chief. . . .

New Civil Chief Lafontaine, about thirty-one years old, was described as a "tall, spare, athletic" youth "noted for fleetness of foot," but he became "robust and corpulent" and in his later years weighed about 350 pounds. He was at least half—or perhaps three-quarters—Indian. He usually wore Indian clothing and followed Indian customs, which practices, along with his tendency to avoid contact with the whites, indicate he accepted Richardville's pattern of cautious and reticent behavior. Between his eighteenth and twenty-first birthdays, he married Richardville's daughter Catherine (Poconaqua). Lafontaine and his family probably stayed at the Forks of the Wabash most of the time, but he may have spent at least part of the 1830's on his reserve opposite the mouth of the Aboite River. After his election as principal chief of the Miamis, he lived at the Forks west of present-day Huntington.

Lafontaine had not received as many sections of land through treaty grants as had some of the other prominent Miamis, but he was later able to acquire other large holdings. He also operated Richardville's old trading post at the Forks, conducting a successful business there. As a family head-man and chief, Lafontaine had legal control of the extensive property of his dependents, and as principal chief, he secured, through the courts, the guardianship of Richardville's minor heirs. The old chief had provided well for the security of his family. Under the terms of his will, Lafontaine's wife, Catherine, inherited two sections of land at the confluence of the Mississinewa and Wabash rivers and one section at the Forks of the Wabash. The section at the Forks included her father's houses and store next to the tribal council house. Lafontaine's oldest son, Louis, received a section of land opposite the mouth of the Mississinewa. Each of the old chief's grand-

From *The Miami Indians* (1970), pp. 213–221, 224–228. Footnotes in the original have been omitted.

Miami chief Francis Lafontaine
Courtesy of the Fort Wayne Public Library

children and great-grandchildren—including Lafontaine's five younger children—inherited a half-section of land.

Lafontaine's election as principal chief made him the major spokesman for all of the Miamis and the guardian of all the financial affairs of the Richardville village. He followed the Miami practice of making the village subchiefs the agents for peaceful settlement of claims for damages committed by Indians against white property. The legal status of the Indians was changed in the first year of Lafontaine's leadership when the Indiana General Assembly passed an act removing the necessity of bail for those accused persons with one-eighth Indian blood or more and prohibiting whites or Negroes from contracting or collecting debts from Indians. While this law may indicate the confidence the local courts placed in the ability of the tribal chiefs to produce any erring member of a village at a court session, it may also reflect the reluctance of communities to furnish jail lodging and provisions for impoverished Miamis during the long periods of court recess.

More important, the law required Indian merchants to conduct legal phases of their business through the white men—not a new practice, but one which this process made mandatory.

The career of an Indian chief was closely bound to the motives and actions of the white men who cooperated with or influenced him. Fort Wayne banker and merchant Allen Hamilton was probably the most important adviser associated with the Miamis. He had worked closely with Chief Richardville and had participated in the 1840 treaty council. Hamilton became intimately involved in Richardville's commercial affairs, but he could only attempt to influence the old chief, who was astute in the ways of both white and Indian negotiations. At the tribe's request, Hamilton was appointed Miami agent in 1841 before Richardville's death and continued in this post after Lafontaine's election until 1845. . . .

Matters of land ownership and transfer and the disposal of property were the major problems blocking emigration and absorbed most of Lafontaine's time. His duties increased in number and urgency as the time of emigration approached. Earlier, he had been able to conduct his affairs with one secretary-clerk; in 1844, he added a chief clerk, John Roche of Huntington, a young Irishman with experience in Wabash and Erie Canal construction and maintenance. In 1846, Roche was made a partner in Lafontaine's business to circumvent the legal restrictions that harassed the Indian merchants. He also continued Lafontaine's enterprises when the latter traveled to Washington and later to Kansas.

The preparations were timely, for on May 6, 1844, Thomas Dowling of Terre Haute was granted a contract to move the Miamis to their western lands. The document provided $55,000 for the expenses of emigration, including salaries for conductors and physicians, the cost of assembling the tribe, and the expense of one year's subsistence for the Miamis in their new location. Dowling immediately traveled to the Wabash country for consultations with Hamilton and Lafontaine; then, on October 6, during a second trip, he met with the tribe and its chiefs. Hamilton's cooperation and understanding of the problems connected with the undertaking impressed the contractor, but the Indians countered Dowling's haste with amiable and frustrating procrastination. They wanted more time to complete the sale of their property but agreed that if additional time were not granted by the federal government, they would empower Lafontaine to dispose of it after their emigration. Dowling reached the conclusion that traders would foster the Indians' efforts to remain in Indiana as long as annual payments were made there.

Since the Miamis had agreed in the treaty of 1840 to emigrate within five years, preparations for the impending event accelerated in 1845. Secretary of War William Wilkins told Crawford there would be no further extensions of time and ordered Hamilton to press the Miamis for a definite commitment to move. There were still sporadic maneuvers to create delays, however. Lafontaine tried to divert the attention of the Bureau of Indian Affairs by suggesting to Hamilton that the Meshingomesia band might be troublesome. He indicated its members feared they might be evacuated from their reservation of ten sections along the Mississinewa, even though the land had been granted as a communal holding under their chief's guardianship until it should be alienated. Lafontaine thought their fear was based partly upon the fact that only the family of Meshingomesia had been specifically exempted from emigration. He suggested that the government try to purchase all of the reserve except a section or two which could be retained for Chief Meshingomesia. Although Commissioner Crawford approved Lafontaine's suggestion, it was not implemented. Hamilton added that the area was increasing in value. Land valued at $1.10 an acre in 1840 was bringing $3.00 by 1845, and the Richardville family had received as much as $5.00 an acre. While one Miami group had asked for $3.00 an acre, Hamilton thought the tribe would set a price of about $1.25 an acre.

During the summer of 1845, Lafontaine's oldest son, Louis (Wah-pahsapanah), and several village chiefs were sent to the proposed Miami reservation on the Marais des Cygnes River (which becomes the Osage River at its confluence with the Little Osage in western Missouri) in what is now eastern Kansas. On their return, they reported their satisfaction with the land's natural features; the valley of the Marais des Cygnes bore a striking resemblance to the Wabash Valley....

The federal government's eagerness for the emigration was evident in the authorization it gave in 1845 for the selection of a commission of three arbiters to review the Miamis' claims and debts to their traders. The Indians were instructed to select two traders, and the claimants named the third man. This unusual agreement was made October 27 and later approved by President James K. Polk. William L. Stuart and Dr. Graham N. Fitch, two residents of Logansport, were chosen by the Indians, and Elias Murray of Huntington was named by the traders who had claims against various members of the tribe.

Sometime in 1845, Joseph Sinclair of Fort Wayne was appointed agent to the Miami, replacing Hamilton. Sinclair sent Crawford's successor, William Medill, a petition from Lafontaine requesting reassurance that the Chief's family would be exempt from emigration. "I will remark that Lafontaine married the favorite daughter of the late chief.... Lafontaine has relatives and connections to the number of thirty-four," wrote Sinclair, who thought anything which protected the prestige of the Chief would expedite the emigration, since the Miamis gave unusual obedience to their paramount officer and members related to chiefs were extremely proud of that relationship.

In spite of the terms of the treaty of 1840, the Miami emigration did not take place in 1845. Several factors contributed to the delay. Miami debts were not yet liquidated, and the Indians were dispersed among their villages and refused to assemble. In addition, it is doubtful that Dowling had ever intended to attempt the removal, but had instead entered into the contract as a speculative venture. Nevertheless, by 1846, emigration was inevitable, and the events leading to its culmination occurred with increasing frequency as the year began. Using his removal contract as security, Dowling negotiated a loan of $6,000, then sold the contract to Robert Peebles of Pittsburgh. Peebles notified Commissioner Medill of the purchase, acknowledged his legal obligation to conduct the emigration in the name of Dowling, the original contractor, and informed Medill that Allen Hamilton had aided him in securing a conference with Lafontaine at which they had arranged for a council to be held at the Forks of the Wabash in March, 1846.

Agent Sinclair was appointed superintendent of the emigration in March, 1846. On March 30, Peebles reached the Forks, where Lafontaine approved the new contractor and his appointed physician, Dr. Fitch. Sinclair believed the only remaining obstacle was the final debt accounting, but again the removal contract was sold, this time to a group of four men. The Ewing brothers, William G. and George W., bought one-third of the joint venture; Samuel Edsall of Fort Wayne bought another third; and Alexis Coquillard of South Bend bought the remaining third. Coquillard was designated the "active partner," or actual conductor.

While there is no hint of the circumstances which motivated Peebles' withdrawal, subcontracting was a common practice and the actual removal of Indians was usually performed by experienced men like Coquillard. The contract—it was still the one originally granted to Dowling—contained the customary terms required by the Bureau of Indian Affairs: the contractor was obligated to issue rations to Indians waiting at the place of assembly, to assume the expenses of the actual migration, to provide rations to the tribe for one year after its arrival at the western reservation, and to pay the salaries of all of the conductor's assistants.

Sinclair and the new contractors immediately moved to liquidate Miami financial affairs, using the procedure devised the previous October. Arbiters Stuart, Murray, and Dr. Fitch met the Indians and their debtors on May 4, 1846, and completed the settlement in five days. During the conference, there were rumors that some traders received preferential treatment from the Indians or from the arbiters and that many claims were fraudulent. The arbiters, however, were able to obtain an immediate settlement, leaving individual traders who were dissatisfied to make their charges of corruption to the commissioner of Indian affairs or their congressmen. . . .

The emigration finally began at Peru on October 6. Three canalboats were loaded with baggage, Indians, and white officials. Although no military action was necessary—partly because of the Lafontaine family's presence—Sinclair cautioned Medill that it would be expedient to have the semi-annual payment ready for distribution to the Miamis as soon as they reached their western reservation. On the second day, the three boats reached Fort Wayne, where the remainder of the tribe was awaiting the conductors; two more boats were added to accommodate them.

There is no reliable account of the Miamis' departure in 1846. October 1 to 6 must have witnessed veritable madhouse scenes at Coquillard's camp near Peru as families assembled and exempted relatives came to say farewell. Even greater confusion must have reigned on the St. Mary's and Eel rivers while families packed to join the large contingent at Fort Wayne. The curious gathered along the canal to watch "The Indians" leave for the west: relatives, friends, and sensation seekers, the latter hoping to witness violence or grief. Once again the observers reported that which they wanted to see: disorder or dignity, unrestrained grief or stoic behavior. At least it was a ceremonial exodus—more humane, more worthy of both the federal government and the Indians than the herded caravans of the 1830's.

The party followed the Wabash and Erie Canal to its junction with the Miami and Erie Canal in Ohio, then passed through Dayton to Cincinnati, where the entire party was transferred to the steamer *Colorado* on the Ohio River. In a report from Evansville, Indiana, Sinclair wrote that a few Indians had eluded the conductors at Peru but that Coquillard had hired Ezekial French, an experienced trader, to find as many as possible and take them west via a land route. The agent suggested placing these fugitives—some of whom had been involved in murders on the Mississinewa in 1844 and 1845 and thus were also fugitives from their own tribe—on the western reservation of the Potawatomis when they emigrated.

The expedition reached St. Louis on October 20, 1846, transferred to the *Clermont II,* and three days later steamed up the Missouri River. The Indians and baggage were unloaded at Kansas Landing (now Kansas City) on the first of November and reached the Osage subagency reservation eight days later. Meanwhile, Joseph J. Comparet of Fort Wayne, who had contracted with the conductors to deliver the Miamis' horses to the western reservation, arrived there on November 5. He had left Peru one day after the boat party and had lost only nine of the original herd of ninety-nine animals in crossing Indiana, Illinois, and Missouri.

At the reservation, Indian Agent Alfred J. Vaughan certified the arrival of 323 Miamis. A few were ill when the journey began; during the first part of the trip, there had been six deaths and two births, and the conductors had acquired a few additional Indians on the way. The party included 142 men and 181 women; 51 males and 53 females were under eighteen. Vaughan also prepared lists of the names and relationships of the family or village of each subchief. . . .

Sinclair began his return journey to Fort Wayne on November 10, leaving Vaughan and the Indians with the assurance the Miamis would have subsistence for another year under terms of the Dowling contract. After Sinclair's departure, the Miamis called a council at which Lafontaine told

Vaughan the Indians wished to apologize for their fractiousness at Peru and said they were pleased with their new home. He praised Coquillard's supervision, accused Sinclair of neglect and inattention during the emigration, and charged Dr. Fitch with drunkenness. Lafontaine spoke of other Miami grievances. The Miamis had been disappointed in the past with the results of training received by some of their children at the Choctaw Academy in Kentucky. The Chief criticized the continued use of tribal school funds at the school, to which they had sent no pupils for about ten years, and indicated that in their new home they now wanted a school operated by the Roman Catholic church.

When Thomas H. Harvey, superintendent of Indian affairs at St. Louis, sent $10,000 for the relief of the new arrivals in December, he ordered that the money be paid to the heads of families. Later, when Harvey accompanied the officials who transported the March, 1847, annuity payment of $33,500 to the Miamis, he found Lafontaine still with the tribe. They refused to accept their money as individuals and voted to pay their remaining debts out of their next two annuity payments.

"Lafontaine's influence on these peoples," Harvey insisted, "is unlimited. He will leave in a few days for Indiana after which I hope they will begin to think and act for themselves. . . . It is due Mr. Lafontaine to say that he expressed himself warmly in favor of ample provision for education of their children. . . . Lafontaine says he will send his own children to school here." Harvey soon changed his opinion of Lafontaine's prestige in the tribe; after the Chief's departure, the western Miamis immediately held a meeting, selected a new chief for themselves, and declared they would no longer listen to Lafontaine. Harvey was sure, however, that Lafontaine and the Indian traders would continue to exert a great influence on the tribe, even though the emigrants had declared themselves no longer dependent upon their former leaders.

4: Transportation Problems

Transportation development is one of the keys to understanding pioneer history, or indeed the history of any period. The struggles of the pioneers to join farm and marketplace and to improve their access to the commerical and cultural centers of the region were continuous ones. The first settlers in Indiana relied on the natural routes supplied by rivers and streams and by animals and Indians of previous generations. The Buffalo Trace, for example, a route traveled by wandering herds across southern Indiana between New Albany and Vincennes, became an early pioneer road, probably the one used by the Lincoln family on their way to Illinois in 1830. The major north-south route of the pioneer period was the Michigan Road, laid out in the 1820s and constructed during the 1830s; the major east-west route was the National Road, also known as the Cumberland Road, which began at Cumberland, Maryland, reached the Ohio River at Wheeling, Virginia [now West Virginia], and then crossed Ohio, Indiana, and part of Illinois as it headed toward St. Louis. In Indiana it connected Richmond on the eastern border with Terre Haute on the western. A route modification after Indianapolis became the state capital brought the road through that city on Washington Street, and it was one of the factors in Indianapolis' subsequent commercial development.

The state, however, was in need of additional transportation routes, a need that became pressing as its population and agricultural production continued to grow. In 1827 the state authorized—and the federal government helped subsidize via its first internal improvement land grant—a canal across northern Indiana through Fort Wayne and Peru to Lafayette and beyond. Construction began in 1832 and proceeded slowly, but it was buoyed by the example of numerous internal improvement projects in other states, particularly the spectacular success of the Erie Canal in New York and the promising experiments with a new and revolutionary form of transport, the steam-powered railroad. Although, as Professor Carmony points out in the following selection, the mammoth internal improvement program which the state undertook in 1836 was a monumental failure as a state enterprise, its various parts were eventually constructued by private— or a combination of public and private—enterprise, and the state was at last well supplied with a system of roads, railroads, and canals. The canals, basically the 453-mile-long Wabash and Erie Canal and the shorter Whitewater Canal, were not profitable to their owners, but they made a contribution to the economic development of the state. And the railroads, delayed almost a decade by the Panic of 1837 and the depression that followed, had an even greater impact in the decades before and after the Civil War.

In the following pages Professor Carmony not only describes the constitutional impact of the failure of the internal improvement program but also contributes to our understanding of the transportation needs of the state, the internal improvement mania that emerged, and the psychology of the people in supporting a program that, in the cold light of the morning after, left so much to be desired. Professor Carmony, a foremost authority on the history of Indiana, has specialized in the study of the pioneer period and the financial history of Indiana during its territorial and early statehood periods. For additional information on Indiana's transportation history, see Logan Esarey, *Internal Improvements in Early Indiana* (1915); R. Carlyle Buley, *The Old Northwest: Pioneer Period, 1815-1840* (2 vols., 1950); Paul Fatout, *Indiana Canals* (1972); Elbert Jay Benton, *The Wabash Trade Route in the Development of the Old Northwest* (1903); and Philip D. Jordan, *The National Road* (1948).

The Mammoth Internal Improvement Fiasco

DONALD F. CARMONY

One of the more significant provisions of the present constitution of Indiana is Section 5 of Article 10: "No law shall authorize any debt to be contracted, on behalf of the State, except in the following cases: To meet casual deficits in the revenue; to pay interest on the State debt; to repel invasion, suppress insurrection, or, if hostilities be threatened, provide for public defense."

These restrictions are probably unwise but their inclusion in the Constitution of 1851 stemmed directly from Indiana's experience with the Internal Improvements System of 1836 and the catastrophic fiscal consequences which resulted therefrom. Such limitations on state legislatures are characteristic of the state constitutions formed at mid-century under the spell of Jacksonian Democracy. Indiana's experience with her internal improvements debt differed only in degree from the experience which Ohio, Illinois, and Michigan had with the same problem. These three states, and many others, also have constitutional restrictions against state debts.

From "Historical Background of the Restriction Against State Debt in the Indiana Constitution of 1851," *Indiana Magazine of History*, XLVII (June 1951), 129–138, 142. Footnotes in the original have been omitted. Reprinted by permission.

We are conditioned to thinking in terms of millions of dollars when viewing state finances and of billions when considering federal revenues and expenditures. This makes it almost impossible for us to comprehend the limited expenditures and revenues required to support the territorial and early state government. The total cost of the territorial government, during the sixteen years from its establishment, in 1800, until statehood in 1816, averaged less than ten thousand dollars yearly and approximately two-thirds of this amount was provided directly from the federal treasury. During the first decade of statehood it cost about twenty-five thousand dollars annually to operate the state government, while the average yearly cost increased to about one hundred twenty thousand dollars by the mid-thirties, including expenditures arising from the sales of land received from the federal government as subsidies for various purposes. The annual reports of the state treasurer have not been carefully analyzed and tabulated for the mid-thirties but it is roughly estimated that the "ordinary" expenses of the state government which were provided by landholders and citizens of the state did not exceed a maximum of seventy-five thousand dollars annually. The preceding totals and estimates for territorial and state expenditures do not include the costs arising from local government.

These very limited expenditures are merely an index of the meager economic, political, and social resources of frontier Indiana. Indiana was a debtor area and its people were engaged in the laborious and exhausting task of conquering their physical environment. Further explanations for these exceedingly small expenditures are to be found in the low price level, the meager population and the fact that the role of government was in accordance with the laissez-faire traditions of Adam Smith and Thomas Jefferson. From the establishment of Indiana as a separate territory in 1800 until the adoption of the Internal Improvements System in 1836, Hoosier revenue payers provided considerably less than one million dollars to finance the territorial and state government. Direct appropriations from the federal treasury and liberal subsidies through land grants loomed large in the fiscal affairs of the frontier commonwealth. New Dealers increased and made new uses of federal subsidies; however, federal subsidies were gratefully accepted by the early Hoosiers who often complained that the federal government could, and should do more to foster and support internal improvements and other desirable projects for improving their economic status.

If the expenditures for internal improvements be measured against this background, and with general regard to frontier conditions, their magnitude becomes apparent. To understand the internal improvements muddle and the resulting constitutional restrictions against state debt we must look back from 1851. Comparison with our present state finances will blind us to the realities and limitations of the half century preceding the adoption of the 1851 constitution. Historians continue to argue whether history really teaches men anything; certainly the debt restriction section of our constitution is ample evidence that historical experience at least greatly influences human conduct and policy.

The frontier faced many problems. Perhaps the basic economic problem was that of transportation. Until arteries of transportation could be developed it would not be possible to exchange the surplus produce of the soil for imports or dollars necessary to pay for land, establish business, support government, build roads and canals, raise the standard of living and bring about gradual improvement in the social and cultural life of the pioneers. It was natural that an isolated and debtor society should bend its efforts toward solving the all-important transportation problem.

Under these circumstances the attempts to improve conditions of transportation were perhaps discussed with as much interest and intensity during the two decades between 1816 and 1836 as any other subject in any two decades of our history as a state. Every message of every governor during this period mentioned internal improvements. Committees of the assembly studied the problem and made numerous reports with increasing vigor and enthusiasm in the 1830's. Newspapers included many articles concerning the need for the improvement of river travel, for better roads through the forest, for better methods of road building, and watched with interest and growing absorption the building of canals, roads, and railroads in other states. The pro and con of railroads versus canals was debated and as the internal improvements movement gained momentum it swept the Hoosiers with greater intensity and with more permanent effects than some of the agues and fevers which took a heavy toll among the pioneers.

It was generally agreed that something should be done and for years they talked about "the system," and although there was Clay's American System, the movement for a system of common schools, and other "systems" yet "the system" meant internal improvements by the 1830's as clearly as "the revolution" means the revolution of the 1790's to a Frenchman. But how could a debtor society which lacked available funds provide such a system and what would be the results of the proposed system? Some thought that the federal government should build at least the national arteries for river and land travel but the policy of Andrew Jackson in the early 1830's made it necessary for the states to assume primary obligations for building internal improvements if such were to be provided by governmental action. Even so it took some time for Hoosiers, even some of the Democratic leaders, to realize that appropriations from the federal treasury for improvement of the "noble Wabash" were also scheduled for the discard so far as Old Hickory was concerned. During the twenties the federal government started the National Road across Indiana, approved a grant of land to build a road from the Ohio to Lake Michigan via Indianapolis, and made a liberal grant of land to finance the building of the Wabash and Erie Canal. The latter was expected to provide continuous navigation from the Wabash through Lake Erie and thence by way of the Erie Canal down the Hudson to

New York City. Meanwhile, Indiana opened many highways for land travel, assisted by the three per cent fund received from the federal government. River traffic via flatboat, keelboats, and steamboats was of great importance but the flatboat trade took Indiana's surplus to the southern markets. The "system" was designed to connect Indiana with eastern markets where prices were higher and a better selection of goods could be exchanged for the products of the soil.

As early as 1822, Governor William Hendricks, in addressing the assembly, rather safely said: "Let us not lose sight of those great objects, to which the means of the state should at some future day be devoted—The Navigation of the falls of the Ohio—the improvement of the Wabash, the White rivers, and other streams, and the construction of the national and other roads through the state. But to these objects, great as they are, the fostering hand of government cannot be extended, while its finances are embarrassed by a state debt."

In 1825, New York successfully completed the Erie Canal and Ohio began the construction of two important canals. The internal improvements fever was moving westward and it was easily caught by the Hoosiers. On November 18, 1825, the Lawrenceburg *Indiana Palladium* reported the following toast as having been given at a public meeting: "The Fair—while they cultivate their *external* graces, may they not forget that the spirit of the age is in favor of *internal improvement*." Early in 1825, John Ewing reported from a select committee of the Senate: "The statesmen and philosophers of the age, have exerted their best faculties to establish the theory and the practicability of this system [internal improvements by canals], combating in their progress, ignorance and prejudice, timidity and heedlessness, in all variety of forms. They have moved fearlessly on, demonstrating by successful experiment its importance and advantages.... The scintillations of these mighty geniuses ... have visited every hemisphere, and the benign influence will continue to unfold and expand the beauties of a God of nature, and the mysteries of political economy, until the *Danube* like the *Nile*, the *Mississippi* like the *Thames*, and the *Wabash* like the *Hudson*, shall exhibit one great theatre of splendid and successful exertion.... No part of the Union has a greater interest at stake in the final success and accomplishment of this system, than the state of Indiana, and ... greater facilities for, or prospective advantages from internal improvements, are no where to be found."

The next year Governor James B. Ray gave much consideration to internal improvements in his annual message and in his grandiloquent and flowery style pointed to the outlet through Lake Erie as the best "to reduce western produce into money." The governor predicted that Indiana would sustain a population of ten million and shortly Indiana's granary would be overflowing and wasting for lack of a market outside the state. Indicating an awareness of the vital role of transportation Ray continued: "It is evident that the settlers of a new country, must be subjected to many privations and a heavy indirect tax, imposed upon them by the rude deformity of surrounding nature. . . . Although this kind of a tax [transportation costs] exceeds ten times the amount which is yearly paid for the support of the government, yet it appears that it has escaped with less consideration, and more indifference. . . . *The rough appearances of nature, must be overcome, and made to yield to human enterprize. Our waters must be imprisoned in new channels, and made to subserve the essential purposes of commerce.*" In concluding the governor exhorted: "Whilst our sisters around us are rearing eternal monuments of their energies and public spirit, we have looked and admired, but have been too timid to imitate!!!" In spite of this florid oratory the governor was cautious about recommending specific steps to be taken but did urge that further attention be given to the improvement of the roads.

By the mid-thirties the state was reaching the peak of a decade of prosperity. Population and resources had greatly increased having jumped from about seventy-five thousand when statehood was achieved to approximately one hundred forty-seven thousand in 1820 and then more than doubled during the twenties to reach about three hundred forty-three thousand in 1830. By 1840 the population totaled over six hundred eighty-three thousand. In 1832 the Wabash and Erie Canal was begun and advocates of internal improvements prepared for an early inauguration of a system of railroads, roads and canals which would bring the markets of the east to the farmers and townsmen of Indiana.

In 1834, Governor Noah Noble, a Whig, indicated to the assembly the kind of financial magic which he thought would make it possible to build the system by tapping the available and painless resources which would flow from appropriate use of public credit: "Since the beneficial policy of engaging in public works for the advancement of the agricultural and commercial interests of the country has been so frequently and clearly demonstrated, and while our credit is justly such as to command any amount of capital at an interest of five per cent or less, no good reason can be assigned why we should longer hesitate to follow the successful examples of other States. New York, Pennsylvania and Ohio had, at the commencement of their works, which have enriched their citizens . . . but little more means or resources than their public credit. . . . The money thus procurred . . . immediately benefitted the people by being thrown into circulation in payment for labor, materials and subsistence, and as soon as the works were completed, the people and the States were repaid many fold by the increased demands and higher prices for their produce; by the activity imparted to every branch of industry, and by the enchancement [*sic*] of the landed property of the country. The additional value alone of the lands in the district of the country intersected by the Miami Canal in Ohio, far exceeds the cost of construction. The actual wealth of a state or nation, does not consist of the sums hoarded in the Treasury, but in the wealth of the citizens

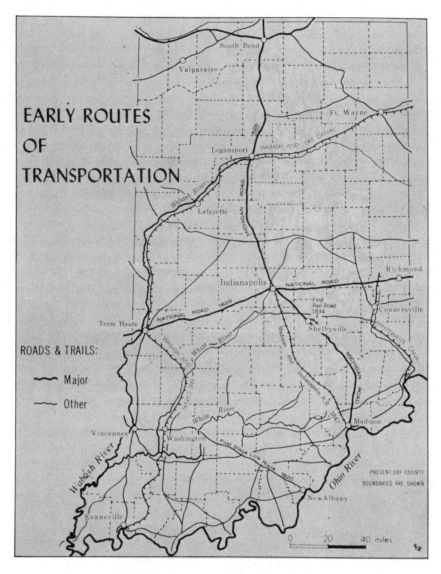

Indiana's early roads and canals

Courtesy of Robert C. Kingsbury, An Atlas of Indiana, 1970

and their ability to pay whenever the exigencies of the Government make contributions necessary. The Treasury of a well managed Government, is the pockets of the people, in which something should be placed by wise legislation, before much is required."

The *Indiana Journal,* principal Whig organ of Indiana, indicated that the spirit of internal improvement was abroad in the land: "It remains for the people of Indiana to say whether we shall fall behind our sister states in public spirit and enterprize. So far as we have had an opportunity to mingle with the people we have found them prepared for the commencement and energetic prosecution of a liberal and judicious system of internal improvements. Our state needs nothing but outlets, by means of canals and railroads, to make her a populous, wealthy, and influential member of the confederacy."

Early in 1836 the mammoth internal improvements system was approved. The *Indiana Journal* without waiting for the governor to sign, or for the two houses of the assembly to iron out the differences between the bills which had passed their respective houses, gleefully announced: "On Saturday night Indianapolis was most brilliantly illuminated as a manifestation of joy for the passage of the bill. The only cause of regret . . . is the fact that a respectable portion of the members of both houses . . . felt constrained to vote against the bill on the ground that equal benefits are not extended to the whole state." The *Journal* then prophesied: "We doubt not that population and capital will flow into our state, in consequence of this bill, with a rapidity hitherto wholly unexampled, and we believe many of the present generation will live to see Indiana the third state in the confederacy."

Later the *Journal* received a report concerning the celebration at Peru: "No sooner did intelligence of the passage of the General Internal Improvements Bill reach us, than the expression of general joy was manifested by the symultaneous glow of light from every house, hamlet, and shantee, within the town and vicinity, presenting one of the most beautiful illuminations we have ever witnessed. . . .

"From a spot where but twelve months ago, little else was to be seen save the dense wilderness and the red man of the forest, now sending forth streams of light from at least one hundred houses, accompanied with the cheer of civilization, none could fail to foster and cherish the most lively hopes, for the future of a town so flourishing as Peru, on an occasion like this."

Dr. R. Caryle Buley, who has spent many years in a study of the Old Northwest, stated: "Passage of the law was celebrated from one end of the state to the other; other states hailed the enterprise and spirit of Indiana. Enthusiastic advocates of the 'System' had promised that not only would no additional taxes be necessary, but that soon the tolls and receipts would provide the state with revenue for all purposes. Few people seemed to note that the young state had voted itself a program far beyond its means."

Whigs and Democrats vied for popular favor in their support of the system. During the ensuing annual session of the legislature some in both parties made strenuous efforts to broaden the system to include some neglected parts of the state. When failure came, and the inability to pay principal or interest haunted the taxpayers, the Democrats made effective efforts to blame the Whigs for the financial ruin which existed in stark contrast to the promised arteries of commerce with revenues therefrom sufficient to provide for upkeep, payment of debt, and perhaps even allow a surplus for ordinary state expenditures.

Possibly the most effective pen among the Democratic editors in the 1840's was that of E. W. H. Ellis, editor of the Goshen *Democrat*. Ellis reviewed the flattering promises of improvements past local doors to transport produce and roll back a tide of wealth. Ellis was partisan as he poured forth his satire against the Whigs: "But what have we instead? Half-finished canals, which will not pay for keeping themselves in repair—detached portions of railroads—dilapidated bridges—here and there a straggling frog pond, whose dismal echoes seem to forebode the wreck and ruin of which they are the monuments; and these are the riches of Indiana!" Editor Ellis pinned the responsibility upon the Whigs, and with his eye toward the state elections for the ensuing August, asked: "CHANGE! CHANGE! Is it not time for a change? Can our situation not be bettered?—Of what use is it to plod on in the old beaten path, and sink deeper at every step into the yawning gulf of ruin. For twelve long years have the Whig party had possession of Indiana. They found her in her virgin beauty, the pride of the Western forests. Her hardy yeomanry were free and independent. Her rich soil teemed with valuable products, and the husbandman received a rich reward from her toil. But they beggared her—they ruled and they ruined her—they piled a debt mountain high upon her—they crushed her energies—they sapped her credit, and they gnawed like hungry dogs at her vitals."

The failure of the system and the resentment of the electorate was the most important single factor leading to the landslide victory of the Democrats in the election of a governor and state assembly in 1843. The stigma attached to the failure of the internal improvements system was a basic reason the Whigs never regained political control in Indiana.

During 1846 and again in 1847, approximately a decade after the system had been adopted and commenced, the assembly approved legislation which brought about an understanding with the state's creditors and a plan for debt settlement. The Butler bills, as the legislation was called after Charles Butler who carried on the negotiations on behalf of many of the creditors, provided that the Wabash and Erie Canal should be given to the creditors as payment for one-half of the debt due. A definite plan was arranged for payment of principal and interest on the remaining debt. It was a compromise arrangement which salvaged as much for the creditors as it appeared possible to secure and made it possible for the state to begin the long process of debt liquidation. Some creditors were dissatisfied with the arrangement but they either agreed or were forced to make the best of the legislation. Eventually in 1873 a constitutional amendment was adopted to make certain that no further claims be paid except as agreed to in the Butler bills.

In 1849 there was a constitutional referendum regarding a proposed convention to revise the constitution. In the agitation arising over this referendum many, both Democrats and Whigs, insisted that if a new constitution be framed there must be strict limitation against another state debt. Schuyler Colfax, Whig editor at South Bend and later vice-president under Grant, thought there should be no important debt except by vote of the people. Colfax explained: "The past history of our State is the best argument in favor of this amendment."

. . . .

In 1851 the new constitution was submitted to the people at a popular referendum and overwhelmingly approved. The restrictions against state debt were generally considered as desirable and wise. In an address to the people, authorized by the convention and distributed among the voters during the ratification contest, the restrictions against public debt were reviewed and the comment made: "Had this provision, brief and simple as it is, been inserted in the Constitution of 1816, it would have saved the State from a loss of six millions of dollars. Upon that sum we are now paying, without any return, some three hundred thousand dollars of interest annually; that is, about eight hundred dollars a day; more than enough to maintain in perpetual session ... such a Convention as that which has been engaged, for the last four months, in framing a constitution, which shuts out for the future, all possibility of similar folly."

No doubt we will generally agree that in the long run the political ability and maturity of a people, or lack of the same, are more basic in the struggle for successful government than mere constitutional restrictions. In any event it is abundantly clear that it was the catastrophic fiscal consequences arising from the System of 1836 which directly caused the rigid restrictions against state debt in our present constitution.

Chapter V
PIONEER CULTURE AND AGRICULTURE

The primary economic activity of the Indiana pioneers was agriculture. By 1850 the state had become a major supplier of the national granaries, ranking high particularly in the production of corn (4th), wheat (6th), and oats (8th); Indiana was also a major producer of hogs and sheep. Although some mills and factories existed in the state, these activities were "neither an important nor typical part of the scene during the first half of the nineteenth century."[1] Rather, the economy was characterized by the curious combination of self-sufficiency and cooperation common to frontier conditions, and the average family faced a bewildering variety of daily tasks that were required to obtain the necessities of life. Hard work, long hours, and constant activity were the rule. The development of the state fair in the 1850s reflected not only the growing maturity of the state's agriculture but also the usefulness of an exchange of information and a social outlet.

Other activities and interests were essential too, to provide access to market for the crops produced and to tend to the whole person—his educational, religious, and cultural development. In spite of the advanced concept of state responsibility for a "general system of education"—including elementary, secondary, and higher—that was written into the first constitution of 1816, circumstances never did permit its implementation before the plans were adopted for a reduced system in the 1851 constitution. Instead, the public schools of the pioneer period remained a local responsibility, often unmet, that was supplemented in places with private schools operated by churches or individuals. Indiana also became the home of a number of private, usually church-related, colleges during the early nineteenth century, in addition to the two state-supported colleges, now Vincennes University (1806) and Indiana University (1820).

Among the obstacles to the development of a free public school system were the public's denial of the usefulness of education, its aversion to the additional tax burden, and the preference of some for church or private schools. In the late 1840s, however, a concerted campaign for improved

---

[1]John D. Barnhart and Donald F. Carmony, *Indiana: From Frontier to Industrial Commonwealth* (2 vols., 1954), I, 345.

public schools in Indiana, spearheaded largely by Professor Caleb Mills of Wabash College, finally resulted in much-needed constitutional and legislative reforms. Although the 1851 Constitution did not provide for free higher education, it did—together with the Free Public School Law of 1852—authorize the establishment of a free public school system. But little progress was made during the 1850s because of controversies and lawsuits challenging the authority of the state to levy taxes for educational purposes; finally, during the 1860s and after, the basis for a system of free elementary and secondary schools was laid.

In religious matters, the individualistic system of the Baptists and the itinerant circuit-riding system of the Methodists proved to be most suited to the needs of the predominantly Protestant Hoosiers. The Presbyterians, committed to an educated ministry and the development of educational opportunities for all, trailed the other two denominations in members; but they contributed to the stability of the communities they served and to the educational resources of the state, especially in higher education.

Other major Protestant denominations in Indiana were the Disciples of Christ (Christians), Episcopalians, Lutherans, and Quakers. Roman Catholicism, the oldest religious persuasion in the state, saw its numbers swell with the increased immigration, particularly from Germany and Ireland, of the 1840s and 1850s. The Catholics established not only their own elementary and secondary schools but also colleges and universities, most notably the University of Notre Dame in 1842.

For additional information on the economic and cultural activities of the Indiana pioneers, see John D. Barnhart and Donald F. Carmony, *Indiana: From Frontier to Industrial Commonwealth* (2 vols., 1954); Logan Esarey, *A History of Indiana* (2 vols., 1915, 1918); and Paul Wallace Gates, *The Farmer's Age: Agriculture, 1815–1860* (1960).

1: Farming

The Farming Seasons

LOGAN ESAREY

The selection below comes from Logan Esarey's delightful little book *The Indiana Home,* which might be considered the distillation of Esarey's experiences and learning in and about Indiana over a lifetime. The book is a collection of Professor Esarey's unpublished lectures, notes, and papers as arranged by a junior colleague, Professor R. Carlyle Buley, and published posthumously in 1943. In the passage below, taken from the chapter entitled "Farm Life in the Fifties," Esarey describes the never-ending round of chores and the seasonal acitivites of the Hoosier farmer in the prosperous last decade before the Civil War.

    The author, to a degree at least, lived the life of a pioneer farmer during his youth. He was born in 1873 in a log cabin in Perry County, a rugged rural area in southern Indiana where primitive methods and practices were slow in being abandoned, and he remained in the county until 1903. In the introduction to a 1970 reprint of Esarey's major book, *A History of Indiana* (2 vols., 1915, 1918), Professor Donald F. Carmony, a student of Esarey at Indiana University, wrote: "When Esarey wrote or talked about butchering, sheep-shearing, blacksmithing, grist milling, churning, drying fruits, making maple sugar and syrup, tanning, spinning, weaving, and the like, he drew upon information gained from personal experience and observation. When he explained the use and importance of the ax, frow, broadax, cross-cut saw, sickle, maul, cradle, wedge, and walking plow, he was describing tools which he, himself, had used." For a fuller appreciation of his character and career, see R. Carlyle Buley's tribute, "Logan Esarey, Hoosier," *Indiana Magazine of History,* XXXVIII (December 1942), 337–381.

The farmer's most important job in early spring was breaking for corn. The work began as soon as the ground was thawed. A side or turning plow

From *The Indiana Home* (1943; 4th ed., 1976), pp. 86–99. Copyright © 1953, 1976 by Indiana University Press. Reprinted by permission.

was in general use, though a few of the more conservative farmers still used a big shovel plow, especially if oxen were used. During this decade [1850s], there was about one yoke of oxen in Indiana for each farm. The big gentle, lazy, liquid-eyed oxen were still in favor among the farmers. An ox team would break about an acre per day while horses or mules could break as much as two acres. All good farmers hoped to have their corn land, except the new ground, broken and harrowed by May 10. Planting was more rapid. The field was "laid off" with a one-horse shovel plow into squares about three and a half or four feet and the corn dropped by hand in the intersections and covered with hoes. The dropping was often done by women, but men or grown boys handled the hoes. A planting crew usually consisted of one man and a horse to lay off the rows, and two droppers and two coverers with hoes. They planted about eight acres per day. Corn drills—not check rowers—were on the market but they were not favored because the farmers perferred to plow the corn both ways. Corn planting was finished by the middle of May and the new ground by the last of the month. If planting was finished in good time everybody had a holiday, usually spent in fishing.

There followed a busy month cultivating or plowing corn. All farmers hoped for a rain as soon as the planting was done and then two or three weeks of dry weather. Just as soon as the corn was up enough to show the row the alert farmer went over it with a "harrey" (harrow), removing the front tooth and straddling the row. Then at week or ten-day intervals he plowed it with a one-horse double-shovel plow. It is still undecided whether the crop should be "laid by"—that is, given the final plowing—with a shovel or a side (turning) plow. The latter left the corn ridged high and braced it against wind and storm. If a dry summer followed, however, it was just too bad. If two or three weeks of wet weather followed the planting, the weeds and grass "got the jump" on the corn and it had to be "barred" out. This meant weary days with the hoe. In any case the good farmer went over his cornfields after they were "laid by," or perhaps after harvest, and cut out all the weeds. This was done by the Fourth of July at latest, and we must now leave our cornfields for "harvest."

By the last of June the sun was riding high at its summer solstice, the wheat fields on the southern slopes were taking on a golden glow and the heavily whiskered heads were bending with the weight of the ripening grain. The farmer took down his grain cradle, sharpened the scythe, tightened the nib and mended the weak or broken fingers. Like the logrollings, wheat-harvest was a neighborhood job, and required the united help of all the men, women and children. All other work waited because the wheat wouldn't; not even on Sunday. The hands began with the ripest wheat and changed from farm to farm, day by day as the fields ripened. It took from five to a dozen men. One shocker could keep up with two cradlers and two binders. The binders tied the bundles with bands of straw. At best the harvest lasted only ten days and an untimely wet spell meant heavy loss. Three acres was a

Cradling grain
Courtesy of the John Deere Company

good day's work for one cradler and a squad of five men usually shocked five acres of wheat.

In the logrolling the short, stocky men had the advantage, but in the wheat-harvest the tall, deep-chested, rangy men were in their glory. Some trusty cradler set the pace, the others followed, each ten steps behind. Occasionally there were tests of endurance but sensible men would not risk the loss of a good hand by overwork to satisfy a foolish whim. Today we admire the endurance of a two- or four-mile runner but such activity is child's play compared to swinging a cradle in heavy wheat "from sun to sun."

After the spring work the winter fat was worked off and the men were in good training. The first swath in the morning sun started the sweat trickling down their faces and by ten o'clock there was little dry clothing. At the ends they met the water boy with a jug of fresh water from the spring. And how the barefoot urchin longed for the time when he could set his cradle down, reach for the jug with his left hand, flip it up on his shoulder and drink while he mopped his red, manly face with his right. "Gee! Only to be a man!" There were chicken, cake and pie on the dinner table and at ten in the morning and four in the afternoon the women brought out more pies and perhaps buttermilk for a short lunch under the shade trees. So the gay but tiresome work proceeded day by day from farm to farm until the wheat was all in shock. Then all gathered in a circle, gave the "stubble call," retired to the nearest swimming hole, performed the necessary ablution, laid aside their sweaty clothes full of prickly wheat beards, and wheat-harvest was over.

But the golden age of the cradler was passing. Already at the county and state fairs McCormick reapers were giving demonstrations before wide-eyed and open-mouthed Hoosiers. The cradle artist, who could leave the wheat stubble as level as if it had been clipped by a modern lawn mower, was disgusted but the "machine" was on his trail. The noblest art of the pioneer farmer was lost to his own sons.

In 1856, middle of the "glorious Fifties," Indiana raised 9,350,971 bushels of wheat, about ten bushels per head. This, perhaps, was as much as could be harvested by the cradle.

The farmer usually let his wheat stand in the shock until the hay was cut unless an untimely wind blew the shocks down. Then while the big hay frame was still on the wagon he hauled the wheat to the barn and stacked it. Sometimes he stowed it away in the barn but it was much easier and pleasanter to stack. Nobody wanted to get up in the barnloft under the hot roof and put away wheat, and then in a few days get up and dig it out again when the thresher men came. The days of the threshing floor and winnowing, as previously practiced, had passed, and even the "ground-hog thresher" was no longer used. The horse power separator had taken its place.

Threshing was the most spectacular event of the year. The "horse power" was a circular cog machine driven by eight teams hitched to sweeps. The power was carried to the separator by a long iron rod, perhaps four inches in diameter, called the "tumbling shaft." The crew consisted of two drivers and two feeders, working in shifts of two each. The driver and the feeder were the heroes. Every distinguished visitor had to step up and feed a shift to show that he was a real man. The envy of the young boys was the driver who stood on a central platform, a long whip, the "stalk" about five feet long, in his hand. This would crack like a rifle and that was the signal for the horses to step off. The driver never dreamed of striking a horse with the whiplash. Instead, he sang to his teams in a monotone, much as the cowboys used to sing to the "dogies." His voice had to be raised above the general hum of the machine as he sang: "Jack, Jill, Kate, Bill, up here, up here!" followed by two or three short whistles. He kept one eye on the feeder who might signal for more power or stick up a finger to stop. The other eye was on the horses. Some horses were lazy and had to be encouraged; a limp or flinch indicated a sore foot or shoulder. So long as the sweat flowed freely and the white lather formed where the harness touched the hair, all was well, but when a horse quit sweating it was time to take him out. The driver could make a hit with a boy by taking him up on the platform for a "heat."

The other hero was the feeder. He took the bundles or sheaves one by one, shook them to pieces and fed them in so evenly that the gentle hum of the cylinder was never broken. A "chug" brought everybody to attention. It might mean an uncut band or wet wheat had gone through. About once in a season someone dropped a monkey wrench into the cylinder. The result sounded like a railroad crash; a dozen or so teeth were gone from cylinder and concave and the work was stopped for a half-day or so.

On the right of the feeder stood the band-cutter; two men laid bundles on the table before him; one or two pitched from the stack. An elderly man filled the half-bushel measure and kept the tally; a man poured the wheat from the half-bushel measure and two boys carried the wheat to the bins. Four or five men who took the straw from the separator screen finished the crew. The machines of that day had no strawstackers. The threshing crowd usually numbered not less than thirty and the food exceeded in abundance that for the logrollings. The older men consulted the tally to see what the "turn out" or yield was. Apparently the average for the state was about as at present, 18 to 20 bushels per acre.

Hay-harvest was unimportant in early Indiana. Some timothy and more redtop grew on the wet lands, yielding at best one ton per acre. This hay was cut right after wheat-harvest with a light, long-bladed or mowing scythe. The mower had to bend over all the time making it tiresome on his back. An acre per day was good cutting. The scythe left the hay in a small windrow and if the mower was not careful a wisp of grass was left uncut at the end of each stroke. This made miserable work for the person who came along with a small hand or garden rake to gather the hay into bunches for the pitchfork, or to scatter it so the sun would cure it. When cured it was either built into shocks, "haycocks," or loaded on a sled and hauled to the mow. Much of it was stacked in the field, as you may yet see on many farms. Hay presses and mowing machines were coming onto the market as well as revolving horserakes. Red clover, now so common, was a novelty. It was considered good pasturage for stock cattle but would make horses "slobber" the same as white clover. If cut for hay there would be sure to be some ripe heads and the seed would "dry up" the milk cows. It was generally considered a good cover crop to turn under for wheat or corn.

The farmer had a breathing spell during the "dog days" of August. If he was "ornery" he hunted squirrels or loafed at the country store or blacksmith shop. If he was not "ornery" he "sprouted" the new ground, went through his cornfields with a hoe, or cut out the briers and weeds from his fence corners and pastures with the brush scythe. Poison ivy grew prolifically in the fence rows and those who were not immune often enjoyed a good case of ivy poison. This job of cutting the fence rows usually fell to the boys. Apparently all the hornets, "yaller" jackets, bumble-bees and wasps nested along the fences, and by the middle of the summer each nest was an enemy which no boy would pass up.

Those boys who were fortunate enough to live near the streams spent a large part of each day in the swimming hole. Curiously enough, girls were not permitted to go near a swimming hole. There were, of course, no bathing suits and if there had been the sight of a woman in a bathing suit would have caused a panic in any neighborhood and mobilized every deacon in the township. A woman who could even swim was of doubtful character. She was not supposed to go fishing with her brothers.

As soon as the fall rains had softened the ground the fall breaking for wheat began. A prelude to this was a week or so of manure hauling. The feverish rush of the springtime was over. All kinds of fruits were ripening and the women were busy making apple butter, drying apples, making marmalades, jelly and preserves. The horses were lazy from the green pastures, and all the folks were so full of food it was hard to keep in training. For two or three weeks the team or teams trudged slowly 'round and 'round the narrowing wheat field. The oxen with harrow or drag followed still more leisurely until the field was ready for the wheat drill or, more often, the sower. Many of the old farmers were still "skittish" of machinery and sowed the wheat broadcast. The children and turkeys chased the fat grasshoppers in the green meadows while the forest slowly put on its holiday dress of yellow and red. The fat frisky squirrels were cutting the hickory and beechnuts and spring chickens had passed through the frying stage. These were the "halcyon days" the poets speak of, unless the baby took the "summer complaint" or the older folks the "ager" or "fever" or granny came down with "yaller janders."

In the meantime the farmer had hauled his surplus wheat to the mill and either sold it to the "merchant miller" or had it ground and packed in barrels for the eastern or southern market. Store-keepers came back from the East about the first of October with a brand-new line of "hats, caps, boots and shoes," not to mention silks and satins, just beginning to rustle in Indiana society. A little later all climbed into the big wagon some bright morning and drove off to the big store to lay in the winter supplies. Real cash money was beginning to circulate among the folks. Homemade goods fell off one-half during the decade. "Store clothes," now ready made, soon crowded out the homespun, except with the deacons who mourned over the sinfulness and extravagance of the new times.

But the corn was ripening. The tassels and silks dried up, the "shoots" gradually bent away from the stalks and as they filled modestly bowed toward Mother Earth. If an early September frost did not play havoc, by the closing week of September the shucks were dry and corn was ready for the shock. The ordinary farmer cut eight or ten acres of fodder for his cattle during the winter. Nobody "hankered" for the job of cutting corn. It was hard, tiresome, uninteresting work. The dry blades cut one's wrists and neck until they were raw and bleeding; the big "woolly worms" crawled down under the worker's shirt and the sharp stubs skinned his shins as he staggered to the shock with a load of heavy fodder on his shoulder. No one who has not cut heavy corn all day knows how tired the left arm can become. No one came with a jug of water, no one brought pies and cakes to the field as in wheat-harvest. The long V-shaped lines of wild geese "honked" on their way to Florida, the last mellow specimens of the Rambo, Yellow Belleflower, Maiden Blush and Carolina Sweets hung temptingly on the rapidly coloring apple trees, and all nature called from the near-by woods. But still the corn had to be cut on time. It was just plain work.

With the fodder in the shock and the wheat in the ground came the fall chores. The onions and potatoes, long ago lost in the wild grass, had to be dug out and placed in a cool place until freezing weather threatened. Then they were either "holed up" in the garden or stored in a dry part of the cellar, if such a part existed. The big late Drumhead cabbages were through growing in October and a day was set aside when all hands made sauerkraut. If it were a German or Dutch family nothing less than four to eight barrels would do; otherwise a couple of barrels would answer. In any event it was at least an all-day job. The cabbages had to be pulled up, beheaded above the ears and the loose leaves carefully removed to get rid of all worms and traces of worms. Then the heads were placed in a big box which slid over three or four knives. After a few hours of vigorous "sawing" and salting and tamping one had a barrel of slaw which in time became "kraut." All of this made the mouth water profusely. Surplus cabbages, onions or potatoes were given to less fortunate neighbors. No one thought of selling them.

Every farmer had an orchard and every orchard had from eight to twenty varieties of apples. The Early Harvests, Red and Yellow Junes, Summer Queens, Pearmains and Sweet Bows ripened in summer; those named previously ripened in the fall. During October the Imperial Winesaps took on a fiery red, the Baldwins became red-streaked, the Romanites speckled, the Russets golden and the Northern Spies a golden green. All had to be picked from the trees and carefully laid away in a dry cool place to season for the cellar or apple hole for winter use. The best were sorted out for this purpose and the remainder given to the neighbors or run through the cider mill—come to think of it, a glass of sweet cider along about nine o'clock on winter nights after one had eaten a dozen hickory nuts or walnuts was considered healthful.

There remained the corn husking. It might be husked on the stalk or snapped off and husked in the crib shed—a husking bee, for instance. Whatever the procedure it has not changed with the years. Tractors and gang-plows have sent Buck and Bright to the showers; the cultivator has put the mules and double-shovel out of business; the corn-cutter and shredder have superseded the corn knife, but the champion corn husker of a century ago no doubt would walk right along with the champion of today—in fact Old Nokomis shucked Mondamin no differently. Human ingenuity has not yet invented a machine which can satisfactorily cut the weeds and grass from the corn rows or husk the ripened corn on the stalk.

The season ended—or began, according to the weather—with hog killing or "butchering." We may sing the praises of all the heroes of Indiana from LaSalle or George Rogers Clark to the present, but the prosperity of our state through the century has depended on Mr. Hog. In fat years and lean years, until his late unmerited humiliation (when he was ordered to be destroyed by the government) he has come up with his part, even though he does grunt about it considerably. The hog population of the state during the Fifties was about two and one-half millions, two for each person, or a dozen for each family. Both the day and the glory of the old "razorbacks" were passing but stock hogs in general ran at large and fed on the mast. During the summer when the range was poor for hogs the prudent farmer cultivated their acquaintance by giving them a few ears of corn; or perhaps out in the lane he prepared a slop trough where the hogs might come and get the garbage and skim milk or a basket of bad apples.

About the tenth of December hogs selected for the winter killing were penned up and fed corn for two or three weeks until they were fat enough to kill. As a rule they were two or three years old. On the appointed day three or four of the neighbors, each bringing "his old woman," gathered for the killing. Large kettles of water were heated to the boiling point, the water poured into large barrels or meat tubs set at an angle. The hogs were shot, one by one, stuck so the blood would drain out, then doused in the hot water until the hair was loosened, scraped with knives until free of all hair and dirt. Then tendons of the hind feet were raised, gambrel sticks inserted and the hog hung up on a pole so his nose was a foot or two from the ground. He was then gutted, the heart and liver hung up to dry, the leaf fat taken out for lard, the guts washed to be used as sausage casings. The Germans likely saved the blood for blood wurst which they stuffed in the hog's stomach after it was washed. As soon as the carcass dried it was carried into the smokehouse, where the head was cut off for "souse" and the body cut into shoulders, middlings (bacon) and hams, which left the knuckles, ribs and backbones for immediate use. Each neighbor returning home took enough "bones" to last a week. If the butcherings in the neighborhood were properly distributed each family might thus have fresh meat—spareribs, pigs' knuckles and sauerkraut, or backbones—for a month. During this month the men put on the weight they had lost in harvest. Coming near the Christmas holidays it was a time of feasting.

The women's work did not vary so much with the changing seasons. The kitchen program was varied only slightly by the season's menu. Bread and meat came on the tables three times each day. The first garden vegetables, onions, lettuce and radishes, came in early in June and went out with frost. The first berries came in about wheat-harvest and apples hung on the trees until November. From two to five milk cows had to be attended to morn and eve the year 'round; the milk was strained into crocks, in due time skimmed and the cream churned into butter and the skimmed milk served at table while still sweet, or made into cheese. As stated above, the wool furnished year 'round work. Early in the spring a dozen hens were set, half as many geese and a like number of turkeys. All these had to be nursed through the summer season.

Wash day monopolized one whole day each week and ironing and mending another. The children went barefoot half the year but it was no relief to mother. What time she saved in darning she lost in picking out briers and splinters and binding up misused fingers and toes. There was always someone ailing—"under the weather." Colds, sore throats, croup and winter fever were succeeded by summer complaint, sore eyes, chills and fevers. The mother was both doctor and nurse. And all this while she rocked the cradle with one foot. It took the Civil War to break this deadly monotony of women's lives but few mothers of the "glorious Fifties" lived to see the day.

The First State Fair

GEORGE S. COTTMAN

George S. Cottman, the founder and first editor of the *Indiana Magazine of History* (established in 1905), wrote many of the first articles that appeared in the journal. In 1907, Cottman, an Indianapolis journalist and amateur historian, contributed a short essay describing the first Indiana state fair at Indianapolis in 1852. As indicated, the site of the earliest fairs changed from year to year, but soon Indianapolis became the permanent home of the event. The present State Fairground on the near east side of the city above 38th Street, to which the fair moved in the 1890s, is its third location in Indianapolis. Two contemporary accounts of the 1852 state fair are from *The Diary of Calvin Fletcher, Vol. IV: 1848–1852* (1975), edited by Gayle Thornbrough, Dorothy L. Riker, and Paula Corpuz, pp. 496–500, which also reprints a map indicating the layout of the grounds; and from *The Indiana Farmer* (November 1, 1852), pp. 65–69. For an account of the Indiana State Fair nearly a century later, which is still going strong after more than a century and a quarter, see the selection by John Bartlow Martin on the 1946 fair in Volume II of this publication.

Indiana's first fair was held in Indianapolis, October 19–23, 1852, on the old military reservation, west of West street, now known as Military Park. It was largely through the efforts and influence of Joseph A. Wright,

From "First State Fair in Indiana," *Indiana Magazine of History*, III (September 1907), 144–145. Reprinted by permission.

then governor of the State, that the institution was brought into being, and the hearty response when the movement was once under way showed that the time was right for the focussing of the State's industries.

The newspapers, which at that day reviewed local affairs but sparingly, devoted an unusual amount of space to advertising the fair both before and during its progress, and the following extract from an editorial shows the hopeful enthusiasm that greeted the occasion:

"A just pride in the utility and greatness of their pursuits will be generally infused among our farmers, mechanics and manufacturers. Standards of excellence in stock, of utility in machines, and of true taste in the elegant articles of comfort and luxury will be fixed in the minds of all. Progress in their respective pursuits will take the place of indifference in their minds. A laudable ambition to have the mantel decorated with a silver cup will actuate all, and thus feeling and acting, who can calculate the ultimate result?"

The people responded no less enthusiastically. By that time railroad communication was established to Madison, Terre Haute, Lafayette and Peru, and with the eastern counties by the Bellefontaine and Indiana Central (Panhandle) roads. These admitted of easy access to the capital from the various sections of the State. Half rates were given; the plank roads let animals pass free of toll, and the exhibits and the crowds came.

There were 1365 entries, with quite a showing of improved agricultural machinery. Among the greatest curiosities of the time were three sewing-machines (the Home, Wilson, and Singer). There was much live stock exhibited, especially hogs, sheep and cattle, and of the latter the Durham were by all odds the most in evidence. By reason of this feature the attendance was augmented by many stockmen from Kentucky. According to the report of one paper, there were about 15,000 visitors the first day; on the second 25,000, and on Thursday, the third day, there were more people in town than the grounds could hold, and the other shows outside caught the overflow.

Among other features there was an address on Thursday delivered by John B. Dillon, the historian; and Friday and Saturday plowing matches were held out on Calvin Fletcher's farm. The gate receipts at twenty cents a head, for the five days of the fair amounted to something over $4,600, which, according to the local papers, not only defrayed expenses but allowed the return of $2,000 that had been borrowed of the State.

Altogether it was undoubtedly the liveliest week Indianapolis had ever known. In anticipation of the unusual crowds, side shows, great and small, flocked hither, all eager to catch the surplus Hoosier small change. The "Yankee" Robinson's "Athenæum," otherwise vaudeville troupe, gave three performances daily in a tent near the fair grounds, and Wells' Minstrels lured the crowds with time-honored jokes and burnt cork. A man named Diehl put up what he advertised as an "enormous pavilion" near the State House, where he let off fireworks a la Pain of modern pyrotechnic fame.

Toward the last came P. T. Barnum's Museum and Menagerie. Then there was a "grand exhibition of the World's Fair"—a reproduction by illuminated views of the famous Crystal Palace exposition; "Beard's Hoosier Panorama of 'Paradise Lost'," at one of the churches, and divers other catch-pennies.

Added to all this the Democrats had a big torch-light procession which was to close with speaking at the Wright House where the New York store now stands. The Whigs, however, objecting to the Democratic program, gathered in numbers to howl down the speakers, and pandemonium resulted. Out of this affair a difficulty sprang up between George G. Dunn and W. A. Gorman which all but resulted in a duel.

The original intention, out of deference to the other leading towns of the State, was to shift the fair from place to place, giving Indianapolis every third year. In accordance with this idea Lafayette had it in 1853 and Madison in 1854, but this plan proved financially disastrous, and it was finally decided to hold it permanently at Indianapolis.

Land Laws and Speculators

PAUL WALLACE GATES

Paul Wallace Gates, the nation's leading historian of the public lands, the policies governing their distribution, and the consequences of those actions, has written extensively about the concentration of land ownership, the role of speculators on the American frontier, and the growth of tenancy in the Midwest. In an address presented at the twentieth annual Indiana History Conference in Indianapolis in December 1938, Professor Gates focused his attention on the lush prairie counties in northwestern Indiana, where high rates of farm tenancy and poor tenant housing contrasted sharply with the richness of the soil and the larger-than-average size of the farms. In attempting to explain the apparent paradox, Gates focused on the history of land sales in the area during the nineteenth century. As early as 1835 Solon Robinson, an influential agricultural editor then living in Lake County, Indiana, had warned against permitting nonresidents to obtain large bodies of land, something "which always injures the rapid growth of a country,"[1] but both absentee ownership and the tenancy system were fastened on the prairie counties early. Gates is led to the conclusion that "the much vaunted land system" of the United States failed to meet its

[1]Gates, "Land Policy," p. 2.

From "Land Policy and Tenancy in the Prairie Counties of Indiana," *Indiana Magazine of History*, XXXV (March 1939), 3–13, 18–26. Footnotes in the original have been omitted. Reprinted by permission.

objectives in the Wabash Valley. Rather than fostering the establishment of democratic farm ownership, it "had produced a system much
at variance with American democratic ideals."[2]

For additional information on Indiana agriculture, see William
Latta, *Outline History of Indiana Agriculture* (1938), and Herbert A.
Kellar (ed.), *Solon Robinson: Pioneer and Agriculturist* (2 vols., 1936).

The Land Ordinance of 1785 and subsequent laws had placed no
restrictions upon the amount of public land that individuals or groups could
acquire at the government offices, and it was not until after 1862 that any
serious attempts were made to restrict land entries. The policy of unlimited
sales and unrestricted transfer of titles made possible land monopolization
by speculators, who acquired most of the choice lands in certain areas,
notably in the Military Tract of Illinois, the prairie sections of Indiana and
Illinois, and the timber areas of Michigan, Wisconsin and Minnesota. This
resulted in the early disappearance of cheap or free land and the emergence
of tenancy. In Indiana the dead hand of the speculator created many problems which were to stunt the growth and waste the resources of some
sections of the state.

Unimproved lands and town lots were the chief items of speculation in
the United States before the era of wide scale stock distribution. In the
nineteenth century, New England, the Middle States, and the older Southern
States poured great sums of money into land investments in the new territories and states as they were opened to settlement. In the boom years
1835 to 1837 and again in 1847 to 1857 whole townships were swept into
the control of absentee proprietors and holdings of 5,000 and 10,000 acres
were widely established while holdings of 50,000 to 100,000 acres were not
unknown. The fertile state of Indiana naturally attracted the attention of nonresident capitalists and hundreds of thousands of acres of its lands were bought
by people who had no intention either of settling upon or improving them.

It was in southern Indiana that the lands were first opened to entry
and here they were generally taken up before the speculative boom of the
middle eighteen-thirties got under way. This section was early overrun by
squatters who settled promiscuously over the land before it was offered for
sale, made improvements, and organized claim associations to provide a
quasi-legal land and title registration system in the absence of government
action. The claim association was also a mutual protective organization to
assist its members against claim-jumpers or speculators who might try to
seize or buy their homes. Having settled, the squatters petitioned Congress
to grant them preëmption rights, and Congress, responsive to appeals from
pioneer farmers, granted the coveted preëmption privilege in a series of special
acts. When squatters' appeals did not bring congressional action, the pioneers

[2]*Ibid.*, p. 26.

had another means of safeguarding their homes against outsiders who might attend the auction sale to buy the choice claims. This was to appear *en masse* at the sale and by intimidation or force prevent competitive bidding. Of course, the squatters had to purchase their lands at the minimum price of $1.25 per acre and when they lacked the cash they had, perforce, to borrow from "loan sharks" at extortionate rates of interest—thirty-two and forty-eight percent—but they preserved their equity, at least temporarily. Thus squatters got title to their lands in southern Indiana, even though they took the law into their own hands to protect their "rights," and they made the land system more democratic in its operation than its framers intended. . . .

In central Indiana there was even less large-scale speculative purchasing than in the south. Here most of the land passed directly from the government to actual settlers.

The land system worked the least satisfactorily in northern Indiana, especially in the prairie counties. Here the speculators, both absentee and resident, acquired enormous tracts of land before the actual settlers appeared and when the immigrants began to come into the country they found that the lands had long since passed into private hands and could only be acquired at high prices. An area which from the outset had labored under numerous handicaps to its settlement had now added to them the retarding effect of large speculators' holdings.

From the first appearance of the white men in Indiana the prairies were regarded with disfavor and they were slow to attract settlers. Their streams were sluggish, meandering and difficult of navigation; their soil was suspected of being infertile; their lack of forest cover gave them no protection against the wintry blasts and greatly increased the costs of building, fencing and fuel; their low relief and poor drainage made parts of them difficult to cultivate until they were drained, and the constant existence of surface water that was used for drinking purposes, produced fevers, chills and other bodily disturbances which were attributed to the unhealthy nature of the prairies. The unfavorable character given to this section by some early writers likewise proved a handicap to the settlement of the region. As Richard Power has well shown, immigrants preferred to go farther west in their search for land rather than settle in an area in such disrepute. Central Illinois and even far off Iowa and Minnesota drew settlers while such prairie counties as Benton, Newton, Jasper and parts of White, Tippecanoe and Warren were almost completely avoided. But if actual settlers disdained the prairies one man from Connecticut had an almost sublime faith in them from his first visit—Henry L. Ellsworth. . . .

In 1835 Ellsworth became Commissioner of Patents to which position he was strongly attracted as it enabled him to witness all the important mechanical progress that was being made in the country. He was especially interested in farm machinery such as ditching machines, steam plows, and fencing devices. But more than anything else he wished to make this bureau an agency which would aid the farmers as well as industry. He felt, perhaps, rightly, that "For commerce and manufactures, much has been done; for agriculture . . . much remains to be done. Husbandry sems to be viewed as a natural blessing, that needs no aid from legislation. Like the air we breathe, and the element of water, which sustain life, the productions of the soil are regarded by too many as common bounties of Providence, to be gratefully enjoyed, but without further thought or reflection." Ellsworth urged Congress to establish an agricultural museum, recommended that a part of the Smithson bequest be used for vocational education for farmers, and requested that funds be provided for the collection and dissemination of information on agricultural practices at home and abroad. The beginning of the publication of an annual volume on agriculture by the Patent Office, and the free distribution of seeds resulted from his efforts and entitle him to be called the "father of the United States Department of Agriculture."

Ellsworth was no swivel-chair farmer, nor did he undertake a mere speculation in lands. He was confident that the prairies of Indiana and Illinois would be dotted with prosperous settlements in a few years time and he became the great advocate of prairie farming. The prestige of his official position as Commissioner of Patents and the *entree* he had to farm journals enabled him to give wide publicity to his ideas. Ellsworth's tremendous enthusiasm for the prairie induced him to abandon his ancestral home in Connecticut and to throw in his lot with the Hoosiers.

During the thirties when credit was easy and the land speculative boom was at its height, numerous eastern and southern capitalists bought large tracts of land in the western states which they tried to develop into great estates operated by numerous tenants paying rent to the landlord. Daniel Webster, the Wadsworths of New York, Thomas Ludwell Lee Brent of Virginia, and Romulus Riggs of Philadelphia are among those who bought large tracts for such a purpose. Ellsworth had a similar plan in mind but, unlike some of the others, he moved into the area which he proposed to develop and gave it his personal attention.

It was the Grand Prairie of Indiana and Illinois that most attracted Ellsworth as a field for investment and he centered his attention on that portion embracing Benton and Tippecanoe Counties, Indiana, and Vermillion and Iroquois Counties, Illinois. This area, he believed had "the best soil and the most favorable climate." He began buying land in June, 1835, when he visited the Danville, Fort Wayne, and Crawfordsville land offices and entered 18,000 acres, 10,000 of which were in Tippecanoe County. He chose the city of Lafayette for his home and made a substantial investment in lots and improvements there.

Ellsworth began to farm his extensive holdings in Tippecanoe in 1836. Laborers were employed to make improvements and they, in turn, were encouraged to become tenants upon the improved sections. There was a ready demand in the southern states for hay and this became Ellsworth's first commercial crop. Like most prairie residents, he plunged into the cattle and hog business in a large way but prairie cultivation interested him more than livestock production. Here he found exercise for his ingenious and fertile Yankee mind. Before part of the prairie could be cultivated it had to be drained and Ellsworth tinkered with various ditching devices, one of which combined ditching and fencing. This machine was designed to provide cheaply for two of the most expensive requirements of prairie farming. He was also fascinated by the new improvements which were being made in the plow in an effort to adapt it to prairies. The first plowing of the tough prairie sod was an expensive operation as it took a special kind of a plow which had to be drawn by three or four yoke of oxen. Only a few pioneer farmers could afford to buy or hire such equipment, but on a large farm the cost per acre of breaking the sod was of course considerably reduced and Ellsworth found his cost of prairie breaking much less than he had anticipated. When the steam plow was introduced in the fifties he was as delighted as a child with a new toy and he was a firm believer in its future importance. Large scale operations and the use of machinery for seeding, cultivating, and harvesting further reduced Ellsworth's costs of production and convinced him for a time that the prairie could be expensively cultivated and at large profits but far better in large farm units than in small ones. . . .

Ellsworth wished to attract both capital and settlers to the prairies. He reasoned that each additional investment whether by absentee proprietors or settlers would make the prairies better known and further their development. To call attention to the prairie country he prepared a booklet with the title, *Valley of the Upper Wabash, Indiana, with hints on its agricultural advantages: Plan of a dwelling, estimates of cultivation and notices of labor saving machines,* which was published in 1838. Restrained in tone in comparison with some of the current guide books, the work cannot be considered too optimistic in its description of the prairies. True, the cost of fencing is seriously understated and the probable profits from prairie farming are equally overestimated. Also too much space is devoted to discussions of the cultivation of flax, sugar beets, tobacco and hemp and not enough to problems of pioneer life on the prairies. Nor is the description of the Wabash Valley as well done and as valuable for the historian as are Peck's and Mitchell's guides to Illinois. One is also troubled by the numerous references to large scale farming and the inadequate attention given to the needs and problems of the average settler. But, after all, the book was written not so much for them as for men of capital. It is obviously the work of Henry L. Ellsworth whose hand is seen on practically every page although Henry William Ellsworth, his son, appears as the author on the title page. Included in the book is a letter of the former, written on January 1, 1837, and apparently first published in the Sangamo *Journal* of Illinois. It was also published in S. A. Mitchell, *Illinois in 1837*, and in A. D. Jones, *Illinois and the West*. The following quotation from this letter shows Ellsworth's unbounded enthusiasm for the prairies:

> If it be asked, what are the profits of cultivation? I answer, if the land is rented for five years, the profits accruing during this period will repay the capital advanced in the commencement, with 25 per cent. interest per annum, and leave the farm worth $20 per acre at the expiration of the lease. Probably the profit would be much greater.

The book announced the formation of a partnership between John Curtis and Henry W. Ellsworth and advertised the purpose of the new firm as follows:

> They propose to purchase of Government and individuals, lands in Indiana and Illinois, for such persons as are desirous to make investments, and to take charge of the same, or of *other lands* already purchased; pay taxes, and, when requested, to put lands into cultivation, and generally to promote, in the best possible manner, the interests of their employers.
>
> The undersigned will take capital to invest in new lands, and allow the capitalist the legal title and a deduction of 8 or 10 per cent. interest, and divide the extra profits, which, it is confidently believed, will not be less than 25 per cent more.

One of the first persons whom Ellsworth induced to make an investment in the Wabash Valley was William J. Grayson of Charleston, South Carolina. Grayson was an eminent literary figure and a successful politician. He served Congress for two terms and while in Washington he met Ellsworth. In 1836 Grayson entered into a partnership with Ellsworth for an investment in Indiana lands. Grayson was to furnish $10,000 for the purchase of lands, was to pay taxes and for such improvements as were jointly deemed advisable; Ellsworth was to manage the lands and to share equally in the profits after deduction of all costs plus six per cent interest on the investment. This type of contract was used by Ellsworth with some variations in his land deals with dozens of eastern and southern people who were persuaded to invest their savings in prairie lands.

Southerners from Maryland, Washington and even from Texas invested with Ellsworth in Indiana and Illinois lands. Two Baltimore capitalists, Ramsay McHenry and James McHenry Boyd furnished $20,000 and the Washington banking firm of Pairo and Nourse which had large land holdings in seven western states and territories bought 11,000 acres through Ellsworth, in Benton County.

Most interesting of the absentee investors who were attracted to Indiana lands were the members of the "Yale Crowd," so-called by the local abstractors and attorneys of Benton County. Ellsworth, a faithful alumnus of Yale, had intermarried with the Goodrich family and had close relations with the Chauncey family, both almost as well known in Connecticut as the Ellsworths, and likewise loyal sons of Yale. Six of the members of these families with associates bought 95,000 acres in Indiana and Illinois, of which 45,000 were in the Wabash Valley. Elizur and Chauncey Goodrich bought 5,340 and 3,960 acres respectively in the Crawfordsville, Fort Wayne and Danville districts. Elihu and Nathaniel Chauncey invested $40,000 with Ellsworth in lands, acquiring thereby 16,500 acres in Indiana and 5,720 in Illinois, together with a valuable farm near Lafayette which was intended as an addition to the city. Isaac Chauncey and Peter Schermerhorn of New York entered 5,800 acres at Crawfordsville and 7,000 acres at Danville. Other Connecticut Yankees who invested in prairie lands through Ellsworth were Robert and David Watkinson, who bought 9,500 acres, Noah Webster and dozens of others, who entered from forty to 2,000 acres.

By 1855 all the public land in Indiana had been disposed of and yet vast stretches of the state were totally unimproved. Absentee proprietorship and high land prices were to a large extent responsible for the tardy development of such areas, especially the Grand Prairie. By the eighteen-fifties, when the agricultural pattern of central and southern Indiana was already well established, Benton, Newton, and Jasper counties remained almost untouched by settlers, and White, Warren and Tippecanoe still contained a large proportion of undeveloped land. As late as 1860, scarcely six per cent of the land in Benton County was improved and but thirteen per cent was improved in Jasper and Newton. Only two other counties had a smaller population than Benton in 1860. It was not until well into the eighteen-sixties that these counties began to develop and much of their land was not improved until after 1880. The words of Solon Robinson, written in 1841, in which he deplored the unfortunate effects of land speculation were proving only too true:

> It is evident that no man can cultivate such large tracts as many have been anxious to possess, of such a soil as ours. It were better by far that our uncultivated lands were occupied by hardy and industrious laborers, whose every stroke of plough, hoe, or spade, would add intrinsic value to it, than to lie dormant, waiting some hoped for rise in value. It is a subject well worthy of our careful inquiry, whether our greediness has not driven many good citizens to look further, without faring better, while we have fared worse. Our settlements are too sparse, and we ought to use all honorable means to invite immigrants to fill up our waste lands. To do this we must be more liberal.

Many of the absentee proprietors bought their tracts as simple speculations. It was their intention to hold the land until rising prices, which they could reasonably expect within a generation, should enable them to sell at a profit. They had no intention of improving their land or in any other way aiding in their development of the prairies. When taxes were assessed against their property for local improvements many of them delayed payment as long as possible. The Ellsworth lands and those of other easterners were delinquent in tax payments in Benton County in 1860 as much as eight years. Thus the speculators not only kept the land out of the hands of actual settlers but prevented the collection of taxes which were needed for road improvements, school expenses, and other local government costs. Where actual residents insisted upon public expenditures for schools and roads they were forced to tax their own property more heavily to compensate for the unimproved lands of the nonresidents who paid little or nothing into the treasury.

Farm tenancy early appeared in the prairie counties of Indiana and developed rapidly there in contrast to the southern counties where its growth was slow. From the outset Ellsworth had planned to improve his possessions by placing tenants upon them who would after the initial start, continue to break up and cultivate new land, construct fences and buildings and otherwise increase the value of the property. Meantime, they would be paying rent amounting to one-third of the crops they raised. Ellsworth's *Valley of the Upper Wabash* described his plan of placing tenants upon the land and it was set forth as an inducement to attract capitalists to prairie investments. It is remarkable that Ellsworth was criticized neither by the press of Indiana, including the farm journals, nor by politicians for proposing to introduce into pioneer Indiana an institution which all agreed was un-American. Indeed, until well after 1860 one finds politicians praising the American land system because it was, according to them, building up a nation of farm owners, and was not permitting such an alien institution as tenancy to develop. Yet here was Ellsworth publicly inviting capitalists to invest funds through him in Indiana where tenants could be attracted to the lands.

Ellsworth was not solely responsible for the introduction of tenancy into Indiana. As early as 1823, Lazarus Noble of Lawrenceburg advertised his farm for rent, and, after 1835, one finds scattered advertisements in the Indiana papers of farms for rent. The Pottawatomie and Miami reserved sections, lying adjacent to the Wabash River and the route of the Wabash and Erie Canal, were regarded as choice lands and were much in demand by the early settlers. The Ewings of Fort Wayne who, with Cyrus Taber, Allen Hamilton and Senator John Tipton had succeeded in wresting most of these lands from their untutored owners, rented them to incoming settlers who preferred to settle upon them, temporarily, rather than to take up more remote locations back from the river. Elsewhere in Indiana, lands were being rented by local proprietors to new arrivals, some of whom, after a short period of tenancy, were able to purchase farms of their own.

Nor were Ellsworth and the "Yale Crowd" the only nonresident capitalists who intended to develop their estates through tenants. In fact, in practically all the western states easterners bought tracts of land as permanent investments to be developed by tenants. When such easterners appeared in a community where the land office was located, they were welcomed by the local press, feted by the "prominent citizens," and encouraged to invest in the area provided they did not attempt to encroach upon the rights of squatters who had claims on public lands. Thus as early as 1825 the *Michigan Sentinel* of Monroe, Michigan, exulted over the fact that a number of "robust capitalists" from western New York had arrived to purchase lands. . . .

It may be argued that it was not the speculators but the wet lands which deterred immigrants from settling in the prairie counties. It is true that the extremely wet lands could not be cultivated until they were drained and that their drainage would call for heavy financial expenditures. Unfortunately, the absentee proprietors were either unable or unwilling to invest more capital in lands which still brought them no revenue, and the tenants, as has been seen, could scarcely afford to invest their money or very much of their labor in improvements of which they might be dispossessed at any time. Had the lands been democratically owned by farmers operating quarter-section tracts coöperative ditching systems might have been arranged, the reduced costs would not have been insurmountable, and the wet lands would doubtless have been brought under cultivation much sooner.

Absentee ownership not only kept both the impoverished immigrants and those supplied with capital away from the prairie counties but it also delayed the construction of railroads. Many Indiana counties aided materially in their own developments by liberally subsidizing the construction of railroads through grants or loans. But absentee proprietors were loath to make contributions for this purpose, even though they might be benefitted greatly by the transportation lines. Furthermore, the virtually non-taxable lands of the absentee proprietors so reduced the tax base of the area that the counties could not sell bonds to finance railroad subsidies. Railroad lines which did not need to depend upon local aid for their construction, such as the Wabash, the Monon, and the Logansport and Peoria, were built through the prairie country in the fifties but there yet remained vast stretches of land so far from railroads that transportation costs were prohibitive. Other railroad schemes were proposed but they had to wait until the 'seventies and 'eighties when prairie development had progressed sufficiently to make possible their financing. Before 1870 Benton County could not boast a single mile of railroad. Settlers who would have worked hard to secure them by voting county subsidies and by exchanging mortgages on their own lands for bonds of the railroads were not encouraged to settle in Benton or other prairie counties, despite the publication of the colorful advertisements of Ellsworth and Sturges.

In the late fifties most of the prairie land still owned by the original speculators was sold to another group of capitalists who took their places as great landlords. Ellsworth's eastern associates had grown tired of waiting for their promised $10 and $20 per acre and were glad to sell for much less rather than to continue to suffer tax penalties and especially further loss of income from their capital. This second stage of large land ownership was not characteristically speculative in its nature but was more constructive. The new owners were generally Hoosiers who lived in the prairie counties where they had already built up considerable fortunes from the cattle trade, railroad construction, banking and the sale of town lots. They were a part of the community, had grown up with it, and were now showing their confidence in it by investing their surplus at home. They were an aggressive group of men who had the capital and the driving force to make the prairies productive.

One of the most able of this later class of landlords was Moses Fowler, Lafayette banker, cattleman, partner in a large meat-packing firm and railroad contractor.... Edward C. Sumner, another of the great cattle kings of Indiana, bought 30,000 acres in Benton County, the greater part of which was acquired from Ellsworth and other members of the "Yale Crowd." ... Lemuel Milk and his associates operated on an even larger scale than Fowler or Sumner. They are said to have owned 65,000 acres of land in Indiana and Illinois of which 40,000 were in the Beaver Lake region of Newton County, Indiana. Here, after a part of the tract was drained, there were pastured 10,000 sheep, 2,500 cattle and 300 horses. One field of corn contained 2,000 acres.

Other large holdings in Benton County, most of which were established in the 'fifties were: those of Parnham Boswell, 12,000 acres; of Cephas Atkinson, 12,000 acres; and of Adams Danforth Raub, 6,000 acres. In Newton County James M. Gaff of Cincinnati bought 11,000 acres and Alexander J. Kent acquired 25,000 acres. In Warren County perhaps the largest landholder was James Goodwin who built up an estate of 10,000 acres. In White County John Kious owned an estate of 4,000 acres and Miller Kenton one of 5,000 acres....

The land system which had worked fairly satisfactorily from the settlers' point of view in southern Indiana in the early part of the nineteenth century failed in its objectives in northern Indiana where great landlords first acquired titles to the land and democratic ownership was subsequently impossible. The preëmption law of 1841 was a gesture to actual settlers (squatters) but it did not check speculation, and the homestead act of 1862 came too late. By then all the public lands in Indiana had passed into private hands. There yet remained a large acreage of undeveloped land which, however, was withheld from impoverished immigrants by its high price. Indiana could no longer be a refuge for the poorer class of immigrants who were seeking free or cheap land.

The first generation of speculators contributed nothing to the development of the prairie country. Even Ellsworth, less a speculator than a promoter, did more harm than good by helping to bring about a speculators' monopoly in the prairie country. When these speculators sold their land it went to a second, more dynamic group of promoters who could partially develop their holdings but who still prevented democratic ownership. When the second series of owners divided their estates into tenant holdings, it was too late for tenants or other small farmers with little capital to buy the land. Rising land prices, $50 per acre and more for improved sections, fastened the tenancy system and absentee ownership upon the prairie counties. The much vaunted land system had failed of its objective in the Wabash Valley and the prairie farther west. It had not established democratic farm ownership but had produced a system much at variance with American democratic ideals.

2: Education

Establishing the Public Schools

VAL NOLAN, JR.

Caleb Mills is recognized as the father of the public school system in Indiana. Not only did he campaign effectively for constitutional reform and new educational legislation during the late 1840s and early 1850s (described in the pages below), he also served a term as Superintendent of Public Instruction, an elected office, and as such helped establish the system for which he had labored very diligently over a number of years. For too long, in Mills' opinion, the easterners' jibe that "Hoosier" was a synonym for "ignorant" was too nearly true to be humorous; and the college professor was moved into action when he read the 1840 Census and its alarming report that Indiana ranked at the bottom of the northern free states in literacy, and was even surpassed by several southern slave states.

The Constitution of 1851, while moving away from the first constitution's attempt to set up a system of free higher education, did authorize the establishment of a free public school system at the lower levels. The Free Public School Law of 1852 embodied the General Assembly's first attempt to carry out its new constitutional mandate, but litigation over the right of the state to tax its citizens for educational purposes delayed the actual establishment of an adequate school system until after the Civil War. Gradually, however, during the late nineteenth century, both elementary and secondary school programs were started, and these were supplemented by a growing network of private colleges throughout the state and by two new state schools—Purdue University, the state's land grant institution established for agricultural and mechanical training in 1870, and the Indiana State Normal School, now Indiana State University, authorized in 1865.

The contributor of the following piece is Val Nolan, Jr., professor of law at Indiana University in Bloomington. For further information on Mills and nineteenth-century schools, see Charles W. Moores, *Caleb Mills and the Indiana School System* (1905), and Richard G. Boone, *A History of Education in Indiana* (1892, reprinted 1941).

From "Caleb Mills and the Indiana Free School Law," *Indiana Magazine of History*, XLIX (March 1953), 81–90. Some footnotes in the original have been omitted. Copyright © 1953 by the Trustees of Indiana University. Reprinted by permission.

Historians have long assigned to Caleb Mills the leading role in Indiana's free school movement of the middle 1800's, a movement that culminated over one hundred years ago in the passage of the state's first truly systematic free school law. Mills' most enduring claim to generalship in the victory lies in his six widely-read "Educational Messages" written under the nom de plume "One of the People." Why he preferred to conceal his identity, and how and when his secret eventually became public are facts not revealed in the rather meager biographical materials. A recently discovered letter from Mills to John Barron Niles is interesting therefore, both because in it Mills divulges his identity as "One of the People" and because it reveals how thoroughly Mills was a fighter and not simply a philosopher of the revolution. A brief narrative will place the letter in its setting.

Despite the truly memorable educational article in its Constitution of 1816, Indiana approached mid-nineteenth century with its ideal of free popular education still a lofty concept rather than a reality. Most common schools, where they existed at all, were locally maintained and therefore cheaply administered and poorly taught, their doors open for brief periods each year only to those who could afford and were willing to pay tuition. County seminaries, on their level, were no better; and Indiana University reached only a few. Private academies and colleges[1] brightened a little the gloom of the state's educational picture (some were good, and the mere existence of private schools indicated considerable interest in education); but they were not, of course, free. The harvest of such apathetic cultivation is not surprising. The 1840 census revealed that one of seven of Indiana's adults could not read or write, and its illiteracy rate exceeded that of all northern and of three slave states.[2]

"Among all those who saw the calamitous ignorance of the people and were ambitious of better things for the State ... was one whose contributions to the question were sufficiently definite and sound to be recognized as the chief factor in its solution." On the day following the opening of the 1846 session of the General Assembly, *The Indiana State Journal* carried "An Address to the Legislature" over the signature "One of the People." The writer pointed to Indiana's lamentable inadequacy in the vital field of education, then passed to concrete consideration of particular evils and of remedies. Public funds at that time devoted to schools came largely from the federal land grant of one section in each congressional township. The money derived from these sections was not consolidated and then distributed equally throughout the state; instead each township kept whatever it could

---

[1]Private colleges in Indiana prior to 1850, the dates of their foundations, and the religious sects that controlled them were: Hanover, 1827, Presbyterian; Wabash, 1832, "Christian in spirit" but nondenominational; Franklin, 1834, Baptist; Earlham, 1837, Quaker; Asbury (DePauw), 1837, Methodist; Concordia, 1839, German Evangelical Lutheran; St. Mary of the Woods, 1840, Catholic; University of Notre Dame, 1844, Catholic; and Taylor University, 1846, Methodist.

[2]*Sixth Census of the United States, 1840*, pp. 373–74, 475. Of a total population of 685,866 (678,698 whites), illiterate whites over 20 years of age numbered 38,100.

realize from its own section. Thus the very communities that most needed public assistance and could least afford to support schools from local funds, *i.e.,* communities where land values were low and farms poor, in fact received the least help from the land donation; prosperous townships got the highest incomes from their more valuable lands. Such inefficient use of the funds must be rectified, said the Address, by equal state-wide distribution. Furthermore and even more significant, the really basic support for free schools must be raised by taxation. Finally, only if higher schools improve will well-trained teachers be available; therefore let the county seminaries and the state university be reorganized. Sell all the physical facilities of the seminaries and of the university; distribute the interest on the proceeds to one private seminary in each county and to every college whose governors will agree to maintain certain stipulated standards, to train teachers, and to devote the money received to provide prospective teachers with free tuition.

Eight days after the address appeared, Governor James Whitcomb in his annual message to the legislature urged that body to revise the entire school system and place it under the charge of a state superintendent. The General Assembly passed no such statute, but it indicated its interest by adopting a joint resolution calling upon the friends of education in Indiana to meet at Indianapolis in a convention to consider the school problem.

Mills' second address, to the 1847 legislature, expanded upon many of the points already made, called taxation a necessity not only as a money raising device but also as the most effective way to insure public interest in education, and explored problems of requisite buildings, adequate salaries for teachers, books, and integrated school superintendence. Probably at least partly in response to the messages, the General Assembly ordered a referendum to determine the public will on a free school bill introduced at the session; the referendum vote was in favor of the bill.[3] The third address analyzed this vote by counties, pointing to the close correlation between a county's high illiteracy rate and its hostility to the bill. The 1848 legislature to which the third message was addressed passed a new school law adopting taxation as a means of support of common schools and equalizing the periods of instruction in all schools in each congressional township. But this step forward was largely vitiated by a local option provision whereby each county could decide for itself whether to operate under the new system. The act also failed to consolidate the school funds and to require equal distribution. The fourth address was therefore a criticism of this statute, which had meanwhile been rejected by twenty-nine counties.

"One of the People" directed his fifth appeal, in the form of four letters in *The Indiana Statesman,* to the men who assembled in Indianapolis in October, 1850, to draft a new constitution for the state. Like so many in his time and since, he sought to incorporate the details of the particular project close to his heart in the fundamental law of the state, where it would

[3]Fifty-nine counties favored free schools, thirty-one opposed. Of 140,410 votes cast, 78,523 favored, 61,887 opposed.

be relatively secure from future legislative tampering. The only real novelty of this address, which reiterated all the familiar arguments, was a proposal to divide the permanent public education money into three parts, the Common School, the Literature, and the University Funds. The interest from the Literature Fund was, in addition to being used to subsidize private academies, to be spent to establish and increase common school libraries, a recently recognized instrument of public instruction.

It was after his fifth address that Mills wrote Niles and revealed himself as "One of the People." How the Wabash College professor and the influential lawyer delegate had become acquainted can be conjectured: Mills graduated from Dartmouth College in 1828, Niles in 1830. Mills' reference to "scenes of bygone years" has just that touch of nostalgia which supports the inference of an undergraduate acquaintanceship. Obviously Mills expected sympathy from the well-educated Niles, himself a former teacher of chemistry in the medical department of the Indiana Medical College of La Porte.

John B. Niles Esq.,
(Constitutional Convention)
Indianapolis, Ind.
[Postmark Crawfordsville, Dec. 10.]

Wabash College
Dec. 7, 1850

John B. Niles Esq.
     My Dear Sir:
     You may perhaps be surprised to receive a letter from me. It would be pleasant to sit down and chat over scenes of bygone years, but we revolve in such different orbits that it is utterly impossible to calculate when two such bodies will be in conjunction. Were it certain that the convention would not complete their labors by Christmas & that the portion of the constitution pertaining to Education would not be disposed of before that time, I think I should confer upon myself the honor of a lobby membership for a few days. But I presume that period would be too late for the accomplishment of the principle object of such a visit and therefore I will venture to propose a conference on the subject of constitutional provision for popular Education. I presume you feel a deep interest in this subject & are prepared to favor any plan that bids fair to accomplish the object in the most effectual manner. There is a strong disposition among timid polititions & demagogues to skim along the surface and ask what will be popular, disregarding whatever is essential to their success, providing it is not grateful to the more ignorant or selfish of the dear people. Presuming that you do not sympathize with such & are willing & desirous to embody in the fundamental law of the commonwealth educational provisions of an enlightened and liberal character, I will proceed to communicate to you what I wish to be considered a *secrete,* vis, that the Educational Addresses to the Legislature, under the signature of One of the people, for the last *four years,* and the *fifth* published in the Indiana Statesman, addressed to the Constitutional Convention came

from me. They have been extensively circulated and read, & have done something to awaken & increase the interest in fact in popular education. I presume you have read the one addressed to the Body, of which you are a member. I flatter myself that the plan suggested in that address, will commend itself to your favorable regard, and if so, I wish you would give it the benefit of your influence and support when the subject of Education comes up for discussion. Now is the time to strike, and in the right spot. Can you not make a *great speech* on the subject and show shallow heads that academies and colleges are as indispensable to a good educational system as common schools? Show them that these higher institutions are the intellectual reservoir from which proceed the controlling influences of society. Whence proceed inventions and improvements in every department of human industry, but from awakened, cultivated intellects? Will you carefully read the several nos. if you have not already done it & suggest any difficulties & modifications & thus give me an opportunity to explain, obviate & demonstrate the soundness & wisdom of the scheme. No one, who has *seen* the operation of free schools in New England, will question for a moment, the wisdom, nay, the necessity of a partial support at least by taxation, & the undesirableness of a fund so large as to superseed the necessity of taxation. This point being established, where is the necessity of a public fund larger than I have shown we should have from the three sources indicated. Let the Literature fund derived from the fines & forfeitures, bank tax & saline funds be consolidated & appropriated for the encouragement of academics, common school libraries & apparatus. New York has appropriated $90,000 annually & for a series of years on the plan suggested securing the raising an equal sum by the recipiants of the grant. The fine and forfeiture funds, bank tax and saline funds would go but a little way in sustaining the common schools of the state, not amounting to 25 cents per head on all the children in the state; but for the purpose proposed, they would be sufficient, abundantly sufficient to secure a library of 150 or 200 vols such as you will see in the state library room, to every school district in the state. What a glorious point gained to secure such a result. Such a library would educate parents as well as children [and] prove of untold value to every neighborhood. I hope you will both take hold of it yourself and endeavor to enlist others in its support. I have urged Jernigan to do what he can with the members of his acquaintance and hope you will stand up and support the Educational Committee should they propose it. Could you not get a dozen of your most intelligent & influential members to unite & push it thro' with a rush. In respect to the University plan, I see no objection at all. The funds are all in the possession & under the *sole & exclusive control* of the State on my plan. It proposes to alienate not a dollar but to make every dollar tell on cultivated mind[s]. It proposes nothing but what is just, liberal & wise. You can see at a glance that the influence of its operation would be most happy & efficient. It would do more to expose imposition & elevate the standard of collegiate education than anything that could be done. The adoption of the plan suggested in its threefold division would both bless & honor us as a state. The facts & statistics embodied in that address & its predecessors, would furnish you with unanswerable arguments. I will send you a copy of the second & third for perusal. I should rejoice to see that plan, or something substantially like it, incorporated into the organic law of the state. Let me hear from you at an early date & know the result of your recruiting service. Could you not return by this place & spend a day with us? Yours truly

Caleb Mills

P.S. Let this all be "*sub rosa.*"

While Niles may have given his silent support, or may have subscribed to Mills' views but not thought the matter one to be embodied in detail in a constitution, certain it is that he never made a "great address." Nor was the article reported by the committee on education and passed after amendment by the convention in any sense an embodiment of Mills' plan. True, the new constitution called for "a general and uniform system of Common Schools, wherein tuition shall be without charge, and equally open to all"; a perpetual Common School fund was established and the office of Superintendent of Public Instruction created. But county seminaries were abolished,[4] with no attempt to find a substitute in private institutions, and Indiana University was left unscathed.[5] All details of the school system to be effected under the new government were left to the legislature.

To the 1851 General Assembly, then, Mills directed his last appeal, calling attention to the peculiar significance any law passed at this time must have as a sort of interpretation of the spirit of the new constitution. Buttressing his call for immediate action by presenting even more depressing data from the recent 1850 census,[6] Mills asked for a law embodying those details of his plan which were still permissible under the new constitution. Fundamentally, the statute must provide three essentials; freedom, competence, and supervision.

The legislature's response must have been gratifying, for the comprehensive School Law of 1852 was a long step in the march to organize in the state a system of uniform public-supported schools. A taxing provision

---

[4]Section 2 provides simply that the funds derived from sales of the seminaries and their lands, and money and property heretofore held for them, be made part of the Common School Fund. The convention intended to abolish seminaries. *Debates and Proceedings of the Convention,* II, 1867–68, 2044.

[5]The status of Indiana University was the subject of perhaps the most vigorous debates on education of the entire convention. Some members wished to abolish the university and divert the federal funds donated for university purposes to the common school fund. Others wished to make it possible for the legislature to do so. *Debates and Proceedings of the Convention,* I, 171; II, 1862–67, 1884–93. The university fund was left inviolate by the Constitution as finally adopted. Article 8, Section 7.

[6]*Seventh Census of the United States, 1850,* pp. 756, 788–89, reveals that 72,710 white adults of Indiana were illiterate in a total population of 988,416 (977,154 whites). Only 3,265 of the illiterates were foreign-born.

William C. Larrabee, Indiana's first superintendent of public instruction
Courtesy of the Indiana Department of Natural Resources

contained no such escape clause as ruined the 1849 act; and school funds were to be consolidated and equally distributed. Administrative organization too was revamped; the congressional township was abolished as an administrative unit and local control of schools given to civil townships, under the supervision of a state Board of Education presided over by the Superintendent of Public Instruction. Other sections of the law taxed for the purpose of establishing township libraries, regulated the examination and licensing of teachers, and sought to provide for the erection of school buildings. The influence of Mills, or at least the general conformity of the act to many of Mills' most important suggestions, is clearly apparent.

The fate of the statute in the courts is another and more discouraging story. But despite the fact that Supreme Court decisions during the next few years "almost destroyed the school system," legislative tenacity and a change of the judicial heart eventually gave Indiana a workable school law. In the long war for effective free schools ultimate victory was Caleb Mills'.

Little Red Schoolhouse Days

PAUL VAN RIPER

Although the following selection describes events at the turn of the century, its depiction of conditions in the typical one-room schoolhouse—of which hundreds, mostly made of logs, square-faced and chinked with clay, dotted the landscape of nineteenth-century Indiana—has validity for the earlier period too. What is different, of course, between mid-nineteenth- and early twentieth-century education is teacher qualifications and training. Only the most rudimentary means for preparing teachers existed in the mid-nineteenth century. They were hired by local township officers or sometimes even by groups of families, who both boarded the teacher around and paid the meager salary. The rudiments were supplemented by township and county institutes, one or two weeks long, designed to upgrade to whatever extent possible a teacher's knowledge of subject matter and pedagogical methods. Eventually, in the latter part of the century, a number of supposedly permanent normal schools or teachers' colleges were established in the state; most notable among the surviving institutions is the state school at Terre Haute (now Indiana State University).

Paul Van Riper (1876–1944) was born in Kansas but spent his youth and most of his adult years in Indiana. Educated in the township schools of Jennings County in southern Indiana in the 1880s and 1890s, Van Riper studied and then taught in such schools. Subsequently Van Riper attended Indiana University and Franklin College, graduating from the latter in 1907. He served as superintendent of the Lebanon, Indiana city school system from 1920 until 1942.

Professor Victor Bogle, who edited Van Riper's reminiscences for publication, points to a basic conflict between Van Riper's description of southern Indiana schools and the one presented by Edward Eggleston in *The Hoosier School-Master*, a fictional account set in the 1850s. The two writers "present opposing value judgments on the life and culture of rural southern Indiana. . . . Eggleston's 'Flat Crick deestrick' is one that a schoolmaster, or anyone else, would prefer to flee from at the first opportunity. Van Riper's Hardenburgh, Glixver, and Butlerville, however, are all attractive places, inhabited by 'friendly, hospitable, frugal and thrifty' people." Bogle concludes that accounts such as Van Riper's may present "more balanced appraisals of the Hoosiers who have been rather seriously maligned in Eggleston's widely-read novel" (p. 208).

A long-time student of Indiana history, Professor Bogle is the former chancellor of Indiana University at Kokomo. He has written extensively about urban and economic growth in Indiana during the early nineteenth century. For another view of the pioneer teacher in

From Victor M. Bogle (ed.), "Reminiscences of a Hill-Billy," *Indiana Magazine of History*, LXI (September 1965), 214-217. Some footnotes in the original have been omitted. Copyright © 1965 by the Trustees of Indiana University. Reprinted by permission.

Indiana, see James Albert Woodburn, "James Woodburn: Hoosier Schoolmaster," *Indiana Magazine of History*, XXXII (September 1936), 231–247.

In the early eighties education had made great strides from the old log cabin schools of early Indiana. It was the day of the little red school house. These little frame one room buildings, and strange as it may appear rarely painted red, dotted every township. They were topped with a cupola in which hung the bell. On a clear cold day the pealing of the bell summoning the children to school could be heard from all points in the school district.

The furniture was simple. In front sat the teacher's desk and chair. The recitation bench where the pupils sat to recite was just in front of the teacher's desk. Back of the recitation bench and placed in rows were the double pupils' study desks, the smaller desks in front and those for the older pupils in the rear. A large box stove that would burn three foot lengths of wood sat in the middle of the room. The larger boys carried in the wood and in cold weather helped the teacher fire the stove. The stove pipe rose from the rear of the stove to a point near the ceiling, then took off at right angles, supported by wires from the ceiling, to the chimney at the front end of the building. When the weather was cold the pupils nearest the stove burned and those over by the windows shivered. If the teacher had a yen for the comfort of his pupils, on a cold day there would be a constant movement of pupils to and from the stove. But woe unto the pupil who dropped a piece of rubber or other evil smelling stuff on the stove.

The blackboard, usually just the plaster painted black, ran across the front of the room. Two or three chairs for visitors also sat in front. In one corner there was usually a high stool for disciplinary purposes. Sometimes a primary chart stood on a tripod by the side of the teacher's desk. Nearly always a few switches cut from nearby trees stood in the corner opposite the stool. If the teacher was unusually enterprising he secured a home made book case and a few books bought from a school exhibition or from a box or pie supper.[1]

Occasionally a picture of Abraham Lincoln or George Washington adorned the walls.

The playground was fenced off from the surrounding fields by a rail fence. One half was devoted to the use of boys and the other part to the girls.

Back of the schoolhouse or to one side was the woodhouse. This was filled with wood during the summer months. Sometimes the wood shed was large enough to house the teacher's horse when he rode to school.

On opposite corners of the lot and well back from the road were built "Chic Sale Houses" what Chic would call "three seaters" with one seat a

---

[1]At pie or box suppers girls of the community brought pies or boxes of food which were auctioned off to the highest bidder. The purchaser then had the privilege of eating with the owner. Quite often there was keen competition between the young men who wished to eat with a certain girl, and a pie or box would sell for several dollars. Proceeds for the supper were usually used for school equipment, books, or similar community project[s].

little lower and a little smaller than the other two seats for use of the smaller pupils. These houses were open to flies in spring, summer and fall and were usually in a sad state of sanitation.[2]

Water for drinking purposes was drawn from a well on the school yard or more often carried from a spring or from a neighboring farmhouse. As a special favor about four times a day, the older pupils were permitted to get a bucket of water and pass the water along the aisles to the pupils. All drank from the same cup or dipper. If a pupil did not drink all handed him, the water remaining in the dipper was thrown out the window or more often put back in the bucket.

The schoolyard was not covered by stone or gravel as are schoolyards now, nor were there many gravel or stone walks. What was the need when the school yard was less dusty or muddy than the roads the children tramped to school?

The pupils comprised all the children of the district sometimes numbering fifty or more, and varying in age from five to twenty-one years. Many of the older boys would not enter school until after wheat sowing and corn cutting and after the winter supply of wood was cut. Frequently some of the pupils were older than the teacher. The school term was rarely more than six months.

The teacher of this district school might be either a man or woman. A license to teach was secured by taking an examination on the common school subjects and the "Science of Education" at the county seat under the direction of the County Superintendent of Schools. A teaching position was secured by applying to the Trustee of the Township.

The curriculum was as simple as the building. The emphasis was placed on reading, writing, spelling and arithmetic or ciphering. The upper grades studied geography, history, grammar and physiology. There was little time for music even if the teacher could sing and it was a brave teacher who dared to attempt to teach drawing or art.

The games played by the pupils at recesses and noon were also simple: town-ball, two or three cornered cat, shinny, duck-on-Davy, fox and geese, follow the leader, whipcracker, piggie, running, jumping and wrestling were indulged in by the boys. The girls played drop the handkerchief, blackman, blind man's bluff, three deep and similar games. Occasionally the older boys and girls joined in some of the singing, dancing games as Old Dan Tucker, weevley wheat and skip to my Lou.

The teacher must needs be a good disciplinarian. If not there was soon a vacancy. Often pupils were older and larger than the teacher. Corporal punishment was meted out on the slightest provocation. Many of the

[2]"Chic Sale Houses" were outdoor privies, so called because a rural humorist of the 1920's, Charles (Chic) Sale, used them as one of the chief themes in his repertoire of stories. For example, see Charles (Chic) Sale, *The Specialist* (St. Louis, 1929). Van Riper has applied the term which did not become prevalent until the second decade of the twentieth century to an earlier period in his life. The society which he describes here would not have recognized the phrase.

District school houses in Dearborn County
Courtesy of the Indiana Historical Society

punishments administered were unique. Whipping with a good tough switch was perhaps the most common. For minor infractions of the rules there was the stool in the corner with its dunce cap, or the pupil was stood in the corner facing the wall and made to stand on one foot. Some teachers were very ingenious in thinking up unusual punishments. Some used a ruler and smacked the pupil on the palms of one or both hands, or had children stand and hold out one or both hands, or made them kneel on a round stick, or sit on the teacher's desk. Pupils were frequently cuffed with a book on the side of the head or given a good shaking or slapped soundly on the ear. Occasionally a teacher would throw a book or a piece of chalk or an eraser at a youngster who was idling away his time. I knew one teacher who had a dictionary with all the pages loose. Woe to the pupil that incurred that teacher's ire. With unerring aim that dictionary would hit the luckless urchin on the head or shoulder and the loose leaves would fly to the four corners of the room. Then the poor kid had an all day job gathering up the leaves and placing them in order between the covers.

But all honor to the little red school houses and the district schools. They served the people well. They met adequately the needs of the time. They laid the foundation for the finest citizenry of any age. Many of the teachers were men and women of fine character, intellect and personality. Many successful men and women received their inspiration and outlook from faithful but unsung teachers in the district schools.

3: Religion

The arrival of organized religion on the Indiana frontier followed closely the arrival of the first settlers. Although the Roman Catholic Church was established first, at Vincennes in the mid-eighteenth century, most of the frontiersmen of the early nineteenth century were Protestant. The Methodists, Baptists, Presbyterians, and Christians (Disciples of Christ) had the most followers, but other denominations were also present—as well as freethinkers and agnostics. Perhaps the best-known symbol of frontier religion is the Methodist circuit rider, a courageous and toughened man of the cloth who undertook the seemingly impossible task of preaching regularly, if infrequently at any one point, to parishioners scattered over an immense and often trackless area.

As Professor William Warren Sweet has pointed out, practically all of the early circuit riders were single men, for Bishop Asbury discouraged marriage among his preachers because of the increased hardships this would cause. When one of the circuit riders did marry, he usually ceased "to travel," as it was called, and instead "located" and began serving the locality in which he settled. Sweet has also commented on the living arrangements of the itinerant ministers: without permanent homes, they lived in the cabins of the settlers around their circuits or in the saddle. "It is no wonder," he concludes, "that the Methodist preacher got a reputation as a horse trader, and as a judge of good horse flesh, for the ease and comfort in which he traveled his circuit depended upon the kind of horse he rode, and the preacher and his faithful horse were necessarily constant companions."[1]

The Baptist preacher, unlike his Methodist counterpart, was usually a farmer-settler himself, who took to the pulpit on the Sabbath to preach the gospel. Both the Methodist and Baptist systems were more suited to frontier conditions than the Presbyterian one, which required a highly educated clergy and organized churches from which "calls" to specific ministers to serve a specific congregation could be made. In part because of the difficulties involved with this approach,

[1]W. W. Sweet, "Early Methodist Circuits in Indiana," *Indiana Magazine of History*, X (December 1914), 367–368.

the American Home Missionary Society had more than sixty men from the East working in Indiana as late as 1851. The detailed reports of these missionaries, which were sent back to the East periodically, form a major but virtually untapped source of information concerning life on the frontier in the early nineteenth century.

Among the scholars who have used the Home Missionary Society records is the Reverend L. C. Rudolph, a theologian and historian now at the Lilly Library of Indiana University at Bloomington. Rev. Rudolph is the author of a study of Indiana Presbyterianism in its earliest period, and he has carefully examined both the people and the preachers, their origins, their way of life, and their theology. In the selection below Rudolph analyzes the motivations and achievements of the Presbyterian missionaries to Indiana and discusses the constructive tension between the back country culture of the typical frontiersman and the different cultural and religious standards of the ministry.

For additional information on Indiana's religious heritage, see the many works by William Warren Sweet, particularly *The Story of Religion in America* (1930); Jane Shaffer Elsmere, *Henry Ward Beecher: The Indiana Years, 1837-1847* (1973); and various denominational histories such as Henry K. Shaw, *Hoosier Disciples: A Comprehensive History of the Christian Churches (Disciples of Christ) in Indiana* (1966); John Frank Cady, *The Origin and Development of the Missionary Baptist Church in Indiana* (1942): and John C. Wenger, *The Mennonites in Indiana and Michigan* (1961).

Religion on the Frontier

L. C. RUDOLPH

There had been a long history of cooperation between Congregationalists and Presbyterians. They had both been dissenters from the state church in England and in 1690 had actually agreed to merge their operations there under the name of United Brethren. There were many Presbyterians among the early Puritan settlers in America, and New England church government often had a Presbyterian look, the Saybrook Platform of Connecticut (1708) being an excellent example. When the need arose for ministers for the West, it was natural that Presbyterians and Congregationalists should work together. They approved the Plan of Union in 1801. Under this plan Congregational ministers could serve Presbyterian churches, or Presbyterian ministers could serve Congregational churches wherever that was convenient. There were generous provisions for representation in church courts and for church discipline.

Indiana's settlement had been just beginning in 1801 when the Presbyterians and the Congregationalists entered into their Plan of Union for joint operation in the West. The effect of this was to make the college and seminary graduates of the Congregational schools available for "destitute" Indiana. They were sent out with Presbyterian and Congregationalist money through the mission societies. Since so few of Indiana's settlers were from New England, these eastern missionaries founded Presbyterian churches under the Plan of Union. By 1850 there were but three Congregational churches in the whole state and one of them was the congregation at Bath, Indiana, a Presbyterian splinter group which had borrowed the Congregationalist name. Isaac Reed's history is an interesting example of how Presbyterianism was furthered on the frontier by one with Congregationalist backgrounds. Reed attended Middlebury College in Vermont, was taken under the care of Long Island Presbytery in New York, and was licensed by the Fairfield Congregational Association in Connecticut. He served under various eastern societies, including the Connecticut Missionary Society and the American Home Missionary Society. Reed founded more churches than any other eastern missionary to Indiana—all of them Presbyterian churches!

It is fascinating to speculate on the motivation of these eastern societies and their missionaries to Indiana. In their calls for funds back East they made a bald appeal to political security, suggesting that new states were being carved out of this western empire and their representatives would one day rule the land; New England might be outnumbered and she had better see to it that this new West was both wise and good:

> Facts place the subject beyond a doubt, that within a generation to come, the millions of the Atlantic states will be under the stern necessity, by the federal compact of this Union, to surrender their destinies to the outnumbering millions who will soon throng the Mississippi valley . . . Should the United States continue to populate for years to come, with a rapidity equal to years past, there will then be a population in this country, within an hundred years of 320,000,000. Such in general is the superiority of soil in that great valley, that a given portion of land is capable of sustaining three times greater amount of population, than the same portion in the Atlantic states. Hence there is reason to believe that the excess of population in the valley, over the Eastern section, will exceed within a century the expectations of those who are at present most sanguine in their calculations.

The call to frontier adventure must also have been a real factor at work on the young seminary graduate. If a commission from a missionary society could allow him to tour the great West, serve an apprenticeship in preaching among the destitute, and at the same time pay off his educational debts, a licentiate found it attractive. A real concern for the unchurched was a prime mover among these missionaries, especially in the early nineteenth century, when widespread revivals heightened the concern. Crucial as any motivating factor was a kind of Calvinistic meddlesomeness, a special variety of community concern, maybe more basic to historic Calvinism than technical theories of predestination or the decrees. The easterner had come from a more genteel culture, even more lately improved by temperance societies, Bible societies, tract societies, and Sunday schools. Whenever he saw or even heard about the mud and illiteracy and grossness of the frontier, the need overwhelmed him. He felt the call as one of the elect to do something about it. Perhaps the most persistent theme of the frontier missionary letter was "building up Zion." It was progress in building Zion that the executive secretary of the society wanted to hear about. It was for this cause that eastern capital would flow. The purpose of the missionary in Indiana was building up Hoosier Zion—a segment of the kingdom of God. This was to be done for the good of every man, even if some men did not like it. Certain pressures ought to be brought to bear on the common life of all. Everything must give way before God.

When one considers that as late as 1846 the uncouth frontier preacher Peter Cartwright was running for national Congress against another unpolished frontiersman, Abraham Lincoln, it is not hard to understand the Yankee concern. Also both religion and morals needed help on the frontier. The Wild West (the term originates on the Wabash) was destitute of "sound and proper" religious institutions. "The Home missionary movement was the resultant of many forces: Christian idealism, denominational rivalries, humanitarianism, nationalism, and enlightened self-interest all had their effect in producing and directing a movement designed to mold the West according to orthodox Protestant standards."

First there was a tendency to proliferation in missionary society work. Indiana received missionaries from the Connecticut Missionary Society, from the Young Men's Missionary Society of New York City and from others as well. Then came consolidation. Several societies in the State of New York combined in 1822 to form the United Domestic Missionary Society. By 1826 this body had 127 missionaries, four of whom were in Indiana. That year the United Society combined with the Connecticut Missionary Society, the Massachusetts Missionary Society, and others to form the American Home Missionary Society. "At the outset most of the financial support for the Society came apparently from Presbyterians. Of the $20,000 received in the second year (1827–28), $16,121.27 was credited to New York and only $1,641.34 to four New England states." The American Home Missionary Society grew mightily until in its tenth year its receipts were over $100,000. That year 191 of 755 missionaries were in the West and twenty-four were serving in Indiana.

The American Home Missionary Society never sent many men into the South. The missionaries were from New England or the Middle Atlantic states and disliked slavery. Officers of the Society found that missionary operations in the slave states were more expensive and less fruitful than in the Northwest. Among the states of the Northwest, Indiana was the most "southern" and proved the hardest field for the American Home Missionary Society. Calvin never had it so hard in Geneva as some of the Presbyterian missionaries had it in Indiana. "Exotic" is the literal word for Presbyterian ministers in early Indiana. It was not that they had lost out; they had never really been there at all. Now they came late and mostly from the East, entering as Yankees into the hog and hominy belt. If the Appalachian settlers were culturally limited, it led them not so much to regret their limitation as to demand that their churches conform to it. These frontiersmen had no basic aversion to doctrine, but it had to appeal to their ego and be presented movingly "in a storm."

Presbyterian missionaries looked upon the Indiana frontier as a great sea of destitution. They were shocked and often showed it with condemnation. They tried to preach traditional doctrine only to find that a favorite sermon of the backwoods preacher was a denunciation of all "biggity" and educated preachers who were assumed to hold themselves above the people. The missionaries proceeded at once to organize temperance societies, Sunday schools, Bible societies, and missionary auxiliaries, only to find that folk resentment could solemnly declare all these to be not only unnecessary but an affront to God. They tried their hand at community reform and were promptly accused of alliance of church and state. Presbyterian ministers on the Indiana frontier were not original shapers of tradition. They arrived late and their number was small. Upon arrival they met an exclusive revivalism and folk "frontierism" already occupying the land. Whenever the Yankee preacher and the southern settler met in Indiana, the shock was mutual. Some of the preachers stayed at their work, though the field was "like plowing upon a rock." Missionaries were often shoddily treated. Nothing short of an ideal of Zion could have kept them going.

Just because the lot of the missionary was so hard there, Indiana did not get her numerical share of the missionaries sent. The missionary societies were inclined to bypass Indiana in favor of northern Illinois or Michigan or Wisconsin, where Presbyterians were more appreciated. This was simply a matter of spending mission funds at the point of greatest opportunity. Alert Indiana missionaries were quick to notice the policy. Benjamin Cressy of Salem wrote to the American Home Missionary Society that he felt they were actively favoring Ohio and Illinois over poor Indiana as a promising missionary field. Moses Wilder made the same point:

> I intend *Deo Volente* to write some things about Indiana shortly in order to remind you that "there is such a state as Indiana" and that while it has almost double the population of Illinois it is receiving but little more than half the aid, and has only about the same number of ministers. Illinois is supposed to have 375,000 inhabitants and Indi-

ana 700,000. Illinois has 70 ministers and Indiana 76. In 1833 three years before Illinois had 38 ministers and Indiana 72 ministers. Why is this?

Missionaries to the Hoosiers were often discouraged. By the time of the Civil War they felt they had made very little impression on Indiana. It is true that growth seemed slow and progress small, but they were building better than they knew.... It is not entirely a biased view which Joseph S. Clark, Secretary of the Massachusetts Home Missionary Society expresses to William Badger, Secretary of the American Home Missionary Society, 29 April 1844, "There is not a church in Indiana of the Presbyterian or Congregational order that did not spring from missionary efforts. The same is true in Iowa, only one or two in Wisconsin, less than a dozen in Illinois, and not more than twenty in Ohio that do not owe their origin to home missions. Strike out the American Home Missionary Society and you strike the sun from the heavens."

. . . .

Because the American Home Missionary Society contributed substantially to the salary of frontier ministers, those ministers were expected to spend full time in ministerial duties. Farming, merchandising, or even teaching was frowned upon. These were not unworthy occupations, but for a missionary they were diverting. At the point of full support for a settled ministry the Society flew in the face of frontier folkways and earned for its men the frequent epithet "hireling." Nevertheless, the Society upheld its position that its missionaries should give themselves entirely to the work of the ministry and avoid overfrequent changes of parish. [M. A. Remley wrote in 1833:] "You seem to regret my frequent changes of location and say that 'nothing more discourages the efforts of the Society than the frequent changes of ministers.' No one is more sensible of the evil tendency of such changes, than I am; or more deeply deplores the necessity of having to make them; yet such is the heterogeneous character of society, and the fluctuating state of things here in this 'far West' that changes of this kind are often unavoidable however undesirable." By 1829 the Assembly's Board of Missions had adopted a similar policy of supporting a settled ministry rather than appointing itinerants.

. . . .

Baynard Hall jokes about the eastern mission societies and their greenhorn missionaries to the West, but he pays tribute to those "true missionaries" in the New Purchase as very excellent men. He praises their self-denial, zeal, tireless labors, and disinterestedness, and observes that though they were considered Domestic Missionaries they endured as much as their brethren in foreign fields, and without the incidental excitement and support derived from foreign mission work, especially when the woods preacher came to depend for his entire sustenance on two or more weak settlements once the aid of the missionary society was declined or withdrawn. Hall has no sympathy with eastern attacks on secular employment for the clergy. He says such employment was the woods preacher's only hope of getting any money at all. As an alternative he suggests a new society, "The-make-congregations-pay-what-they-voluntarily-promise Society," because he found that most clergymen were doing all they promised and more but the congregations were not.

John Dickey's average annual salary for his first sixteen years in Indiana (1815–31) was eighty dollars. Mrs. William Martin remarked to a guest at the Martin House in 1823 "that for seven entire years she had never seen together ten dollars either in notes or silver." Isaac Reed asked the presbytery for release from Bethany Church in 1825. Among the reasons for moving was the fact that he had not received a dollar in money from his congregation for almost two years. The American Home Missionary Society put pressure on western congregations to pledge at least half a minister's support (generally $400 per year after 1830) before the Society would give aid for the remainder. One of the first things a young missionary had to learn was that the congregational part of this pledge was likely to be made with "Kentucky enthusiasm." It would be paid in part with produce and in part not at all. Most settlers did not have cash. As missionary Samuel G. Lowry phrased it, "Money is not to be had for anything that people have got." Besides, the settlers were always being harangued about the unfitting association of wages and the clergy. Many missionaries agreed with what Moses Wilder reported in 1834, namely that the Baptists and Methodists had served these Indiana areas until even they became disheartened. Their ministrations had left no mark on the people except a determined prejudice against supporting the clergy. This grew to the point where the entire income of Methodist circuit preachers for a full quarter was only $5.50. It was small wonder they left the circuit. Ulric Maynard, having encountered the same prejudice, expressed the wish that he were some sort of craftsman so that he might make the Gospel available without charge to these people who needed it but were against supporting it. But such enthusiasm would hardly fill the need. Samuel Lowry of Rockville became so hard pressed that he had to request a missionary barrel: "We have 8 children. The first four sons 20-18-16 and 14 years of age. The oldest 3 I have had at college. The 2nd has just graduated. The next 3 are daughters 12-10 and 8 years old. The next a son near two years old. Besides these I have a widow sister with three children that I have to provide for. She has two sons 8 and 5 years and a daughter 6 years old. I shall not say what kind of clothing I want. There is no kind that can come amiss in such a family."

The plain impression is that Indiana's early Presbyterian churches were quick to seek mission aid and slow to leave it. To accede to the cries for more missionaries was only to increase the need for support. The churches founded were too weak to support a ministry but too important to neglect entirely. Over the years the mission societies paid the larger share of salaries. In 1837 Moses Wilder provided a summary of the situation in Indiana. He stated that there were eighty-five Presbyterian and eleven Congregational ministers, seventeen of whom were teachers and eight others secular businessmen. Only thirty-two preached to a single church, many to two churches, and some to three or more. Only eleven of the churches were able to support ministers without aid. Asa Johnson had a theory to explain such small progress, which he voiced in 1841 when he applied for renewal of his commission at Peru. He felt definitely that there was a difference in the kind of people who were settling Michigan, Illinois, and other new states from the kind who had come to the Indiana Territory; had the latter been like the former, the Indiana churches would have been independent long ago.

. . . .

The State of Indiana had changed by 1850. Her population had reached 988,416 according to census records. A public school system seemed assured and every Indiana youth might expect to receive a modicum of education. Along with the whole of the Old Northwest, the state had formed commercial ties with the East instead of the South; facile transportation had made this possible. In a few years the Civil War was to create the impression that southern influence north of the Ohio had been swept away. To some it must have appeared that the Ohio Valley was truly a suburb of Boston and a great new day had come.

Richard Power has pointed out that this Yankee victory was apparent but far from complete in the Old Northwest: "It has already been noted that the Yankees after about 1850 regarded themselves as victors in a 'thirty years war.' There was much to make this view plausible. It was easy during those years to be swept into overstatement by the delirious intemperance of Manifest Destiny. But the New England triumph, however large, was never so complete as the zealots believed." This was especially true of Indiana, where southern back-country culture was so predominant. Settlers from the northeastern states and immigrants from Europe settled beside the southern stock. There was intermingling but at a stage far short of Yankee victory or even homogenization. Indiana remained Hoosier in her language, in her moods of isolation, in her resentment of outsiders, and in her toleration of local demagogues.

Indiana is different now than she was in her early days, but she is also much the same. The immigration corridors of Indiana have remained open from south to north. A common saying in mid-twentieth century is that Kentucky has taken Indianapolis without firing a shot. In these days of high mobility, Indiana shares this population stream from the Appalachian South with her sister states of the Old Northwest and with the urban centers of the whole nation. As in the early days, there is a minority of genteel and educated southerners who are welcomed everywhere. But there are hosts of so-called "southern whites" who are poorly trained technically and socially. These latter are the modern upland southerners seeking their place in the sun. That place is less in the squatter's cabin in the woods now than in the wilderness of the industrial cities. But the hovels are the same. The drive to make a new economic start and the resentment of the "educated big bug" are still there. Extensive Southern Appalachian studies have just been made with the aid of a grant from the Ford Foundation. The results are even more vivid than some had guessed: high birth rate, low income, poor education, small economic opportunity, high mobility. Indiana has changed, but in view of this migration her population problems will be much like those of the century and a half since 1800.

The church in Indiana changed too. The Christian faith did keep pace with the early settlers in a way. All the churches grew, but they did not grow equally by any means. The Roman Catholics, the Episcopalians, the Lutherans, and the Moravians grew slowly, more by immigration and by increase from natural birth rate than by evangelization of the unchurched settlers. In 1850 Indiana had eighty-nine congregations of Friends, ranking fourth in the nation in the number of Friends' churches that year. But it was evangelical Protestantism which carried the day, especially the denominations which were identified with the folkways of the upland South. In 1850 the Methodists in Indiana had 779 churches with accommodations for 266,372 worshipers; their church property in the state was valued at $492,560. The Baptists reported 403 churches, with accommodations for 138,783 and property valued at $212,735. The Christian Church, now but an infant among the denominations, had 187 churches in Indiana, some of them honored as the first churches to be established in the pioneer communities.

The Presbyterians also grew. By 1850 they had 282 churches in Indiana, with accommodations for 105,582 worshipers (about ten times the official membership of the Old School and New School combined) and church property valued at $326,520. Since the earliest frontier days, there had been little change in the requirements for the ministry, except that graduation from college and theological seminary became quite generally expected. The Presbyterians had set themselves to their mission in the West with a small body of trained clergy. That decision meant that they had to be sharply limited in the breadth of their ministry; in the case of Indiana it meant that the Presbyterians could not really occupy the state in the crucial early years.

Since 1850 the major denominations have grown more and more alike. Presbyterians have learned more flexibility and have learned to carry their ministry to the people more winsomely. The popular frontier churches—Methodist, Baptist, Christian—have moved admirably to raise their standards. The itinerant minister, the uneducated farmer-preacher, and the "see-saw-hum-and-spit" manner are nearly gone. The pattern in each denomination is an educated ministry with a deliberate plan of community ministry. However pleasing these changes may be, they must be recognized as expensive. Many Hoosiers who felt at home with the older folk churches have failed to make the transition to the new. There is a painful gap between them and their educated clergy; they keep murmuring about the old-time religion. Some have withdrawn to sect groups with the old, comfortable, rural, southern ways.

As for the new southern white who is now migrating to the North, he finds little to attract him to the major denominations. Studies show that in his southern home he is the least church connected and the poorest church attender of all Americans. If he is church connected at all, it is likely to be with a sect group which relates him very little to a well-rounded community life. When he moves north, he attends his church even less than he did back home.

Early Presbyterians in Indiana did not fail when they refused to identify with back-country culture. They were a healthy corrective on the frontier because they presented another cultural and religious standard which the frontiersmen needed to remember and to face. Nor did the early folk religions in Indiana fail because they were so close to the woods dwellers. At least they kept a vital form of Christianity alive as an option for thousands who might never otherwise have met the faith. The peculiar mission of the churches of Indiana today is much less clear. All the major Protestant denominations have become alike and minister to the same population strata—strata in which the new southern settlers are not included. But the persistent back-country mentality and the continuing immigration from the South are a problem to all these churches. The perennial Hoosiers, even the urbanized ones, are no easier to win than their forebears were.

Chapter VI
SECTIONALISM AND WAR

The decade of the 1850s in Indiana was both a time of extraordinary progress economically and socially and of increasing sectional tension, a national trend that culminated in civil war. At first it appeared that the decade would be one of unprecedented prosperity and growth, with virtually unlimited economic progress the likely result of the considerable agricultural advances, transportation improvements, and the number of new manufacturing establishments then underway or completed. A new constitution, hammered out by a convention in Indianapolis during the winter of 1850–51, seemed to mark Indiana's departure from its pioneer period into a more politically and economically advanced state. The document provided for more elective offices, including a superintendent of public instruction, for biennial sessions of the General Assembly, limited in duration to sixty-one days, and for an end to the type of local and special legislation—such as divorces—that had been so time-consuming previously. It also prohibited the state from going into debt except in emergency situations such as foreign invasion. And it contained the infamous Article XIII, a Negro exclusion section prohibiting any further influx of Negroes into the state. Voted on separately by the people of the state, Article XIII was adopted with a slightly higher majority than was the remainder of the constitution; but of course the article became a dead letter in 1865 and was formally removed from the constitution in 1881. Otherwise, the Indiana Constitution of 1851, with only a few amendments, is still serving as the fundamental law of the state.

As Professor Harvey L. Carter suggests in the first selection below, however, the 1850s were not a true "golden age" for the people of Indiana. Many problems remained for a state standing on the brink of growing industrialization and urbanization. Carter has attempted to paint a realistic portrait of the life of a typical Indiana farmer, a "moderately profitable occupation" during the decade. The future did appear extremely bright, nonetheless; and perhaps nothing reflects this better than the story of railroads in the 1850s. Barely 200 miles of track were in operation in the state in 1850, the major line being a connection between the thriving river town of Madison on the Ohio and the still struggling political capital at the center of the state. By 1860, however, more than 2,000 miles of track had been laid and put into operation. The second selection below describes the three-step process by which the general enthusiasm for railroads, often unreasonably high, led to legislative authorization and sometimes resulted in actual lines being built. Other major economic activities of the decade included a variety of manufacturing, generally milling and other types of food processing, but also an important cotton mill in Cannelton, several large shipyards in Jeffersonville and New Albany, wagon works and farm machinery plants in South Bend, and various mills, mines, and factories in other parts of the state. There were, in addition, significant banking changes, not all leading to improvements in the system.

The 1850s were also a time of significant political change. In the early years, following the Compromise of 1850 with its controversial Fugitive Slave Act (which was followed, as noted above, by Indiana's adoption of a Negro exclusion article in its constitution), the divided opinions in the state reflected its divided but strongly southern population. As the national antislavery movement slowly gathered momentum, Indiana remained more antiblack in its attitude than antislavery. However, events such as the John Freeman case, discussed below, helped create a distaste for the slavery system; and the distaste was stimulated even more by the Kansas-Nebraska Act of 1854. Another extremely controversial piece of legislation, this act repealed the Missouri Compromise line of 1820 and, theoretically at least, opened the territories of Kansas and Nebraska, which were created by the same act, to slavery on the basis of popular sovereignty—that is, allowing the people of the territory to decide for themselves whether or not to have slavery. There was an immediate outcry in the North against the Kansas-Nebraska Act and its potential for extending slavery into places previously closed to it. And this outcry was institutionalized by the formation of a new political party in 1854, the Republican party, an almost immediate power in the country. At first this new coalition of former Whigs, Know-Nothings, and northern Democrats was known in many states, including Indiana, as the Fusion or People's party; but the name Republican was generally adopted by 1856.

In Indiana, despite the continued domination throughout the 1850s of the increasingly southern-oriented Democrats, who had also controlled the state offices and the legislature since 1843, the late 1850s were marked by increasing political conflicts. The election of 1860 was an especially memorable one for both the state and the nation: the Republicans won in both but were immediately faced with the secession of South Carolina and then other states. President Lincoln confronted a divided nation when he took office, and within six weeks the Civil War had begun.

Oliver P. Morton, Indiana's peppery Civil War governor and one of Lincoln's most ardent supporters, directed Indiana's enormous contribution to the northern war effort. Although often officious and even dictatorial, Morton presented Lincoln with some of his earliest volunteer soldiers in

1861, and Indiana stood second overall among the states in both the absolute number and in the per capita percentage of troops provided. Morton also proved equal to the political challenges of the war years, which were made more difficult after the 1862 election returned a Democratic majority to the General Assembly. The majority refused to pass an appropriations bill in 1863, but the governor managed to operate the state on personally borrowed funds during 1863 and 1864. And he was able, using some questionable tactics and exploiting the presence of a small group of "copperheads," particularly the Knights of the Golden Circle, to bring Indiana back into the Republican column in the 1864 election.

There is an extensive literature on Indiana during the late antebellum and Civil War years. The best single source is Emma Lou Thornbrough, *Indiana in the Civil War Era, 1850-1880* (1965), part of a projected five-volume sesquicentennial history of the state, which contains an extensive bibliography. See also the work by Kenneth M. Stampp, *Indiana Politics during the Civil War* (1949); and W. H. H. Terrell, *Report of the Adjutant General of Indiana* (8 vols., 1869). Volume I of that report is a narrative of Indiana's role in the war, and it was reprinted by the Indiana Historical Bureau and the Indiana Historical Society in 1960 under the title *Indiana in the War of the Rebellion: Report of the Adjutant General.*

1: Economic Patterns

Farming in the 1850s

HARVEY L. CARTER

Indiana was still a predominantly agricultural state in the last decade of
the antebellum period. Harvey L. Carter, a professor at Colorado College at the time this essay was written, has analyzed various economic
and social aspects of rural Hoosier life during the 1850s. Making careful use of federal census returns as well as contemporary newspapers
and correspondence, he has described patterns of land ownership,
constructed an economic profile of average rural families and communities, and commented on crops, work routines, and the movement
toward county and state fairs that swept the nation during the period.

Professor Carter is also the author of studies dealing with the Far
West, Zebulon Pike, and the Pike's Peak area, where Colorado College
is located. For additional information on agricultural life, land tenure,
the rural press, and other aspects of agriculture prior to the Civil War,
see Paul Wallace Gates, *The Farmer's Age: Agriculture, 1815–1860*
(1960).

The idea has been advanced that the decade of the 1850s was a golden
age in the history of Indiana—an era in which life for the majority of
Hoosiers, especially in the economic sphere, was better than before or since.
The basis of this belief may be stated thus: during the decade, the pioneer
effort flowered into an equitable life which lacked the crudities and hardships of the frontier and also contamination from the evils of industrial
civilization.

There is, indeed, much evidence to support this view. Taken as a
whole, Indiana had emerged from frontier conditions. It is true that communities were still being opened up and settled in the prairie counties of the

From "Rural Indiana in Transition," *Agricultural History*, XX (April 1946), 107–113, 118–
121. Footnotes in the original have been omitted. Reprinted by permission of the
Agricultural History Society and the author.

northern part of the State and on the recently drained swamp lands of the same section and that many vestiges of the earlier way of life remained in the older parts. Generally speaking, however, rural Indiana of the 1850s was no longer part of the American frontier but a product of it. Although half of the rural population still dwelt in log cabins, few new ones were being built, and the other half already had brick or frame houses. Half of the farm land was under cultivation, and half of the men were farmers who owned their holdings; the rest carried on all the other occupations, urban, and rural, skilled, unskilled, and professional.

Although plausible at first glance, it is dangerous to consider the 1850s as a golden age in the sense that the people themselves felt that they had achieved the *summum bonum* of existence. There was a great deal of self-complacency, but this feeling was more evident in political than economic life. The latter was far from static, and there were frequent expressions of desire for change or progress. It is with a view to delineating the actualities of the social and economic life of rural Indiana during the 1850s that this historical reconstruction is undertaken. In addition, it is expected that the details of this survey will provide the bases for accurate generalizations concerning the agricultural history of more extensive regions of the country in a corresponding stage of development.

Farming in Indiana during the decade under review was a moderately profitable occupation. There was a ready market for the surplus of wheat and hogs, and the newly built railroads furnished transportation at rates made reasonable by virtue of canal and river competition. Although farmers were interested in keeping their soil fertile, they were not yet compelled to do so, and there was still another fourth of the total farm land that could be brought under cultivation as needed. The average farm contained about 130 acres, and more than one-third of the counties had no farms larger than 500 acres. The typical farmer had a wife and four children whom he supported by the cultivation of 65 acres, and although he farmed for a surplus, his farm was still very much a self-sufficing unit. As a contemporary English traveler observed: "A backwood farm produces everything wanted for the table, except coffee and rice, salt and spices." When dry goods, shoes, and farm implements are added, the list of things the farmer ordinarily bought is complete. The farmers already had binders and threshing machines. Although the spinning wheel and loom were still in common use, many wives made clothes for the family from purchased goods. Sewing machines and coal-oil lamps were also coming into more widespread use. Tenant farming and mortgages were still uncommon.

The towns of the State were doubling in size every decade, but there were no large cities. The typical manufacturing establishment had a capital investment of $3,500 and employed four men. Considering capital and labor, it was, therefore, the equivalent of two average farms of the time. The economic status of an industrial laborer was probably as good as that of a farmer, except for the ownership of land. Most laborers supplemented their earnings by cultivating a few acres. The number of industrial workers about equaled the number of farm laborers but was only one-eighth the number of independent farmers. The principal industries were flour milling, sawmilling, pork packing, and the making of shoes, furniture, liquor, and machinery. The return on the capital investment varied but averaged about 50 percent in these leading industries. There was, however, almost no concentration in any industry, so the profits were widely distributed and there were no large fortunes. Landownership rather than industrial profits was the chief source of wealth, and the largest amount of taxable property owned by any one individual was valued at about $250,000. In short, practically all individual effort was being rewarded with moderate success through the exploitation of abundant opportunities and expanding markets. One might almost be tempted to conclude that the Jeffersonian ideal of a predominantly agrarian democracy was realized by the Hoosiers during the pre-Civil War decade.

A general spirit of optimism pervaded all communities and groups. Every town expected to be a metropolis; every banker hoped to be a captain of finance; and every debtor looked forward to the day when he would be free from financial stringency. One individual, when sending money to pay claims against himself, wrote: "By the constant exercise of the graces of humility and perseverance and the blessings of Providence I hope to get along. My income may now with safety be put at $400 a year. This may with industry be indefinitely increased." Even a serious economic crisis could not dampen the optimism of the Hoosiers during the decade. Recuperation was regarded as certain, and as one editor insisted: "We are headed not for another crash ... but for the hey-day of prosperity and money making." Confidence in the future rather than satisfaction with the present was the keynote insofar as material well-being was concerned.

Originally Indiana had for the most part been heavily wooded. This was true, without exception, for the region between the Ohio and the Wabash rivers, but the land north of the Wabash was covered with moraines and morainal lakes and small prairies or forest openings. In the real prairie region lying between the Wabash, the Tippecanoe, and the Kankakee rivers and the Illinois line, there were only infrequent and inconsiderable hardwood groves. About two-thirds of the trees of the State were oak and beech. Next in order came maple, hickory, ash, walnut, poplar, elm, sycamore, and cherry. In the southern and central parts, the smaller trees like dogwood, pawpaw, thorn, persimmon, plum, and crab apple were plentiful.

Southern Indiana, having been settled some twenty to thirty years longer than any other section of the State, was in many ways the best developed economically, but its position was already being challenged by the central section. Both were heavily wooded, but the soils of the southern part were of varying degrees of desirability, whereas those of the central part were of more uniform richness, although they probably had poorer natural drainage. By 1860, the ratio of improved to unimproved farm land in the central part was 3,118,000 acres to 2,610,000 acres as compared with 3,787,000 acres to 4,023,000 for the southern part.

The northern part, which contained most of the swamp lands and was settled mainly from 1840 to 1860, made the poorest showing with 1,211,000 acres of improved and 1,401,000 acres of unimproved farm land. Taking the State as a whole, there were about 8,000,000 of improved and an equal amount of unimproved acres. There were about 5,500,000 acres, mainly composed of swamp lands in the north and barren hills in the south, that were not in farms. In 1850, the Federal Government had turned over 1,286,827 acres of swamp lands to the State which were then drained and sold so far as possible in the early years of the decade. In 1853 there were only 246,339 acres in the entire State that were unsold and unappropriated.

Probably the best farms were in the Whitewater Valley and southeastern Indiana generally, which in many ways reached its maximum development in this period. However, in all southern and central Indiana, farming was making rapid strides, and on the better farms, log cabins were being replaced by frame houses and larger barns were being built.

The northern, and more especially the northwestern, part was not so far advanced. Horace Greeley, after a ride by handcar from La Fayette to Westfield, wrote: "I doubt that all the houses visible on the seventy-eight miles would amount to one hundred, and I am sure they would be dear at two hundred dollars each on the average. Yet there is much fine timber and excellent land on that route, and he who passes ten years hence will see a different state of things." Greeley also expressed the following opinion of the more fertile and more settled regions of northern Indiana.

> The most eligible wild lands are those combining timber and prairie in about equal proportions so interspersed that the one is rarely more than a mile or so from the other. Northern Indiana, embracing La Porte, St. Joseph, Elkhart, and one or two other counties, is admirably favored in this respect. Here the population is already quite compact and the land has a fair value apart from the influence of speculations. I think farms in the counties above named would now average twenty dollars per acre above the value of the buildings and the fences, which are often worth as much more. There are farms adjacent to villages which would command $100 per acre, or even more; but these are few.

Another observer pointed out the difference between the development of wooded and prairie lands. "La Porte county is a prairie county and came to an acme all at once; and not advancing any they continue all the old habits. The timbered counties are fast developing themselves, and perceptibly improve in morals as well as agriculture and science."

The grand prairie was the last area to be settled. Prior to 1850, it had few settlers, but during the decade, large parts of it were brought under cultivation. A young lawyer, soon to be elected to Congress, described it thus: "Here [Monticello] begins grand prairie, and extends to the Mississippi. From the court house steeple one can see around one hundred fifty miles of prairie; now a waving sea of flowers." Speculators like Henry L. Ellsworth, believing in the utility of the prairie, had bought large tracts which they endeavored to sell to settlers. In the 1850s their judgment was vindicated, and they began to realize returns on their investments. . . .

It is difficult to give an adequate economic portrayal of an average rural community in Indiana in the 1850s. An approximate view may be gained by a detailed study of a township in one of the counties of the east-central section of the State. It had one small village of the type to be found in almost any township of the State. Otherwise it was completely rural. There were 988 people, comprising 183 families. Of the heads of families, 136 were farmers, 17 were laborers, probably on farms in most cases, and 5 were widows. This listing leaves 25 families for the village, or a total population of 104. In the village were 3 merchants, 1 grocer, 1 innkeeper, and 1 clerk, to represent the retail trade; 2 tailors, 1 shoemaker, 2 wagonmakers, 1 blacksmith, 2 tanners, 2 coopers, 2 cabinetmakers, and 1 miller, who, taken together, represented manufacturing; 1 joiner and 3 carpenters who comprised the building trade; and 2 medical doctors—the sole representatives of the professions. The fact that the enumeration included no preacher or teacher may mean that there was no church or school in the community, but more probably it indicates that these institutions existed but were served by itinerants.

The wealthiest farmer in the township had real estate worth $6,000, while the wealthiest man in the village was a merchant with $4,700 worth of real estate. Forty-four families had no real estate whatever, and 64 owned less than $1,000 worth each. A percentage distribution of landownership would show that 24 percent of the heads of families owned no real estate in the township; 35 percent owned 16 percent of the wealth in real estate; 34 percent owned 56 percent and 7 percent owned 28 percent.

The farm families were larger than those of the village, the average being 4.3 as compared with 2.6. Of the 183 families in the township, 18 were childless, and the largest family had 11 children. The 115 families with 4 or less children had an average wealth of $740, whereas the 68 families with 5 or more children averaged $1,323. From these figures, the deduction might be made that children were an asset rather than a liability in an economy based on land. When the comparison is made in terms of individuals the disparity is not so great, for the 494 people belonging to the small-family group possessed a total wealth of $85,090 and 492 people of the large-family group had a total wealth of $87,985. Still, considering the fact that the children constituted a larger portion and cost less to support the balance was in favor of the large families.

Glimpses of the diverse human factors impinging upon the economic scene add further interesting details. A certain William Gray had bought land in central Indiana but for some reason did not occupy it, lingering on in Ohio. His friend, James Mix, having moved to Indiana, began a campaign by letter in the late 1840s to persuade him to move to his farm. "You could not expect to make a dollar per day—still there is plenty of work if you wish to labour out." The implication is clear that Mix looked down on hired labor and wished to point his friend's ambitions somewhat higher. A half year later he wrote:

> I was afraid you would fool your land away—I had about gave you out—if you move out here in time I have about Nine akers of ground to sow in Wheat on good terms . . . and corn ground for a small Family a while by some little Fixing at least till you could get up a Cabin— You may expect to put up with some hardships for a while but perhaps nothing more than you experience there and then a home of your own will urge you forward to exertions—property is rising in value.

Thus Mix argued and in so doing exhibited several qualities typical of his kind and time. He was not afraid of hard work, nor of privations, and he was willing to share what he had in order to help a friend. In the same letter, he added that the wheat crop was a failure and that his family would have to live on corn bread for a year. Thus, it may be said that he also had courage and optimism.

Another good description of farming conditions is supplied by a letter from a resident of Brewens Cross Roads in Parke County, Indiana, to friends back in Virginia.

> I am very well pleased with my situation out hear. I have 85 akers of land for which I paid eight hundred and twenty dollars it is a first rate peace of land to the size of it all the falt it has there is two little of it . . . it has a cumfortable one story dwelling house on it wetherboarded on the outside and plastered inside it has a kitchen to the end of it. it has a stable & corn crib smoke house etc there was about 20 akers cleared and in cultivation when I bought it there was about 24 akers deadened and ready for clearing up and fencing I have had one of my brothers sons highered since the 25th of March at ten dollars per month wee have cleared and fenced about 12 akers since that time we have about 16 akers in corn. . . . I have earnt nine dollars harvesting besides cutting 84 dozzen on the shears I put it up in shock and get one half (wheat) a man that is able to work and is so disposed neadent ever be idle . . . I did loose half the day yesterday fishing with a sane . . . there was seven in company we had between a peck and a half booshel a

peace my mooving out here and fixing up to farm has cost me a good deal but I am better fixed than ever I have been.

These sentences clearly reflect a man who had worked hard, improved his situation, and was proud of his achievement. However modest his success might appear to others, it was a worthy reality to him, and he must have been typical of thousands of his contemporaries.

Regardless of how well newcomers to the State may have succeeded economically, there were some who felt that they could do better elsewhere. Iowa, in the early 1850s, and Kansas, in the later years of the decade, attracted many Hoosiers. An Indiana farmer, referring to the fact in a letter to his brother who had already moved to Iowa, wrote: "You said something about my not having the Iowa fever yet. I am clear of it yet I think that Harrison has got a light attack of it." He continued:

> You said something about hog raising. I want to make five hundred dollars at it this fall   hogs are worth $3.50 here now . . . I can tell you that I have got a full match for my brown mare, they are worth one hundred dollars apiece. I have been clearing ground this winter and spring and have just got ready for the twenty acres I want to go to sowing oats tomorrow morning . . . I am going to plant fifty acres of corn 16 acres of oats and 5 of timothy.

By implication, this Hoosier was saying: why go to Iowa when one can clear an additional 20 acres on the Indiana homestead as new ground was needed? The letter also shows appreciation of the opportunities afforded by hog raising, and pride in matched teams of valuable horses.

Similar problems were discussed in a more pessimistic tone by another farmer in 1859.

> I have a right smart crop of corn planted some seventeen acres and have cleared up some ground and made fence . . . I am doing my best but luck seems to be against me . . . we are too far north here I would go west but Iowa is too cold Kansas not settled and Missouri a slave state. Indiana is good enough for me and if I can get a home here that suits me I will stay.

Here, in essence, was the problem of the pioneer farmer—getting a home. Adverse weather, crop failures, ill health, and poor management were the factors, all lumped together under the term "bad luck," which might hinder him in this objective. No matter how hard he might work, he had to use intelligence and also have a reasonable amount of luck in order to succeed.

As a generalization for the period under discussion, it is reasonable to say that the good seasons with bumper crops and the bad ones with a consequent scarcity evened up in the long run, and the increasing foreign and domestic market for foodstuffs kept up with production.

The first growing season of the decade was not good. A severe drought

Hand and hoe cultivation
Courtesy of the John Deere Company

in the early summer affected most of Indiana as well as other States nearby. The wheat yield was poor, and grass was unusually short. The oat crop was a total failure, and much of the corn failed to come up. Except for early potatoes which were all right and the fruit crop which was fair, it was a bad season. On the other hand, 1851 seems to have been a good year, and in 1856 the corn crop was so large that the farmers did not have enough hogs to consume it. In 1858 the season was very wet. Corn planting was held up, and some was scalded or washed out.

The farming methods of the 1850s were such as might be expected in a period of transition from frontier to modern conditions. Horses were used far more commonly than oxen, but the latter were by no means rare and were preferred for breaking the tough prairie sod. New ground totaling 3,000,000 acres was brought under cultivation during the decade. This fact alone meant a great deal of work with ax and saw; it meant splitting rails for additional fences and difficult cultivation for a few years. Because of the stumps, the corn had to be planted by hand and cultivated with a hoe. It was also cut, shocked, and husked entirely by hand, and the bulk of it was stored in open cribs made of rails. The corn planter could be used where the ground was relatively free of stumps. With wheat there could be more recourse to machinery, but it was still sown broadcast. The same was true of oats. The reaper had been introduced, and it was being used increasingly to harvest grain. It was a genuine labor and time saver, for handling a cradle was very arduous and slow work. Threshing machines had also appeared, but the more common method was trampling out the grain on the barn floor. The fanning mill had largely replaced the old practice of winnowing the grain from the chaff by hand. Marketing, however, was still difficult with country roads almost impassable during much of the winter and spring.

. . . .

Indiana was the greatest pork-producing State in the Union, both in 1850 and 1860. In 1850, the Illinois farms were better stocked with hogs than those of Indiana—each Illinois farm averaging one more hog than a corresponding Hoosier farm. By 1860, however, Indiana's supremacy was unchallenged, its average per farm having been lowered by one half pig while Illinois had lost 7½ pigs per farm. There were 2 hogs and an extra ham for every man, woman, and child in Indiana in 1860, or a swine population of about 90 to the square mile. Hog production decreased somewhat in all five States during the decade.

There are at least two explanations for Indiana's greater progress in this decade. One is that the State had been more backward than the others before 1850, and the improvement was somewhat overdue. There is probably some truth in this. If it has any validity here, however, it must be restricted to the raising of cattle and wheat and cannot possibly apply to hogs and corn. A more plausible explanation is that Indiana's great rural advance was the result of slower industrial progress than the other States. In 1860, farmers made up 47 percent of all men employed in Indiana as compared with 40 percent in Wisconsin, 39 percent in Illinois, 37½ percent in Michigan, and 34½ percent in Ohio.

What role did the various sections of the State play in these agricultural advances? In general the answer may be stated thus: each section paid particular attention to increasing the production of those commodities which had previously been neglected. Earlier the tendency had been to grow the crop that was easiest and most naturally adapted to the land of a given section. In the fifties, without giving up specialties entirely, the trend was to develop the less natural characteristic products. Thus the north and central sections doubled wheat production during the decade, but the south, hitherto a poor wheat-growing area, tripled its production. Similarly corn and hog production which had been preeminent in the southern part remained nearly stationary. At the same time there was a material increase in the central and northern sections.

. . . .

The agricultural progress of the fifties found expression in the movement for county and State fairs which swept the United States at that time.

These fairs may be taken as an indication of an increasing pride in the quality and quantity of farm produce. No longer was the farmer simply bent on making a living; he was now producing for a profit. Hence his interest in improved farm machinery, increased yields per acre, and better livestock through breeding. Insofar as Indiana was concerned, there is no doubt that most of the credit for furthering these interests must be accorded to Governor Joseph A. Wright, who was not and had never been a farmer, but who made agricultural improvement his hobby because he appreciated the fact that four-fifths of the people of the State which he governed made their living by farming. Only his political enemies said that he advised farmers to improve their sheep by the use of hydraulic rams, but even his friends had to admit that he sent a ball of hair from the paunch of a cow to the world's fair. He liked to speculate concerning this ball of pig bristles, which he regarded as a scientific curiosity, but his enemies said that it was an unfair specimen of the resources of the State. However, Wright did organize the State Board of Agriculture on February 14, 1851 and became its first president.

A few county fairs had already been held, but the State Board of Agriculture sponsored the demand for a State fair. The legislature appropriated $2,000 toward the project, and the first State fair was held at Indianapolis, October 19–25, 1852. The attendance was estimated at 15,000 on the first day and 25,000 on the second. It was thought that the agricultural exhibits were not so extensive as they might have been although mills from all over the State had flour on display. All told there were 3,100 entries of exhibits ranging from plows to pickles and from sorghum to steam engines. Among the mechanical exhibits, patented and made within the State, were Reynold's Indiana bran duster and regrinder, Hollingsworth's patent washing machine, Hewitt's patent hay and cotton press, Mendenhall's Excelsior churn, and Coffin's ice cream freezer. Singer, Wilson, and Howe sewing machines were prominently displayed. Wayne County took most of the awards for fine cattle, but the other livestock prizes were widely distributed over the State. Another feature was an agricultural essay contest in which prizes were given to Benjamin Reynolds of White County, who wrote on the reclaiming of swamp land; J. T. Smith, of Rush County, who submitted a plan for a farmhouse and barn; and B. Lawrence of Monroe County, who discussed the best ways to use hilly lands.

The first State fair was assuredly a success, and other cities felt they should be allowed to hold one. Indianapolis was not yet large enough, and transportation facilities were too bad to give the capital city, with its central location, a clear advantage over its rivals. In 1853 the fair was held at La Fayette, the principal attraction being an address by Horace Greeley to the members of the Indiana State Agricultural Society. The next year the fair was held at Madison, but compared to the two previous gatherings, it was financially a failure. Charges were made that the Madison merchants and innkeepers profiteered at the expense of those attending, so for the next four years it was again held on the military grounds at Indianapolis. In 1859 the fair was held at New Albany, but it soon became a fixed custom to have it at Indianapolis.

County fairs became more prevalent during the fifties. In 1858 it was reported that 37 were held in Indiana, 34 in Ohio, and 14 in Illinois. At these fairs a favorite competition was the plowing match, in which the contestants were both to hold and drive and were judged on skill and workmanship. Another common feature and great attraction was the riding contest for ladies. By 1858 a great many farm implements were shown at all the county fairs including the subsoil plow, harrow, cultivator, corn plow, grain drill, horse rake, corn sheller, straw cutter, threshing machine, farm wagon, corn planter, reaper, mower, and the reaper and mower combined. Farmers had an opportunity to see all of these implements actually at work, because the fairs provided a convenient place for manufacturers to display their products in the most convincing way.

Newspapers began adding agricultural columns as regular departments. In 1850, Chicago promoted a Great National Agricultural Fair, which numerous Hoosiers attended, since the railroads reduced their fares by one half for the occasion. One Indiana pioneer farmer, Solon Robinson of Lake County, who had formed a squatters' union there in 1834 became a

An early Studebaker
Courtesy of the Indiana Historical Society

nationally known agricultural authority in the fifties. After an unsuccessful effort to found a monthly farm magazine of his own, in 1853 he accepted Horace Greeley's invitation to become agricultural editor of the New York *Tribune.*

The formation of agricultural societies stimulated a great deal of interest in improving livestock and in using fertilizers and better methods of cultivation to produce larger crop yields. Some of the inquiry and experimentation went into unfruitful channels, as when a farmer of Wayne County made a gallon of molasses from a bushel of Broadwell apples, or Henry L. Ellsworth attempted to fatten hogs on meal made from ground corncobs.

The improvement in cattle was genuine, although it met with some opposition. This is rather dramatically portrayed in the report of the Marion County Agricultural Society. "The old race of long-legged, slab-sided, sharped-backed, big-horned and long-haired quadrupeds is rapidly disappearing from the land." This was an assuring prospect, but the writer continued: "The truth, however, compels us to say that we have many men among us, men of ample means, who are such perfect 'know-nothings' that they cannot see the necessity for good stock ... and for the good of the country turn out a bull of their peculiar stock to improve the various breeds in the neighborhood, especially in their milking qualities, for these gentlemen sagely remark that, 'if the Durhams replace the scrub stock our children will starve for milk.'" The farmers who were really interested in blooded stock had their own effective way of dealing with the menace, however, for the writer continued, "it sometimes happens that when their fine animals— emulating the knights of old—go forth glorying in their strength and beauty, announcing their coming in trumpet tones to the denizens of the pastures, they return with drooping heads and sadly marred in their fair proportions."

Hogs were also improved by more attention to breeding and feeding. "The stock of hogs is also receiving attention, and the breed of 'land sharks' is passing away." When pigs ranged the woods and fed on acorns and beech mast, they were bound to be razorbacks, but when they were penned and fed on milk and corn they were sure to round out, and the amount of lard was greater and the meat more tender.

Horses, too, were improved and more attention was given to the pedigrees of animals used for riding and driving. In the fifties people were beginning to go more than formerly, and this was reflected in the interest in better horses. The first Percherons are said to have been imported into Indiana by the Whig congressman, George G. Dunn.

Taken all in all the 1850s may be regarded as having ushered in a stage in the development of agriculture and rural life which was destined to remain, and continue to improve, for about sixty years.

Beginning the Railroad Network

VICTOR M. BOGLE

The railroad was introduced into the United States in 1830—with the initial Baltimore and Ohio Railroad charter dating from 1827—and almost immediately there was talk of building railroads in all parts of the country. Indiana had its share of early railroad boosters but, as Professor Bogle points out, very little was done in the way of actual construction until the 1850s. The planning and promoting of lines in the 1830s and 1840s, however, was important in that a more realistic appraisal of which routes to build was possible afterwards. Three factors influenced the layout of the state's rail network: market requirements, existing transportation (largely natural waterways), and the location of the state capital. By 1850, in Professor Bogle's phrase, "the building era of Indiana's railroads had arrived" (p. 217), with three-quarters of the railroad mileage constructed in the 1850s completed and in operation by 1855. By that time, too, the first "union station," a depot used in common by all the railroads serving Indianapolis, had been constructed in the capital city.

For more information on the history of railroading in Indiana, see Emma Lou Thornbrough, *Indiana in the Civil War Era, 1850-1880* (1965); Wylie Daniels, *The Village at the End of the Road* (1938); and George W. Hilton, *Monon Route* (1978). See also the delightful anecdotal article about the early days of the Monon by Thomas Carter Perrin, "The New Albany-Salem Railroad—Incidents of Road and Men," *Indiana Magazine of History,* XV (December 1919), 342-362; and the excellent general introduction by George Rogers Taylor, *The Transportation Revolution, 1815-1860* (1951).

With increasing frequency these days back-page stories in Indiana newspapers indicate that rail service is to be discontinued on sections of the Pennsylvania, the New York Central, and the Monon—or that a few of the remaining giant corporations are negotiating to bring about the ultimate in railroad consolidation. Most Hoosiers who grew up before World War II can recall when railroads were somehow different, if not more important, then they are now. Some may already be looking back nostalgically to days when the steam locomotive and sleek diesel were dramatic symbols of commercial progress, or when a train ride was the standard means for making a trip to Chicago, New York, or Denver. A moment's reflection will prompt the realization that these are but signs of a new chapter in the railroad

From "Railroad Building in Indiana, 1850-1855," *Indiana Magazine of History,* LVIII (September 1962), 211-224, 226-227, 230-231. Some footnotes in the original have been omitted. Copyright © 1962 by the Trustees of Indiana University. Reprinted by permission.

history of the state, and that, if it is not the concluding chapter, certainly it is one falling near the close of a long and fascinating story.

The phases of Indiana's 130 years of railroad history can be capsuled into a few simple statements. From the late 1820's until around 1850 there was much *talking* but not much *building*. From 1850 to the early 1870's the basic network was established, very much along the lines projected by the earliest promoters. During the latter decades of the past century, consolidation of major lines took place, and many branch and feeder lines were built to supplement the basic network. Since World War I consolidation has continued while the network has retrenched due to competition from other forms of transportation. With minor modifications, this summary might be applied to the history of railroads in most of the states between the Appalachians and the Mississippi River. But such generalizations obviously ignore the unique and multitudinous steps which Indiana and other states have pursued in fitting themselves into the nation's railroad pattern.

The present study is concerned primarily with railroad developments in the state of Indiana during the period 1850–1855 when, after a somewhat lengthy prelude, the rail network of the state finally began to take shape. In a sense this presentation is a "progress report" on a more ambitious research project designed to encompass the story of Indiana's railroads from their origins to their current operations. Because of the abbreviated scope of this report, developments preceding and following the first half decade of the 1850's have been dealt with in a cursory manner only; and although a judicious effort has been made to base conclusions on defensible data, this study must naturally suffer from a lack of perspective because of incompleted research. It is hoped, nevertheless, that what is presented here will serve as a sample of the kind of study that railroad history in the state and nation gives rise to and, in fact, demands.

The decade of the 1850's began with little actual railroad construction accomplished in Indiana. The eighty-six-mile connection between Madison and Indianapolis—the state's pioneer railroad—had been in operation between its terminal towns since 1847, but even this pre-1850 success had not come easily. The dream of a railroad between these points went back to the agitation of the early 1830's when the Indiana General Assembly granted charters to mushrooming "rail road" companies all over the state—even before anybody was sure just what a "rail road" was. The Madison and Indianapolis Railroad has deservedly received much attention from Indiana's historians for its initial achievements; but the fact that it required fifteen years for Indiana to build its first operable railroad is certainly indicative of the times.

There may be, on the other hand, a tendency to dismiss too lightly the period of the 1830's and 1840's as a background for later construction. A study of the projected routes outlined in the hundred or more separate railroad charters issued from 1832 to 1850 reveals that these fragmentary lines, prompted largely by local interests, did make some sense when plotted on a composite map of the state. Of the more than four thousand miles of railroad authorized in these early charters, most lines were designed to connect geographic points which, in the perspective of 125 years ago, should have been connected. In fact, some of the routes were of such intrinsic importance that companies to construct railroads over them were authorized again and again after earlier charters became obsolete.[1] The route from the Falls of the Ohio River to Lake Michigan, over which the New Albany and Salem Railroad company eventually completed its road, was one which figured in many separate pre-1850 charters.[2] Another route was that of the Buffalo and Mississippi (later the Northern Indiana) Railroad company; it meandered over the northern tier of counties toward Chicago, sending its projected tributaries in all directions to catch infant villages along the way. Still other routes consistently regarded as important were those from Evansville to Terre Haute, from Richmond to Terre Haute, from Lafayette to Indianapolis, from Peru to Indianapolis, from Lawrenceburg to Indianapolis, and from the Ohio Falls area to Indianapolis. Once railroad building began in earnest in the early 1850's, these routes were among the first started.

The general assembly was usually quite lenient in the time it allotted companies to complete their roads, but legislative authority alone was not enough to get them built.[3] In many instances in which a company was little more than a flare-up of "rail fever," the project normally died soon. Apparently this was the fate of such unbuilt roads as the Levenworth [sic] and Bloomington (1834), the Charlestown and Ohio (1835), the Perrysville and Danville (1836), and perhaps 40 percent of all those chartered in the 1830's

[1]The mileage total is the writer's own estimate based on study of the routes authorized in the charters. Although many of the points to be connected by the proposed roads were at the time only villages, it would have been impossible to predict with certainty in the 1830's and 1840's which of them might eventually become key urban centers.

[2]The original charter for what was to become the New Albany and Salem Railroad was probably that approved February 3, 1832; it authorized a "rail-road" from New Albany to Indianapolis via Greenville, Salem, Brownstown, Rockford, Columbus, and Franklin. In the comprehensive Internal Improvements Bill of the mid-thirties a "Rail Road" or "McAdamized Turnpike" was authorized between Jeffersonville and Crawfordsville, via New Albany, Salem, Bedford, Bloomington, and Greencastle. In 1845 a charter was granted residents of Montgomery County to build a railroad from Crawfordsville to Lafayette; it was re-granted the following year, "revived" in 1848, and amended in 1851 to include an extension south to Greencastle. Another significant charter amendment relating to this route was that granted to the New Albany and Salem company in 1848 which gave its officers the "right and power to extend their work or road to any other point or points, than those indicated by the location heretofore made by authority of the state...."

[3]For example, the Andersontown, Greenfield and Shelbyville company was given three years to begin work and ten more to have it completed. The Ohio and Mississippi company was allowed twenty-five years to complete its road.

and 1840's. It is impossible to determine how many other companies were stillborn before they even reached the charter stage, but it is likely that at one time or another through the thirties and forties almost every settlement in the state at least dreamed of an all-important rail connection.

Stripped of certain emotional overtones which accompanied the formation of the early railroad projects, the problem the planners and promoters tried to solve with their schemes was an economic one. Paraphrased in a single word, it was *markets*. They wanted means to dispose of their surplus commodities and facilities to obtain products their own economy was not advanced enough to provide. In simplest terms, this meant they must somehow attach their locality to a point or points where the advantageous exchange could take place. When the railroad fever first hit the Hoosier State, waterways were the accepted mode of transporting bulky materials over long distances. The initial purpose of the railroad was to supplement the waterway system. Since the state's population was weighted toward the Ohio River, towns along its banks had a strong priority as terminals for the earliest chartered roads. Of the hundred or so authorized before 1850, twenty-five were to have points on the Ohio as one of their terminals. Almost this many more were to touch the Wabash and Erie Canal, while others were to tie in the northern portion of the state with the natural waterway supplied by the Great Lakes. A few of the more ambitious routes, most notably the one to be followed by the New Albany and Salem Railroad, attempted to link all three of these east-west waterways.

If it had not been for the establishment of the state's capital near the geographic center of the state, this plan of using railroads chiefly as a means of linking waterways probably would have prevailed somewhat longer. The location of the capital town itself came to be an important factor in railroad planning. To plan a railroad of any significant length and not somehow have it reach the promising capital became almost infeasible. Though by 1850 Indianapolis was little more than the political center of the state— noticeably behind Madison, New Albany, and other communities in industrial advancement—this town was ideally situated for the kind of transportation revolution now beginning. It served as a magnet to draw to a central point what otherwise might have been dangling lines. The foresight, promotion, and sheer good luck which combined to create Indianapolis into the rail hub of the state make up one of the intriguing stories in Indiana's history.

By the close of the 1840's Indiana was recognized as a valuable hinterland for any established marketing center which could arrange to tap it. The larger Ohio River towns, and some of the not-so-large ones, early visualized themselves in this highly profitable role. Promoters in Evansville, New Albany, Jeffersonville, and Lawrenceburg consciously or unconsciously worked toward this end. Madison, having the first success in getting a railroad into the interior, actually came closest of the river towns to being a regional distribution center.[4] Ultimately, however, it was larger, out-of-state cities which exerted the real gravitational pull: Cincinnati and Louisville to the southeast; Cleveland and Toledo to the northeast; and the phenomenal Chicago to the northwest. There may have been an awareness on the part of Indiana's early railroad promoters that anything they might accomplish would eventually fall as gain to commercial interests in distant cities, but there is little to indicate that by the early 1850's they were seriously disturbed about it.

Although there was no sharp break between rail developments of the late 1840's and those of the beginning 1850's, the new decade did promise certain advantages over the previous period. The state had gotten over most of the financial shock resulting from the internal improvements fiasco of the late thirties, and relatively prosperous times were back again. Along with a large increase in the state's population there had undoubtedly been a commensurate increase in property values and investment capital.[5] Also, managerial and technical talent had no doubt evolved as a result of the trial-and-error experiences of the recent past. Still another important stimulant was the example of the Madison and Indianapolis Railroad. Its success proved that railroads could be built and operated in Indiana; here was the encouragement needed to goad planners of other roads into action.

At the beginning of the 1850's many earlier charters were still legally in effect, but no more than ten of the companies authorized to construct railroads showed serious inclinations to start building.[6] These companies were surveying their routes and attempting to accumulate sufficient funds to begin construction. At least two of the railroads were at the track-laying state; before the year 1850 closed, the Indianapolis and Bellefontaine Railroad company laid down twenty-eight miles of track between Indianapolis and Pendleton, and the New Albany and Salem completed its track thirty-five miles to Salem.

The year 1851 brought further proof that the building era of Indiana's railroads had arrived. The vigorous Terre Haute and Indianapolis Railroad company almost completed trackage over its seventy-three-mile route within this single year; the Northern Indiana Railroad company opened a twenty-five-mile stretch from the Michigan state line, near White Pigeon, to South Bend; the Indianapolis and Bellefontaine company moved its line sixteen miles farther east to the village of Chesterfield; and the New Albany

---

[4]Urban rivalry in the state of Indiana is a subject that has not yet been adequately explored, but as early as 1907 one writer pointed out the competition among the Ohio River communities for supremacy.

[5]Indiana's population in 1840 was 685,866; in 1850, 988,416—an increase of over 40 per cent. See U.S., Census Office, *Seventh Census of the United States: 1850*, p. 781.

[6]Among the many charters legally in effect were those providing railroads between Pendleton and Indianapolis, Rockville and Montezuma, Brownstown and Scipio, Indianapolis and Cincinnati (the "Junction" road), Peru and Goshen, and Mount Vernon and New Harmony.

and Salem finished an additional twenty-mile section beyond the original terminus of Salem to the village of Orleans. Two other companies began laying track; the Peru and Indianapolis had the twenty-one-mile section from Indianapolis to Noblesville ready for use in March and the Jefferson-ville road, heading northward to Columbus, completed twenty-seven miles of track to Vienna, in Scott County, before the year's end.

The following three years (1852, 1853, 1854) showed the same kind of tangible results. Early in 1852 the Northern Indiana company joined with the Michigan Southern Railroad company to open a route curving through the northwestern corner of the state into Chicago. During 1852 the Lafayette and Indianapolis company, blessed with ideal terrain, built its entire seventy-three-mile line, and by the close of the year the Jeffersonville company had finished its road to Columbus and added an eleven-mile sec-tion to Edinburg. Meanwhile, the twenty-five mile Martinsville and Frank-lin Railroad was opened for business in November.

In January 1853 the Indianapolis and Bellefontaine company cele-brated the opening of its track to Union (now Union City) on the Indiana-Ohio state line and joined with finished roads in the neighboring state to give Indiana its first rail link to major cities on the eastern seaboard. The Indiana Central Railroad company opened its line from Indianapolis to Richmond in the fall of 1853; and a few weeks later, after more than two decades of false starts, the Lawrenceburgh and Upper Mississippi Railroad company finally got its road completed between Indianapolis and Law-renceburg. Largely as a result of the growing rivalry of the older Madison and Indianapolis company and the newer Jeffersonville company, another feeder line was completed in December in southern Indiana; this was the twenty-three-mile Columbus and Shelbyville.[7]

The New Albany and Salem Railroad, longest of all the pioneer roads, moved forward methodically and completed its 288-mile route across the state from New Albany to Michigan City by the middle of 1854, thus realizing the dreams of early promoters to tie by rail the Ohio River and Lake Michigan. During 1854 two other companies managed to open service between key terminal points; the Peru and Indianapolis did this in the spring, and the Evansville and Illinois (from Evansville to Terre Haute) in the following November.[8]

Also during the same three-year period other important lines were either in the advanced planning or early construction stage. These were: the

[7]The corporate name of the Lawrenceburgh and Upper Mississippi Railroad company was changed to Indianapolis and Cincinnati Railroad company in October, 1853.
[8]Francis F. Hargrave in his study of the New Albany and Salem Railroad (which later became the Monon) discusses in some detail the agreement by which the New Albany and Salem and the Michigan Central railroads arranged a rail line into Chicago. He indicates that this line was open early in 1852, more than a year before the completion of the New Albany and Salem. See Francis F. Hargrave, A Pioneer Indiana Railroad, the Origin and Development of the Monon (Indianapolis, 1932), 109, 128.

Ohio and Mississippi, from Lawrenceburg to Vincennes (actually a segment of the Baltimore to St. Louis trunk system); the Cincinnati, Logansport and Chicago, which was to join the rail complex in western Ohio to roads converging on Chicago; and the Lake Erie, Wabash and St. Louis (known later as the "Wabash"), destined to run from Fort Wayne along the Wabash Valley into Illinois.[9] These roads, all designed to span the state from east to west, would eventually comprise a significant part of Indiana's rail network, but their completion did not occur until some months after the period directly considered in this report.

By the close of the year 1854 over fourteen hundred miles of railroad had been completed and were in operation in Indiana.

. . . .

No systematic study has yet been made of the eighteen completed roads' financial statements, but fragmentary evidence indicates that the average cost per mile was well over $15,000.[10] This includes the costs of right of way, surveying, preparing the roadbed, rolling stock, and station facilities. Therefore, a conservative estimate of the investment in Indiana's completed roads by 1855 is more than $21,000,000—roughly twice the estimated cost of the whole projected internal improvements system of the 1830's and 1840's. Some companies, such as the Lafayette and Indianapolis, had little difficulty in preparing a roadbed and thereby cut initial engineering costs to a minimum. Other roads, confronted with rough terrain and numerous streams to bridge, were obliged to spend considerably more. Obtaining sufficient capital to finish a road once construction began was a sore problem with several of the roads. Others arranged adequate financing of the entire line before beginning construction.

No really standard procedure was followed in raising the necessary funds to construct these railroads of the early 1850's, but certain common features did prevail. Usually the charter specified the amount for which the road could be capitalized; depending on its length this might vary from $150,000 to more than $1,000,000.[11] Since the charters governing the roads constructed in the 1850–1855 period had been issued some years before, when practical information on costs was unavailable, the capitaliza-

---

[9]The Cincinnati, Logansport and Chicago was initially chartered and known as the Newcastle and Richmond.

[10]The following cost per mile examples are based on data supplied by the contemporary companies: Lafayette and Indianapolis, $9,709; New Albany and Salem, $14,000; Indianapolis and Bellefontaine, $17,784; Lawrenceburgh and Upper Mississippi, $20,777. The $37,000 estimated cost per mile for the 385-mile Ohio and Mississippi was reported to be "nearly double what Western roads usually opened for."

[11]Authorized capitalization for the Martinsville and Franklin Railroad was $150,000, for the Knightstown and Shelbyville $200,000, for the Peru and Indianapolis $500,000, and for the Jeffersonville $1,000,000. For the Ohio and Mississippi, which extended across three states, a $5,000,000 capitalization was authorized by the Indiana General Assembly.

tions specified in these charters obviously were little more than guesses. On the other hand, increases in capitalization were apparently obtained with ease. From evidence thus far studied, it appears that the capital to be raised by selling stock in a new company was intended to cover about 50 percent of the railroad's total cost. The other half was to be procured from the sale of bonds, frequently with an interest rate as high as 10 per cent.

A "typical" case of the procedure followed in planning and building one of the early Indiana railroads might be depicted as follows. A number of persons in a region of the state decided that they should have a railroad. A mass meeting was then held in a courthouse where articles of association were drawn up, the more affluent or vocal members of the area were designated officers of the company, and an application for a charter was forwarded to the state government. The charter, running anywhere from a few summary statements to several dozen paragraphs, included information about the route, time allowed for building, amount of capitalization, gauge of track, permissible arrangements with other railroad companies, and directors of the newly formed corporation.

Once the charter was approved, solicitation began for the sale of stock. This was one of the crucial phases in the destiny of the new company, for if officials failed to sell enough initial stock to build up momentum for their enterprise, the venture halted right there. A strong appeal was made to residents at all points along the proposed line to purchase or to make pledges for stock. In exchange for stock certificates the buyer might give cash, real estate, equipment of various sorts, or his promise to contribute so many days labor. When enough stock was thus distributed to indicate to officials that the project was likely to succeed, the president and his agents began their campaign to sell bonds to larger investors, usually at an attractive discount, and a man was selected to supervise the engineering. Hereafter the president spent much of his time in eastern commercial capitals peddling bonds and seeking bargains on rails and other needed equipment. This was another crucial point in the affairs of the project. If times were good and the president could make a convincing case for his railroad, money from the sale of bonds poured in and the road was brought to completion with a minimum of delay; if times were bad and money tight, the project slowed up or was indefinitely postponed.

The eighty-four-mile Bellefontaine line (Indianapolis to Union) may serve as an example of railroad financing in the 1850's. The road's 1848 charter authorized a capitalization of $1,000,000 with a stipulation that this amount might be increased at the pleasure of the company. The line was completed early in 1853 at a reported cost of about $1,300,000. A little over half of this initial indebtedness was in the form of stock; the remainder was divided between 7 per cent foreign bonds and 10 per cent domestic bonds. During its first six months of operation (July–December, 1853), the Bellefontaine had gross earnings of $118,000. Almost $40,000 of this amount went for running expenses, $27,000 for paying interest on bonds, and $31,000 for paying 4 per cent dividends on stock; a little less than $20,000 was designated as "surplus." Since the Bellefontaine's connections were excellent, earnings could be expected to increase dramatically within the next few years. In the case of other roads not so favorably located, the margin of surplus profits left little for maintenance, improvements, and removal of bonded indebtedness.

Income for the completed or partially completed roads consisted of receipts from the transport of passengers, freight, mail, and baggage.

. . . .

Approximately half of the gross receipts of most early Indiana railroads came from the transport of freight.[12] Freight rates were so flexible during this period that no accurate estimate on charges as they applied to various commodities can yet be given, but considerable data exists about the types and quantities of freight carried on several of the roads. During the months when the road was running only to the nearest town to which track had been laid down, the usual pattern was a flow of farm commodities from the smaller terminal to the larger and a simultaneous flow of finished goods from the larger to the smaller. For example, during a three months' period when the Peru road was operating only between Noblesville and Indianapolis, Noblesville shipped southward to Indianapolis 1,000 barrels of flour, 218 barrels of eggs, and over 21,000 pounds of bacon; in turn Indianapolis shipped northward 25 plows, 126 barrels of salt, 36 kegs of powder, and 20,000 feet of lumber. This pattern was soon altered if the rural terminal became a junction point for one or more other roads. It then served as a trans-shipment center where all kinds of goods from a wider region were accumulated for shipment to more distant markets.[13]

Although corn and wheat were among the most important items of freight transported by the Indiana railroads to Cincinnati and other eastern cities, hogs were probably the most important single commodity. During the weeks of late fall and early winter carload after carload of "porkers" was gathered from outlying areas and sent to the slaughtering centers. In the early 1850's the Madison and Indianapolis road probably carried the bulk of this traffic, transporting as many as thirty or forty loads in a single day, but the Lafayette, the Bellefontaine, and the Lawrenceburgh lines also had their share. Some of the longest and most heavily loaded freight trains during these years were those carrying rails and other building equipment

[12]There were exceptions: for example, the Bellefontaine company reported for the latter six months of 1853 $38,790.90 in passenger receipts and $73,398.85 in freight.
[13]Greencastle, at the junction of the Terre Haute and Indianapolis and the New Albany and Salem roads, was such a clearing point. In one instance, 15,000–20,000 barrels of pork accumulated there for eventual shipment to New York via Lafayette and Detroit.

for roads under construction. Again this was the type of business from which the Madison road benefited greatly, since its southern terminus was a principal landing point for heavy river shipments from both east and west. But in the long run the Madison road paid dearly for helping to supply its future competitors.

. . . .

By 1855 most completed roads had telegraph service extended along their routes, but it is not clear from available reports just what this facility contributed to the operation of the railroads. Most companies also were granted contracts for carrying mail over the area of their routes. Although mail was thus speeded to distant points, postal service to smaller communities which had been regular stops on stage lines was sometimes slowed. Express service, operated principally by the Adams Company, became an important adjunct of the railroads. Express cars were included in some of the larger trains, and the company's agents were kept busy transferring more valuable freight at important junctions.

Confining the account of railroad developments to a description of track laying and scheduled train service would seriously distort the history of Indiana's early railroad building. The classic iceberg example is certainly applicable here, for what is concealed below the surface may be immeasurably more important than what is visible; for example, the number of railroad proposals of the early 1850's almost defies enumeration. Distinguishing between projects which were more and those which were less serious in intent requires the utmost vigilance from the later investigator. Just about everybody wanted to build railroads whether the building made sense or not. "There seems to be a kind of Railroad mania abroad," remarked the editor of the *Indiana Journal* in the spring of 1853. "In almost every newspaper within our own and adjoining States, we find some new Road projected. The last one is from Covington through Pinhook to Lafayette! There are at least a dozen talked of from the Atlantic to the Pacific."

As yet no attempt has been made in the present study to determine precisely how many separate companies were chartered in the 1850's to build railroads in Indiana, but a day by day survey of the *Indiana Journal* reveals scores of newly projected roads. A conservative estimate of their proposed mileage would be over thirty-five hundred—more than double the amount of track laid during the 1850–1855 period. The peak of railroad optimism and agitation was reached in 1853; during this year alone at least twenty-five new roads, with a total distance of over seventeen hundred miles, occasioned some degree of discussion or action. If all the railroads created on paper had materialized, the cost for the times would have been astronomical. The more serious-minded planners, faced with the prospects of a tightening money market, began to realize this, and there was a sharp decline in new proposals during the latter months of 1854 and on into 1855.

Columbus, Edinburg and Franklin Business Guide, 1865, 1866

A Terre Haute & Indianapolis Railroad ad
Courtesy of the Indiana Historical Society

"Railroad talk" certainly continued, but it came to center upon a few favored projects, most notably the Evansville Straight Line Railroad, promoted as Indiana's link in the vital transportation chain binding the South
to the Union.

Early Banking in Northern Indiana

JOHN ADE

The story of banking in Indiana is a mixed one. Probably the banks in
the state were operated as responsibly as in any other part of the Old
Northwest, but their quality "ranged from the fraudulent and reprehensible practices of the First State Bank to the conservative and creditable
operations of the Madison Farmers and Mechanics Bank and of the
Second State Bank."[1] The Indiana Constitution of 1816 prohibited the
establishment of private banks in the state; instead, it provided for a
state banking system. Since only two incorporated banks were then
operating in the territory, the option was given the banks at Vincennes
and Madison to join the state system. Only the bank at Vincennes did
so; but soon both it and the corruptly managed First State Bank had
failed. The Madison bank, more soundly operated, survived into the
1820s. In the meantime Congress had established the Second Bank of
the United States, with branches to be established throughout the
country. None, of course, was situated in Indiana because of the constitutional prohibition, but the state's business community was served
to some extent by national bank branches in Cincinnati and Louisville.

A new state banking system, soundly conceived and capably
operated, was established in 1834, when the "bank war" between
President Jackson and Nicholas Biddle foreshadowed the demise of the
Second Bank of the United States. But in the face of increasing criticism of monopolies and state control of banking, the new constitution
of 1851 relaxed the prohibition on private banks. Consequently, under
the Free Banking Act of 1852, a phenomenon known as "wildcat
banking," which had come to other parts of the country long before,
now also arrived in Indiana. Governor Wright, in his message to the
General Assembly in 1853, described the situation:

> The speculator comes to Indianapolis with a bundle of bank notes in one
> hand and his stock in the other. In twenty-four hours he is on the way to
> some distant part of the Union, to circulate what he denominates as

---

[1] John D. Barnhart and Donald F. Carmony, *Indiana: From Frontier to Industrial Commonwealth* (2 vols., 1954), I, 299.

From *Newton County: A Collection of Historical Facts and Personal Recollections Concerning Newton County, Indiana, from 1853 to 1911* (1911), pp. 46–53.

legal currency authorized by the legislature of the State of Indiana. He
has nominally located his bank in some remote part of the State, difficult
of access, where he knows that no banking facilities are required, and
intends that his notes shall go into the hands of persons who will have no
means of demanding their redemption.[2]

By 1855 ninety-one banks had been opened under the provisions of
the 1852 law, but few such banks survived long, and during the Civil
War a new national banking system was established.

In the brief passage below, John Ade describes the type of
"wildcatting" operations possible under the free banking law. Ade, an
early settler in Newton County, the last county of Indiana to be established, is perhaps best remembered today as the father of writer and
humorist George Ade. In 1910, when the fiftieth anniversary of the
county's establishment was being celebrated, John Ade was prompted
to "set down" certain facts concerning the history of the area "that
have come under my observation." As one who had helped organize
the county in 1860, Ade was particularly qualified for the task. He
wrote in a simple, straightforward fashion, lacing his factual reporting
with numerous anecdotes. The result, not originally intended for publication, was turned over to a printer on the request of friends. "This is
the only excuse I have," wrote the 83-year old farmer and banker, "for
joining the long procession of Indiana authors" (p. iv).

For further information on banking in Indiana, see Logan Esarey,
State Banking in Indiana, 1814-1873 (1912); John D. Barnhart and
Donald F. Carmony, *Indiana: From Frontier to Industrial Common-
wealth* (2 vols., 1954); and James H. Madison, "Businessmen and the
Business Community in Indianapolis, 1820-1860" (Ph.D. dissertation,
Indiana University, Bloomington, 1972). There is a brief section on John
Ade in Fred C. Kelly, *George Ade: Warmhearted Satirist* (1947).

One of the most noted and far-reaching laws enacted by the legislature
of 1853 was the adoption of what was known as the free banking law.
Under its provisions, any person or persons depositing with the secretary of
state bonds of any state in the union, were authorized to issue currency for
an equal amount. The object of many of the founders of banks under this
law was to establish them as far away from the lines of travel as possible and
put the money into circulation at points far distant from the banks of issue.
As Morocco was then forty miles from the nearest railroad, and the intervening country was very sparsely settled, Morocco made a very desirable
point for the establishment of such a bank.

The first intimation to the citizens of Morocco that the Bank of
America had been established came in 1854. I had been to Cincinnati on a
visit, and while there saw some of the money in circulation. Shortly after my

[2]Quoted in Emma Lou Thornbrough, *Indiana in the Civil War Era, 1850-1880* (1965), p. 429.

return from Cincinnati, in company with John Murphy, I went to Rensselaer on business in connection with the new post-office, of which I had been appointed postmaster. Shortly after our arrival in Rensselaer we were called into the office of George W. Spitler, who informed us of the fact that a bank had been established in Morocco and told us of some of the advantages that would accrue to the country by reason of the same—that our school funds would be increased and the county developed by inducing persons to locate in that vicinity, also that within a short time some of the officers of the bank would be among us and erect a bank building and take charge of the business in general. In the meantime, before these things could be attended to, he requested Mr. Murphy to take home with him one thousand dollars in gold to redeem any bills that might be presented before the regular officers arrived to take charge of things. Mr. Murphy said that was more money than he wanted to be responsible for, but finally he consented to take one hundred dollars for the purpose named.

As time passed, Mr. Murphy redeemed what few bills were presented, until the amount brought from Rensselaer was exhausted, and still no one put in an appearance to establish the bank. But, having entire confidence in the stability of the bank, he redeemed other notes until he had paid another hundred dollars out of his own money. Then he sent David Pulver to Rensselaer with a request for some one to come down and attend to the business or else send more money. On arriving at Rensselaer, Mr. Pulver was informed that the bank had changed owners and there was no one there authorized to speak for the further action of the institution. There was no clue to the proprietors and Mr. Murphy had two hundred dollars of the paper of the Bank of America on his hands, without any assurance that he would ever realize anything for his money expended. It is safe to say he did no further banking business, but when the affairs of the bank were eventually wound up by the secretary of state he made a reasonable salary besides the return of his money, as the issue of the bank, amounting to about seventy-five thousand dollars, was redeemed at eighty cents on the dollar. No one ever appeared to make settlement with Mr. Murphy, nor is it known that there was ever any person in the town of Morocco that had any right of ownership in the same. I was not president of the bank, although there is an outstanding joke to that effect.

This is not an exceptional case, for the state was full of banks that had but little, if any, better foundation on which to rest. This was almost a fair example of the condition of the finances of the state under what was known as the wild-cat banking system.

It is impossible for us to-day to realize the difficulties of doing business under that system. Whenever a bill was offered, you had to get the latest Bank Note Reporter and find the quotation. It might be worthless or show any shade of discount. When one crossed the state line no one in another state would accept his local currency.

To illustrate, I had a note for fifty dollars, due in six months without interest. One of my neighbors bought it, taking the note at its face, and discounted his money ten per cent.

A great many stories are told of the bank at Morocco. Many have but little foundation in truth, but the following, I have every reason to believe, is an actual fact. During the time the bank was supposed to be in operation, the town of Bradford (now Monon) was the railway station nearest to Rensselaer. The railroad line extended north to Michigan City. A stage coach from Rensselaer met the north-bound afternoon train at Bradford and then returned to Rensselaer, so that most of the return trip through a very lonesome region had to be made after night.

One afternoon five men got off the train at Bradford, made their way to the hotel and called for supper. Two of them were attorneys from Lafayette going over to Rensselaer to attend to some legal matters. Two of the others were citizens from Rensselaer—one an attorney and the other a doctor. These four were well known to each other, in fact old acquaintances. Also, all of them were well known to me. The other was a stranger, and although he ate supper at the same table, he seemed to keep as far away from the others as possible. It was noticed that he kept a small satchel on his lap all the time while eating supper. This, and a few remarks he made to the landlord in regard to the location of Morocco and the manner of getting there, satisfied one of the party at least that the stranger's objective point was the Bank of America at Morocco. He communicated his suspicions to the rest of the company. After supper the hack drove up and all got in. After a few miles had been traveled, by a preconcerted arrangement, the two Lafayette gentlemen commenced an attack on the two citizens of Rensselaer for the bold and terrible system of outlawry allowed to exist in their county, especially in the neighborhood of Morocco. They cited many cases of murder and horse-stealing and called attention to the gang of counterfeiters said to exist in that neighborhood. The Rensselaer gentlemen defended themselves as best they could from these charges, claiming that they were no more responsible for violations of law in their county than the gentlemen from Lafayette were for crimes committed in Tippecanoe county. These charges and counter-charges were kept up until late at night, when Rensselaer was reached and all went to bed.

Early the next morning the livery-stable keeper was posted by one of the passengers of the night before, so when he was approached by our friend with the black satchel, he refused to take him to Morocco for less than thirty dollars, and asked for a guard of four men. He told the stranger that he (the stranger) would be held responsible for all loss or damage to team and wagon. About this time one of the fellow passengers of the night before called the stranger aside and told him he supposed his business at Morocco must be of the greatest importance, and, as a friend, he would advise him how to go there. In the first place, it would never do for him to go there in the clothes he had on, for he would be almost certain to be murdered. He proposed letting the stranger have an old suit of clothes and a rifle, so that, in the disguise of a hunter, he might make his way on foot to Morocco and back, with at least some prospect of safety. Our friend thanked him for his kindness, went back to the hotel, and in a short time the hack for Bradford drove up and he secured passage for that point. And the bank at Morocco was thereby saved at least one demand for specie.

2: Political Developments

The Fugitive Slave Law in Operation
EMMA LOU THORNBROUGH

The place of the Negro in Indiana, ostensibly a free state, was an insecure one. Confronted with a legacy of slavery and involuntary servitude, and either open hostility or studied indifference on the part of most Hoosiers, the small number of Negroes in the state (approximately one per cent of the total population in 1820 and even smaller in 1860) lived in constant danger. According to the federal constitution, as well as an act of Congress in 1793, runaway slaves were to be returned to their owners. The worst feature of the law was its failure to protect free Negroes from illegal seizure and enslavement, something that happened many times. In Indiana such "kidnappings" occurred most frequently in the southern counties; but no area was immune and no one knows the full extent of the practice. Professor Emma Lou Thornbrough, in her fine study of *The Negro in Indiana*, describes many such episodes as well as the efforts of primarily the Quakers in resisting this practice. And in a few cases, particularly in the antislavery (and Quaker) strongholds of Wayne and Randolph counties, their resistance was successful. In the passage below Professor Thornbrough describes the way in which John Freeman of Indianapolis thwarted an attempt to have him declared a runaway and sent to Kentucky. This occurred after a new Fugitive Slave Law had been enacted in 1850, something the South had insisted on, perhaps foolishly, since the attempted enforcement of its provisions increased northern opposition to the entire system of slavery.

For a detailed account of the John Freeman case, see Charles H. Money, "The Fugitive Slave Law in Indiana," *Indiana Magazine of History*, XVII (June 1921), 180–197; see also William M. Cockrum, *The Underground Railroad in Indiana* (1915); and Eugene H. Berwanger, *The Frontier Against Slavery: Western Anti-Negro Prejudice and the Slavery Extension Controversy* (1967).

From *The Negro in Indiana: A Study of a Minority* (1957), pp. 114–118. Footnotes in the original have been omitted. Copyright © 1965 by the Indiana Historical Bureau. Reprinted by permission.

The procedure for the retaking of runaway slaves was modified by the Fugitive Slave Act of 1850, an amendment to the law of 1793 adopted in response to the demands of the representatives of the slave states. The principal change was that the 1850 measure relied for enforcement upon Federal rather than state officers. Federal commissioners, appointed by Federal judges, had concurrent jurisdiction with these judges in hearing fugitive slave cases. Testimony of the persons claimed as slaves was expressly prohibited from being admitted as evidence at these hearings. If the commissioner decided in favor of the claimant, he issued a certificate for the removal of the fugitive out of the state, and if the claimant had reason to fear that there would be an attempt to rescue the slave by force, it was the duty of the commissioner to give him protection in escorting the slave out of the state, the cost being borne by the United States government. The commissioner also had the power to deputize any private citizen to assist in the capture of a fugitive.

This act, which was one of the series of measures known as the Compromise of 1850, was supported by a majority of the Indiana delegation in Congress as necessary for quelling the sectional bitterness which threatened to disrupt the Union. In most parts of the state the measure did not evoke the immediate and universal condemnation which it brought forth in some Northern states. Abolitionist groups branded the "blood hound fugitive slave bill" as unconstitutional and pledged themselves to prevent its enforcement, but Governor Joseph A. Wright told the General Assembly that it must be carried out in good faith. Although Wright and most Indianans hoped for the "finality" of the Compromise of 1850 and the end of agitation on the slavery question, the operation of the new fugitive law had the effect of converting men who had heretofore been moderates into outspoken opponents of the slave system.

A notorious case in Indianapolis in 1853 caused a wave of revulsion against the system of slave catching. The central figure was John Freeman, a Negro who claimed to have come to Indianapolis from Georgia about 1844, and who through hard work and thrift had acquired some real estate, including a house and garden and a restaurant. In 1853 a Missourian by the name of Pleasant Ellington, who professed to being a Methodist minister, appeared in Indianapolis and filed a claim with the United States commissioner that Freeman was his slave, Sam, who had escaped in 1836 when Ellington was residing in Kentucky. Freeman was arrested, but before a hearing could be held friends learned of his plight and the commissioner was persuaded to allow him to have legal counsel. One of the ablest lawyers in the city, John L. Ketcham, came to Freeman's aid, and the commissioner, much to the disgust of Ellington, agreed to a delay. The case soon attracted wide attention in the newspapers, and public opinion apparently compelled the commissioner to see that Freeman was given a chance to prove his right to freedom. A postponement of nine weeks was granted for the securing of evidence. Efforts to secure the release of Freeman on bail were unavailing, although some of the most prominent men in Indianapolis helped raise the bond. The commissioner decided that bail was not permissible, and the Negro was kept in jail for nine weeks, and as an added injury was compelled to pay the cost of a special guard that was hired to see that he did not escape.

Two other lawyers, John Coburn and Lucian Barbour, joined Ketcham in the case, and the three worked tirelessly and brilliantly to secure evidence. Correspondence with persons in Georgia corroborated Freeman's claim that he had resided there and was free, while witnesses from Georgia were brought to Indianapolis to identify him. Meanwhile, the real Sam, who had escaped from Ellington, was traced to Canada. He freely confessed his identity, and witnesses who had known him in Kentucky went to Canada to identify him and brought depositions to Indianapolis. This sworn testimony showed that the physical characteristics of Sam and Freeman were quite different as to both height and color; nevertheless Ellington and three witnesses whom he had brought with him had not hesitated to swear that Freeman was Sam after compelling him to submit to a physical examination.

To clinch the case for Freeman his old guardian arrived from Georgia to identify him, and six other witnesses from Georgia arrived on the day set for the final hearing of the case. Their testimony was not called for because Ellington had given up and left the city. The commissioner dismissed the case, and Freeman was released. He was free, but the cost of proving his freedom in the face of a wanton and unscrupulous attempt to enslave him had cost him everything that he had saved from a life of hard work. The only redress which the law afforded for the financial loss and the indignities which he had suffered was a damage suit. He won an award of two thousand dollars in a suit against Ellington, but this was a hollow victory. The award was never paid since Ellington sold his property and left St. Louis to escape payment. Freeman also brought suit in the Marion County Circuit Court against the United States marshal who had imprisoned him. The case was taken to the Indiana Supreme Court which upheld the right to sue the United States official since the acts with which he was charged—assault, forcing the prisoner to strip naked, and extorting money from him for the pay of the guard—were not part of his official duties and were unlawful. But again this was only a technical victory since the court ruled that the suit should have been brought in Rush County, the residence of the marshal. In the end Freeman was able to save his home and a garden plot through the help of many persons in both Indiana and Georgia who had become interested in his case. Nevertheless, he left Indianapolis and moved to Canada at the outbreak of the Civil War, apparently because he feared a southern victory.

Freeman's case was watched with intense interest throughout the state, and there was widespread relief and satisfaction when his freedom was assured. The case showed more forcibly than all the speeches of antislavery orators the woeful inadequacy of the Federal law to protect the rights of free Negroes. As a Fort Wayne newspaper observed: "A more flagrant case of injustice, we have never seen. It appears to us in such cases, that if the person swearing to the identity of the accused and seeking to consign a free man to slavery, were tried and punished for perjury, a wholesome lesson would be given which might prevent injustice to free persons of color. The fugitive slave law evidently needs some amendment, to give greater protection to free persons of color. As it now stands, almost any of them might be dragged into slavery. If Freeman had not had money and friends he must inevitably have been taken off into bondage. Any poor man, without friends, would have been given up at once and taken away, and it was only by the most strenuous exertions that Freeman was rescued. A law under which such injustice can be perpetrated, and which holds out such inducements to perjury, is imperfect and must be amended or repealed. The American people have an innate sense of justice which will no longer allow such a law to disgrace our statute books."

Cases such as this, which were widely publicized, hastened the final extinction of slavery. But in the meantime, as the editorial observed, in spite of his ordeal, Freeman was more fortunate than many members of his race. No one will ever know how many anonymous Negroes were carried off into slavery without the benefit of counsel or a fair hearing simply because they were without friends or money.

Birth of the Republican Party in Indiana

ROGER H. VAN BOLT

An insight into the confused political situation of the mid-1850s is provided by Roger H. Van Bolt of the Alfred P. Sloan, Jr., Museum at Flint, Michigan. Van Bolt's doctoral dissertation at the University of Chicago, large portions of which were published in the *Indiana Magazine of History* in the 1950s, was an examination of Indiana politics from 1840 to 1856 and focused on the rise of the Republican party. In the chaos that existed after the demise of the Whig party following the 1852 election, a number of groups attempted to become the second major party in the two-party system and thus provide the opposition to the Democratic party. In the elections of 1854 the various factions in Indiana coalesced into a "Fusion" party, made

From "The Rise of the Republican Party in Indiana, 1855–1856," *Indiana Magazine of History*, LI (September 1955), 185–187, 191, 206–213. Footnotes in the original have been omitted. Copyright © 1955 by the Trustees of Indiana University. Reprinted by permission.

up of former Whigs, Free Soilers, Americans (Know-Nothings), and northern—or antislavery—Democrats. Surprisingly, this "conglomeration of antagonisms" routed the Democrats "Horse, Foot, and Dragoon" (p. 185) but then found it impossible to carry through a legislative program in 1855. Some elements of the Fusionists then organized themselves into the People's party, and as such later participated in the first national convention of the new Republican party in 1856. But disagreements over policy positions shattered the temporary unity and paved the way for a Democratic victory in 1856. Ashbel P. Willard, a brilliant young politician from New Albany, defeated Centerville's Oliver P. Morton in the gubernatorial race, and the Democrats also regained control of the Indiana General Assembly.

For a general overview of the political scene in the 1850s, see Emma Lou Thornbrough, *Indiana in the Civil War Era, 1850-1880* (1965); Charles Roll, *Colonel Dick Thompson: The Persistent Whig* (1948); Willard H. Smith, *Schuyler Colfax: The Changing Fortunes of a Political Idol* (1952); and Ralph D. Gray (ed.), *Gentlemen From Indiana: National Party Candidates, 1836-1940* (1977), especially the essays on Julian, English, Colfax, and Hendricks.

The fusion of the anti-Democratic elements in 1854 had been accomplished under intense heat; the resulting amalgam was yet to be tested for durability. With no elections in 1855 to keep the political fires burning, the manipulators of Fusionism were cautiously observing the cooling-down process, waiting to see what they had created. The year 1855 would reveal whether the result was a new compound or merely a mixture.

Shortly after the fall elections of 1854, while the Democrats were still smarting under their defeat by the conglomeration of antagonisms that had routed them "Horse, Foot, and Dragoon," the Fusionists called an outdoor meeting at Indianapolis for November 1, 1854, to celebrate their victory. Thomas Smith of New Albany was chairman; among the speakers were Henry S. Lane, Samuel W. Parker, Oliver P. Morton, and Godlove Orth. The theme of their speeches was by now a familiar one: to forget all past political affiliations and to forward the new movement. They declared that freedom, temperance, and pure elections should be the watchword of the party. The "people" resolved that the Declaration of Independence, the Constitution, the Ordinance of 1787, and the resolutions of July 13 were long enough and broad enough planks with which to build a platform capable of supporting all the American people.

When the meeting adjourned, the Know Nothings in the group stayed on to hold a conclave of their state council. After many arguments, they chose Godlove Orth as their candidate for United States senator and Milton Gregg of the *New Albany Tribune* for state printer. The action of the council indicated trouble ahead for the brittle new party, for the politically experienced realized that organization should come before a search for party spoils. Men like Jacob Chapman and Michael C. Garber had hoped that strong organization would be developed.

When the legislature convened in January, 1855, the new party was given its first opportunity to carry out its political promises. The first obstacle to hurdle was the election of a United States senator. Rather than permit the choice of a Fusionist, the Democrats refused to caucus. Some Fusionists who reasoned that the so-called old liners could not refuse to go into an election felt that the stalemate was temporary. As Orth wrote: "For this would, more than anything else [serve] to drive us together & Keep us together for the next campaign—nor will the Prest. Election swallow up this dereliction of duty as they confidentially hope."

A week went by, and with it went the hope of ending the deadlock. Orth's optimism was gone; now he wrote: "If they [the old liners] had the assurance that a Natl. Whig—who didn't fuse, don't fuse, and who is anti-Sam, could command the necessary strength—they would, in my opinion, give him the old line vote—and elect him." Thus in its first political skirmish with the Democracy the Fusion lost the encounter. As a consequence of this stalemate, Jesse Bright alone represented Indiana in the United States Senate until 1857. In the meantime, the legislature attempted to co-operate on other matters.

The temperance advocates of 1854 were still to be satisfied. Early in February, 1855, the general assembly approved an act which prohibited the sale of liquor in the state, following the Maine law principle. The new law passed with a comfortable majority and in the senate, where the Democrats held a slight advantage, seven members of that party supported it. Popular reaction among the "cold water" boys was spontaneous. Indiana had again joined the ranks of the reformers. Governor Joseph A. Wright's faithful correspondent, John Hunt, reported that "the people here are Laughing all over their faces on account [of] the passage of the Temperence Bill: we have had 2 illuminations. They are becoming intemperate on temperence."

The so-called Whiskey Democrats were not yet defeated, however. Within a short time, an Indianapolis saloonkeeper named Roderick Beebe opened for business. His immediate arrest made possible a test case. The Indiana Supreme Court received the case in the November term, and Judge Samuel E. Perkins, who had declared the legislation of 1853 unconstitutional, handed down the same decision on this temperance bill. Thus the door was opened once again for unhampered liquor traffic. Politically, the Democrats had won another victory, this time in the courts of the state.

. . . .

The adjournment of the legislature brought to an end the political maneuvers in the general assembly, but the organization of the parties continued throughout 1855. The session had revealed that the politicians were not out of the troubled waters of the previous summer. The Democrats were busy reorganizing their efforts for the coming presidential year while the Fusionists needed to maintain the semblance of political organization they already possessed, meanwhile hoping that structure could be given to the amorphous mass.

During 1855 the state Democracy was not very active, since the elections were local in nature. At a meeting in Indianapolis in April, the party reiterated its claims of 1854, with particular emphasis given to anti-Know Nothingism.

The Fusionists had more difficult problems. After the elections of 1854, the once harmonious elements became suspicious of one another. The Free Soil elements had begun to "feel quite offish" after Milton Gregg was nominated for state printer, while the temperance forces generally lost interest once the new law was in the legislative mill. Under the guidance of Joseph G. Marshall of Madison the old Whigs had aspirations of their own for senatorial nominations. Finally, there was the question of what would become of the Know Nothing movement. Among the leaders of 1854 who were in the state capital attempting to weld the Fusion more firmly was Schuyler Colfax, the congressman-elect from South Bend. Some "'outsiders,'" he reported from Indianapolis, "'ought to be expected to be preaching concord rather than attempting to sow disunity.'" He was not sure that the Know Nothings might not be the chief opposition of the Fusion. The ex-Whigs themselves, after the initial success, felt that instead of remaining in the background they should come to the fore to manage affairs for the Fusion.

. . . .

Reactions to the People's convention varied. The "South" Americans refused to stand by the nomination and a platform that was so strongly "Republican" in character. One American editor blamed William Sheets, the president of the state council, for the failure of the party. He bitterly growled: "The officiating head of the American party in Indiana is rotten to the core! He has sold us to our enemies." Such reports as these, however, were exceptional.

On the other hand, to such radicals as George W. Julian, the party had not gone far enough in its denunciations. Julian was unable to find a single true antislavery man on the whole ticket. He called the People's party a "combination of weaknesses, instead of a union of forces." One of Julian's friends, Daniel Worth, despondently described the Indianapolis convention thus: "A poor miserable truckling concern without either soul or body. . . . You will mark the fact that our wise-acres at Indianapolis ignored even the name of Republican as well as all antislavery principle. This was done for the benefit of Knownothings and old fossil Whigs who have just emanated from their old political graves where they have been 'persevering to rot,' and are now ready to take office at the hands of antislavery men provided they are not compelled to take more antislavery than they might safely take of *arsenic*." The old abolitionists who sought a political home among the factions of the new party were sorely disappointed.

The People's convention, however, was antislavery enough in sentiment to frighten away the more conservative elements of the Democratic opposition. The friends of William H. English felt that the stand of the party assured them of success in the coming canvass. One wrote confidently, "I see by the proceedings of the peoples Convention that Black Republicanism was triumphant, no elector was appointed for this District. Gregg [the local American editor] has been unhorsed, I think the whole affair a miserable abortion, the policy of nominating a broken down set of renegad Democrats, because they love niggers more than white folks will not win in Indiana. we Shall beat the whole tickett by thousands."

The tremendous importance attached to national questions in the progress of the state party brought the question of the national Republican conventions into sharp focus. The first meeting of the Republicans was held in Pittsburgh in February. The role of the Hoosiers in this initial assembly is rather vague. According to the various writings of George W. Julian, he played an important role. He did serve as chairman of the committee on organization and was one of the vice-presidents. William Grose of Henry County was appointed to the executive committee, and Oliver P. Morton was a member of the resolutions committee. Julian explained later that the Fusion had "subordinated every question of principle to its desire for political success. The situation was most humiliating." This preliminary meeting, which served primarily to formulate more solid propositions upon which a permanent organization could be established, was an impetus to the Philadelphia convention in June.

Henry S. Lane was elected president of the second convention. In his address the former Whig extolled the virtues of Henry Clay. Had the Kentuckian been alive, he would have been leading the Republican party, declared Lane. The disunion cry, he claimed, came from South Carolina "unhung" nullifiers who still had the halter of General Andrew Jackson about their necks. Caleb Smith, another ex-Whig, formerly of Indiana but at this time a resident of Cincinnati, also spoke. This retired legislator called the Republican party the true national party. He was careful to state that his party would not interfere where slavery already existed, yet since the institution was always aggressive, the Republicans were the only party that would maintain the principles of freedom. These two Hoosiers permitted the speakers who followed them to express more radical views. One was Owen Lovejoy of Illinois, who spoke of the divine inspiration of the Declaration of Independence and its mission in America. Henry Wilson of Massachusetts was allowed to shout: "Sir, our object is to overthrow the Slave Power of the country, now organized in the Democratic party of the country."

It is interesting and significant to compare the list of delegates selected at Indianapolis to attend the Philadelphia convention with the list of men who answered the roll call of the credentials committee at the convention. The first and second districts, which were strongholds of the Americans, were represented at Philadelphia by Hoosiers who lived outside these constituencies; apparently those appointed did not attend. There were also substitutions in the seventh and eighth congressional districts. The replacements were often men of prominence from other areas in the state.

The Indiana delegation was indicative of a mature party leadership. There was a sprinkling of editor-politicians: William G. Terrell of Lafayette, an ardent ex-Whig; Thomas H. Bringhurst, Whig editor of the *Logansport Journal;* Charles D. Murray of Kokomo, another Whig editor; and John Defrees, a member of the platform committee, the leader of the state press as well as of the People's party. The lone ex-Democrat was the Bright antagonist, Michael C. Garber of the *Madison Courier.*

Another significant group was made up of businessmen—merchants, bankers, and railroad promoters. Defrees was connected with the Central Bank at this time. Henry S. Lane of Crawfordsville was a banker with his father-in-law, Isaac Elston. Daniel R. Bearss of Peru, a Henry Clay Whig, was a retired mercantilist, one of the wealthiest men in the county. Benjamin F. Claypool of Fayette County was president of the state bank in Connersville. Jacob B. Julian of Centerville was a sometime banker and railroad promoter. Henry County sent Martin L. Bundy, a wealthy citizen. From Terre Haute came L. A. Burnett, a leather and hide dealer. Finally, Samuel Hanna was a delegate from the Fort Wayne district. This Allen County Whig was a frontier capitalist and one of the wealthiest men in Indiana. Hanna had begun as an Indian trader and was president of the Fort Wayne and Chicago railroad.

A few of the ardent exponents of the various isms were also represented, but they were in the minority. One of these was Jonathan W. Gordon of Indianapolis, whose law practice was such that it had given him ample time to edit the *Temperance Chart,* a publication appearing under the patronage of the Sons of Temperance. James Ritchey of Franklin County, who was named to the national executive committee, was another reformer devoted to many causes. Judge William Peaslee of Shelbyville had been an original member of the Know Nothings in the "dark lantern" stage.

Taken as a whole the membership indicated Whig entry into the leadership of the National Republicans of Indiana. The respected and prosperous of the now defunct party were gaining control of the new organization. For the most part it was a conservative leadership, replacing the more radical elements that had rushed into the Fusion in 1854. This Whig group, however, did not include the old Whigs of the river counties but came rather from the northern and central sections of the state, the areas in which significant economic and social change was taking place in the fifties. These

Hoosiers, who were taking strides to secure political advantage, were to determine the character of the future Republican party of Indiana.

With the nomination of John C. Fremont, the Indiana delegation, Republican in fact if not in name, returned home to stump the state in the new party's first national campaign. Back in Indiana, as a result of the problem of the course of the Americans, the important political question was the matter of support. Before the convention met in Philadelphia, John Defrees, chairman of the state central committee, called for a ratification meeting to be held at Indianapolis on July 15, 1856. The Americans, however, decided to await the results of the People's convention before meeting; consequently they called their gathering for July 16. The decision was of some significance since it seemed to mean that no longer were the Know Nothings, now Americans, attempting to set the pattern for the Fusionists.

The People's convention on July 15 was little more than a ratification meeting. Henry S. Lane and Stephen S. Harding were among the speakers. The afternoon program included a few Kansas speeches as well as a parade of young men attired as "Border Ruffians" and "Buford's Thieves."

By the time of their state convention on July 16 the Americans had been reduced largely to the position of an irreconcilable minority of the old Whig party. The seceders of the conventions of the previous year had brought many of the Indiana Americans into the People's party; those left behind were chiefly from southern Indiana. An important leader of the party in Indiana was Richard W. Thompson, who was made permanent chairman of the state party. In June, Humphrey Marshall of Kentucky had written Thompson: "'We must have a *separate* Fillmore ticket in Indiana. You must go to the Convention—and you must head the movement and go on the Electoral ticket—there is no time for trifling... *we must not fuse.*'"

The activities of Dick Thompson were reported to the People's chieftain, Henry Lane, by one of his correspondents: "'We are peculiarly situated here [Terre Haute]. R. W. Thompson is using extraordinary means to prevent an organization upon Frémont.... He maintains that the Planter has the same right to occupy the territories with his slaves that the northern farmer has with his horses. Thompson is making desperate exertions to carry his points, he does what he has seldom done before; he is on the streets and at the corners in season and out of season, trying to inveigh old Whigs into his scheme of resuscitating the Whig party.'"

The convention itself was not particularly impressive as compared with the People's meeting of the day before. Only about one-fourth of the counties were represented, for the Americans had become a sectional party within the state with the chief centers in New Albany, Jeffersonville, Terre Haute, and Vevay. The Democratic pocket and the American pocket were almost the same. A last attempt to endorse Fremont was put down hurriedly, and the support of the state ticket was left open, a policy which amounted to a handicap for Morton and the People's party. With the conclusion of the meeting the battle lines of the coming presidential campaign were drawn: the Democracy, with Buchanan, had divided opposition. After the convention, Thompson labored to organize Fillmore clubs over the state; only one of these, at Lafayette, was north of the National Road. But the Americans lost more than they gained in press support. Perhaps the greatest blow was the defection of John W. Dawson of the *Fort Wayne Times*, who was also a candidate on the state People's ticket.

The campaign during the summer and fall of 1856 was a test of the new People's party. No longer an impetuous upstart nor a purely offensive party, it was now a political organization which was beginning to operate as a responsible group and which had to resort also to defensive actions in the rough and tumble tactics of the canvass. At the state level and in Congress its leaders had the opportunity to carry out the demands and promises of 1854.

In the Kansas situation the People's party in Indiana and the Republicans in the nation had a firebrand that was capable of igniting men's emotions. Jim Lane, who had promised to carry the truth to every corner of the North, dramatically rushed back to Kansas just before the campaign reached fever pitch. At the end of May, he announced to the electors of Indiana, " 'You have heard the late thrilling news from Kansas. I am hastening there, then, either to relieve, or perish with that gallant bleeding

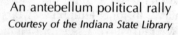

An antebellum political rally
Courtesy of the Indiana State Library

people.'" Whereupon he cancelled a series of speaking engagements that would have taken him to many corners of the state.

The numerous letters and dispatches from Kansas that appeared in the press and the speeches of those who had recently returned served to arouse the citizens. Editors gave the latest happenings high priority. Wheeler in South Bend reported to Colfax: "The subscribers were anxious for Kansas News, and I gave them Kansas news. Kansas news would spoil by laying over; Day's Speech would not." Schuyler Colfax's wife was the happy recipient of "Governor Robinson's Polka," the gift of her husband's political ally, Nathaniel P. Banks. She commented that the governor was then "suffering imprisonment in Kansas at the hands of those vile despots, the border ruffians, for the crime of loving Freedom better than Slavery." In the Whitewater Valley an even more powerful impact of the Kansas affairs was felt, for the news came that a member of a party of Hoosiers who had gone to Kansas had been killed in an attack.

The political capital in firing the emotions of those who were already enlisted in the ranks of the People's party was one matter, but when the "fagenders" began to fall under the spell of the Kansas dispatches, the Democracy began to worry. One of Governor Wright's political friends hoped the excitement would end. "The Kansas troubles afford the theme for about all the declamation of the opposition, and at this moment they effect the creation of some prejudice to our injury. May we not reasonably hope for a conclusion of those disturbances soon?" Then the Democrat expressed an interesting point of view that was not exactly high doctrine in Democratic circles. He wrote: "Anything that Congress would with propriety do ought to be done—Confidence once restored, that Kansas will probably be a free-state, and all is well with the Democracy, for the people, I am persuaded would gladly see this constant agitation of the subject of slavery driven out of the Halls of Congress."

The campaign centered about the sectional issue, and with the cry of "Black Republicanism" ringing in their ears, the excitement of the people grew as the October state election day approached. The Democrats made the most of the American People's party split as well as of the fact that most Hoosiers hated the Negro. In one Democratic neighborhood, in Dubois County, it was reported that several young ladies of the community, dressed all in white, paraded through the streets carrying a banner, "'Fathers, save us from nigger husbands!'" Less dramatically but with effective results, the Democrats stressed the theme that the Black Republicans were plotting abolition and the bestowal of full social and political rights upon the Negro. The brunt of the state campaign was borne by Oliver P. Morton, an anti-Nebraska Democrat. He was rather evenly matched on the stump with Ashbel P. Willard, who was a brilliant speaker.

The results of the local campaign were indicative of the events to come in the November elections. Willard carried the state by almost 5,000 votes.

Examination of the results in the congressional districts reveals the sectionalism of the state. Morton carried the Whitewater valley and the northern districts. The congressional election resulted in a sizeable increase in the number of Democratic victories. Indiana now had six of the old liners back in Congress, while the People's party had lost four seats.

3: And the War Came

Indiana in the Civil War

JOHN D. BARNHART

The Civil War was one of the great watersheds in American history. Its fury extended beyond the great battlefields of war and reached into the homes and businesses and daily lives of almost every American. Its total impact is immeasurable, but the attempt to measure it must still be made, as Professor John D. Barnhart has done for one state in the essay below. Originally a part of his larger work, *Indiana: From Frontier to Industrial Commonwealth* (2 vols., 1954), written in collaboration with Donald F. Carmony, the chapters on the Civil War were recast and republished at the request of the Indiana Civil War Centennial Commission.

As Professor Barnhart indicates, the people of Indiana played major roles in almost all phases of the war. Militarily, the state provided officers, troops, and equipment, while at home the state offered political leadership, unswerving loyalty to the Union cause, and vital agricultural and industrial support. There was some concern about the true sentiments of the Democrats in Indiana and whether or not they would support the Union wholeheartedly; but that was a needless worry. Political differences over local issues continued to be aired, but Hoosier Democrats generally followed the leadership of men like Thomas A. Hendricks, a conservative Democratic senator whose devotion to the Union equaled that of any Republican.

The most comprehensive report on Indiana's military contributions to the war is the *Report of the Adjutant General of Indiana* (8 vols., 1869). A recent study examining both military and home-front activities is Emma Lou Thornbrough, *Indiana in the Civil War Era, 1850–1880* (1965); see also Kenneth M. Stampp, *Indiana Politics during the Civil War* (1949); Frank L. Klement, *The Copperheads in the Middle West* (1960); Alan T. Nolan, *The Iron Brigade: A Military*

From "The Impact of the Civil War on Indiana," *Indiana Magazine of History*, LVII (September 1961), 185–193, 198–201, 212–213, 221–224. Some footnotes in the original have been omitted. Copyright © 1961 by the Trustees of Indiana University. Reprinted by permission.

History (1964). For the colorful Oliver P. Morton, see both the older study by William D. Foulke, *Life of Oliver P. Morton* (2 vols., 1899), and the unpublished doctoral dissertation by Lorna Lutes Sylvester, "Oliver P. Morton and Hoosier Politics during the Civil War" (Indiana University, Bloomington, 1968).

The Civil War was the greatest challenge Indiana's democratic government had met. The war affected all of the citizens of the state, penetrated their vital social relations, and threatened their necessary and cherished organizations. The way the people met that challenge constitutes much of the history of the war years in Indiana.

That all patriots yield obedience to the voice of the people when expressed in a constitutional manner and that all citizens unite in preserving the Union and the Constitution was the message of Abraham Lincoln to the people of Indiana as he journeyed from Springfield, Illinois, to Washington, D.C., for his inauguration as president of the United States. The next day, February 12, 1861, his fifty-second birthday, he was escorted to the railway station where he entrained for Cincinnati. Lincoln's Indianapolis appearance and speech were the subject of favorable comment by the Republican *Daily Journal,* but the Democratic *Daily Sentinel* declared him to be a theorist, a dreamer, and an impractical man who lacked the will and purpose to be a leader.

The attack upon Fort Sumter, April 12, 1861, stunned the people of Indiana and its sister states. When the news came over the wires, small groups gathered to discuss the ominous deed. Some were gloomy because of the portent of war. Others were angry because of the insult to the flag and the threat to the unity of the nation of which the flag was the symbol.

Angry or sad, the people responded immediately. In two mass meetings in Indianapolis on the evening of the following day, the people promised to defend the government with their lives, fortunes, and sacred honor; and on Sunday, April 14, ministers of various churches gave their sanction to these same loyal sentiments. When President Lincoln and Governor Oliver P. Morton called for troops, volunteers came forward in such numbers that Indiana's quota could have been filled twice.

South Carolina had seceded from the Union on December 20, 1860, and five other states joined her on February 4, 1861, to organize the Confederate States of America. Jefferson Davis was elected president, and the raising of one hundred thousand troops was authorized. Texas soon came into the Confederacy, and after Lincoln's call for soldiers four additional states seceded.

The border states were in a difficult position, for their people were divided in sentiment, and none relished the prospect of their land becoming a battleground of contending armies. Indianans were particularly concerned

Indiana volunteers "Rallying 'Round the Flag"
Courtesy of Harper's Weekly

about the decision of Kentucky because it was separated from Indiana only by the Ohio River and citizens of the two states had been friends since frontier days. The decision of Kentucky might determine how close the fighting would come to Hoosier soil.

A large number of Indiana citizens were natives of southern states or the children of transplanted southerners. Many of them had relatives or friends among the people of the Confederacy. Former southerners were not so numerous in the northern counties of Indiana, but they were quite numerous in the southern and central counties where the danger of invasion was greater. Richard Thompson, of Terre Haute, received letters from relatives in the South appealing to him to try to stop the war. But Hoosiers who had been born in the states on the south side of the Ohio River had helped to make Indiana a free state in 1816. They knew from experience some of the injustices involved in slavery, and they did not want them in Indiana. They did not object, however, to this institution in the southern states until efforts to preserve it threatened the unity of the nation.

War issues tended to divide the people of Indiana, to break the unity of families, to form groups with different ideals, to split political parties into factions, and to prevent representative government from functioning smoothly. A few Hoosiers who were pro-southern were willing to acquiesce in disunion. Jesse D. Bright, whose influence was dominant in the Democratic party for some years before 1860, shared these views. He was expelled from the United States Senate on February 5, 1862, because he had written a letter to "His Excellency, Jefferson Davis, President of the Confederation,"[1] in which he recommended a friend who wished to sell an improved firearm. Other Peace Democrats opposed the use of force and insisted that the Union could be preserved by concessions to the South. Included in this faction were Lambdin P. Milligan, John C. Walker, and Horace Heffren, individuals associated with the secret political societies.

More numerous were the Constitutional Union men who wanted to preserve the Union and therefore supported the war, but who opposed such measures as the tariff and the National Banking Act. Many of these Union men were willing to offer some concessions to prevent a war or to bring an early peace. When they realized that the destruction of the Union might leave Indiana a part of the interior nation—without free access to the sea and with her trade subject to taxes imposed by a southern or eastern confederacy—their nationalism increased perceptibly. Nevertheless they declared that they were unwilling to fight an abolition war.

A few War Democrats openly supported the state and national administrations and joined with the Republicans in forming the Union party. Among the War Democrats were former Governor Joseph A. Wright, James Hughes, of Bloomington, Lew Wallace, and Allen Hamilton.

The firing on Fort Sumter not only started the Civil War but made it necessary for Indiana Democrats to readjust themselves rather quickly. They had recently been engaged in state and national political campaigns with considerable intensity and had continued their criticism of and hostility toward the Lincoln and Morton administrations. After April 12, vigorous hostility began to assume the aspects of disloyalty, which the Republicans were quick to turn to their advantage. Such action only increased the anger of the Democrats and made their protests more vigorous. Although the remarks of the Democrats were often tactless, the Republicans did not prefer charges in a civil court against them, much less secure a conviction in a criminal court against anyone.

The war not only embarrassed Democrats, but it also divided Republicans. The latter differed about the concessions they would make to avoid war, but the real division came later in respect to the Emancipation Proclamation. Was the preservation of the Union the sole purpose of the war? At the beginning the answer was almost always in the affirmative. A few Republicans, however, like George W. Julian, "had no love for a proslavery Union." He regarded liberty as more desirable than the Union. Radicals of

[1]Indianapolis *Daily State Sentinel*, August 20, 1861. It is very difficult to classify Bright accurately. He favored negotiation, but that seemed a broken reed. He also opposed the use of force. His was a peculiar type of loyalty, if it were loyalty. Wayne J. Van Der Weele, "Jesse David Bright: Master Politician from the Old Northwest" (Ph.D. disseration, Dept. of History, Indiana University, 1958), 266.

this type demanded that no concessions should be made to the South and that they were insisting that slavery should be destroyed. Julian said on January 14, 1862, that

> the disturbing element has uniformly been slavery. This is the unclean spirit that from the beginning has needed exorcism. . . .
>
> This rebellion is a bloody and frightful demonstration . . . that slavery and freedom cannot dwell together in peace. . . . I believe the popular demand now is, or soon will be, the total extirpation of slavery as the righteous purpose of the war and the only means of a lasting peace. . . . Never perhaps in the history of any nation has so grand an opportunity presented itself for serving the interests of humanity and freedom.

In the naming of his cabinet, Lincoln tried to counteract the division within the party. He chose party leaders who represented different elements and sectional groups in order that he might keep the support of all factions. For secretary of the interior, Lincoln chose Caleb B. Smith, of Indianapolis, who had been a lawyer, a newspaper publisher, and a railroad president. An advocate of internal improvements, Smith was elected to the state house of representatives from 1832 to 1842. From 1843 to 1849 he served Indiana as a member of the national House of Representatives. He was a skilled stump speaker, and his appointment came to him at least in part because of his support of Lincoln in the Republican national convention in Chicago. His appointment was also a recognition of the important role played by Indiana Republicans in Lincoln's nomination and election. It has also been alleged that the choice resulted from a pre-nomination pledge made by Judge David Davis and Joseph Medill to secure the selection of Lincoln by the Chicago convention and which Lincoln felt obligated to carry out although it was made without his knowledge. Smith remained in the cabinet for less than two years; his resignation became effective on January 1, 1863.

Indiana's congressional delegation was divided between seven Republicans and four Democrats. All of the latter were from the vicinity of the Ohio and lower Wabash rivers. William S. Holman, of Aurora, was a War Democrat who was later better known as the "Watchdog of the Treasury." John Law, of Evansville, the historian of Vincennes, was a War Democrat who vigorously opposed emancipation as a war aim. James A. Cravens, of Washington County, was also a War Democrat. Daniel W. Voorhees, of Terre Haute, has been called a Constitutional Union Democrat whose sharp tongue led many to consider him a Peace Democrat. "To him abolitionism and secession were equally hateful; and he bewailed the breaches of the Constitution and the tyranny of the war Government in terms of unmeasured [opprobrium]."

The seven Republican members of the National House of Representatives ranged from radicals to moderates. Schuyler Colfax, editor of the South Bend *St. Joseph Valley Register*, had been elected to Congress in

1854, and was re-elected until he became vice president of the United States in 1869. He was considered in 1860 for a post in Lincoln's cabinet, but was passed over for Caleb B. Smith. Colfax served as speaker of the House of Representatives from 1863 to 1869 and was known as a Radical Republican. George W. Julian, of Wayne County, already noted as a radical, had been a Free Soil member of Congress from 1849 to 1851 and a Free Soil candidate for vice president in 1852. Now he was a Radical Republican deeply interested in the abolition of slavery. Albert S. White, of Tippecanoe County, was more conservative than Julian but was very energetic in trying to secure adoption of gradual emancipation of slaves and indemnification of their owners. Albert G. Porter, of Indianapolis, had been a Democrat but had joined the new Republican party, which elected him a congressman in 1858 and 1860. After Sumter he favored a vigorous prosecution of the war. William M. Dunn, of Madison, was elected in 1860 but defeated in 1862. He entered the army and became assistant judge advocate general in 1864.[2]

Although Oliver P. Morton had been elected lieutenant governor, he became the chief executive on January 16, 1861, when Governor Henry S. Lane resigned to accept a seat in the United States Senate. Believing that war was inevitable, Morton was foremost in preparing the state to do her part in support of the national administration. After Sumter was fired upon, he appointed Lew Wallace adjutant general, Colonel Thomas A. Morris quartermaster general, and Isaiah Mansur commissary general. The state fairground at Indianapolis was transformed into Camp Morton, where Indiana volunteers were trained, equipped, and organized into regiments. . . .

Indiana's geographical position, her large population, and her large crops of agricultural products made her support of the war important. Since the state was located between the Great Lakes and the Ohio River, railroads connected her cities, villages, and farms with Atlantic ports. Other railroads which ran from north to south were prepared to carry troops, supplies, and food to the armies which were soon located in the south central states. Indiana was a part of the great production area for wheat, corn, and hogs. Hoosier farmers raised more hogs than those of any other state and were second in the production of wheat. Only four loyal states had a larger population or more members in the national House of Representatives.

Most of the state was in the drainage basin of the Ohio River, which with the Mississippi River formed the natural outlet for her surplus products. Although the east-west railroads opened the way to other markets, commerce to New Orleans had not diminished. Consequently the outcome of secession was of vital importance because it threatened Indiana's most natural route to the markets of the world.

The state, however, lacked the funds necessary to organize and equip

[2]John P. C. Shanks was elected in 1860 but defeated in 1862. He served in the military forces during the remainder of the war. William Mitchel was also defeated for re-election in 1862. Dunn became judge advocate general in 1875.

regiments and to send them to the front. Temporarily the need was supplied by private persons and banks, among which was Winslow, Lanier, and Company, of New York. James F. D. Lanier, formerly a banker of Madison, Indiana, and a founder and principal stockholder of the Second State Bank of Indiana, was largely responsible for the interest this firm took in Indiana affairs. Although he left the state in 1851, he was much concerned about Indiana's part in the Civil War. His company loaned Governor Morton $420,000 at this time. Since this loan and other actions required legislative approval and cooperation, Morton called a special session of the general assembly which met on April 24.

The new governor undertook the great task of guiding the state through the war years. He addressed the special session of the legislature with an appeal that politics be forgotten and that all act as patriots. The members of the assembly responded quickly and vigorously, divided legisla-

Indiana's war governor, Oliver P. Morton
Courtesy of the Indiana Historical Society

tive offices between the two parties, authorized an issue of $2,000,000 in state bonds for the defense of the state and nation, and appropriated $1,600,000 for military purposes.

The Indianapolis *Daily Sentinel,* which on April 13, hailed the firing on Fort Sumter as the "Abolition War of Seward, Lincoln and Company," and advised on April 15, "Let Them Go in Peace," promised on April 25 that "there will be no factious opposition on the part of the Democratic members." Four days later it urged: "The Legislature of Indiana should promply provide for all the requisitions of the General Government." The ultimate was reached on May 10 when it commented on the possibility of war or peace: "There is now no choice in the matter. The Government must be sustained." It actually used "Webster's Reply to Hayne" against the arguments of the secessionists. The call to action seemed to have brought unity to Indiana—at least the dissident elements became quiet, but this temporary unity was not to last long.

Since the markets for many products of southern Indiana had been in the southern states and trade continued after Sumter, the legislature appointed committees to investigate the possibility that aid was being given to the Confederacy by the continuation of trade. Acts were adopted defining treason, prohibiting correspondence and trade with the Confederacy, and providing penalties for violation of these measures. The federal government also intervened to prevent commerce with the enemy. Interference with the normal economic activity of this part of the state resulted in hardships for the people.

The governor was authorized on May 6, 1861, to organize six additional regiments from the volunteers. They were formed into a brigade under Brigadier General Joseph J. Reynolds, a graduate of West Point who had several years of military experience. The regiments were soon in federal service. To safeguard the immediate defense of the state, a militia was provided under the title "Indiana Legion." Its organization was confined largely to the southern counties, and inevitably much of the burden of local defense fell upon the citizens of this part of the state.

A debate over the purpose of the nation in waging war also revealed elements of disunity. Both houses of the general assembly adopted resolutions which declared that the men and resources of the state should not be employed to destroy slavery or the constitutional rights of the states. Some of the legislators wanted to add pledges stating that the preservation of the Union was the sole aim of the war, but radicals asserted that only the abolition of slavery would bring permanent peace.

. . . .

A rancorous partisan conflict without precedent in Indiana also took place in 1862. The Democratic state convention met in Indianapolis on January 8 in the midst of discouraging circumstances. Divided among themselves in respect to support of the war, their attitude towards slavery, and the methods of preserving the Union, Democrats were associated in the minds of many people with the rebellion of the South. Thomas A. Hendricks, president of the convention, promised support of the war for the preservation of the Union, but warned against abolitionists and complained about economic changes which the war stimulated and which worked to the advantage of the East. The platform promised support of a war for the "integrity of the Union under the Constitution" but opposed emancipation of the Negroes or the subjugation of the southern states. The platform was unrealistic in demanding the preservation of the Union as it had been before the war.

The Union party, a coalition of Republicans and War Democrats, met in convention on June 18, anticipating an easy victory. Governor Morton as president of the convention again urged the abandonment of party for the duration of the war. He also spoke of treasonable societies in the state and of the possibility that strong measures against them might be necessary. Another speaker likened the Democratic convention to the Hartford Convention in which the Federalist party had opposed the War of 1812 and by so doing had destroyed its own usefulness. The nominations for offices were divided between the War Democrats and the Republicans. The platform declared in favor of vigorous prosecution of the war, which should be waged for the preservation of the Union and not for the abolition of slavery.

Developments that occurred between the meeting of the Union party convention and the election caused a sharp reversal of sentiment. Economic measures of the Lincoln administration—the growth of the national debt, the Pacific Railroad Act, with its large land grant and loan of money to a private corporation, and especially the raising of tariff duties to aid manufacturers—seemed to be a return to Hamiltonian policies. Arbitrary arrests, interference by the military in civilian affairs, violation of freedom of speech and the press, and the suspension of the writ of habeas corpus for all persons charged with disloyal practices caused the people to fear that their constitutional liberties were in danger. The failure of the military to win the war was very disappointing. Hoosiers had expected the opening of the Mississippi River, but they were not prepared for the failure of McClellan's Peninsular Campaign, the call for more volunteers which followed, and the disaster at the Second Battle of Bull Run.

One of the causes of dissatisfaction in the state was the conscription of soldiers. Volunteers had enlisted in 1861, but in December the War Department, fearing that it could not equip and use so many soldiers, ordered governors to cease raising troops. When resumed in 1862 recruiting became increasingly difficult. In June urgent appeals were sent to the governors for more regiments, and early in July Lincoln issued a call for three hundred thousand additional soldiers. Fervent appeals, promises of money for the support of soldiers' families, and bounties for volunteers brought only languid recruiting. On July 17, 1862, Congress passed an act authorizing the states to resort to conscription if necessary to meet their quotas. In each county a commissioner was appointed, who in turn named a deputy in each precinct. The latter was to make a list of all resident male citizens between the ages of eighteen and forty-five. The commissioners and deputies then passed on all pleas for exemption and sent the final lists to the general commissioner in Indianapolis. The general commissioner determined whether each township had met its quota and then ordered those that had not to draw names from the list and send the draftees to the capital. Substitutes could be employed.

In conformity with this measure, on August 4, Lincoln requested another 300,000 men. Because of inadequate records, Indiana officials assumed that the state had failed to furnish its quota, although later investigation indicated that the state had furnished 8,008 more men than had been required. The draft was administered by state officials and was applied only to those townships which had not furnished the number of volunteers required of them. A total of 3,003 men were conscripted. Dissatisfied persons destroyed a draft box and delayed the officials in Blackford County for two days, while threats and misdemeanors marred the record of Fountain County. "Few events did more to strengthen the opposition [to the state Republican administration] than this first crude attempt to administer a draft." It seemed to confirm fears of arbitrary government.

The reassertion of abolitionism raised again the question of the purpose of the war and of the sincerity of the original statements of the war aims of the administration. Although Lincoln had revoked the military orders of General John C. Frémont, in Missouri, and General David Hunter, in South Carolina, both of whom sought to abolish slavery in their military districts, the President suggested that Congress pass a measure for compensated emancipation in the border states. Congress accepted this proposal only insofar as it applied to the District of Columbia and excluded slavery from the territories. After the Battle of Antietam, Lincoln issued the preliminary Emancipation Proclamation, September 22, 1862, which declared that slaves would be free in all states resisting the Union on January 1, 1863. Since the proclamation applied only to the people of the Confederacy—who would not obey the order—it was in reality only an announcement of policy and may not have freed a slave. Although very pleasing to the Radicals and to English liberals who helped prevent English interference in the American war, to many in Indiana the proclamation meant that the war had become a means of ending slavery as well as a struggle to preserve the Union. To numerous citizens who had migrated from south of the Ohio River and who were not willing to fight for the abolitionist cause, this proclamation was very objectionable.

The New Albany *Ledger,* along with many War Democrats who had been affiliated with the Union party, transferred its support to the Democrats. As the strength of the Union party weakened, its leaders resorted to charges of disloyalty and treason and to a stimulation of emotions by means of horror stories which told of cruelty on the part of Confederates. The report of a federal grand jury on a secret political society was circulated as a campaign document. Republicans cultivated the impression that only Union party members were loyal and that only their candidates could safely be entrusted with official positions.

The grand jury report just mentioned exposed the existence and activities of the Knights of the Golden Circle. This organization, which originated before the Civil War, was said to have been devoted to the conquest of Mexico and its acquisition by the United States. As secession became [im]minent, the South took the place of the nation in the organization's ritual and purpose, and the order expanded into the Ohio Valley. Castles or local chapters were organized in Indiana, but the revelation of the group's existence and the charges of its supposed treason were so inextricably involved in the efforts of the Union party to win the state election of 1862 that the grains of truth cannot now be separated from the chaff. The charges were often so extreme as to discredit themselves. Many of the people undoubtedly believed that the order was an organization of traitors, and, perhaps, some of the members were. Other observers asserted that such allegations were not only false but were made for the purpose of winning the election. The existence of the society has been questioned, but the persons said to be its leaders were critical and unfriendly towards many of the methods which the state and national administrations were using to win the war.[3] The KGC was said to have protected individuals against arbitrary arrest and mob action, opposed Hamiltonian economic policies, and insisted that the draft was unconstitutional. Its friends asserted that it was only a harmless political club, but its enemies attributed to it all kinds of disorders, murders, resistance to conscription, and treason.

. . . .

In addition to alarms about secret societies, resistance to conscription, and other disorders, Indiana suffered invasion in 1863. Captain Thomas Hines, one of the officers of the famous Confederate cavalry leader, John H. Morgan, crossed the Ohio River above Cannelton, pushed northward as far as Paoli and Hardinsburg, and returned to the Ohio above Leavenworth. Most of his men were captured, but Hines swam the Ohio and escaped.

A month later, on July 8, Morgan crossed the river at Brandenburg,

[3]"The Republican constructed myths about Copperhead secret societies served their purposes well. It was a political apparition which appeared on the eve of elections. It was a figment of Republican imagination." Frank L. Klement, *The Copperheads in the Middle West* (Chicago, Ill., 1960), 205. The importance of Copperhead organizations has undoubtedly been exaggerated.

Kentucky, with nearly three thousand cavalry, advanced to Corydon, divided his forces and took Paoli and Greenville, united his troops again at Vienna and Lexington, moved northeastward to Versailles, and left the state near Harrison, Ohio. He had little trouble securing food, money, and fresh horses and was able to defeat the small bodies of militia that opposed him. Governor Morton called on the men of the southern half of Indiana to organize, arm, and take the field. In the northern part of the state, citizens were asked to organize military companies and hold themselves ready for action. In two days, twenty thousand men assembled in Indianapolis and another forty-five thousand were nearly ready to serve. Morgan destroyed railroads and bridges to delay his pursuers. The damage he wrought in the state has been estimated at $500,000, but in return he left a host of stories—many humorous, others tragic—that have enriched the traditions of the state. Because he feared to try crossing the Ohio River at Madison and because the militia was closing in, he fled into Ohio. On July 26 he was captured at Salineville in eastern Ohio. He had expected the people of Southern Indiana to come to his aid, but their efforts to capture him should have quieted the fears of various officials about thier loyalty.

. . . .

Indiana had furnished 208,367 men, of which 11,718 were re-enlistments. If the average family contained four persons, more than half of the families furnished one of its members to the armed forces. Almost 12 per cent of the soldiers, 24,416, were killed or died during the war. A few over 5 per cent, or 10,846, deserted from the service. Although the deserters were a blot on the state, the military record of Indiana soldiers was otherwise very creditable.

One of the near-casualties of the Civil War years in Indiana was the Democratic party, which had enjoyed an almost uninterrupted series of victories before 1860. Although badly beaten by Governor Morton and associated in the minds of many people with treason, the Democracy staged an early revival in the election of Thomas A. Hendricks to the governorship in 1872. Possibly the Jacksonian wing, which might have furnished liberal leadership, was even less popular than the party. But Jacksonian principles became more popular in the person of "Blue Jeans" James D. Williams, who was elected to succeed Hendricks. The lack of progressive leadership was also revealed in the weakness in Indiana of the Granger movement, which laid the foundations for the state regulation of railroads and utilities in four upper Mississippi Valley states, but did not produce such results in Indiana. Little progressive legislation, aside from that regarding education, was passed until near the end of the century. How much of this conservatism was due to Morton's war on the Democracy and changes which occurred during the war can only be estimated.

Economic changes of the war period also tended to diminish the influence of the old Democratic areas. The river interests were injured by the closure of the Mississippi, the destruction of southern markets, and the competition of railroads. Serious reductions were recorded in the building of steamboats, the sale of agricultural products to the South, and the distribution of goods by merchants of river towns. In general, counties south of the Wisconsin Moraine continued to grow, but at a slower rate than northern and central counties. The southern area in 1860 contained 45 per cent of the total population of the state, but five years after the close of the war the percentage had declined to 39 per cent.

On the positive side, the prosperity that accompanied the war and the rise of the new industrial order paved the way for the acceptance of the changes. During the war the Republican administration had enacted the National Banking Act of February 25, 1863, and repeatedly raised the tariff. Aided by war contracts, the tariff, and railroad transportation, a new economy in which manufacturing assumed an increasingly important role began to achieve significance. The new national banks, some of which replaced former state banks, also became a part of the new order. Railroads enlarged the markets that were available for Indiana farmers, while the feeding of the soldiers required vast quantities of supplies from western states. High prices raised considerably the standard of living in rural areas and small towns, where many new houses were built. These homes were in part made possible by the prices received from raising wheat. Whatever remained of frontier self-sufficiency disappeared along navigable streams and railroads. A less frugal way of life developed. Labor, too, gained, for recruitment of men for the armies produced a shortage of manpower. Towns and cities grew more rapidly....

A conflict which lasted four years and involved so many people, either directly as members of the armed forces or indirectly as civilians who supported the armies, could not possibly have left the nation unchanged. The early promises, demanded by the Democrats and so readily given by the Republicans, that the nation should be preserved as it was appeared at the end of the war to resemble the early notion that the conflict would last only a few weeks. In addition to the casualties, the handicap placed upon the Democratic party, the growth of cities, the increase in manufacturing, and sectional fears and animosities had effected a breach in the mental and spiritual life of the nation that could not be healed quickly. The Union had been preserved, but at a terrible price! The questions of the nature of the Union and the right of secession had been answered. Although the guns became silent and the soldiers came home, politicians were unable to make peace with defeated fellow citizens for ten additional years. The reconstruction which followed the fighting was not a separate process, but the time required to check the forces released by the firing on Fort Sumter.

Political posters of 1866 in Delphi, Indiana
Courtesy of the Indiana Historical Society

Morgan's Raid into Southern Indiana, July 1863

WILLIAM E. WILSON

The single episode of the Civil War which most directly involved Indiana, and which lives on in legend and lore, is Morgan's Raid through the southeastern quadrant of the state in July 1863. General John Hunt Morgan, a cavalry officer who had long harbored plans to operate north of the Ohio River, crossed into Indiana at Mauckport, moved northward through Corydon and Salem, then eastward through Vernon and Versailles and on into Ohio, where he and his men were captured. The purposes of the raid have been variously explained: to relieve the pressure on Confederate troops in Tennessee, to aid General Lee in his northern invasion (Morgan had not yet learned of Lee's defeat at Gettysburg on July 3), to encourage the "copperhead" sympathizer element in southern Indiana to support the South openly, or simply to ransack and plunder the region, thereby obtaining horses

From "Thunderbolt of the Confederacy, or King of the Horse Thieves," *Indiana Magazine of History*, LIV (June 1958), 119–130. Footnotes in the original have been omitted. Copyright © 1958 by the Trustees of Indiana University. Reprinted by permission.

and supplies. Whatever its purpose, the raid terrorized the state momentarily and brought a massive—if disorganized—outpouring of men from all parts of the state to resist the invasion. W. H. H. Terrell estimated that 65,000 citizens gathered within forty-eight hours to defend their state, and Emma Lou Thornbrough concludes that this response "belies the tradition of widespread disloyalty and sympathy for the Confederacy."[1]

In the selection below Professor William E. Wilson takes a minority position concerning both the purposes and effectiveness of the Morgan raid, but his review of the events, the opposing interpretations concerning Morgan himself, and the impact of the invasion is a useful one. For a detailed study of this episode by a participant, see Basil W. Duke, *History of Morgan's Cavalry* (1867). See also W. H. H. Terrell, *Indiana in the War of the Rebellion* (1869, reprinted 1960), pp. 209–254; and Edison H. Thomas, *John Hunt Morgan and his Raiders* (1975). For a brief treatment of Morgan's Raid in fiction, see Chapter Five of Jessamyn West, *The Friendly Persuasion* (1945).

Zigzagging across southern Indiana and Ohio in the summer of 1863, John Hunt Morgan wove a trail as raddled as turkey tracks. Although his pursuers were never more than a few hours behind him, they were never sure of the whereabouts of the man known variously as The Thunderbolt of the Confederacy and The King of Horse Thieves, until they stumbled upon him.

Today, plaques and monuments mark Morgan's route from Mauckport, Indiana, where he crossed the Ohio River on a July day almost a century ago, to Salineville, Ohio, near the Pennsylvania line, where he surrendered eighteen days later. But the modern tourist who attempts to follow that trail of some six hundred miles will find himself almost as confused as the Federal cavalrymen Morgan was dodging in 1863. The legend of Morgan's Raid along the north shore of the Ohio has grown as ubiquitous as Morgan himself once seemed to be.

At times, the vitality of the legend gives the visitor the impression that the country has not changed since Morgan swept across it. There have been changes of course, but off the main highways there is much that remains the same. If those slumbering, isolated hill-villages dream at all, they can dream now only of the past. On their quiet streets the houses where Morgan dined and slept have a certain lustre upon them, and nearby, at crossroads and along creekbanks, the old battle sites remain as they were when home guards stood and fought or, more often, dropped their inadequate arms and fled. In the back-country lanes where Morgan rode, it is possible still to imagine that distant thunder on a sultry summer day is the echo of his horsemen's passing. And all along the way there are, still living in that

[1]Emma Lou Thornbrough, *Indiana in the Civil War Era, 1850–1880* (1965), p. 204.

country, men and women whose forebears sat on rail fences in their child-hood and watched the raiders gallop by.

Surviving also in southern Indiana and Ohio, almost as vital as the legend of Morgan, are the bitterness of 1863 and the contempt that was added to it when at last the Confederate raider was captured and impris-oned in the Ohio State Penitentiary, head shaved and beard shorn like a common criminal's. In that country, The Thunderbolt is only The Horse Thief, and the descendants of the people he robbed console themselves, like their forebears, with the conviction that his unauthorized invasion was a failure.

Actually, it was not.

It is true that Morgan lost to the Confederacy an organization of 2,400 seasoned cavalrymen. He did fail to rally to his support the Copper-heads believed numerous in the area through which he passed. He turned eastward only sixty miles south of Indianapolis, which indeed he might have captured and where he might have released and armed from the city's arse-nal some three thousand Confederate prisoners. And he failed to unite with Lee in Pennsylvania, as some say he intended to do.

But the arguments in Morgan's favor are stronger.

The damage to railroads, steamboats, bridges, and public stores in-flicted by the raid amounted to at least ten million dollars. The cavalry unit of 2,400 was disintegrated, but most of the men escaped and lived to fight for the Confederacy again. In contrast with their own small losses, the raiders captured and paroled six thousand Federal home guards and regu-lars and killed or wounded some six hundred more, they kept thousands of Yankee citizens in a paralyzing state of panic for a fortnight, and by their penetration behind the lines they immobilized 28,000 troops under General Ambrose Burnside, who otherwise would have joined General William S. Rosecrans three weeks before the battle of Chickamauga.

On only one score can Morgan's raid be truly said to have failed, and here the argument, like most of the arguments against him, must rest on hypothesis. Since Morgan was destined to disobey the orders of his com-manding officer and cross the Ohio eventually, it is too bad that he did not disobey nine months earlier, when he first conceived and proposed the Indiana and Ohio raid. Then, even with the same tactical mistakes and the same losses, he might have accomplished much more than he was able to accomplish in 1863.

Nine months earlier, Morgan's men were less war-weary, less starved for luxuries, and better disciplined. Although the number of Copperheads in Indiana and Ohio was probably exaggerated by the Republican canard that all Democrats were traitors of one degree or another, what Southern sym-pathizers there were in the states north of the Ohio might have welcomed the raiders more warmly if Morgan had been able to keep them under control.

Of more significance was the opportunity which lay within the grasp of General Braxton Bragg in 1862 and which was never to come again. That summer Bragg invaded Kentucky. If he had joined forces with General Kirby Smith while Morgan harassed the Federals' rear on Northern soil, he could easily have taken the entire state out of the Union. All that was needed was to prevent General Don Carlos Buell's being reinforced at Louisville, and Morgan could have accomplished that, just as he prevented Burnside from reaching Rosecrans in Tennessee a year later. But Bragg said no, and Morgan obeyed him. Buell got back to Louisville, consolidated his forces, and returned to the offensive; and the Confederates' opportunity was lost.

All this is based on the assumption that Braxton Bragg would have acted swiftly and vigorously in conjunction with a raid by Morgan in 1862, and that of course is a large assumption. Still it can be soundly argued that the tragedy of Morgan's disobedience lies in its postponement. Morgan's original proposal was a good one, but when finally his patience with his over-cautious and short-sighted chief was exhausted and he took matters into his own hands, the most propitious times for insubordination had passed.

By the best accounts, Morgan was an even better strategist than tactician. Nature had endowed him with "gifts which she very rarely bestows, and which give the soldier who has them vast advantages; a quickness of perception and of thought, amounting almost to intuition, an almost unerring sagacity in foreseeing the operations of an adversary and in calculating the effect of his own movements upon him, wonderful control over men, as individuals and in masses, and moral courage and energy almost preternatural."

These are the words of Basil W. Duke, who commanded the first of the two brigades Morgan led across the Ohio. In his *Reminiscences* and his *History of Morgan's Cavalry,* General Duke regards his commanding officer always with admiration and respect. So, in *The Partisan Rangers,* does Adam R. Johnson, who commanded the second brigade. Both these men were able and intelligent soldiers and both lived after the war to become distinguished and respected citizens, Duke as a prominent lawyer in Louisville, Johnson as the founder and patriarch of a prosperous town in Texas.

Their estimates of Morgan should prove that he was neither the lawless brigand that his enemies in Indiana and Ohio called him nor the unruly hothead that some historians have concluded he was because of his insubordination on the banks of the Ohio. By all standards of military conduct there is no justification for his action of course, but if he had disobeyed Bragg earlier and achieved a greater success, the insubordination would have been more generously regarded afterwards. . . .

Although John Hunt Morgan was born in Alabama, he regarded himself as a Kentuckian. He grew up in Lexington, Kentucky, a member of a slave-owning family. After a year of service in the Mexican War, he returned

General John Hunt Morgan
Courtesy of Leslie's Newspaper

to Lexington and married a young woman of delicate health who was soon to die. In business, he was a successful manufacturer of hemp and woolen goods, and he was active in many civic affairs. . . .

When Morgan embarked upon the Indiana and Ohio raid, he was thirty-eight years old, married for the second time, a brigadier general, a cavalryman of two years of arduous service raiding in Kentucky and Tennessee, and a veteran of the battle of Shiloh. By the time he reached Brandenburg, Kentucky, on the banks of the Ohio on the morning of July 8, 1863, he had completed his raiding mission under Bragg's orders. Capturing Columbia, Lebanon, and Bardstown, he had destroyed large quantities of Federal stores in Kentucky, had thoroughly confused the Union command as to the intention of the Confederates, and had already delayed Burnside's march into East Tennessee to join Rosecrans. By that time, too, he had long since made up his mind to cross independently into the rich country north of the Ohio.

Morgan's reasons that July morning were not so cogent as they had been nine months earlier when he first contemplated the raid, but they were still valid. Bragg and Rosecrans were facing each other now in Tennessee, neither ready to strike. They had already engaged in one major battle, at Stones River, and each could claim a sort of victory, Bragg's statistical, Rosecrans's strategic, but neither's decisive. Bragg's force was smaller than Rosecrans's, but it was in top condition, had the advantage of shorter supply lines, and was maneuvering on familiar terrain. If Burnside could be kept in the North, the chances of the Confederates holding their own at least were still good.

Elsewhere, conditions seemed to favor a bold Confederate action of the sort Morgan was about to undertake. Down the Mississippi, Grant was still hammering at Vicksburg and had not yet overpowered it when Morgan left Tennessee. In the East, the Confederate Army had won two major victories, at Fredericksburg and Chancellorsville, and, so far as Morgan knew when he stood on the banks of the Ohio, Lee was still marching into Pennsylvania. Finally, in the North, there were draft riots and a growing weariness of the war.

How much these last two considerations weighed in Morgan's decision is a matter for conjecture. He spoke on several occasions of joining Lee in Pennsylvania, but at the same time he was making definite plans to recross the Ohio at Buffington Island above Cincinnati. The project of union with Lee was probably only an alternative to be resorted to if the crossing at Buffington Island failed. As for the dissidence in the North, he would naturally have welcomed a large-scale revolt, but there is no good evidence that he counted on support from Copperheads, in spite of attempts to prove that he was deeply involved in "the Northwest Conspiracy." For one thing, Morgan's first raid into Kentucky the year before must have taught him not to expect recruits from Southern sympathizers. If his fellow Kentuckians would not rally round him, certainly few disaffected Hoosiers and Ohioans would do so. Morever, his treatment of the few Copperheads who approached him in Indiana and Ohio demonstrates his lack of confidence in the Knights of the Golden Circle.

"Good," he is reported to have said to one of them, as he took the Copperhead's horse. "Then you ought to be glad to contribute to the South."

The crossing of the Ohio got off to a bad start. Although two steamboats were easily captured for the ferriage, a party of home guards were established on the Indiana side behind houses and haystacks. The raiders' Parrotts had to be put into action to silence the single Hoosier field-piece before the crossing could commence. Then, after the Second Kentucky and the Ninth Tennessee were over the river and the home guards were retiring, a Federal gunboat steamed round the bend and began tossing shells alternately at the raiders on the Indiana shore and those who had not yet left Brandenburg on the Kentucky side.

The appearance of the gunboat brought the ferrying to an abrupt halt. Worse still, it put the entire Confederate force in a hazardous position. Delay was dangerous, because pursuing Federal cavalry would soon be coming up from the south. Yet if the crossing was abandoned, half the troops would be left stranded on the Indiana shore. Morgan opened up on the gunboat with every piece of artillery at his disposal, but for two hours he could not drive her off. When the situation had come to seem most desperate, however, she suddenly turned tail and fled, her ammunition exhausted.

That night, after firing the two steamboats and setting them adrift, Morgan's men camped at Frakes Mill six miles north of the river. Behind them, one of the boats, the "Alice Dean," did not burn completely, and until only a few years ago a part of its carcass was still visible in the water where it sank.

The next day, the raid was on in full swing,—and *swing* is a good word for describing its progress. Morgan had what the English call "a good eye for a country," but he amplified his vision and prehension by using his troops as an insect uses its tentacles. They rode usually in fours, and at every crossroad those at the head of the column fanned out, foraged and scouted for several miles on both sides of the main force, and then rejoined it in the rear. Thus was Morgan not only kept informed of any threat on his flanks, he kept the countryside in a wide area through which he passed in constant alarm and confusion as to his whereabouts and the direction he was taking.

A Canadian telegrapher named George Ellsworth, but called Lightning by the raiders, further extended Morgan's vision and his knowledge of the purposes of his adversaries. Ellsworth had the priceless skill of mimicry at the telegraph key. By watching a captured operator work or by listening to one on a tapped wire, he could soon imitate the man's style so well that he was able to deceive other operators and get information from them. Better still, he could send out false information and even false orders. His expert faking made it possible for Morgan virtually to assume command of the enemy forces surrounding him and to put them almost anywhere he wanted them.

At Corydon, once the capital of Indiana, the raiders met their first serious resistance. Outside the town, four hundred home guards barred their way. Before the defense could be broken, sixteen Confederates were killed, but Morgan was able to enter the town in time for noonday dinner at the Kintner Hotel. It was while he was dining there, on July 9, that he learned from the innkeeper's daughter that Lee had been defeated at Gettysburg almost a week before. There is no evidence that he even considered turning back when he received this disheartening information.

After Corydon, the men were in the saddle twenty-one hours out of

Morgan's raiders at Salem, Indiana
Courtesy of Leslie's Newspaper

every twenty-four for the next two weeks. They advanced to Salem, Vienna, and Lexington, but nine miles below Seymour they began to swing eastward toward the Ohio line.

When the news of the invasion came to Indianapolis, its people were panic-stricken, and if Morgan had pushed straight on from Salem on July 10, he might indeed have captured the city. In another twenty-four hours, however, it was too late. By that time, Governor Oliver P. Morton had the situation in hand, General Lew Wallace, home on leave and on a fishing trip on the Wabash, was back in uniform and on his way downstate to help General Edward H. Hobson, who was hot on Morgan's trail, and General Henry M. Judah, whom Burnside had dispatched in Cincinnati to head the raiders off if he could. More damaging to Morgan, however, than the combined maneuvers of all three of these generals was the thing that was happening to his own men. They had begun to loot and to straggle.

Horses had been taken as needed from the beginning. This was the custom of cavalrymen, both Union and Confederate. It not only gave the raiders fresh mounts along the way, it denied them to their pursuers. Morgan tried to see that the exchanges were as fair and as legal as possible under the circumstances, but in his swift, zigzag movements he lost contact with many of his men, and by the time they reached Salem, the plenitude of the shops and stores after impoverished Dixie was too much for them. To use Basil Duke's euphemistic words, they developed "the propensity to appropriate beyond limit or restraint."

General Duke could be—and was—more specific. Describing the raid for *Century Magazine* in January, 1891, he wrote:

> The weather was intensely warm,—the hot July sun burned the earth to powder, and we were breathing superheated dust,—yet one man rode for three days with seven pairs of skates slung about his neck; another loaded himself with sleighbells. A large chafing dish, a medium-sized Dutch clock, a green glass decanter with goblets to match, a bag of horn buttons, a chandelier, and a birdcage containing three canaries, were some of the articles I saw borne off and jealously fondled.

At Harrison, Indiana, twenty-five miles from Cincinnati, all detachments that could be reached were drawn in and thereafter a strong provost guard kept the stragglers under some control. They would not throw away their loot, but from there on their holiday was ended. Morgan was no longer a wolf on the prowl; he was now a fox in flight, and the hounds were baying all around him.

Still, he was able for another two weeks to dodge, turn, stand at bay, turn and dodge again, and even vanish for several hours at a time. He circled round Cincinnati in the night, the men in the rear lighting torches every few yards to pick up the trail of the vanguard in the foam dropped from the mouths of the horses and the dust kicked up by their feet. Then on to Buffington Island, in as straight a line as he dared to follow.

Halfway to the proposed point of crossing the river, he learned that Vicksburg had fallen and that Lee was retreating across the Potomac. At 1:00 P.M. on the eighteenth, he reached Chester, Ohio, eighteen miles from his destination. He knew that the river was rising and delay was dangerous, but his men were exhausted and he was encumbered with two hundred wounded so he postponed the crossing till the next morning and stopped for a two-hour rest that would allow the stragglers to come up.

This decision proved disastrous. The next morning, at the riverside, General Judah's whole force was upon him. Then came Hobson's advance under General James M. Shackelford. And after that, Federal gunboats appeared and began shelling the raiders from the river.

Duke's brigade was lost in the ensuing battle, but Morgan and Johnson succeeded in leading a thousand men out of the trap; and twenty miles farther up the river they began to cross. Johnson got over with three hundred men, but when Morgan himself had swum his powerful mount half way over, he turned back. Too many of his men were behind him, and gunboats were approaching that would cut them off. He preferred to remain with them to the end.

Yet the end did not come for another six days, during which Morgan traversed the eastern half of the state; and when finally he surrendered, he surrendered voluntarily.

He was riding along with Captain James Burbick of the Union militia near Salineville. He had persuaded Captain Burbick to guide him to the Pennsylvania line in return for his promise to leave the district unharmed. Suddenly he asked Burbick whether he would give him and his men paroles if he surrendered, and the startled militiaman agreed. When the word was passed around to the 364 men remaining with Morgan, they must have dropped from their saddles in unison, like the crew of the Ancient Mariner's ship falling to the deck, for when Colonel Shackelford came along a few minutes later, they were all sound asleep.

Shackelford refused to honor the terms Captain Burbick had granted Morgan, and Morgan and his men were taken back to Cincinnati as prisoners of war. When they were incarcerated in the Ohio State Penitentiary at Columbus two days later, they were treated as common criminals.

Four months after their imprisonment, Morgan and six of his captains tunneled their way out of the penitentiary and escaped. Morgan fought again, in Virginia, but never again so boldly or successfully. As one contemporary put it, "The plain truth is that Morgan never had a fair chance after he escaped from prison." He was given only the meanest troops to command, and his requests and proposals fell upon deaf ears in Richmond. There were many in authority there, too, as in the North, who thought him a failure; and among them, quite understandably, was Braxton Bragg.

John Hunt Morgan was finally shot dead at point blank by a Union soldier in Greeneville, Tennessee, on the fourth of September, 1864, and the soldier is said to have cried out after he fired the fatal shot, "I've killed the damned horse thief!" By that date, Morgan was indeed no longer The Thunderbolt, but it mattered little to the Confederacy then what he was. The war was already lost, and the time for such feats as he could once accomplish had passed.

Chapter VII
INDIANA AFTER THE CIVIL WAR

The dual nature of Indiana politics continued into the Reconstruction period, when problems associated with the Civil War dominated the scene. The loyalty of the state to the Union blended imperfectly with the program of "Radical Reconstruction" designed to bring about complete political and social equality for the former slaves. This duality is reflected in the state's two most prominent postwar leaders: Republican Oliver P. Morton, governor and then senator, who ardently supported Radical Reconstruction policies while maintaining his control of state politics; and Democrat Thomas A. Hendricks, senator and then governor, who just as strongly opposed efforts to remake the Constitution during a time of inflamed passions. As a result, Indiana offered only lukewarm support to the Radical Reconstruction program, giving successively smaller margins of victory in its ratifications of the Thirteenth, Fourteenth, and Fifteenth amendments. Then, in 1872 it elevated the conservative Hendricks to the governor's mansion. In so doing Indiana became the first northern state after the Civil War to elect a Democrat to its highest office. The gradual revival of the Democrats stemmed from a general weariness with wartime issues; dissatisfaction with Reconstruction policies, particularly regarding Negro rights; unhappiness over the growing centralization of power in Washington; and concern about economic and monetary matters.

The last issue became of even more pressing importance in the wake of the Panic of 1873 and the widespread depression that followed. A central question in national politics had long been what to do with the unbacked paper currency, known as "greenbacks," issued during the war. Some politicians, chiefly Republicans, favored a rapid contraction in the amount of currency; this would be achieved by withdrawing the greenbacks from circulation and returning to a specie payment system as quickly as possible. Others, chiefly Democrats, favored the permanent retention of the greenbacks as an aid to debtors. Obligations that had been incurred with a depreciated currency were to be paid in the same currency. The positions of the political parties in Indiana on this issue were murky, however, in that Senator Morton favored only a gradual return to specie payment. The greenback-retention idea, known as the "Pendleton Plan," did become part of the Democratic program in the 1868 election, and the issue was revived during the depression of the early 1870s. Eventually—in 1875—a political party known as the Independent party, later called the Greenback party, was organized in Cleveland, Ohio, and its first national convention was held in Indianapolis in May 1876.

The depression of the early 1870s was also the backdrop for one of the most interesting and significant elections in the state and the nation, which also coincided with the national centennial. In the first essay below, Professor W. T. K. Nugent describes the mood of the people, the nature of the centennial celebration, and the transitional significance of events at this time. The second essay, by Howard R. Burnett, is a memorable portrait of the man elected governor in 1876, a farmer-politician known as "Blue Jeans" Williams. This was also the year of the famous "disputed election" for president, in which the Republican team of Hayes and Wheeler was declared victorious over Democrats Tilden and Hendricks by an 8–7 vote of a special electoral commission. Thomas A. Hendricks, the Democratic vice-presidential nominee, was only one of several Hoosiers accorded this honor in the post–Civil War period. Schuyler Colfax was elected as Ulysses Grant's vice-president in 1868, and Hendricks himself was elected with Grover Cleveland in 1884. William H. English was an unsuccessful vice-presidential nominee with Winfield S. Hancock in 1880, as was John W. Kern, William Jennings Bryan's running mate in 1908. However, Charles W. Fairbanks was elected with Theodore Roosevelt in 1904, and, of course, Thomas R. Marshall enjoyed two full terms as Woodrow Wilson's vice-president from 1913 to 1921.

There were many other burning political, social, and economic issues of the Reconstruction period. Foremost among them were the somewhat related questions of temperance and women's rights, and state organizations for the promotion of both were established. Resolutions leading to woman suffrage never cleared the Indiana legislature, but several temperance laws were passed, and a number of temperance organizations, including the Women's Christian Temperance Union and the Prohibition party, were established during the 1870s. More positive results came in the economic field, despite the depression of the 1870s and the national railroad strike of 1877. The state's railway network was largely completed by 1880, and a beginning was made toward railroad regulation helpful to farmers and other shippers. Professor Emma Lou Thornbrough, author of the most comprehensive study of Indiana during the Civil War and Reconstruction periods, describes below the significant railroad developments of the 1860s and 1870s.

For more information on the immediate postwar period in Indiana, see Emma Lou Thornbrough, *Indiana in the Civil War Era, 1850–1880* (1965); John D. Barnhart and Donald F. Carmony, *Indiana: From Frontier to Industrial Commonwealth* (2 vols., 1954); Ralph D. Gray (ed.), *Gentlemen from Indiana: National Party Candidates, 1836–1940* (1977); William D. Foulke,

Life of Oliver P. Morton (2 vols., 1899); and John W. Holcombe and Hubert M. Skinner, *Life and Public Services of Thomas A. Hendricks* (1886). See also William G. Carleton, "The Money Question in Indiana Politics, 1865–1890," *Indiana Magazine of History,* XLII (March 1946), 105–150; Robert P. Sharkey, *Money, Class, and Party: An Economic Study of Civil War and Reconstruction* (1959); and Dee Brown, *The Year of the Century: 1876* (1966).

1: Political Developments

The 1870s in Context

WALTER T. K. NUGENT

Professor Nugent, a specialist in late nineteenth-century American history, discussed America during the time of the centennial at an annual meeting of the Indiana Historical Society in 1972. Organized in a series of concentric circles, the lecture considered first the "Centennial Fourth," then the year 1876, a somber backdrop to the festivities in July, and finally the "broader context" of the 1870s, particularly the depression which lasted from 1873 until the end of the decade. In addition to the well-publicized events of the period, such as Custer's Last Stand and the controversial centennial election, Nugent points to many basic changes during the decade that foreshadowed the major problems and configurations of American society in its second century. In Nugent's phrase, the decade constituted a "seed time of modern conflict."

Nugent, a professor of history at Indiana University, is the author of *The Tolerant Populists: Kansas Populism and Nativism* (1963); *The Money Question During Reconstruction* (1967); *Money and American Society, 1865–1880* (1968); and *Modern America* (1973). For more information on the American centennial, see Dee Brown, *The Year of the Century: 1876* (1966); see also C. Vann Woodward, *Reunion and Reaction: The Compromise of 1877* (1956); and T. Harry Williams (ed.), *Hayes: The Diary of a President, 1875–1881* (1964).

My purpose in speaking to you this afternoon is to tell you something about the shape and structure of American society at the time when the nation ended its first century and began its second. As I shall try to show,

From "Seed Time of Modern Conflict: American Society at the Centennial," *Indiana Historical Society Lectures, 1972–1973* (1973), pp. 31–44. Footnotes in the original have been omitted. Copyright © 1973 by the Indiana Historical Society. Reprinted by permission.

that society was a proud and in many ways a confident one, yet also one which confronted some very serious difficulties. I like to regard the 1870s as Act I, scene 1, of a long epic which we can call "America in the Modern Age," in which the nineties provided Act I, scene 2 (an even more troubled time), and in which, of course, later acts are still in progress as we approach the bicentennial.

First I want to talk about the first day of the United States' second century, the Fourth of July of 1876. Then we can take up its immediate context, and then the general context of the seventies. The Fourth in 1876 was the "Centennial Fourth," and everybody seemed very much aware of that fact. In much of the country it was celebrated as a three-day holiday, a very rare thing for that time, beginning with preparations on Sunday the second, much activity on Monday the third, especially Monday evening, and climaxing on Tuesday the Fourth. Celebrations took place for three days from San Francisco to New York. The biggest affair was at Philadelphia, then hosting the Centennial Exposition: as five hundred thousand people lined the streets, a great torchlight parade of ten thousand workingmen and five thousand G.A.R. veterans, still black-haired and straight-backed only eleven years after the Civil War, passed before the presidential candidates, Hayes and Tilden; the Emperor of Brazil, Dom Pedro, and lesser foreign dignitaries; and several governors and mayors, marching beneath triumphal arches not used in Philadelphia since La Fayette was received there in 1824.

In Indianapolis the celebrating was no less intense. For weeks, L. S. Ayres & Co. had been advising ladies to buy new hats and dresses for July 4, "this day of days," and an editorial warned that "those only who wind up the day in sobriety are worthy to be citizens of a repulic [sic] one hundred years old." There could have been an ominous symbolism in the appearance of a bad electrical storm late in the evening of July 3, literally the eleventh hour of America's first century, and threatening weather continued until mid-morning on the Fourth. But the skies cleared, and by 2 P.M. the celebrations were enjoying fair skies, westerly winds, and (if it had been invented yet) a comfort index of about 72. The day lengthened into a delightful evening, with the temperature 70° at sunset.

Special trains had brought an estimated twenty-five thousand people into Indianapolis from out of town for the festivities, and we presume that they were not disappointed. A "monster balloon," called "America" and guided by one Professor Shotts, ascended from the Indianapolis Exposition grounds, rose to a height of three miles, and landed about an hour later north of Greenfield; while aloft a "young theatrical couple" were married in it. A gala parade brought out marchers from a long list of voluntary associations: the Schwarzer Ritter Order Band preceded the Veterans' Association, the Fraternité Française, the Emerald Society, the Liederkranz Society, the Turnverein, the Society of St. Joseph, the Männerchor, the Free-Thinkers' Society, the Beer Brewers' Association Band, and many others; it took almost a full newspaper column in six-point type to list the program and the marching order of the parade. Governor Hendricks, recently nominated for Vice-President by the Democrats, presided, while the Hon. Byron K. Elliott gave the main speech.

On the fifth, the newspapers devoted column after column to minute descriptions of the parade, of house decorations along the route, of the tableaux (the "floats" of those days), and to verbatim transcripts of all the Indianapolis speeches as well as, in five-point type for a page and a half, William M. Evarts' principal address at the Philadelphia celebration. What were they talking about? "Fourth of July oratory" has long since become a cliché, but there is no reason to doubt the sincere pride of these people when they said: *rejoice, rejoice.* A few lines from an editorial will serve: "The nations of the Old World look on in wonder at our achievements, and while there is a proud victory there, all over the land a patriotic thrill stirs the American heart, as the people gather, as prophesied by the fathers of the republic, to render grateful shouts of rejoicing over the heritage that is ours. Let the day be festal for all. Let the rich and poor, who alike enjoy the blessings of freedom, rejoice together. Let the old rejoice in the inheritance of their children. Let the young rejoice in the promises of the future. Let all render grateful thanks to the God of nations for our free and peaceful land from the Atlantic to the Pacific, from the lakes to the Gulf." Pride, indeed; and beyond that, optimism, and confidence in the future. I do not get the impression that these were a fearful people, shouting down the wind to suppress their own insecurities. Nor do I think they were being particularly naive or hypocritical; they were expressing something they believed, in a manner partly ritual, partly evangelical.

And they were not blinded by fervor. One of the most accurate and revealing sentences written on that occasion was the following, from a *Sentinel* editorial: "It was hard times yesterday, and will be to-morrow, but to-day is the Centennial Fourth of July."

Indeed there were many hints, amid the festivity, that all was not Arcadian in the America of 1876, and that the celebrations on the Fourth provided a decided contrast in mood with the run of life in 1876. The same newspapers that described the Centennial so glowingly also confirmed that a few weeks before, on a branch of the Yellowstone River called the Little Big Horn, Maj. Gen. George Custer and a sizable U.S. Army detachment had been massacred by the Sioux under their great chief, Sitting Bull. Another news story on July 4 reported that the Chicago Common Council had had to abolish the Health and Public Works Boards of that city because expenses were running $2 million ahead of tax income. A classified advertisement promised that Drs. Johnson and Laubach, of the American Opium Institute at 247 North Tennessee Street, would "cure the opium habit in ten days," with "no charge whatever until the patient says he is cured." In another and more frightening manifestation of the depression, the newspapers stated that a horde of two hundred tramps had infested and taken over Milwood, Illinois, a small town thirty miles south of Springfield, and "sundry depredations have been committed at various points," the most serious being the wreck of a passenger train because a switch was thrown the wrong way. The assumption was that the tramps did it. "The train men on the Toledo, Wabash, and Western railroad," the papers said, "are supplied with arms, and the company guarantees the legal expenses of defending any of its employees who are obliged to use force in defending the property of the company against the tramps. There is no doubt that some vigorous action is necessary to protect farm houses, small villages and railroad trains against this late development of villainy." Tramps have not been seen very much in the past couple of decades, but those of us who can recall the depression of the 1930s will remember those sometimes menacing figures. They were no novelty in the thirties, but I suspect that they were in the 1870s—for the reason, as I will suggest in a moment, that the seventies were the first decade in which the kind of social dislocations and problems which we think of as "modern" became apparent and widespread.

During that summer which was brightened momentarily by the "Centennial Fourth," politics continued in its tawdry way. The Republican party, forced to pay attention to the reformers within it because the scandals of the Grant Administration would not down, nominated the virtuous (and empty-headed) governor of Ohio, Rutherford B. Hayes, for president. The Democrats, expecting to benefit electorally from the "Republican" hard times, and smelling their first presidential victory since Buchanan's in 1856, nominated the spotless Samuel Tilden, governor of New York. Some months later, the irony became apparent that these two paragons had headed the only presidential election in American history in which the will of the electorate was almost certainly thwarted by outright vote fraud, the inconclusive and scandalous disputed election of 1876. . . .

Thus, to summarize for a moment, we are confronted with a contrast when we look for the content of the public press and public debates of that summer of 1876. The festive celebration of the Centennial Fourth had a context. The context included unsatisfactory relations between white Americans and American Indians (especially unsatisfactory to General Custer, admittedly, but unsatisfactory also to Sitting Bull and indeed to all concerned); a disastrously poor resolution of the problems of the freedmen; financial crises in urban government; the need for opium cures, reflecting some degree of drug abuse; instances of semiorganized violence against persons and property, and a climate of fear resulting from such instances (which could be multiplied); political corruption, not only in executive agencies, tarnishing the mighty figure of General Grant, but in the presidential election itself; and finally, a profound disagreement over the future

A soldiers' rally in Indianapolis, 1876
Courtesy of Harper's Weekly

shape of society, having its specific focus in debates over the money question, but ramifying much more generally. Such was the more-or-less immediate context of the Centennial celebration.

The broader context was even less happy. The Centennial happened to
take place in the middle of a bleak, severe, economic depression, the first
since before the Civil War, and the longest since the late 1830s. The depression of the seventies began in the manner typical of nineteenth-century
reverses in the business cycle, of which it was the fourth but not the last....

Indeed, financial hardship or outright disaster struck many people
between 1873 and 1879, and unfortunately the worst effects of the depression were visited upon those least able to withstand them. Thus the economic events of the seventies fortified the prevailing nineteenth-century
conviction that panics and depressions, like tornadoes or crop failures, were
natural, inevitable calamities—whether of an angry Deity or of a blind
Nature made little difference. In addition, the depression of the seventies
was felt in such a peculiar way as to disguise the crisis for some, yet make it
especially hard on others. Retained profits and dividends were not greatly
disturbed; total national output in mining, manufacturing, and agriculture
actually increased rather than decreased; the balance of trade improved,
since the depression was less severe here than in other industrializing countries; and the currency continued to stabilize, allowing specie payments to

be resumed as planned in January, 1879. Consequently, two key groups—those we may classify as "capitalists" and those responsible for such national economic policy as there was—while certainly aware that trade had fallen off, could console themselves that in major respects the depression was not all that bad, and actually had a beneficial effect in shaking out reprehensible tendencies toward speculation.

But in the meantime, many farmers, industrial workers, and railroad employees were experiencing layoffs, effective cuts in wage rates, and declining farm prices. The point, therefore, is that among those who needed to know, for the middle and long-run good of society (including themselves), that productivity and wealth were being distributed unevenly, the depression did not provide that knowledge directly; while for farmers and workers the depression experience was direct indeed. Political policy makers, opinion leaders, and businessmen of some magnitude were shielded, in part, from the realization they ought to have had that a crisis was in progress.

This oddly distributed depression of 1873–78 occurred just at a time when major social and economic changes were taking place, and it was a catalyst which intensified the visibility of change, in tangible and unfortunate ways, to many Americans. But because the depression was selective in its effects, it did not help as it might have in teaching people how to cope with these changes.

What were these basic changes which the depression of the seventies intensified yet disguised, or at least did little to make visible? There are at least half a dozen that are relevant. First: Sometime during the early seventies, farmers ceased to be a majority of the gainfully employed. It would be another forty years before any other *single* group—specifically, factory workers—outnumbered farmers, and before more Americans lived in towns and cities than on farms. . . .

Second: Americans in the 1870s were remarkably mobile. We do not know as yet whether mobility was greater in the seventies than in the 1840s and 1850s; historical demography is yet a young field. But it is already clear, for areas that have been analyzed, that mobility was much greater then than it has been in recent decades. The Department of Commerce has been telling us that since World War II, roughly 20 per cent of American residences change each year. In the 1870s the figure was apparently about 50 per cent. . . .

A third change occurring during the seventies was the advent of new difficulties in achieving law and order. We have already mentioned the problem of tramps; they came back in greater force in the nineties, and a Populist governor of Kansas was damned as an anarchist in 1893 for instructing law enforcement officers to treat them more sympathetically as unwillingly unemployed people. We should also notice the retreat from Reconstruction in the South, where 90 per cent of black Americans, the freedmen, lived, a group still 80 per cent illiterate and deprived, not through their own failings but from the inanition of Reconstruction and redeemer governments alike, of land, implements, and education. The white-supremacist Bourbon regimes that followed Reconstruction created a superficial kind of order, but their policies of political co-optation and subtle repression of the freedmen were hardly a real answer to the South's problems of social order, and helped generate later and more bloody protest and repression. We should remember too the shock waves that passed over the nation in the wake of the Great Railway Strike of 1877, the first clash between labor and capital on a nationwide scale, indeed the first major occasion when, as later became habitual, the interests of capital and labor were regarded by both sides and many in between as hostile rather than basically harmonious. When the strike of 1877 erupted at Pittsburgh and state militia fired into a crowd, killing over fifty people, the response of much of the metropolitan press around the country was to approve, on the grounds that though unfortunate in its effects sometimes, armed force was the only way to deal with threats to property. Thus the gut reaction was to nail down the tops of the powder kegs even tighter; and they blew off later at Homestead, at Pullman, and again and again down into the twentieth century.

Technological change made itself felt in the seventies. A few items may be suggestive. Scholes's patent on a workable typewriter was taken out in the early seventies, and later in the decade, particularly after the depression ended, that device promoted significant changes in governmental and business office practices, such as the employment of women in clerical jobs. Developments in refining, mining, and civil engineering allowed precious metals to be brought to market far quicker than ever before, and were one basic reason why the reopening of the Comstock Lode in 1873, bringing with it the prospect of floods of silver bullion inundating the United States Mint, contributed to the fright of "sound money men" and the attractiveness of silver dollars rather than greenbacks as a reflationary device. The introduction of the Bessemer process in steel making, soon to be followed by the use of the open-hearth method, provoked an extremely sharp rise in the average size and output of iron and steel companies. Likewise, the average size of railroad firms rose markedly, as entrepreneurship by leaders like Commodore Vanderbilt and J. Edgar Thomson began to create transcontinentals, trunk lines, and other railroad combinations, and economy and efficiency dictated consolidation of such necessities as round houses, switching yards, terminals, and other elements of railroading.

These processes involved yet another, and very basic, change in the seventies and afterward: namely, a different employee-employer ratio in many occupations from what had existed earlier. Consider for a moment the case of Indiana. It was neither the least nor the most industrial state, either nationally or within the East North Central cockpit of industrialization. Looking back at the sixties, we can see in the East North Central states a doubling or tripling of the number of manufacturing establishments, and a similar rate of increase for invested capital and numbers of workers. But in the seventies, there was a *decline* in numbers of establishments, although investment and numbers of employees continued to rise. This was not simply a consequence of the depression; the pattern continued into the relatively prosperous eighties. . . .

A final change beginning in the seventies, in large part an outcome of the foregoing, and catalyzed by the depression, was in what we might call the self-image of farmers, workers, and manufacturers. Employee-employer ratios and relationships were changing; agriculture was declining in relative strength in the labor force and in share of national income; workers, farm and non-farm, often felt with some justification that they were not getting their fair share of the new wealth they helped produce; and people who owned capital—plant, equipment, or intangibles—reacted with discomfort to farmer-labor unrest and with shock to episodes like the Pittsburgh railroad riot of 1877. For all these reasons, an earlier sense of harmony among economic and social classes disappeared. Instead of a commonalty of producers, a term of self-identification which excluded almost nobody so long as he made some social or economic contribution, we begin to find expressions of polar division between debtors and creditors, capitalists and workers, indeed between rich and poor. This was a development which began very noticeably in the seventies, and was to intensify and continue for decades to come.

So American society at the centennial contained problems and changes of an unpleasant and unpromising kind, more unpleasant and unpromising than was appreciated at that time. Let us descend to a further level of pessimism. American society then possessed neither the ideological nor the institutional tools to cope with these changes. No apposite theory of large-scale enterprise, either business or labor, yet existed. In regard to government, the prevailing attitude was what can be termed "positively negative": a positive, structured belief that governments should not act as regulators or initiators of social adjustment. Institutions were ill-equipped to deal with these changes; the political parties, despite the intense loyalties they generated, were not able easily to absorb new ideas or programs, and the Democrats were even more averse to government activism than the Republicans were. The churches were split on many doctrinal and social issues, and, on balance, the churches reinforced the dominant ethic, rather than criticizing or reforming it. The schools were not yet enrolling many students; elementary education was seldom compulsory, and secondary education was very rare (only in 1874, in the Kalamazoo decision, had it become judicially clear that tax money could be spent on secondary schools, since such a small minority of the public used them).

How did this calamitous situation come to an end? The answer is that it did not end, really, in the seventies. It was alleviated by the conjunction of several events in 1879 and 1880, especially business recovery; but in the nineties it got a good deal worse. These problems, twenty years older and harder, were resuscitated by the more severe depression of 1893–97, were compounded by fears about the new immigration, the end of the frontier, further urban and technological change with consequent social dislocations, and further outbreaks of violence and disorder in the South, the West, and the North. The 1870s, the Centennial decade, were thus a preview, a warning, of a culture crisis. The warning was not heeded, but was only disregarded or temporized with. What had to occur—and did not until after 1900 and beyond—was substantial change in ideology, and substantial change in institutions in the direction of social control.

Thus I find that the seeds of many modern conflicts were sown in the seventies. The Americans of that decade, more than in most others, had reason for profound gloom. Yet we still must remember the hardy confidence, the pride, which was so evident on that beautiful summer day of the Centennial Fourth: when, eleven years after Appomattox, and in the midst of depression and even worse problems, an editorialist could still talk of the American flag as "the emblem of all that is free and noble in government, . . . by its one hundred years of permanence it has attained a proud consciousness of dignity and power that never Roman eagles bore." I submit that, in the face of such a statement made at such a time, an affirmation whose pride and optimism was justified, at least with the long passage of time, we might regard somewhat more calmly and more confidently the crisis of culture which we find before us today.

A Farmer in Politics

HOWARD R. BURNETT

Howard R. Burnett, an Indiana University student from Monroe City, prepared a seminar paper on one of southern Indiana's most illustrious citizens, James D. Williams, in 1926, some fifty years after Williams had been elected governor of the state. Monroe City, a tiny rural community in southeastern Knox County, is located in Harrison Township, near the Pond Creek Mills homestead where "Blue Jeans" Williams lived from 1823 until his death in 1880. Contrary to what might be expected from such a rural and agricultural state, Williams, the state's seventeenth chief executive, "was the first farmer and the last pioneer"

From "The Last Pioneer Governor of Indiana—'Blue Jeans' Williams," *Indiana Magazine of History,* XXII (June 1926), 114–117, 120–128. Some footnotes in the original have been omitted. Reprinted by permission.

to occupy the position (p. 101). He was not, however, a newcomer to politics, having served in the Indiana General Assembly, on the State Board of Agriculture and, for a single term, in the United States Congress. But he remained a Knox County "dirt farmer" all the while. In Congress, where he received both the name "Blue Jeans," his customary garb throughout his life, and a well-earned reputation for frugality, he became the butt of many jokes; but this probably endeared him to his constituency even more. One comment, reminiscent of some of President Lyndon Johnson's remarks about Congressman Gerald Ford, was that Williams couldn't sign his name without biting his tongue.[1]

Nominated for governor in 1876, he defeated Benjamin Harrison (a late replacement on the Republican ticket for a scandal-plagued Godlove Orth) in the fall election, a contest some referred to as one between "Blue Jeans" and "Blue Blood." Tall and gaunt in appearance, Williams bore a striking resemblance to Abraham Lincoln; but his gubernatorial years were undistinguished. Williams died in November 1880, only weeks before his term would have expired. The printed sources on Williams are quite limited, but see William Wesley Woollen, *Biographical and Historical Sketches of Early Indiana* (1883), and the entry on Williams by Christopher B. Coleman in the *Dictionary of American Biography*, XX, 267–268; see also a sampling of the anti-Williams stories in a reminiscing article by W. R. Holloway, "Recollections of the Exciting Campaign of 1876 in which Harrison Was Defeated for Governor," Indianapolis *News*, May 23, 1909.

Williams' activities in state legislative affairs led to his nomination for Congress in 1874, by the Democrats of the Second District. At the district convention, held at Washington, Daviess County, July 23, the candidates were Thomas R. Cobb, a Vincennes attorney, and James D. Williams. Delegates arrived on Wednesday, July 22, and seemed to be about equally divided in their support of the two candidates, but, during Wednesday evening, Williams so out-generaled Cobb and his forces that when the convention convened on Thursday morning Cobb's only chance for nomination was to secure the passage of a two-thirds rule.[1] This proposal was put before the convention, but was voted down by the Williams' supporters. The convention then called both candidates before it and asked each to support the nominee regardless of which was nominated. After each candidate had made a speech to the convention embodying such a promise, they were asked to retire from the hall while the balloting took place. On the first ballot the vote was Williams, one hundred seven, Cobb, sixty-four. The bitterness of the campaign for nomination had disappeared by August 3

[1]Indianapolis *News*, May 23, 1909.
[1]Charges were made by the Cobb delegates that Williams paid the hotel bills of the Martin County delegates in exchange for their support. A prominent lawyer of Pike County, who was a Williams worker, says that money and whiskey were used in Williams' behalf.

when Williams and Cobb appeared together and made speeches from the same platform at a Democratic rally at Montgomery. The Vincennes *Sun,* which had bitterly opposed Williams, said on July 31: "The nomination (of Williams) is such as will command the hearty and cordial support of all Democrats and Conservatives. . . . The writer of this article tried in every honorable way to prevent the nomination of Williams, but since he is nominated, he proposes to march shoulder to shoulder with the friends of Mr. Williams to meet the common enemy, and battle as actively for him as he did against him." Williams' nomination proved to be especially popular among farmers because he was reported to be a member of the Grange, and had the active support of that organization.

The Republicans were unable to agree on a nominee in convention, but Levi Ferguson, of Pike County, announced himself as their candidate late in August. Williams carried every county in the district.[2] This was due partly to his popularity with the Grangers, and partly to the lack of harmony and organization among the Republicans.

Immediately after his election the newspapers of his district began a spirited discussion as to whether Williams would continue to wear home spun, or Kentucky jeans, when he appeared in Congress, as he had done throughout his long career as a state legislator. He soon settled the discussion by sending twenty five yards of "jeans," made of wool from his own flock, to a Vincennes tailor to be made up into two full suits for use in Washington.

Adlai E. Stevenson recalls that:

> While a passenger in a train to Washington, to be present at the opening of Congress, my attention was directed to a man of venerable appearance, who entered the sleeping car at a station not many miles out from Cincinnati. He was dressed in "Kentucky jeans" and had the appearance of a well-to-do farmer. Standing in the aisle near me he was soon engaged in earnest conversation with the porter, endeavoring to get a berth. The porter repeatedly assured him that every berth was taken. He told the porter that he was quite ill, and must get on his journey. I then proposed to share my berth for the night. He gladly did so until other accommodations were provided.
>
> On the Monday following, when the House was in the process of organization, the name of James D. Williams of Indiana being called, my sleeping car acquaintance, still attired in blue jeans, stepped forward, and was duly sworn in as a member of Congress. He soon became known all over the country as chairman of the Committee on Accounts. His determination to economize and peculiarity of dress and appearance soon made him the especial objects of amusement to

---

[2]The Second District has generally gone Democratic since the Civil War. Williams' majority over Ferguson was 7,690.

newspaper correspondents. He was the butt of many cheap jokes,[3] but, even so "Blue Jeans Williams" became a name to conjure with, and he soon became the most popular man in the state.

In Congress Williams was made chairman of the Committee on Accounts, and his close scrutiny of expenditures for minor items became a standing joke during the long session of 1875 and 1876. Due to his activities, the number of clerks for the various committees was reduced, appropriations for lemons and sugar for the usual cold drinks in the cloak rooms were not made, expenditures for stationery, penknives, and various other supplies were cut materially, and he soon received the name of "the two and one half cent member from Indiana."

During this session of Congress Williams was given the name "Blue Jeans"; and from that time forward this name and "Old Uncle Jimmy" vied with each other for first place in popular usage. That he was not entirely averse to the use of such names, probably having in mind their value as a means of political advertising, may be inferred from an event that took place in Congress during the debate on the general appropriation bill. Reduction of expenditures being a fundamental principle of Democratic reform, the items in this bill were cut so low that Congressman Foster, a Republican member from Kentucky, referred to the "home-spun-Kentucky Jeans Statemanship of the Democratic members in their attitude toward government expenditures." James D. Williams took this as a personal affront and rose to make his first and only speech in Congress. After telling a "funny" story by way of getting started, he turned to Foster and in a few scathing remarks closing with, "I am not ashamed of my Kentucky jeans. The people of Indiana are not ashamed of me because I wear it," defended himself so well that Foster apologized to him before the House. The name "Blue Jeans" together with his reputation for honesty and economy, had much to do with Williams' election as Governor in 1876.

Descriptions of "Blue Jeans" went the rounds of the newspapers of the country, and he became an object of curiosity and interest wherever he appeared. A description appearing in the Cincinnati *Enquirer* is typical:

> The name "Blue Jeans" Williams is very appropriate. He is not less than sixty years of age, about six feet three in his boots, and every inch an honest farmer statesman. His avoirdupois is not far from 160 pounds. He has a tremendous reach of arms, and his foot resembles a well developed Borgardus-kicker. In other words, he travels on the broad gauge principle. His habiliments, including coat, vest and panta-

[3]One of these jokes was that Williams objected to the laundry bill for 4,800 towels used in the House washroom. In the course of his objections he was reported to have said, "Why, one towel on a roller on my back porch at home does a family of seven for a week." Such stories, started by Williams' political opponents to discredit him, really reacted in his favor.

loons are of that sterling stuff known as blue jeans. Intimate friends say he wears nothing else. When one suit becomes too threadbare for society use, he immediately has another made of like texture. Notwithstanding his long dusty ride from the Capital his shirt was clean, and his black neck cloth maintained at its proper equilibrium. Except that he is a little more attenuated about the jowl, he does not look unlike the late Mr. Lincoln. Until he stood erect, I did not notice that Mr. Williams's coat was anything more than an ordinary cut, but it is. Notwithstanding the material of which it is made, it approaches the Prince Albert pattern. . . . The color is the only objection I can make. It is too blue for a good greenback man.

. . . .

The Republicans opened their campaign at Greencastle July 10, where Orth, in his key note speech, devoted his time to a review of the Civil War and Reconstruction periods, and the question of national public debt and finances, but said little about state affairs. A general formal opening of the Republican campaign was held July 20, when more than twenty five rallies were held over the state.

Lack of enthusiastic and united support of Orth, because of his connection with the Venezuelian claims,[4] caused him to tender his resignation as candidate for Governor August 2. The Republican State Central Committee met at Indianapolis on August 5 and named General Benjamin Harrison as his successor. Harrison, then on a fishing trip on Lake Superior, returned to Indianapolis on August 5, and took the matter of his acceptance under advisement until August 7, when he sent his letter of acceptance to the Republican State Central Committee. Orth's resignation made a second opening of the Republican canvass necessary. This was held at Danville August 18, where Harrision, standing under the inscription, "The office seeks the man," launched his campaign by discussing the Democratic war record, and Tilden's part in it, but said very little about state affairs. This speech foreshadowed the nature of the campaign to be waged in Indiana in 1876.

The Democratic campaign opening was delayed by the fact that Williams wished to remain at his post in Congress until adjournment early in August. His first appearance in his canvass for Governor of Indiana was made at Salem, August 12, when the Democrats formally opened their campaign for the October election. In the speech at Salem, Williams discussed the question of honesty and economy in national and state governments, justified his record in Congress, declared that he believed in the

---

[4] It was charged that Orth, while in Congress, had voted to legalize certain bonds issued by Venezuela, and held by American capitalists; and that he had, at the same time, accepted an attorney's fee of $70,000 for getting this bill through Congress. A Congressional investigation later declared that Orth had had no criminal connections with the Venezuela claims, but at the time of his resignation from the Republican ticket, his guilt was still an open question.

"Blue Jeans" Williams on the campaign trail
Courtesy of the Indiana State Library

policies of the Greenback party in regard to currency, and defended his record during the war period when he had been a member of the state Senate.

From this time on political excitement in Indiana was at white heat. Monster rallies were held by both parties. Glee clubs were organized in every village, town and city in the state. Great parades led by brass bands were formed at every rally. The greatest Democratic gathering of the campaign was held at Wheatland, August 31, near the home of "Blue Jeans" Williams. Democratic papers estimated that fifteen thousand people attended "Uncle Jimmy's" home coming.[5] Among some of the features of this rally were "huge wagons loaded down with young women dressed in blue jeans, a wagon from Busseron Township drawn by seventy-four mules, and a wagon drawn by fourteen oxen, containing railsplitters, and surmounted by a hickory pole on the top of which was a live rooster bound fast." "Blue Jeans" clubs from neighboring towns sang "Blue Jeans" songs. Williams wore a brand new suit of jeans to grace the occasion. Leading Democrats, including Governor Hendricks and Colonel Isaac P. Gray, were present and

[5] Indianapolis *Sentinel,* Sept. 1, 1876. The Vincennes *Weekly Western Sun* said 20,000 people were present, the Indianapolis *Journal* estimated the number at 7,000. In all probability 10,000 persons attended the celebration at Wheatland.

addressed the people from the two large speakers' stands. "Everybody was satisfied and went away happy."[6]

The Republicans, not to be outdone by Democratic "Blue Jeans" enthusiasm, organized a monster celebration to be held at Tippecanoe Battle Ground, September 26, in honor of "Young Tip." Here the scenes of 1840 were revived. A company of "Old Tip" supporters of 1840 organized and marched about through the crowd, and aroused intense enthusiasm by singing:

> With General Harrison brave and true,
> We'll show what Indiana'll do;
> Blue Jeans Williams can't come in,
> The color's alright but the cloth's too thin.

Log houses on wheels, large wagons filled with young ladies in uniform, canoes on wheels, and wagons carrying banners were a part of the parade, said to have been three miles long. Godlove Orth presided over a great outdoor political speaking in the afternoon at which Harrison made the principal speech.

As the campaign got well under way hundreds of political meetings were held over the state by each party. The Indianapolis *Sentinel* carried a list of thirty five Democratic speakers from fourteen different states who stumped the state for "Blue Jeans" during August and September. The Democrats held over five hundred public meetings in Indiana during July, August and September. Williams made a thorough canvass of the rural portions of the state, but did not often appear in the larger cities; his special strength was to be found among the farmers. Daniel W. Voorhees accompanied Williams about the state to "exhibit" him as the Republicans said. Williams would speak for a few minutes then give way to Voorhees, who made the real appeal to the voters at each Williams' rally. The Indianapolis *Journal* carried a list of forty-five Republican speakers from seven states who spoke at more than six hundred public meetings during August and September of 1876. Harrison proved to be the greatest of the Republican orators; Voorhees the greatest of the Democratic orators in this campaign.

---

[6]Vincennes *Weekly Western Sun*, Sept. 1, 1876. A favorite with the crowd was the "Democratic Rallying Song," one stanza of which was:

> Delighted and hopeful we anchor
> Our trust in all virtuous means,
> For this as a weapon will conquer
> In the hands of our leader, "Blue Jeans".
> Then three cheers for the flag—our old charmer—
> On the "Sage of the Wabash" it leans;
> Three cheers for the honest old farmer
> Who leads us, dressed up in blue jeans.

Members of the "Blue Jeans" clubs wore uniforms consisting of "Blue Jeans pants, with corded seams; white chip hat, with blue cambric band; red flannel belt, three inches wide, stitched to waistband of pants."

The issues discussed in the campaign were for the most part national in their character and application and dealt with the Democratic war record, the question of resumption and the currency, and honesty and reform in public office. The first of these issues, that of the "bloody shirt," was made the subject of many long and fervid orations, by Harrison and Voorhees. Harrison at Greensburg, August 24, declared:

> For one I accept the banner of the bloody-shirt. I am willing to take as our ensign the tattered, worn out old gray shirt, worn by some gallant Union hero; stained with his blood as he gave his life up for his country, and shoulder to shoulder, elbow to elbow, stepping to the music of the old drum taps, we will move forward, eyes to the front, faces to the foe to victory, again under the hallowed banner of the "bloody shirt."

Voorhees' answer to this was, "We are not fighting the war now against the South. We are fighting the battle of honesty and reform in public office." On the question of national currency each party, in the main, advocated the principles set forth in its state platform. The question of honesty and reform in government consumed much of the time of all political speakers of both parties.

Much time was given to a discussion of the qualifications for the governorship possessed by Harrison and Williams. The tone of this discussion can be gathered from the following editorials, the first from the Republican *Journal* is as follows:

> Gen. Harrison, the Republican candidate for Governor so far surpasses his opponent, J. D. Williams, in all the essential points that any attempt at comparison takes the form of contrast. Harrison is a man of large intellect and extensive attainments; Williams a man of narrow mind and no culture. Harrison would take front rank in any assemblage of great men; Williams a rear rank in an assemblage of common ones. Harrison was a brave soldier and patriot; Williams was a Copperhead and fomenter of state difficulties. Harrison discusses questions of state like a statesman; Williams calls attention to his personal appearance. . . . Harrison travels on his brains; Williams on his pantaloons. One would honor the governorship; the other disgrace it.

The Democratic *Sentinel* in speaking of Harrison said:

> General Harrison has nothing in common with the people who hammer at the forge, till the ground or labor with their hands. An aristocrat by birth, he is one in feeling and sentiment. . . . He thinks the blood in his veins is a deeper blue than that which courses in the veins of the mechanic and day laborer. He is as cold as an icicle and has more brains than feelings. He is the best example we know of brains run to seed. He is a stronger candidate than Orth, but he is not strong enough to be elected Governor of Indiana this Centennial Year.

In spite of the seeming harshness of political editorial attacks made upon the candidates for Governor, much good natured ridicule, without personal malice, was current in the press. The best example of this sort of journalism appeared in the Indianapolis *Journal,* September 7, and is as follows:

> He (Williams) is a difficult man to describe. Abraham Lincoln was an Admiral Crichton in comparison, and Richard Smith would look like an Apollo Belvidere along side of him. The English language would never recover from the shock of a detailed and accurate description of his general appearance, and it would take Uncle John Robinson, in his most energetic and capable moments to properly emphasize his political points and peculiarities. He is as handsome as [a] black India-rubber baby drawn out to its greatest possible length and its face pinched out of shape. His head, in shape, is of the sugar-loaf order, and is covered with a short, stumpy growth of bristling, iron-gray hair. His only whiskers is a little bunch of the same description of hair grown upon his "Adam's apple" and sticking out between the hard, yellow-starched ends of his cotton "side-boards," that serve on each side of his head to support the heavy dewlaps of his enormous ears. His eyes are small, and closely set against the high, narrow bridge of his long, sharp, inquisitive nose. His mouth looks as though it had been put on warm and ran all over the lower part of his face before it got set, and it opens like the opening of navigation in the spring. Looking him full in the face gives one the idea of a narrow loaded hay barge, with broad side sails set, coming down stream with the front cabin doors wide open. His long, lean legs part with each other in disgust at the hips and pursue separate and diverging paths to the knees, when negotiations for a reconciliation are entered into which takes place finally at the ends of the toes of two great feet, which join each other lovingly, while the heels still remain estranged and keep as far away from each other as possible.

As the campaign drew to a close both parties extended themselves to the limit to win. The Republicans declared it a matter of state pride to elect Harrison. They appealed to the Irish, the negro, the Independent, the business man, the regular Republican, and the young man, to help save the state from further Democratic misgovernment. The Democrats appealed to the "regular" Democrats, the Independents, the reformers, the day laborers, and the honest Republican farmers and mechanics, "in the name of liberty to lay aside their love of party and unite in electing the faithful old farmer statesman to the office of governor." During the last few days of the campaign James G. Blaine and former Governor Morton made speeches in Indianapolis in behalf of the Republican cause. The Democrats imported men from Missouri, Iowa, and Illinois to save the day for "Blue Jeans."

The State election, October 10, 1876, resulted in a majority of slightly over five thousand for Williams. On the evening of October 11, the Indi-

Governor James D. ("Blue Jeans") Williams
Courtesy of the Indiana Historical Society

anapolis *Journal* declared, "The returns seem to justify the assertion that Harrison is elected Governor. The election was a full, fair and unconditioned expression of popular will." The Democrats were highly elated over the fact that "Blue Jeans swept the Hoosier State from stem to stern" and declared that "Williams will not make a glittering ruler, but he will prove a golden one, enriching the people of the state by his economy and honesty and wise and prudent counsels." By October 13, when Williams' election was assured, the *Journal* had changed its views regarding the election, and professed to believe "Jimmy Williams owes most of his majority, if not his election, to efforts of professional corruptionists and trained repeaters brought in from other states."

Williams as governor-elect became more widely advertised than he had been as congressman or candidate for Governor. He and his family became special victims of newspaper reporters. The Republican press continued to find amusement in his blue jeans and his simple methods of living. They asked the Democrats if Williams' family would attend the inaugural ball barefooted, and if Williams himself would lead the dancing. Even Harper's Weekly sent a reporter to the Williams farms near Wheatland to interview Mrs. Williams in her home. At this time the Williams home was "a story and a half frame house painted white. The parlor had an ingrain carpet, a wide fireplace with daguerreotypes on the mantel, a high post bed-stead with a patchwork quilt, and a portrait of General Jackson hanging on the wall."

When James D. Williams appeared in public he was immediately besieged by reporters seeking interviews on his attitude toward current political questions. He was courteous to all, but as one of them expressed it, "a rather dry pump to work upon." He was never a very good subject for reporters, always expressing himself very clearly and briefly if he said anything at all, but usually during such an interview "his face, when he chose to be uncommunicative, was as unexpressionless as a cast-iron safe, and when he was in such a humor it was useless to try the combination." . . .

James D. Williams was inaugurated Governor of Indiana at the Academy of Music in Indianapolis, January 8, 1876. He was introduced by Governor Hendricks and, after taking the oath of office, read his inaugural address. On this occasion Williams wore a brand new suit of blue jeans lined with silk, a gift from ladies of Louisville, Kentucky. In the evening he gave a public reception and ball at the Occidental Hotel. Here he had engaged a suite of rooms for his home during his term as Governor. This reception was a success in every way. He was greeted as warmly by his political opponents as he was by his warmest political supporters. He had few personal enemies on the day of his inauguration, even though the preceding campaign had been one of extreme bitterness.

It is not the purpose of this paper to discuss at length the executive acts of Governor Williams. Mention may be made of the most important events of his term of office. The great railroad strikes of 1877 tied up freight and passenger traffic for a few days early in July. Williams at first announced that he would interfere in no way with the strike or the strikers, but after some destruction of property by the strikers had led to bitter criticism of his inaction, he called out the militia to protect property and preserve peace. His course pleased the workmen, but brought severe criticism from newspapers favorable to railroad interests. Williams was also severely criticised because of the number of pardons issued to inmates of the state prison. The most notable event of his administration was the law of March, 1877, providing for the erection of a new State House. That this was built and furnished at a cost under the $2,000,000 appropriated for that purpose, is an unusual monument to the honesty and economy of Williams and his associates and successors in the enterprise. No act of Williams' career as Governor gave him more pleasure than the appointment of Daniel Voorhees to the United States Senate in 1877, to fill the seat made vacant by the death of Senator Morton.

Governor Williams took his duties as Governor very seriously, as is illustrated by a toast to the "Governor of Indiana" given at the legislative banquet of 1877, in which he said:

> The honorable position of Governor of a great state should not be sought by any one; and should not be declined by him to whom it is tendered. There are great responsibilities connected with it, and when this office is filled by the selection of the people no one should decline them. His acts should be such that after generations will look upon them with pride and say: "He was faithful and true to his people".

2: Completing the Rail Network

Railroad Consolidation and Legislation

EMMA LOU THORNBROUGH

Prior to the natural gas boom of the late 1880s and 1890s, the most significant economic development for the state of Indiana was the construction of a railroad network. This took place substantially within the period of 1850 to 1880, by which time nearly 4,500 miles of track had been laid; and steady growth pushed the total mileage figure to 7,426 by 1920. During these years too, the railroad exerted considerable political power; but a movement to control and regulate the railroads—the Granger movement—picked up strength in the 1870s and 1880s, when the Interstate Commerce Commission was established. In the passages below, Professor Thornbrough describes postwar railroad construction; problems of the lines in the 1870s caused by growing competition, the depression, and an increasingly hostile public opinion; and the ineffective state measures of regulation which added to the cry for national regulation.

The most valuable sources for railroad history in this period are the primary ones, particularly the annual reports of the various railroad companies themselves. See also Henry V. Poor (comp.), *Manual of the Railroads of the United States* (1868), and *Tenth Census of the United States, Vol. X: Transportation* (1880). More general accounts are in John D. Barnhart and Donald F. Carmony, *Indiana: From Frontier to Industrial Commonwealth* (2 vols., 1954), and Ared M. Murphy, "The Big Four Railroad in Indiana," *Indiana Magazine of History*, XII (June and September 1925), 109-273.

Although the Civil War disrupted normal trade with the South the war proved a blessing to the railroads and gave most lines a chance to recoup their fortunes, at least temporarily. Business furnished by the state and

From *Indiana in the Civil War Era, 1850-1880* (1965), pp. 337, 340-347, 352-361. Footnotes in the original have been omitted. Copyright © 1965 by the Indiana Historical Society. Reprinted by permission.

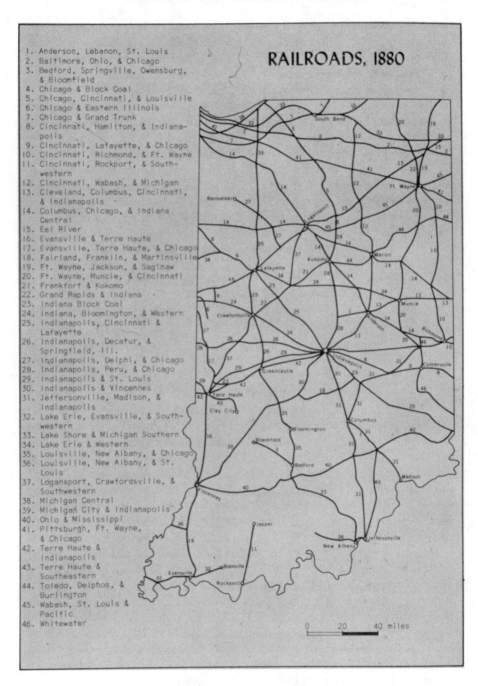

1. Anderson, Lebanon, St. Louis
2. Baltimore, Ohio, & Chicago
3. Bedford, Springville, Owensburg,
   & Bloomfield
4. Chicago & Block Coal
5. Chicago, Cincinnati, & Louisville
6. Chicago & Eastern Illinois
7. Chicago & Grand Trunk
8. Cincinnati, Hamilton, & Indianapolis
9. Cincinnati, Lafayette, & Chicago
10. Cincinnati, Richmond, & Ft. Wayne
11. Cincinnati, Rockport, & South-
    western
12. Cincinnati, Wabash, & Michigan
13. Cleveland, Columbus, Cincinnati,
    & Indianapolis
14. Columbus, Chicago, & Indiana
    Central
15. Eel River
16. Evansville & Terre Haute
17. Evansville, Terre Haute, & Chicago
18. Fairland, Franklin, & Martinsville
19. Ft. Wayne, Jackson, & Saginaw
20. Ft. Wayne, Muncie, & Cincinnati
21. Frankfort & Kokomo
22. Grand Rapids & Indiana
23. Indiana Block Coal
24. Indiana, Bloomington, & Western
25. Indianapolis, Cincinnati &
    Lafayette
26. Indianapolis, Decatur, &
    Springfield, Ill.
27. Indianapolis, Delphi, & Chicago
28. Indianapolis, Peru, & Chicago
29. Indianapolis & St. Louis
30. Indianapolis & Vincennes
31. Jeffersonville, Madison, &
    Indianapolis
32. Lake Erie, Evansville, & South-
    western
33. Lake Shore & Michigan Southern
34. Lake Erie & Western
35. Louisville, New Albany, & Chicago
36. Louisville, New Albany, & St.
    Louis
37. Logansport, Crawfordsville, &
    Southwestern
38. Michigan Central
39. Michigan City & Indianapolis
40. Ohio & Mississippi
41. Pittsburgh, Ft. Wayne,
    & Chicago
42. Terre Haute &
    Indianapolis
43. Terre Haute &
    Southeastern
44. Toledo, Delphos, &
    Burlington
45. Wabash, St. Louis &
    Pacific
46. Whitewater

RAILROADS, 1880

The railroad network, 1880
Courtesy of Robert C. Kingsbury, An Atlas of Indiana, 1970

national governments enabled many lines to pay their debts, buy and repair equipment, and pay dividends, even though wartime conditions increased operating costs. Even the Madison line, which performed valuable services during the war, showed a recovery. The Bellefontaine line, which had been in a state of financial embarrassment from 1855 to 1862, reported that during 1863 and 1864 it was able to make needed repairs and also to declare a 6 per cent dividend. In 1864 the Toledo and Wabash line enjoyed a great increase in both passenger and freight traffic. Its revenues were reported to "have surpassed the conjectures of the most sanguine and hopeful." The company was able to pay interest on all its funded debt, to pay dividends on both preferred and common stock, and to appropriate money for new buildings and equipment as well. In April, 1864, the Indianapolis to Terre Haute paid a stock dividend of 25 per cent, a regular cash dividend of 5 per cent, and an extra dividend of 5 per cent.

The years after the Civil War saw the completion of lines already begun and the construction of new ones. A more striking development was the consolidation of short lines into a few major systems and the transfer of control of most lines to eastern capitalists. By 1880 there were more than four thousand miles of railroads in the state, reaching eighty-five of the ninety-two counties. In the postwar years several new lines were begun and numerous lateral lines were built to connect with major lines. A number of short lines were built to the coal fields in the southwestern part of the state.

. . . .

Subsidies by local governments played an important part in financing the lines built after the war. In some instances lines appear to have been projected primarily as speculative ventures to enable the promoters to collect the subsidies. The early railroad charters which had been granted by special act of the legislature frequently contained provisions which enabled the local governments to take stock in them. The general act of 1852 for railroad corporations contained no such provisions, but even though there was no authorization in the law for subsidies by counties some railroads received public assistance. In 1866, for example, it was reported that some of the counties through which the Indianapolis and Vincennes line ran were making financial contributions. The commissioners of Montgomery County voted to donate $125,000 to the Indianapolis, Crawfordsville, and Danville Railroad. Although there was apparently a great deal of popular support for the subsidy, one taxpayer tried to block it by seeking an injunction. The railroad had the able legal assistance of Joseph E. McDonald and Lew Wallace. The circuit court refused to issue the injunction, but the Indiana Supreme Court reversed this decision. It held that in the absence of a statute authorizing it a county could not make an appropriation to aid a railroad, therefore the entire transaction in Montgomery County was unwarranted by law.

Meanwhile, the legislature acted to legalize subsidies. Acts passed in 1867 and 1869 authorized cities and counties and townships to subscribe money—by buying either stocks or bonds—and to levy taxes for this purpose. Special elections at which voters were given an opportunity to ratify or reject proposals for such subsidies were required before money could be appropriated or taxes levied. But there continued to be sharp differences over public subsidies after the legislature authorized them. In 1869 voters in Indianapolis refused by a wide margin to appropriate $75,000 to aid the proposed Indianapolis, Delphi, and Chicago Railroad, even though the press had strongly urged all who wanted "to make a city of Indianapolis" to vote for the subsidy. A few months later, on the other hand, the voters of Center Township in the same city voted to donate $65,000 to the proposed Indiana and Illinois Central Railroad, which was to run from Indianapolis to Decatur, Illinois. Prior to this all the counties west of Indianapolis through which the road would pass had authorized donations. . . .

The building of new lines after the war brought services to parts of the state hitherto not reached by railroads, but in some cases railroads were built in excess of needs, and ruinous competition resulted. Competition helped to force into bankruptcy many short lines and many weaker lines, which were then consolidated into longer lines. The consolidated giants in turn engaged in cutthroat practices against each other. Longer lines meant intensified competition for "through" traffic. In order to secure freight, rates were slashed below cost on long hauls. The result was a discrepancy between rates for local traffic and through traffic about which farmers complained bitterly. But railroad operators were also unhappy about the state of affairs. The Indianapolis to Terre Haute line complained of "ruinously low" rates on through traffic after the completion of the rival Indianapolis to St. Louis line. It also protested against the "pernicious practice" by which competitors gave free passes in order to obtain shipments. In 1874 the Indianapolis, Cincinnati, and Lafayette complained: "The tendency with railroads for the past few years has been steadily to low[er] rates, until they have been forced below a paying standard in many cases. . . ." It admitted that "great dissatisfaction" was caused "by the disproportion between through and local rates." Farmers who were dependent upon one railroad did not "readily see the justice in paying ten cents a bushel for hauling their corn fifty miles to market, when their more fortunate neighbors. a few miles further on, at the junction of two roads, pay but twenty cents for sending theirs a thousand miles." But railroads tried to justify the discrepancy between local and through rates by emphasizing the high cost of handling grain on short hauls.

A report of the Indianapolis Board of Trade for 1877 declared that competition and discrimination had injured small shippers and diverted traffic from Indianapolis. "Rates, throughout the West, were in many instances established by the shipper according to his influence or the magnitude of his business, to the great detriment of smaller shippers and less favored localities," it complained. Agents at points west of Indianapolis frequently gave lower rates on through traffic than those which the Indianapolis lines charged. For example, a miller reported that he could ship his product eastward from Indianapolis via Lafayette sixty miles northwest of Indianapolis for less than he could ship it directly eastward.

In an effort to put a stop to rate slashing and other cutthroat practices competing lines tried to enter into agreements and "pools" to stabilize rates, but these voluntary arrangements usually proved impossible to maintain. In the late seventies a statistical bureau was maintained jointly by the various lines operating in Indianapolis, and efforts were openly made to form a pool to divide up the traffic and fix rates. But efforts of this sort failed in part because other railroad centers undercut the rates fixed in Indianapolis. There were also complaints that favored shippers were secretly charged rates lower than those fixed by the pool.

During the depression years of the 1870's a large percentage of railroads became bankrupt, but even earlier several had experienced financial difficulties. The end of the war meant a termination of military transportation and wartime profits. This was followed by two years of poor crops of wheat, which meant a further decline in revenue. By 1869 it was reported that practically every railroad was operating at a loss. Some of the new lines were in financial trouble almost before they were begun. Most lines never paid a cash dividend, and many were unable to meet the interest on their bonds.

The most consistently profitable line in the state was the Indianapolis to Terre Haute. It continued to make money when other lines reported deficits, partly because it tapped the coal fields. It reached its peak during the war in 1864 when it declared a cash dividend of 18 per cent, and issued a stock dividend of 25 per cent. In 1868 it paid cash dividends of 12 per cent, and even during the depression years of the seventies paid 10 per cent. The Bellefontaine line, which had become a part of the Cleveland, Columbus, Cincinnati and Indianapolis line in 1868, paid dividends of 7 per cent from 1868 to 1870 but not thereafter for several years. By 1880 it was paying 2.5 per cent. During the seventies the reorganized Jeffersonville, Madison, and Indianapolis line consistently paid 7 per cent. By 1880, after the disastrous years of panic, some other lines paid modest dividends. But stockholders on most lines were paid nothing. Although railroads throughout the country had financial problems and few were really profitable, Indiana railroads in the seventies seem to have been relatively less profitable than those of the neighboring states.

While new lines were being begun, older lines were failing. As early as 1858 the Wabash line was sold under foreclosure. In 1862 the Madison and Indianapolis line was sold under similar circumstances. In 1864 the Evansville and Indianapolis Straight Line was sold by court order to a group of eastern investors. In 1868 it was ordered to be sold again for delinquent taxes, but an agent of the owners was able to buy it back. In 1867 the Ohio and Mississippi line was sold under foreclosure, and in 1876 it was placed in the hands of a receiver a second time. By 1869 the Louisville, New Albany, and Chicago line was in the hands of a receiver. The Peru to Indianapolis road, unable to pay its bonded indebtedness, had been sold, and the stockholders had lost everything they invested. During the seventies financial problems became even more acute, and the number of bankruptcies and foreclosures increased. By 1877 the following were among the lines which were in the hands of receivers: the Ohio and Mississippi; the Indianapolis, Cincinnati and Lafayette; the White Water Valley; the Cincinnati, Muncie and Fort Wayne; the Lafayette, Muncie and Bloomington; the Logansport, Crawfordsville Southwestern; the Logansport and Terre Haute; and the Louisville, New Albany and Chicago.

The bankruptcies and foreclosures of the depression years accelerated a trend which had begun earlier—the consolidation of short lines into a few major systems. An act of the legislature, in 1853, authorized railroad companies to consolidate their stock of railroad companies in Indiana or adjoining states and to connect their roads with the roads of other companies, but it was not until after the war that the trend toward consolidation became pronounced. As a result of reorganizations by 1880 most of the major lines in Indiana had become part of larger systems controlled from outside the state.

. . . .

The impact of the railroads upon economic life in turn produced repercussions in the political realm. As has been seen, the advent of railroads had been hailed with great public enthusiasm. The state legislature had been generous in the terms of the charters which were granted, and local governments vied with each other to extend financial aid. During the fifties there was almost no criticism, but as railroads became more and more powerful and as the lives of many people, especially farmers, became more dependent upon them, complaints began to be heard. Following the Civil War in every session of the legislature there were debates on railroads and proposals to curb abuses attributed to them. Opposition was intensified during the seventies by prolonged depression. But although party platforms condemned the power of railroads and lawmakers introduced many regulatory measures, little legislation was adopted, and railroads remained almost entirely free from governmental restraints. . . .

In 1867 numerous regulatory measures were introduced fixing railroad rates and requiring that they be uniform. There was strong opposition to all the proposals. During the debate it was shown that part of the opposition was led by a member who was an attorney for the Peru line, and by the speaker of the House, who had "been all his life in the railroad interest." In

1869 there were more proposals for rate regulations, but none of them were adopted. At the 1867 session, there were charges that failure to pass regulatory measures was due to the corruption of legislators by railroad lobbyists. In consequence a committee was appointed to investigate evidences of corruption, but, not surprisingly, it failed to report any proof of wrong doing. "God save Indiana from another such Legislature," cried one newspaper at the session's end, "made up of aspiring and venal politicians, old party hacks, bargainers in corruption, tools of wealthy corporations, vassals—labelled and yoked—of rich companies." It declared that members of both parties sold their votes, that "important acts were passed, and important measures and reports suppressed, solely by the power of money." But whether or not members of the legislature accepted money bribes from railroads, there was no doubt that the practice of accepting free passes was widespread. In 1869 a bill to prohibit members from accepting free passes was introduced and referred to a committee but never heard of again.

Editorially the Indianapolis *Sentinel* declared that the greatest threat to the general welfare of the mass of people arose from the growing power of monopolies, and that the most powerful monopolies were the "railroad interest," which represented "a capital equal to, if not greater than the national debt," which sought to control the public policy of the country. "It is well known," it declared, "that these monopolies have a controlling influence over both National and State Legislatures."

Considerable concern was shown by legislators over the trend toward consolidation and control by outside interests. In 1869 numerous petitions were received asking for legislation to remove "the evil growing out of Railroad Combinations" as well as to fix rates. A bill which provided that lines which consolidated lost the special privileges conferred upon them in their original charters passed the Senate in spite of stiff opposition, but it failed of adoption because the House and Senate could not agree on amendments.

At the legislative sessions of 1871, 1872, and 1873 various measures were introduced and debated to curb exorbitant charges. To meet objections that rate fixing was not within the scope of legislative power, constitutional amendments expressly granting the power were introduced in 1871 and 1873. None of these proposals w[as] adopted.

The panic of 1873 and the rise of the Grange in the early seventies intensified the demand for railroad regulation. The newspapers of both political parties were increasingly critical. Even before the depression began the Indianapolis *Journal* editorially attacked the railroad "monopoly." It pointed out that legislatures had been generous in granting favors, but in return railroads had disregarded the public interest—had "managed all their affairs with ... little reference to the needs of the country" and had "worked wholly for themselves and never for the people." As a result of consolidation and outside control, the *Journal* complained, "the transportation of our people is at the mercy of men who never see us, who know nothing of us, and care nothing for us." Railroads should not be surprised "if the public seek some remedy through State or Federal interference."

The Grange, which showed a spectacular growth in Indiana in the early seventies, was made up of farmers who were at the mercy of the railroads. Grange meetings showed concern over railroads, but the resolutions adopted by Indiana Grangers were restrained in tone and emphasized that the interests of farmers and railroads were inseparable. Resolutions adopted at a Grange meeting in 1873 complained of financial mismanagement and the methods by which railroads made "large dividends on watered stock," and urged the construction of more competing lines. The 1874 meeting of the state Grange asked for legislation which would be "just to the railroad interests of the country" but which would make the railroads "serve the people instead of ruling them," and which would compel rates to be fixed according to actual costs.

Grange influence in the 1875 legislature was powerful, and it was expected that some regulatory measures would pass. In his message Governor Hendricks referred to popular complaints and said that railroads should not "take advantage of the absence of competition" in order to make unreasonable charges. He recommended that the lawmakers consider regulation. Several regulatory measures were introduced in both houses. While the measures were under consideration operators of the railroads met with members of the legislature to plead with them not to adopt them. The principal spokesman for the railroads was M. E. Ingalls, of the Indianapolis, Cincinnati, and Lafayette. In his defense of the railroads he pointed out that they were suffering from a decline in business. He insisted that they were "honestly and faithfully managed," and that they had "made every body rich but themselves." He admitted that there was strong public hostility to railroads. This he attributed in part to ignorance, in part to "unwise action" on the part of the railroads, and in part to "political demagogues who hope to ride into power on this feeling and care not who is injured by it." He insisted that the Grangers did not understand the magnitude of the railroad interests nor their contribution to the growth of the state. He warned that to cripple the railroads would injure the prosperity of the whole state. He urged the lawmakers "to prevent such hasty and ill advised legislation in this state" as had been adopted in other states. Instead of fixing rates—which was an arbitrary procedure—he recommended that they consider a railroad commission to hear complaints, similar to the one already operating in Massachusetts. Ingalls' plea was apparently effective for none of the proposed regulations w[as] adopted. . . .

Inability to secure action at the state level was undoubtedly one reason why the 1879 legislature turned to Congress. The idea of Federal regulation was not entirely new. As early as 1869 Indiana's Representative William Williams, a Republican from Warsaw, had introduced into Congress a resolution asking for a commission to inquire into the power of Congress to regulate interstate railroad rates under its power to regulate interstate commerce. At the National Agricultural Congress which met in Indianapolis in 1873 there was a prolonged discussion of railroad problems. A resolution was adopted which declared that whenever a railroad corporation owned or controlled lines in two or more states, it was the right and duty of the Congress to regulate freight rates under the constitutional power to regulate interstate commerce. In the Senate in 1874 Morton urged the adoption of legislation to regulate railroads which were interstate in character. In the same session Democrat William Steele Holman, ordinarily a strong defender of states' rights, also called for Federal regulation and introduced a bill requiring that interstate railroads charge rates which were "fair and reasonable."

These early proposals having come to nothing, the 1879 session of the Indiana legislature adopted a concurrent resolution urging Congress to act. Support for the measure arose in part because of popular opposition to pooling arrangements by which competing railroads kept rates high. One proponent said that the only way the "plain people" could make themselves heard in the face of the powerful lobby of "organized capital" was by an appeal to Congress. "Unless the people can successfully strike against this great monopoly," he said, "no man can ship his surplus produce without bowing in submission to its iron rule."

The resolution as finally adopted declared that "the great transportation corporations," which owned the thoroughfares over which the products of Indiana must pass, had "succeeded in pooling their business, thereby preventing fair competition, and creating a monopoly of the carrying trade." Indiana's delegation in Congress was therefore requested to support the bill then pending in the Senate to regulate interstate commerce.

Congress did not pass the Interstate Commerce Act until 1887, but the debate in the Indiana legislature in 1879 anticipated some of the arguments used in the debate in Congress. Some speakers argued that Federal regulation was unconstitutional. Others expressed apprehension over centralization of power. But many Democrats who were theoretically dedicated to the preservation of states' rights showed themselves ready to accept Federal regulation when vital economic interests were involved. It was also apparent that the railroad question was a sectional one which cut across party lines. In order to protect themselves from eastern corporations both Democrats and Republicans turned to Congress.

INDEX